BRIAN CONNELL

———

REGINA
v.
PALMERSTON

1837–1865

Water colour by Joseph Nash, reproduced by gracious permission of Her Majesty the Queen

King Louis-Philippe of the French, on a State visit to Britain, leads in Queen Victoria to dinner in St George's Hall, Windsor Castle, October 11, 1844.

BRIAN CONNELL

REGINA
v.
PALMERSTON

The Correspondence
between Queen Victoria and Her Foreign and
Prime Minister

1837–1865

LONDON

EVANS BROTHERS LIMITED

First published 1962
by Evans Brothers Limited,
Montague House, Russell Square,
London, W.C.1

Set in 12/13 pt. Bembo
and printed in Great Britain by
Butler & Tanner Ltd., Frome, Somerset

Z5445

In grateful memory of
the late Countess Mountbatten
of Burma

Contents

List of Illustrations

The frontispiece and the illustrations facing pages 34, 82, 98, 130, 242 and 258 are reproduced by gracious permission of Her Majesty The Queen.

For permission to reproduce the other illustrations, the author and publishers are indebted to the British Museum, the Gernsheim Collection, and Radio Times Hulton Picture Library.

List of Illustrations

Foreword

A YEAR BEFORE HER TRAGIC DEATH, COUNTESS MOUNTBATTEN OF Burma placed at my disposal for editing and publication the Palmerston archives she had inherited through her father's family. They had, for many years, been reserved to the eminent historian Sir Charles Webster, who, in 1951, published his two-volume work *The Foreign Policy of Palmerston 1830–1841* (London, G. Bell & Sons, Ltd.). Sir Charles limited his study to Palmerston's first term of office as Foreign Secretary and, although he intended to publish a volume of selected letters, the war prevented him from doing so. I had in my *Portrait of a Whig Peer* (London, André Deutsch Ltd., 1957) edited the papers of the second Viscount, and when Sir Charles surrendered his access to the third and greatest Viscount's papers at Broadlands, Lady Mountbatten most flatteringly consented to my being entrusted with them.

There must be some 50,000 pieces in all. In due course I hope to order them under four further main headings, not dealt with by Sir Charles Webster: Palmerston's early years up to 1830; his influence on Anglo-American affairs 1809–65; the Prime Ministerial correspondence 1855–65; and an exchange of intimate correspondence between Princess Lieven and Lady Cowper, who became Lady Palmerston, supplementary to the letters now in the British Museum. The greatest immediate interest seemed to me to lie in the voluminous exchanges between Queen Victoria and her Foreign Secretary, Home Secretary and Prime Minister from 1837–65.

I found in the Broadlands archives some 1,200 manuscript letters from Queen Victoria, another 150 from the Prince Consort and more than 80 from Sir Charles Phipps, Keeper of the Queen's Privy Purse, who acted as her private secretary for a period after the Prince Consort's death in 1861. The copyright of these letters belongs to the Queen. Her Majesty has graciously permitted me to make use not only of them, but also of the corresponding letters from Viscount Palmerston, together with extracts from certain other relevant papers, in the Royal Archives at Windsor. I am deeply grateful to Her Majesty for her gracious permission to publish this correspondence.

The letters from Lord Palmerston at Windsor amount to nearly 4,500—the discrepancy being explained by the number of daily reports of parliamentary debates which Palmerston wrote during his long years as Prime Minister and which required no direct acknowledgment. I owe an immense debt of gratitude to Mr. R. C. Mackworth-Young, the Librarian at Windsor Castle, who has facilitated my work in every possible way, obtaining further permission for me to transcribe lengthy extracts from personal memoranda by the Queen and the Prince Consort and pertinent entries from the Queen's private journal. I hope the result is worthy of his interest.

The multi-volume John Murray edition of Queen Victoria's correspondence, published in two sections in 1907 and 1926, contains exactly 251 letters out of the total correspondence I have read—or slightly less than five per cent. Even in those published, I found that many interesting passages had been omitted and that in the earlier series some of Queen Victoria's more caustic comments had been carefully excised. Where, in order to maintain the context of a sequence, I have found it necessary to reprint any of these letters, the missing passages have been restored. The material is so abundant that in many cases it has been possible to provide alternative matter from royal memoranda or journal entries in the place of known exchanges.

Otherwise this correspondence is largely *inédit*. The first official Life of Viscount Palmerston, by his heir, Evelyn Ashley and Sir Henry Lytton Bulwer (London, Richard Bentley, 1871), appears to have been written with scant reference to the archives. Professor Herbert C. F. Bell's standard two-volume biography *Lord Palmerston* (London, Longmans, Green & Co. 1936), contains few direct quotes or references to this correspondence, and although Mr.

Philip Guedalla in his *Palmerston* (London, Ernest Benn Ltd., 1926), was the first biographer to appreciate the value of the Broadlands archives, his quotations seldom amount to more than a phrase at a time. Sir Theodore Martin's *Life of the Prince Consort* (London, Smith Elder & Co., 1877) contains a few letters and memoranda to which I refer, as does Mr. Frank Eyck's *The Prince Consort* (London, Chatto & Windus, 1959).

My purpose has been to present this fascinating correspondence in a manner acceptable to those who read for pleasure. I doubt very much if in recent decades any but scholars have ploughed through the five volumes of Sir Theodore Martin or searched for the plums in the John Murray *Letters of Queen Victoria*. I have attempted to give the spirited exchanges between the Queen and her Minister, if not the quality of dialogue, at least the contrast of *demande* and *riposte* through the fluctuations of their relationship. There were, over the years, several tantalising exchanges where differences of opinion must have been resolved in personal interviews, of which there is no record, and, with so much to choose from, I have preferred to omit the inconclusive. Nor did the Queen and Palmerston necessarily correspond on every issue, and where no letters are quoted on some particular subject it may be assumed that nothing of consequence exists. This does not apply to numerous letters concerning Court, administrative and ecclesiastical appointments or recommendations for honours and peerages. Both the Queen and Palmerston frequently commented with such brutal frankness on the personal qualities and otherwise of candidates, that I have been advised not to embarrass their descendants by reproducing some of these passages.

There are no footnotes, which I truly believe drive the ordinary reader to exasperation, especially the lengthy variety which carry him three pages forward and then back to the text. All the information they would have contained is included in the narrative. Necessary identifications are in square brackets. Three dots indicate cuts in the original. Place and proper names have been given their modern form and Queen Victoria's habit of excessive underlining disregarded except where it provides particularly piquant emphasis. Nor is each page cluttered with reference numbers. Academicians will find precise identification of each letter quoted, page by page, in the appendix, indicating whether the original is at Broadlands or in the Royal Archives at Windsor. Occasional references to other letters in the John Murray edition are also identified.

This book is dedicated to the late Countess Mountbatten of Burma. It is a small acknowledgement to make to the many kindnesses I received and the great trust she reposed in me during recent years. I sincerely hope that Lord Mountbatten, who has most generously renewed the permission to edit these papers, will accept this first volume as a token of my gratitude.

I must also thank Mrs. Elizabeth Collins, who was for years Countess Mountbatten's personal assistant, for all her help, and Mrs. Georgiana Blois, whose knowledge of the Broadlands archives and unfailing assistance with transcription work has been so invaluable. My wife, as always, has been my *alter ego*. Without her tireless research work, eagle-eyed editing and unwearied typing this book could never have been produced.

CHAPTER I

'The Queen now comprehends'

AT HALF-PAST ELEVEN ON THE MORNING OF HER ACCESSION, JUNE 20, 1837, Queen Victoria held her first Privy Council in the red saloon of Kensington Palace, where she had led a sheltered life for most of her eighteen years with her widowed mother, the Duchess of Kent. In a brown silk dress, the tiny figure—she was only four feet nine inches tall—was led in by her paternal uncles, the Dukes of Cumberland and Sussex, and her Prime Minister, Lord Melbourne, whom she had just confirmed in office. Bowing to the most distinguished of her subjects—the Archbishop of Canterbury in his wig; the fine, greying, eagle's head of the Duke of Wellington; the tall, formal figure of Sir Robert Peel—the Queen sat very upright on the large chair upon its raised dais at the end of the long table and, in a pellucid child's voice, read her Declaration.

Beside her stood the Prime Minister, in Court uniform, gold-frogged and elegant, with his fine-chiselled, humorous, aristocratic face, holding a pen for her to sign the document. Immediately behind him, to his left, stood the small, eager figure of Lord John Russell, the Home Secretary, who, as the repository of the pure Whig tradition, had piloted the great Reform Bill through the House of Commons five years earlier. To the right, still fresh-faced from the outdoor life he loved, his firm features almost boyish in spite of his fifty-three years, dressed with the careless elegance that was his hallmark, stood the third Viscount Palmerston, Foreign Secretary and the strongest man in the Cabinet.

Lord Melbourne's ministry had four more years of increasingly precarious life before it, a period which this charming, quizzical, cynical man of the world devoted with affection and entire absorption to guiding the inexperienced young Queen through her initiation into statecraft. His two colleagues were to serve her

I

in various ministerial capacities for the best part of the next thirty years. As the Queen acquired maturity and authority, after her marriage to Prince Albert of Saxe-Coburg-Gotha, she was to find herself in recurrent bitter conflict with the two ministers to whom she was one day to refer as 'those two dreadful old men'. Lord John was always the more amenable. For Lord Palmerston she was to develop a deep-rooted antipathy, which survived even their periods of agreement on political issues, while he became established as perhaps the greatest ministerial figure of the nineteenth century.

Their differences were not to emerge in form until Palmerston's second tenure of the Foreign Office from 1846 to 1851. The fundamental cause lay in a contrast of temperament. Both sovereign and minister were well matched in determination, will-power and stamina, but Palmerston was a pragmatist, a skilled politician of infinite resource and guile, a master of diplomatic argument and invective, one of the truly great parliamentarians in British history. Sometimes it seemed as if a triumph over means was as satisfying to him as the achievement of his ends. The Queen's character was much simpler. She possessed a robust common sense, immense resources of character, an honesty almost terrifying in its intensity and a determination to act in accordance with certain clear-cut principles. Palmerston also held certain unswerving political beliefs, but the chief of them, which guided his whole attitude to international affairs, whether as Foreign Secretary or as Prime Minister, ran counter to the Queen's inborn convictions.

Palmerston had seen the French Revolution come and go. The first thirty years of his life had coincided exactly with the agitation that led to its outbreak and the first abdication of the Emperor Napoleon at Fontainebleau. Accompanying his father on a Grand Tour of Europe, the family had escaped from Paris as the mob stormed the Tuileries. All his life he abominated equally despotic monarchies and violent revolution. His panacea for the peace of Europe and social contentment was the installation, wherever possible, of constitutional monarchies on the British model. But after the downfall of Napoleon, autocratic government and the divine right of kings had entered into its own again, semi-permanently in Russia, Prussia, Austria and Italy, fluctuatingly in France, Spain and Portugal. The Queen was to hold that the European monarchs who were her relatives had certain inalienable rights, which even bad government could not diminish. Over the years her correspondence with Palmerston, the Queen's in her quick, slanting, crabbed hand and her minister's in its fluent, lucid copper-plate, was to mirror the great conflict of their times.

The Queen came ill-prepared to such majestic duties. The institution of the monarchy was in disrepute at her accession. The ineffable sons of the poor, mad King George III had brought little honour to the Hanoverian line. The profligate and preposterous Prince Regent, who became King George IV, had more taste in the arts than for the dignity of statesmanship. The brother who succeeded him as King William IV was an old Tory buffoon, whose Whig administrations under Lords Grey and Melbourne had left him increasingly baffled and resentful. Almost the only minister he could tolerate, Foreign Secretary with one brief interruption from 1830, was Lord Palmerston. Of the other brothers, the Duke of Cumberland was an unbridled and hated ultra-Tory, the Duke of York had rendered some service as Commander-in-Chief of the army, the Duke of Sussex had been a more amiable figure, with Whig inclinations, as had the Duke of Kent, Queen Victoria's father, who died a year after she was born. They had all incurred enormous debts, several of them had sired illegitimate children, but when Princess Charlotte, only child of the Prince Regent, married to the Prince Leopold of Saxe-Coburg-Saalfeld who became the first King of Belgium, died in childbed, George III was left without one living grandchild. The Dukes of Clarence, Cambridge and Kent hastily made middle-aged marriages in the hope of providing an heir. The Duke of Kent married Prince Leopold's sister, the widow of Prince Emich-Karl of Leiningen, who already had two children, a boy and a girl. Princess Alexandrina Victoria was born at Kensington Palace on April 25, 1819.

The Duchess of Kent spoke no English, but when her husband died she was persuaded by her brother to bring up Princess

Victoria in England. The Prince was to act almost *in loco parentis* to his niece for nearly fifty years. His sister was so encumbered by her husband's debts that for many years he helped her financially, out of the annuity of £50,000 granted to him by the British Parliament as Princess Charlotte's husband. He was the only royal relative to show much affection for the child. To her credit, the Duchess devoted much care to her daughter's upbringing and education, but the young princess was kept away from the bedizened Court of King George IV, and the Duchess was on such bad terms with her brother-in-law, King William IV, that the only contact between the two households was acrimonious in the extreme. Princess Victoria lived a completely secluded life. She was twelve years of age before she was informed indirectly that she was the heir to the throne and, although instructed in her constitutional duties and acquiring the social accomplishments regarded as proper for a young lady at that period—singing, playing the piano and harp and sketching, at which she showed a neat talent—was almost completely deprived of companions of her own age.

During the 1830's she was taken to concerts and the opera and, as she approached her majority, travelled quite widely around the country, staying at various aristocratic houses. These journeys were arranged with unnecessary pomp and ceremony by the Comptroller of the Duchess' Household, Sir John Conroy, a greatly disliked figure, who attracted much malicious gossip. It was even rumoured that he hoped to become Prime Minister in the event of the Duchess being called upon to act as Regent. However, King William IV survived just long enough to prevent this and his niece had come of constitutional age when he died. The fresh-faced girl, with a glint of gold in her hair, who succeeded him, was still an innocent adolescent. Relations with her mother, in whose bedroom she had slept almost to the last, had become increasingly strained and the chief influence in the formation of her upright character had been the governess appointed when she was five, Baroness Lehzen. As soon as she became Queen, her uncle Leopold despatched to her aid as personal adviser, his own confidant, Baron Stockmar, who had been one

4

of the physicians in attendance at the death of Princess Charlotte. To them, as chief influence in her life, was now joined, providentially, Viscount Melbourne. Independent of her mother at last, the Queen promptly moved into Buckingham Palace, with everything yet to learn.

Her Foreign Minister was as worldly wise as Melbourne and much more forceful. The Temple family had been staunch Whigs for two centuries, until Palmerston's father, whose Irish title permitted him to sit in the House of Commons for the last forty years of the eighteenth century, broke with Charles James Fox over the necessity of fighting revolutionary France and veered to the support of Pitt. His handsome, intelligent elder son was sent to Harrow and then lodged with the leading Whig philosopher of the day, Professor Dugald Stewart, at Edinburgh University. When his father died in 1802, the young man came under the influence of his chief guardian, Lord Malmesbury, nestor of the diplomatic corps, who saw him through a nobleman's degree at St. John's College, Cambridge, and then directed his abundant talents to political life.

The third Viscount had an income of £15,000 a year, large estates in County Sligo and the north of England and one of the most handsome small Georgian houses in the country, Broadlands, near Romsey in Hampshire, a monument to 'Capability' Brown and Henry Holland, who had embellished it for his father. This was not a fortune to compare with the wealth of the great Whig magnates of the time, like the Russells and the Lansdownes, and his continued adherence to the Pittite interest placed him beyond their pale.

After standing twice unsuccessfully for Pitt's old seat at Cambridge University, he was first elected to Parliament for the near-rotten borough of Newport, Isle of Wight, in 1807. An uncommonly attractive young man, with all the social graces, a considerable name and influence, he immediately obtained minor office as a junior Lord of Admiralty in the Portland administration. In 1809, at the age of twenty-five, Perceval offered him the post of Chancellor of the Exchequer, with a seat in the Cabinet. On Malmesbury's advice, he declined the post as exceeding his powers, but accepted that of Secretary at War, in charge of army administration, which he held until 1828. In 1812 he was offered the Chief Secretaryship of Ireland, but declined 'owing to particular circumstances and considerations'. These probably included Emily Lamb, sister of the later Viscount Melbourne and wife of the fifth Earl Cowper. A great beauty, she was long Palmerston's intimate friend, and married him in 1839, two years after the death of her husband.

Known as a gay and amusing London host and man of fashion, wit, and contributor to the *New Whig Guide*, a fine shot and fearless rider to hounds, Palmerston seemed bereft of parliamentary ambition. An effective administrator and devoted adherent of George Canning, the leader of 'Mr. Pitt's friends', his Army Estimates were always models of clarity, but he was an indifferent speaker and intervened infrequently in debate. Then in 1828, his Whig principles had reasserted themselves. He broke with the Duke of Wellington, then serving as Prime Minister, made two great speeches on Catholic Emancipation and British foreign policy, endorsed the necessity for electoral reform, and accompanied the Canningites into the great Grey administration of 1830, in which he became Secretary of State for Foreign Affairs.

His obsession with the superiority of constitutional government was backed by an exalted conception of British power and prestige and an indefatigable capacity for business. His personality could be disconcerting. He retained all his life the exquisite manners and grace of the eighteenth century into which he was born. He was a great favourite in society, gay, buoyant, distinguished, easy. Yet in diplomatic negotiation he could be hard, ruthless, downright offensive. He was an absolute master of detail, and foreign Ambassadors, even such an exponent of his craft as old Talleyrand, quailed before his exhaustive grasp of any subject he chose to discuss. His despatches were remarkable in their force and clarity. He demanded standards of work, application and precision from his own Ambassadors, Under-Secretaries and clerks, which often caused rumbles of near mutiny. As the Whig administration grew lazy under Melbourne's light hand, he emerged as the dominant member of the Cabinet.

6

He was largely responsible, during the European upheaval of July 1830, which had brought King Louis-Philippe to the throne of France, in securing the independence of Belgium with King Leopold at its head and this was to remain one of his most praiseworthy diplomatic achievements. He had assisted the youthful Queens Donna Maria of Portugal and Isabella of Spain to maintain themselves and their constitutionalist parties against the revolts of their absolutist kinsmen, Don Miguel and Don Carlos. He had followed the precepts of Canning and assisted the Greeks to wrench their independence from the Turks, but he had successfully resisted Russian encroachments in the Middle East and renewed French aspirations in Egypt. By the time Queen Victoria came to the throne he was a major figure in international politics, already cordially detested by the absolutist monarchs and their ministers and at odds with the French, whose expansionist intentions, under whatever régime, he suspected and laboured to thwart during most of his ministerial life.

Here indeed was a formidable antagonist, as the Queen was to find, but for the time being, their disagreements lay in the future. Palmerston's first letter to his new sovereign, written three days after her accession, was typical of many exchanged during the first months of her reign—gentle instruction in the protocol of royal duties:

> Viscount Palmerston presents his humble duty to your Majesty and has the honour to submit for your Majesty's signature the accompanying letters to foreign sovereigns, princes and States.
>
> These letters have been prepared according to former precedents and vary in form and style according to the rank and character of the parties to whom they are addressed, but these variations have been rendered strictly conformable with the examples of former reigns.
>
> It is usual that the conclusion of letters addressed by one sovereign to another should be written in the hand of the sovereign by whom the letters are sent, and your Majesty will find in pencil at the end of each of these letters the appropriate words of termination. The pencil marks will be carefully rubbed out, as usual, when your Majesty may be pleased to return the letters to Viscount Palmerston.

The offer of a Russian decoration to the Earl of Durham, British Ambassador at St. Petersburg, required the Foreign Minister's first explanation of certain fundamental principles:

> Viscount Palmerston . . . ventures to think that upon general principles it is desirable and fitting that British subjects should look to their own sovereign and to their own sovereign alone for reward for their good conduct as British subjects, and that the only exception to this principle ought to be cases in which British subjects may have performed specific acts in the service, or for the direct benefit, of some foreign prince.
>
> But if there is any class of your Majesty's subjects with respect to whom it appears to Viscount Palmerston to be more peculiarly important for the good of your Majesty's service that this rule should be strictly observed, it is the diplomatic servants of the Crown. Great national interests are often unavoidably placed in the hands of these persons, important results may depend upon the manner in which one man, at a distance from all supervision and control, may in a critical occasion conduct himself; and the vigilance, the acuteness, or the firmness of a British Minister abroad may often decide matters of considerable moment. It is desirable therefore to exempt such persons, as far as it is possible to do so, from the influence of any motive unconnected with their public duty, by which their minds might in the remotest degree and even unconsciously be swayed . . .'

Most of this early correspondence consisted, however, of quite elementary enquiries and guidance:

> JULY 2: The Queen wishes to know if she can write any day to Paris by the usual post or if she can only do so four times a week.
>
> JULY 3: Viscount Palmerston presents his humble duty to your Majesty and has the honour to state, in reply to your Majesty's enquiry of yesterday, that messengers are sent from this office to your Majesty's Embassy at Paris on the evening of every Tuesday and Friday and that, by such occasions, your Majesty's letters can be safely and expeditiously conveyed. That the ordinary post goes to Paris every day in the week, except Sunday, and that the Post-master-General would be able on any week day to transmit your Majesty's letters to Paris by that post, but that any letter so sent would be liable to be examined at the French post offices.

JULY 18: . . . Your Majesty is also well aware how great a personal favourite of the Emperor of Russia Count Orloff is, and that the selection of the Count for this special mission was intended as an additional compliment to your Majesty, and it might perhaps be well taken if your Majesty were to see fit to remark that the selection of a person who stands so deservedly high in the confidence and esteem of the Emperor must add to the satisfaction with which your Majesty receives the proof, which the letters afford, of the Emperor's desire to cement the friendship which so happily subsists between the two Crowns and which your Majesty is equally anxious to maintain and improve . . .

JULY 22: . . . The Queen imagines that the Prince Christian de Holstein Glücksburg must be a son of one of the Dukes of Holstein (brother to the Princess Christian of Denmark) and cousins to the Queen. Perhaps Lord Palmerston could find out if this is the case before the Prince comes to-day.

JULY 22: Viscount Palmerston presents his humble duty to your Majesty and submits the Gotha Almanach, which your Majesty will find useful as a book of reference and in which, on page 19, No. 5, your Majesty will find the name of Prince Christian of Glücksburg . . .

AUGUST 6: . . . The Queen imagines that she should send back all the formal letters Lord Palmerston sends her from the various sovereigns, etc.

AUGUST 6: . . . Your Majesty is perfectly right in supposing that the formal letters addressed to your Majesty by foreign sovereigns and princes are deposited as public documents in the archives of the Foreign Office.

AUGUST 12: As the Queen has got a great many foreign despatches, which, from time to time she has been unable to read as yet, she requests Lord Palmerston not to send any more until she has done with those which she already has with her, and which she hopes will be the case by tomorrow evening.

AUGUST 18: . . . Viscount Palmerston has desired the Geographer who supplies the Foreign Office with maps to prepare two atlasses which may be useful to your Majesty when reading the foreign despatches, and he has desired those atlasses to be sent to Buckingham Palace in case your Majesty should not already be provided with them . . .

The fashionable world was, of course, agog to know how the young Queen was rising to her new status. There had been much speculation as to the part the Duchess of Kent and Sir John Conroy would play under these new circumstances. The influence of the Queen's former governess and Lady-in-Waiting, Baroness Lehzen, was less feared and the rôle to be played by Baron Stockmar had yet to be appreciated. Countess Cowper, who was much at Court, knew all the gossip and tattled an account of it to her other brother, the Hon. Frederick Lamb, who was British Ambassador in Vienna:

> . . . You are right in thinking the young head has advisers, but there is a good deal of sense wanted to know when to take good advice, for clearly she has had a great deal of bad offered to her, and that for many years. The Baroness Lehzen, who is a very clever woman, has no doubt been of great use to her, but her mother's folly and her constant subserviency to Conroy could hardly have been expected to have a good effect, unless her own judgment and nature had been something superior—and perhaps her fault now, if she has one, will be obstinacy and too great a reliance on herself. Hitherto these characteristics have turned out well, but they a little alarm one for the future, though I hope they will not, because her wish to do right is very great, and her confidence in W[illia]m is unbounded and I am sure she could not have fallen into better hands. Conroy and her mother must be perfectly mad to act towards her as they have done, having always treated her as a child and bullied her, I suppose they had no idea of her real character, but thought a childish obstinacy could be overcome by violence.
>
> And conceive that only a few days before she was Q[ueen], C[onroy] had threatened to shut her up, and she was obliged to put herself in communication with those who could protect her, that in case of such a thing taking place they might come to her rescue. The reason of all this persecution, which had been going

on ever since she was twelve years old, was to make her promise
to promote and take Conroy into favour, he wanted to be a peer
and, above all, to be her private secretary, as Sir Herbert [Taylor]
was to the King [William IV]; but she never would promise anything and this, sleeping every night of her life with her mother,
in the same room, a small bed near hers. It is really quite touching
to think of all she has suffered.

She says that when she came to be 18, people said to her 'now
the happy days of your childhood are over'. In fact she said 'I never
was happy till after I was 18' and I really believe (she said) that all
this worry and torment has made me as little as I am and prevented
my growing. But, she said 'perhaps it did me good in another way,
by forming my mind'. William said 'I am afraid, Ma'am, you
will yet have a great deal of worry to go through.'—'But what a
difference (she said) then I was alone; now I have you to support
me.' She said that C. made her mother do all the things she ought
not, that he made her mother go that tour about the country
receiving addresses, which she, Victoria, very much disliked, and
did all she could to prevent. She said 'I knew it was improper, and
very disagreeable to my uncle, who always behaved very kindly
to me, but it was all Sir John's influence, and what could I do?'

Again she said her mother inviting Hume and O'Connell and
all the Radicals to her party was quite against her wishes and
entirely Sir John wanting to court favour with those people. But
one thing shows her decided character still more than all these.
She has not rode for more than a year and yet is very fond of it. A
year ago Sir John, riding with her, said something either improper,
or which made her angry, so on her return home, she told the
Duchess that she would ride with him no more. The Duchess said
that she must not ride without him. 'Well, then', she said, 'I shall
not ride at all'—and she never did—(what he had said to her she
did not say). So, in the midst of her confidence, she has yet a sense
of discretion or propriety. Is not all this very remarkable?

I would not repeat these things except to you, and feeling that
they are safe by a courier. She likes and admires her uncle [King
Leopold] and behaves with great kindness and attention to her
mother, but evidently is not fond of her and has a great contempt
for her. She keeps her at arm's length in her new Palace, and does
not admit her without her sending up from the ground floor,
which she has assigned to her. The Duchess is of course deeply

annoyed (notwithstanding the £3,000 a year given C. from the Privy Purse). He is left at Kensington and not admitted into the Palace, but the Duchess goes to see him every day. And I believe she cannot help complaining to some of her friends, as she says, having lost her daughter . . . But I hope they will keep their coolness down so as to remain in the same house, as it is better for both parties not to let the real state of the case transpire. Her confidence in William is quite unbounded, she only acts by his advice, and seems to look up to him with admiration and esteem, and certainly she could not be in better hands.

The only person whose advice she takes besides his is Stockmar's, whom her uncle sent over as a friend. And he and William are on the most perfect terms, and he admires William's character and disposition as much as she does. She did not like the feeling of giving the Garter first to a foreigner (Leiningen), and wishes to have given it first to William, but he very wisely refused, said under no circumstances did he wish for it, but under the present [circumstances] he certainly could not accept of it, that the world would say he had used his influence over a young mind for his own advantage. Don't mention the above man's name. Nobody knows he has any influence with her, and it would not look well in England that a foreigner could have any. But he seems from all accounts to be a quiet, wise and unexceptionable person . . .

Victoria is now giving dinners, of which she selects all the company herself, and does the honours perfectly and without the least awkwardness, keeping her servants and Court in great order and constant attendance, but not too much so. Being civil and young, I suppose she thinks it necessary to keep them all in respect. It is a curious thing, and I don't know whether I am most amused or astonished at all I hear of her. She seems to have a very decided will of her own, but so tempered by good feeling and consideration. They say people are all put out, who go to be presented to her, and that even that old stager Orloff looked quite shy and embarrassed at his audience. What you won't say to an old King who helps you must look awkward towards a young Princess, and a child who looks shorter than anybody ever did, though a pretty face and very intelligent look. She always wears a train and so does the Duchess of Sutherland. She is quite charmed with Buckingham House and says she never enjoyed anything like it before, the beauty and privacy of the garden. She has no wish to leave it and

said to Lord P[almerston]: 'I am like Lord M. I like London! !'
She says that sometimes when she wakes of a morning she is quite
afraid that it should be all a dream. (Is not this so natural?) She
enjoys her happiness so much. She has a very beautiful voice in
speaking, and sings well, and sang to one or two of her smaller
dinner parties to their great delight . . .

The Queen did indeed enjoy her parties, and kept up a constant
flow of queries to her Foreign Minister about protocol, the seating
of her guests, when and whether it would be proper for her to
make some small gift to the emissaries who came to congratulate
her and how to sign her official letters. Lord Melbourne had
become her prime favourite and adviser, but Palmerston, with
his gay personality and impeccable manners, clearly earned her
warm regard. Some of the requests from the young sovereign to
her experienced minister were almost deferential in tone:

> If Lord Palmerston could absent himself without inconvenience
> for a short while this evening between 9 and 10 from the House of
> Commons, the Queen would be very glad if he could come here
> as she would wish to talk to him upon several points which can be
> much easily settled verbally than by letter. Should Lord Palmer-
> ston be unable to come, the Queen wishes him merely to inform
> her of it.
> Lord Palmerston should (if he does come) come just as he is, and
> not change his evening dress.

Sometimes the Queen found the Foreign Office despatches difficult to comprehend. One such came from the British Minister in
Persia:

> Should Lord Palmerston however find it impossible for him to
> give the Queen any explanation of Mr. McNeill's despatches in
> writing, she will keep the box till she sees Lord Palmerston, which
> she hopes will be in a short while.

Palmerston's long reply included a preliminary lesson in geo-
politics:

> . . . The geographical position of Persia, interposed as that king-
> dom is, between the southern frontiers of Russia and the northern
> frontiers of British India, has for many years past rendered the

British Government anxious to convert Persia into a barrier to prevent the Russians from invading British India.

With this view, in 1814, a political treaty was concluded between Persia and Great Britain, of which Viscount Palmerston submits a copy, in case your Majesty should wish to refer to it.

The general effect of this treaty was that the King of Persia promised by the first article, which your Majesty may like to read, to prevent any European power (by which Russia was specially meant) from entering Persia for the purpose of invading India; and that in return, the King of England promised to give the King of Persia the aid of his good offices, and of a specified military or pecuniary assistance in case of need.—Some few years ago, however, the King of Persia released Great Britain from its engagement to give succour in men or in money to Persia, in consequence of Great Britain paying down to Persia at that time a certain sum of money, at once; and thus the political engagements between England and Persia, as they at present stand, bind Persia to defend British India by force of arms, but bind England to assist Persia only by good offices, with any power which might threaten to attack Persia . . .

When the late Shah died, and the present Shah succeeded to the throne about three years ago, Mr. Henry Ellis was sent out to compliment the present Shah on his accession; and Mr. Ellis was instructed to press again the commercial treaty, if he should find a favourable opportunity for doing so. Mr. Ellis was unable to persuade the Persians to sign the treaty, but he obtained a decree (called in Persian a Rukhum) from the Shah, declaring that British subjects shall in Persia enjoy all the commercial privileges and securities which the subjects of any other State may enjoy in Persia.

This decree was a considerable advantage to British commerce, because it prevented British subjects from being compelled, as before they sometimes were, to pay higher duties upon English goods, than Russian subjects pay upon similar goods coming from Russia. But the decree is not so full in its details as the treaty would be, and does not distinctly permit the appointment of British Consuls; and besides, the decree may be revoked by the same will which issued it; and at all events, is not binding upon any succeeding Shah.

Mr. McNeill was therefore instructed when he went out to

Persia upon the return of Mr. Ellis, to press the conclusion of a commercial treaty; and the despatches which your Majesty now has give an account of the steps which he has taken with that view.

Mr. McNeill seems to have proceeded with much ability in the execution of his instructions; and he appears especially to have been a match for the Russian Minister in dexterity . . .

The Foreign Minister was also ready with one of his pithy exercises in commonsense, when the Archduke John of Austria sent the Queen a long dissertation on the affairs of Greece:

. . . But the reasoning of the Archduke John is, as Viscount Palmerston would humbly submit, much the same as the argument which is often employed against education by those who dislike improvement. Ignorance, they say, may be bad and perfect knowledge may be a very excellent possession, but a little knowledge is a dangerous thing and as masses of men cannot at once become fully informed, but must begin by having a little knowledge, it is better to leave them in absolute darkness than expose them to the danger of a partial light. But it is unnecessary to expose the fallacy of an argument which, if admitted, would be a bar to all improvement in the condition of nations and which is not more founded in truth than would be the assertion that a little wealth is a bad and dangerous thing and that if men cannot be extremely affluent, they had better be entirely destitute.

After a dinner in February 1838, attended by the French and Turkish Ambassadors, the Queen made a private journal note about the evening's entertainment:

After dinner I sat on the sofa with Mme. Sebastiani and Lady Lansdowne; Lord Palmerston and Lord Lansdowne sitting near me . . . Miss Rice played two games at chess with Sarim Effendi, to our great amusement, and beat him. Lord Palmerston was in very good spirits, and talked a good deal with Lord Lansdowne and me; about Sarim Effendi; pictures—Wilkie—music, for which he said the English had, if he could so say, 'an *untalent*'; of the new way of lighting the House of Commons; said he had seen the Prince of Capua and his wife, who are here again; that she speaks English with a strong Irish accent, and is really very handsome; and that they had shown him their little boy, a fine child of a year old.

Palmerston's clear head and trenchant mind manifestly appealed to the young Queen. Her own developing mental processes also preferred facts to theory and, later in the year, in May, she had occasion to record her appreciation of her Foreign Minister's grasp of detail in another entry in her journal:

> At a quarter-past 3 Lord Palmerston came to me and stayed with me till half-past 4. He first gave me a despatch to read from Villiers relative to that Spanish business Lord Melbourne mentioned to me the other day, and which certainly gives hopes of a final settlement of that unfortunate country by this offer of the Navarrese chiefs to lay down their arms and declare for the Queen. He also gave me his answer to read, which is very right and just, stating that England will act as a mediator and not as a guarantee. Lord Palmerston then went through the whole Belgian affair, beginning from when Holland was made a kingdom, and going through the whole of the proceedings from before uncle became king till now; and I must say, intricate and difficult as the subject is, Lord Palmerston explained it in such a very clear, plain and agreeable manner, as to put me quite *au fait* of the whole thing. The explanation took an hour.

June and July were almost entirely taken up with the festivities attending the Queen's Coronation. Diplomatic activity resolved itself for the time being into endless problems of precedence, and Palmerston good-humouredly found himself acting as the Queen's social secretary, as they exchanged scores of notes as to where and how all the visiting notables should be placed. The Queen was often apologetic about it all:

> The Queen is sorry to trouble Lord Palmerston about what at first appears but a trifle, but which Lord Palmerston knows well enough is the source of much discussion and offence, namely the settling of how all these foreigners are to go in to dinner here tomorrow. The Queen sends the dinner list and would be very thankful if Lord Palmerston would take the trouble of marking on it how these Princes and Ambassadors are to go in. The Queen, of course, will be handed in by the Duke of Nassau and the Duchess of Kent by the Duke of Coburg,—and the Queen's [step]-sister by the next highest in rank. Lord Palmerston would also please settle who is to take in the Lady-in-Waiting and sit on the Queen's left.

16

If Lord Palmerston would let the Queen have the list back at any time before dinner tomorrow it would do very well. The Queen is afraid she is giving Lord Palmerston a very troublesome and tiresome task.

After the dinner was over, the Queen even enquired diffidently what her Foreign Minister thought of it:

... The Queen hopes Lord Palmerston thinks the dinner went off well last night, and that all the people were satisfied; she thought they seemed in very good humour.

His answer lacked nothing in gallantry:

... Nothing could go off better than your Majesty's dinner and evening party yesterday. The foreigners seemed all to be highly delighted and much gratified by the gracious manner in which they were all received by your Majesty.

Nor did he fail to make tactful suggestions about having a young American to another party:

... Viscount Palmerston took the liberty of suggesting to Lord Conyngham yesterday evening that it would be politic to invite Mr. van Buren (whom the young ladies call Prince van Buren from his being son of the President) to your Majesty's ball on the 19th ...

Each winter Palmerston, who was a hearty trencherman, suffered a recurrence of gout, although the attacks were mild as yet and usually responded to life at his country home. The Queen was duly sympathetic:

... The Queen hopes that Lord Palmerston has derived benefit from his stay at Broadlands and feels himself better.

Viscount Palmerston begs to return your Majesty his grateful thanks for your Majesty's kind and condescending mention of his health, and he is glad to say that a fortnight's hunting and shooting in Hampshire has enabled him entirely to shake off the remains of an indisposition under which he had suffered before he left London.

The year had seen renewed crises in Canada and Belgium, but, in contrast to the years to come, Queen Victoria left British policies and the drafting of despatches entirely to her two chief ministers. However, as matters reached a head on the Continent in the spring of 1839, Palmerston sent the Queen formal advice of major developments:

> JANUARY 27: . . . Your Majesty will have seen by Sir Edward Dis-brow's [Minister at The Hague] despatches that the concentration of Dutch troops mentioned in these reports was purely defensive, and was the consequence of the military demonstrations previously made by the Belgians; and it appears, moreover, that the Dutch force is inferior in number to the Belgian force opposite to it; and that affords an additional security against the chance of an invasion of Belgium by the Dutch. It is, however, undeniable that when two armies are drawn up in face of each other, separated by a small distance, and animated by mutual hatred, the chances of collision become great and imminent. But it is to be hoped in the present case that the communication made by the conference to the two parties on Thursday last may avert the danger of hostilities between the Dutch and Belgians.
>
> APRIL 19: Viscount Palmerston presents his humble duty to your Majesty and has great satisfaction in reporting to your Majesty that the treaties between Belgium and Holland and between each of those powers and the five powers have just been signed, so that this long pending matter is at length finally settled . . .

The endless stream of queries about protocol did not deprive Palmerston of his sense of humour:

> . . . The Duke of Lucca has a notion that sovereign princes who have had the honour of dining with your Majesty have been invited by note and not by card; if that should be so and if your Majesty should invite the Duke of Lucca to dine at the Palace before his departure, perhaps the invitation might be made by note instead of by card, as it was when the Duke last dined at the Palace. Your Majesty may think this a small matter, but the Duke is a small sovereign.

The Queen nearly lost her Whig ministry in April. The Govern-

ment resigned when its Bill to suspend the Jamaican constitution
only obtained a majority of five. The Queen was heartbroken and
the letters exchanged with her Foreign Minister lacked nothing
in warmth:

> ... The Queen takes this opportunity to express to Lord Palmer-
> ston how much she laments losing his valuable services, which he
> has performed in so admirable a manner and which have so
> greatly promoted the honour and welfare of this country in its
> relations with foreign powers, which will ever be gratefully
> remembered; as also Lord Palmerston's readiness at all times to
> serve the Queen.
>
> The Queen fears she has detained some Foreign Office boxes,
> but she really has had so much to do, and as Lord Palmerston will
> easily understand, has gone through so much grief and anxiety,
> that it has been impossible for her to read through them as yet.

> Viscount Palmerston presents his humble duty to your Majesty
> and begs to return your Majesty his most grateful thanks for your
> Majesty's gracious communication of this morning. It affords
> Viscount Palmerston the most heartfelt satisfaction to know that
> his humble but zealous endeavours to promote the interests of his
> country and to uphold the honour of your Majesty's Crown have
> had the good fortune to meet with your Majesty's approbation;
> and he begs most respectfully to assure your Majesty that the deep
> impression produced by the condescending kindness which he has
> upon all occasions experienced from your Majesty can never be
> effaced from his mind.

However, Sir Robert Peel, the Conservative leader, made an
issue of principle out of effecting changes in the royal household,
particularly in regard to the Queen's Ladies-in-Waiting, and
Melbourne and Palmerston found themselves precariously back
in the saddle again. The Foreign Minister's boxes were becoming
even further encumbered by constant confidential letters from the
Queen to her uncle in Brussels. Most of them were for forwarding
to her cousin, Prince Albert of Saxe-Coburg-Gotha, on whom her
choice had lighted for a husband. In October, the young man
arrived in Britain for the betrothal. The Queen was in little mood
to concentrate on official business, and when another series of

despatches arrived from Persia, she complained plaintively to Palmerston:

> . . . The Queen received yesterday morning a large box from the Foreign Office, full of despatches from Mr. McNeill, some relating to a Treaty of Commerce, and the Queen regrets that she does not quite comprehend them and would be therefore much obliged to Lord Palmerston if he could give the Queen a slight sketch of what they are about . . .

As soon as Albert had left again, the stream of correspondence resumed and, when Palmerston in his turn, married the lady for whose freedom he had been waiting nearly 30 years, he had first to make arrangements for the forwarding of the Queen's letters:

> Viscount Palmerston presents his humble duty to your Majesty and as he is going down to Broadlands tomorrow for a short time upon the occasion of his marriage to the Dowager Countess Cowper, he has desired Mr. Backhouse to forward during his absence the letters which your Majesty may wish to send to Belgium and, if your Majesty will be pleased to place those letters in a box directed to Mr. Backhouse, they will be despatched without delay.

The royal cousins were married in February 1840, and, during the period that led up to the ceremony, Palmerston found himself more involved in the Queen's private affairs than in official business:

> JANUARY 21: The Queen returns the draft of Treaty of Marriage, which she quite approves, but she did not know if she ought to write 'approved' at the end of it or not?
>
> The Queen also sends a letter which she found in a box which had been put by, and which she has kept near three years, she is shocked to say.

> JANUARY 28: The Queen wishes the accompanying letter to her uncle to go by the messenger tonight. The Queen sends it to Lord Palmerston, for fear there might be any mistake, as she is particularly anxious that this letter should reach the King in safety and run no risk of being opened *anywhere*. Lord Palmerston will therefore be so good as to take especial care of it.

JANUARY 30: The Queen requests Lord Palmerston to be so kind as to give Mr. Thompson (who accompanies the messenger who takes this box) a passport to go to Brussels, where Mr. Thompson (the Queen's tailor) is going to take a uniform for Prince Albert.

The Queen was at pains to introduce her husband to the British people and, in June, took him to the Derby. She reported delightedly:

> The Queen returned about an hour ago from Epsom. A beautiful sight, multitudes of people, I am afraid to say how many,—and a very hearty reception. The weather was very fine. Mr. Robertson's 'Little Wonder' won the Derby, which no one expected would have won. Albemarle [Master of the Horse] told us that I was the first sovereign who ever went to Epsom . . .

But a week later a lunatic pot-boy, named Edward Oxford, fired two shots at her as the royal carriage was driving up Constitution Hill. Palmerston was immediately all concern:

> Viscount Palmerston presents his humble duty to your Majesty and though your Majesty must be overwhelmed with congratulations at your Majesty's escape from the aim of the assassin, yet Viscount Palmerston trusts that he may be allowed to express the horror with which he heard of the diabolical attempt and the deep thankfulness which he feels at your Majesty's providential preservation. Viscount Palmerston humbly trusts that the failure of this atrocious attempt may be considered as an indication that your Majesty is reserved for a long and prosperous reign and is destined to assure, for many years to come, the welfare and happiness of this nation.

> The Queen had no time yesterday to thank Lord Palmerston for his kind letter which, however, she does now. The kindness and attachment shown to her on all sides is most gratifying to the Queen.

The Queen's first inclination was to keep her husband away from the affairs of State. She regarded him as her private companion, and seemed unwilling to allow him to form political opinions which might cause differences between them. In this she was to some extent supported by Baroness Lehzen, who feared the loss of the influence of a lifetime, but the Prince was too intelligent and diligent to be satisfied for long with such isolation. Melbourne, still the Queen's favourite adviser, endeavoured, to his credit, to break down the Queen's imperious intention of reserving to herself exclusive knowledge and control of public affairs. Then there was Stockmar.

The self-effacing baron had already been employed by King Leopold to supervise the final stage of the Prince's education and on many confidential matters connected with the royal betrothal. His influence over the Prince was immense and his undoubted devotion to the House of Coburg made him see in the Queen's consort an instrument for his political and constitutional theories. Stockmar sought no power for himself, which made him an even more effective force behind the scenes. But he believed passionately in certain fixed ideas. His conception of monarchy reserved for the sovereign the political power and position of a permanent prime minister, above party, but adhering to general principles to which the elected representatives of the people must be persuaded to conform. In foreign affairs he was obsessed by the need to combine the heterogeneous German States into one nation under the leadership of Prussia. He was also convinced of the necessity for close relations between Germany and Britain to preserve a balance of power in Europe.

Stockmar could not expect to inculcate these theories directly in the Queen's thoughts, but in the Prince he saw a ready instrument. All the Coburg princes were notable for their intelligence. The marriages of the family were extending their ties and influence all over Europe—Belgium, Austria, Portugal, France. Their own principalities were too small to permit direct intervention in the affairs of Germany, but this left them all the more free to adopt and propagate large political ideas. Throughout his life, Prince Albert was to prove himself an industrious and ready pupil.

The Queen had shown only a superficial interest in and understanding of foreign affairs during the first three years of her reign and had contented herself with brief and benevolent expressions of approval of all her Foreign Minister did or explained to her.

She had not experienced Palmerston at his most turbulent and forceful. The Greek and Belgian crises antedated her accession and his opposition to absolutism in Portugal and Spain, already evident, had yet to cause major repercussions. However, he was at this time engaged in one of the major coups of his whole ministerial career, and must have been distinctly startled at the sudden lucid interest the Court took in his proceedings.

The situation in the Middle East had been bedevilled for years by the revolt of Mehemet Ali, Pasha of Egypt, against his nominal suzerain, the Sultan of Turkey. It was an article of faith with Palmerston that the integrity of the Turkish empire should be maintained as a barrier against Russian incursions in the Mediterranean. He was also determined that the French should not repeat their Napoleonic history of gaining influence in Egypt and control of Britain's overland route to India. He therefore set himself the difficult task of persuading the other four great powers, France, Prussia, Russia and Austria, to agree to a joint guarantee with Britain of the Sultan's sovereignty. For various reasons of self-interest, three of them agreed, but France, hopeful of advantage, refused to discipline Mehemet Ali in concert with the others. So Palmerston, with some assistance from Austria, offered help to the Sultan and placed a British fleet at his disposal.

It was a classic example of his 'gunboat diplomacy'. The French were outraged and threatened mobilisation. Thiers, the Prime Minister, and Guizot, the Ambassador in London, expatiated volubly on their national interests, the other European countries vacillated, the British Cabinet was split on the issue, and only Palmerston, with some backing from Melbourne, stood firm. His gamble came off. Turkish forces with British aid defeated Mehemet Ali before Acre, and a covert hint that Britain might mobilise too, soon brought the French to heel. The Thiers Government was dismissed.

The British Court had taken alarm. In September 1840, the Queen interceded with Lord Melbourne:

> If Lord Palmerston is not in any great hurry for them, might the Queen show these [drafts] to the Prince? Lord Melbourne shall have them by half-past 3 at latest. If Lord Melbourne approves

this, he will be so good as to send them back. The Queen thinks
Palmerston's letter very well done, only a little too severe upon
France, and a little too strong as to her secret schemes and bad
faith; this will I am afraid not do good and only irritate and
wound the King's feelings; could not Palmerston soften that down
a little? Lord M. could say that the Queen thought the King would
feel it.

In October, with his schemes fructifying, Palmerston was able to
start his apologia:

> ... Viscount Palmerston submits to your Majesty some interesting
> letters which he received some days ago from M. de Hummelauer
> [Austrian Minister in London], on his way through Paris, show-
> ing that there never has been any real foundation for the alarm of
> war with France, which was felt by some persons in this country.
>
> Viscount Palmerston also submits a despatch from M. Thiers to
> M. Guizot, which was communicated to him yesterday by M.
> Guizot and which seems to open a prospect of an amicable and
> satisfactory understanding between France and the four powers.
>
> Viscount Palmerston also submits a note from Mr. Bulwer
> [First Secretary at the British Embassy in Paris], intimating that
> the French Government would be contented with an arrangement
> which should leave Mehemet Ali in possession of Egypt alone,
> without any part of Syria, and Viscount Palmerston submits that
> such is the arrangement which it would on all accounts be desir-
> able to accomplish. There seems reason to think that the bombard-
> ment of Beirut and the deposal of Mehemet Ali by the Sultan have
> greatly contributed to render the French more reasonable on this
> question, by exciting in their minds an apprehension that unless
> some arrangement be speedily effected, the operations now going
> on in the Levant will end in the entire overthrow of Mehemet Ali.

But the Queen's letters had suddenly acquired a much greater
authority, although their tone was still conciliatory:

> The Queen, in returning these letters, must express to Lord
> Palmerston her very great satisfaction at the favourable turn
> affairs have taken; and the Queen earnestly trusts that this demon-
> stration of returning amity on the part of France, will be met in a
> very friendly spirit by Lord Palmerston and the rest of her
> Government. The Queen feels certain that this change on the part

of France is also greatly owing to the peaceable disposition of the King of the French, and she thinks that in consideration of the difficulties the King has had to contend with, and which he seems finally to have overcome, we should make some return, and indeed, as Lord Palmerston states, the arrangement proposed is the best which can be desired . . .

At the beginning of November, Palmerston could announce his double triumph:

Viscount Palmerston presents his humble duty to your Majesty and in addition to the good news from Syria, which confirms the defeat and dispersion of the forces both of Ibrahim and of Solyman Pasha, with the loss of 8,000 prisoners, 24 pieces of cannon, the whole of their camp, baggage and stores, followed by the flight of those two generals with a small escort. He has the satisfaction of informing your Majesty that the new French ministers had a majority of 68 upon the vote for the election of the President of the Chamber . . .

The Queen insisted on her point:

The Queen is much pleased to hear of the very good news from Syria and also from Paris. She earnestly trusts that now that the affairs have taken so decisive a turn in Syria, it may render some general agreement between France and the allies for the ultimate settlement of this intricate question easy. The Queen is most anxious to see this done and feels certain that Lord Palmerston and the rest of her Government will be as anxious as she is to support the King of the French and the present Government. The Spanish being so pacific will also make this easier.

In reply, Palmerston for the first time found himself obliged to give a full exposition of his attitude:

. . . There is no doubt a large party among the leading politicians in France who have long contemplated the establishment of a virtually, if not actually, independent State in Egypt and Syria, under the direct protection and influence of France, and that party feel great disappointment and resentment at finding their schemes in this respect baffled. But that party will not revenge themselves on the four powers by making a revolution in France, and they are enlightened enough to see that France cannot revenge herself by making war against the four powers, who are much stronger than she is.

The late French Government, in order to intimidate the four powers, raised a war cry in France and excited the nation by asserting that France had been insulted and deceived and, when a government begins the work of agitation, it cannot fail of being successful. But the King of the French co-operated with his ministers in this agitation and therefore must have felt an inward conviction that the excitement could be controlled if it should not produce the desired effect. It was in fact certain that, when the stimulating action of the Government should cease to act, the excitement created by that action would gradually die away; and this is beginning already to be seen, as is proved by the immense and unexpectedly large majority in favour of the Government on the election of the Speaker.

The French Government, who wish to have the double advantage of the reality of strength at home and of the character of weakness abroad, say that this division is no test of the relative strength of parties on the question of peace or war; but it surely must be an indication that the peace party is much the strongest, although the majority may vary in amount from time to time. For Odillon Barrot was the person intended to be proposed by the Thiers administration and therefore the trial of strength was between the followers of the Thiers ministry and the supporters of the Soult and Guizot ministry, or, in other words, between the war party and the peace party. But Viscount Palmerston would submit that even if M. Thiers had remained Minister, France would not have made war till the beginning of next summer, because your Majesty will see that France would not have had 300,000 men disposable for aggressive war till new levies had been raised, which could not have been completed till next spring or summer; and even that amount of force, large as it is, would have been considerably inferior in number and in composition to the force which Germany could bring into the field . . .

It is very natural that the French Government, after having failed to extort concessions upon the Turkish question by menaces of foreign war, should now endeavour to obtain those concessions by appealing to fears of another kind; and should say that such concessions are necessary in order to prevent revolution in France; but Viscount Palmerson would submit to your Majesty his deep conviction that this appeal is not better founded than the other; and that a firm and resolute perseverance on the part of the four powers in the measures which they have taken in hand will effect a settlement of the affairs of Turkey, which will afford great additional security for the future peace of Europe without producing in the meantime either war with France or revolution in France.

France and the rest of Europe are entirely different now from what they were in 1792. The French nation is as much interested now to avoid further revolution, as it was interested then in ridding itself by any means of the enormous and intolerable abuses which then existed; France then imagined she had much to gain by foreign war, France now knows she has everything to lose by foreign war.

Europe then (at least the Continental States) had also a strong desire to get rid of innumerable abuses which pressed heavily upon the people of all countries. Those abuses have now in general been removed. People in many parts of Germany have been admitted, more or less, to a share in the management of their own affairs; a German feeling and a spirit of nationality has sprung up among all the German people, and the Germans, instead of receiving the French as liberators, as many of them did in 1792 and 1793, would now rise as one man to repel a hateful invasion. Upon all these grounds Viscount Palmerston deems it his duty to your Majesty to express his strong conviction that the appeals made to your Majesty's good feelings by the King of the French, upon the score of the danger of revolution in France unless concessions are made to the French Government, have no foundation in truth and are only exertions of skilful diplomacy . . .

Back came a lengthy memorandum, totally unlike anything the Queen had written before. Another hand was clearly starting to guide her pen:

The Queen has to acknowledge the receipt of Lord Palmerston's letter of this morning, which she has read with great attention. The Queen will make just a few observations upon various points in it, to which she would wish to draw Lord Palmerston's attention; the Queen does so with strict impartiality, having had ample opportunity of hearing both sides of this intricate and highly important question. First of all, it strikes the Queen that even if M. Thiers did

27

raise the cry which was so loud for war in France, (but which the Queen cannot believe he did to the extent Lord Palmerston does) that such an excitement, once raised in a country like France, where the people are more excitable than almost in any other nation, cannot be so easily controlled and stopped again, and the Queen thinks this will be seen in time.

Secondly, the Queen cannot either quite agree in Lord Palmerston's observation that the French Government states the danger of internal revolution, if not supported, merely to extract fresh concessions, for Mehemet Ali. The Queen does not pretend to say that this danger is not exaggerated, but depend upon it, a certain degree of danger does exist, and that the situation of the King of the French, and the present French Government, is not an easy one; the majority too, cannot be depended upon, as many would vote against Odillon Barrot who would not vote on other occasions with the Soult/Guizot ministry.

Thirdly, the danger of war is doubtless also greatly exaggerated, as also the numbers of the French troops, but Lord Palmerston must recollect how very warlike the French are, and that if once roused, they will not listen to the calm reasoning of those who wish for peace or think of the great risk they run of losing by war, but only of glory and revenging an insult, as they call it.

Fourthly, the Queen sees the difficulty there exists at the present moment of making any specific offer to France, but she must at the same time repeat how highly and exceedingly important she considers it that some sort of conciliatory agreement should be come to with France, for she cannot believe that the appeals made to her by the King of the French are only exertions of skilful diplomacy. The Queen's earnest and only wish is peace and a maintenance of friendly relations with her allies, consistent with the honour and dignity of her country. She does not think, however, that the last would be compromised by attempts to soften the irritation still existing in France, or by attempts to bring France back to her former position in the Oriental Question. She earnestly hopes that Lord Palmerston will consider this, will reflect upon the importance of not driving France to extremities, and of conciliatory measures, without showing fear (for our success on the coast of Syria shows our power) or without yielding to threats. France has been humbled, and France is in the wrong, but therefore it is easier than if we had failed, to do something to bring matters right again.—The Queen has thus frankly stated her opinion, which she thought it right Lord Palmerston should know, and which she is sure he will see is only dictated by an earnest desire to see all as much united as possible upon this important subject.

That was the only demonstration of independence for the time being. When, in February, Palmerston forwarded despatches which 'virtually show that the Turkish Question is brought to a close, begs most humbly to congratulate your Majesty upon this rapid and peaceful settlement of the matter which at different periods has assumed appearances so threatening to the peace of Europe', the Queen was duly gracious:

> The Queen has received Lord Palmerston's communication of this morning with sincere satisfaction and she congratulates him on this successful termination of this most important and serious question.
>
> The Queen sends Lord Palmerston a letter from Dr. Kuper to the Duchess of Kent, perhaps Lord Palmerston could do something for the young man. What shall the Queen state to the Duchess of Kent, who is very anxious about this young man? . . .

On such matters as the personnel of his office Palmerston could stand firm:

> Viscount Palmerston presents his humble duty to your Majesty and begs to submit that there would be much difficulty in complying with Mr. Kuper's wishes for promotion for his son in the diplomatic service of your Majesty. It is for many reasons desirable that all your Majesty's diplomatic agents should be entirely and unquestionably British subjects, both by birth and by blood. For first of all there are so many reputable subjects of your Majesty and many of them persons of good family, who are always candidates for every appointment which may anywhere fall vacant, that it would tend to give well-founded dissatisfaction if foreigners were on those occasions to be preferred; and then, in the next place, no diplomatic agent who is not purely and entirely British can represent with full advantage and the necessary weight British interests in foreign countries. Now Viscount Palmerston begs to submit that Mr. Kuper the younger, though he was born

(Viscount Palmerston believes) in England, is by descent and blood a foreigner; and that the foregoing reasons militate against his being appointed Secretary of Legation to a British mission abroad. Viscount Palmerston, moreover, has alway understood that when Mr. Kuper was first appointed as attaché to the Frankfurt mission, it was explained to him that he could not be considered as entering the British diplomatic body and that he was not to look for promotion.

The spring of 1841 was punctuated by trouble in China, but this involved no conflict of opinion between Court and Foreign Office. Then, in May, came an exchange which proved a harbinger of acute dissension between them in the years to come:

> The Queen fears there must be some mistake about sending the despatches, as she has not received one box for the last five days, and she fears that if they delay sending them they will send in a day or two (as they often do) such a number at once that she cannot get through them. It does not signify if they send only one at a time, but sometimes they wait till they have a whole batch to send, by which means they come very late to the Queen. She has also perceived once or twice that they have sent to her drafts to approve when the originals have already been sent away, which of course renders her doing so useless. Perhaps Lord Palmerston could look into this and rectify these mistakes, which may arise from the quantity of business which has to be transacted.

> Viscount Palmerston presents his humble duty to your Majesty and is very sorry to find that the clerks of the Foreign Office have been so negligent, but he will give directions to prevent the recurrence of similar inconvenience to your Majesty. With regard, however, to the circumstance that your Majesty has not received any boxes with despatches during the past few days, it may perhaps have arisen from there having been but few received at the Foreign Office during those days and most of those which did arrive have unfortunately been detained longer than usual by Viscount Palmerston, in consequence of his time having been so much occupied by unavoidable interviews and by attendance in the House of Commons, that he has had less leisure than usual for reading his despatches.

> With regard to the drafts, Viscount Palmerston had given

directions that despatches should never be sent out till the drafts had been returned with your Majesty's approval, and he will pointedly repeat that order. But just at present Mr. Backhouse is away for a short time on urgent private business, and Lord Leveson was obliged to go away two days ago for election matters, and the Foreign Office therefore may not be conducted for a few days as regularly as usual.

But the Whig ministry was tottering to its end. Melbourne was tired, the finances were in a chaotic state and the economy disordered. Defeated on the Budget and a vote of confidence, the Government resigned, the Tories swept in under Sir Robert Peel, flying the banner of protective tariffs, and Palmerston faced five years in Opposition. He and the Queen exchanged warm messages:

... The Queen seizes this opportunity to express to Lord Palmerston her sincere regret at losing his valuable services, and her wishes for his and Lady Palmerston's welfare and happiness.

... Viscount Palmerston begs to be allowed to tender to your Majesty the grateful thanks of himself and of Viscountess Palmerston for your Majesty's gracious expressions towards them. Viscount Palmerston sees with deep regret the termination of those duties in your Majesty's service, in the course of which he has had the honour of experiencing from your Majesty so much condescending personal kindness and such flattering official confidence; and it affords him the highest gratification to have obtained your Majesty's approbation.

CHAPTER II

Seeds of Discontent

SIR ROBERT PEEL'S PREMIERSHIP SAW THE RAPID FLOWERING IN authority, maturity and political insight of the young Queen and her consort. In 1841 they were neophytes. By 1846 they had developed a mind and will of their own. For many months, the Queen continued to lean heavily on her favourite, Lord Melbourne, to a degree almost unconstitutional. Although she came to admire Peel's integrity, she never warmed to him. It was the Prince who found in him a twin soul—upright, industrious, humourless and above all prepared to grant him complete confidence.

It was not long before the Prince was seeing every state paper. With the Queen bearing four children in five years, the Prince found himself representing her at ministerial interviews and conducting an increasing share of the royal duties. If Peel was her elected political adviser, the Prince, with Stockmar's aid, became her private political adviser and secretary. He was diligent, enquiring and indefatigable. He engaged in direct correspondence with ministers, wrote for the royal archives in his own hand a summary of every interview or political conjuncture, and penned innumerable memoranda, for the files, for distribution and attention, or to serve as a basis for the Queen's official letters and, as time went on, began to draft many of the Queen's letters himself.

Not only that, but the Prince maintained a voluminous private correspondence on foreign affairs with his relations: his uncle in Brussels, his brother in Coburg, his cousin at Lisbon, the Queen's half-brother at Leiningen, the Kings of Prussia and Saxony and Archduke John of Austria. He often quoted from British official documents and commented freely on British internal affairs. Stockmar's pupil had indeed become a force in his own right, and

Palmerston was to return to a very different and less malleable Court.

The five years of Tory Government were relatively placid. There was famine and insurrection in Ireland, but in Britain Peel stabilised the finances and appeared firmly in control until his conversion to the policy of repealing the Corn Laws split his supporters irrevocably into two camps.

In foreign affairs, it was a period of conciliation. The Tory Foreign Secretary, Lord Aberdeen, was a temporiser by nature, anxious to restore amicable relations with the European powers which had so often had to feel the lash of Palmerston's more positive policies. The French, in particular, were given occasion to recover from their humiliation over the Syrian affair, successful visits were exchanged between the two Courts, even the French seizure of Tahiti from nominal British occupation was smoothed over. When the liberal and pro-British Government of Spain was overthrown, largely through French intrigue, Aberdeen remained complacent. He allowed his envoy, Lord Ashburton, to negotiate a new Canadian boundary which seemed to make too many concessions to the Americans. He also paid little more than lip service to the suppression of the African slave trade.

All this was anathema to Palmerston, who thought he saw his cherished positions being abandoned one by one. He spent some part of his time in Opposition in well-earned idleness—embellishing his Broadlands estate, maintaining his racing stable, improving the lot of his Irish tenants and repeating, with his wife, part of the Grand Tour of Europe he had first made with his father nearly fifty years earlier. But he had been far too long in politics to surrender to sloth. Not only did he and Lady Palmerston conduct one of the most popular *salons* in London, to which the leaders of political, diplomatic and social life flocked, but as the issues in Parliament hardened, he became one of the Government's most trenchant and forceful critics. Foreign policy was ever his special sphere, but he spoke eloquently in favour of free trade, and roundly denounced the Tories' anti-Catholic policies in Ireland.

His friend and brother-in-law, Lord Melbourne, was in a slow physical decline, but the leadership of the Whig-Liberal group did not devolve on Palmerston, as he might have expected from being its dominant Minister in the previous Government. His long earlier years as a Pittite and Canningite Tory still tainted him with heresy in the eyes of the great Whig magnates, and their support gravitated to that fierce little Reformer, Lord John Russell. Nor had Palmerston's turbulent forays during his ten years as Foreign Minister endeared him unanimously to all the supporters of the Whig coalition. When Peel's Government stumbled in the winter of 1845 over their first Corn Law dissensions, Lord John Russell's attempt to form an alternative administration failed, largely due to the refusal of the Grey faction to accept Palmerston as Foreign Minister, and Palmerston's refusal, as a matter of confidence, to accept any other post. Even the Queen and the Prince, the former basking in the peaceful world of her 'good Aberdeen', the latter in the confidence of his personal friend, Sir Robert Peel, and both reconciled to the French royal family into which three of their cousins had married, rather hoped they might be spared the compulsive Palmerston. His uncompromising support for liberal movements everywhere would only cause exasperation to the absolutist European monarchs who were their relatives. But when the time came for the Tories to go out, there was no other real candidate for the Foreign Office than Palmerston. Their years of conflict with him were about to begin.

Trouble over the Corn Laws finally overthrew Peel and Palmerston returned, in spite of misgivings, as Foreign Secretary under Lord John Russell. Ibrahim Pasha, heir to the Mehemet Ali whom Palmerston had defeated at Acre six years before, was paying a good-will visit to London. The new Foreign Minister warned him against any further attempt by Egypt to break away from Turkey and reported, flatteringly, to the Queen:

> . . . Your Majesty may perhaps have heard that Ibrahim Pasha learnt to write his name while your Majesty's messenger was waiting with your Majesty's album; and that when he had written his name in the book he threw away the pen, saying that as the first time in his life that he had written his name had been for the Queen of England, so it should also be the last, for he would not write it again for anybody else . . .

Water colour by Eugène Lami, reproduced by gracious permission of Her Majesty the Queen

But as Palmerston resumed office the chief threat to European tranquillity came from the other end of the Mediterranean. In Portugal, where yet another Coburg cousin of the British royal pair, Ferdinand, had married Queen Maria II, rebellion simmered. In Spain, the Queen was now aged sixteen and her sister, the Infanta, a year less. In an era of dynastic marriages their hands were coveted, not least, on behalf of his son, the Duc de Montpensier, by the Orleanist King of France, Louis-Philippe. Coburg in-laws he had a-plenty. His eldest daughter had become the second wife of Leopold of Belgium. His son, the Duc de Nemours, and two more daughters were all married to Coburg cousins of Victoria and Albert, who reserved for him their fondest expressions. But his throne was not, for that, more secure. Louis-Philippe suffered a positive epidemic of assassination attempts during his reign and when Palmerston reported the most recent at the end of July 1846 the Queen wrote back:

> The news conveyed in Lord Palmerston's letter and the enclosures (which the Queen had forwarded to the Prince) have shocked us dreadfully, and the Queen cannot be sufficiently thankful for the providential escape of her dear friends, the King and Queen of the French and the royal family. But how awful are these attempts on the lives of such exemplary people! And after all, what can be the object, for the King's death would be no advantage to them,—the dynasty being fortunately so firmly established, that no serious disorder could ensue . . .

To Palmerston, the French were potential revolutionaries and trouble-makers, whoever was at their head, and his reply contained more than a hint of unction:

> . . . It is indeed, as your Majesty observes, difficult to understand what object any set of men in France can imagine they could accomplish by the death of the King of the French, seeing that his dynasty is so firmly established and his family so numerous and that there is no presentable pretender either among the Buonaparte family or in the elder branch of the Bourbons and seeing that a republic is now an impossibility in France. But there certainly is in France a certain number of fanatical republicans, who have persuaded themselves, though without the slightest foundation in

35

truth and justice, that the King of the French entered into some implied engagements with Lafayette and the republicans at the time of the Revolution of July 1830 to make the government of France more democratic than it is; and that those engagements have not been kept.—Viscount Palmerston believes that there is no ground whatever for this opinion but he has been informed that it does exist among a small set of men.

The Queen was about to receive a rude shock to her confidence in the 'dear good' King of the French. The question of finding a suitable husband for the adolescent Queen of Spain had reached a juncture comparable to the succession problem which had led to Marlborough's wars. Under the Treaty of Utrecht, the crowns of France and Spain were never to be united in one person. Louis-Philippe and his Prime Minister, Guizot, hoped to circumvent this by arranging for Queen Isabella to marry her Spanish Bourbon cousin, Francisco, Duke of Cadiz, who was reputed to be effeminate and impotent. His brother, Enrique, Duke of Seville, described as 'a horrid little monster', was another possible candidate. In the hope that Isabella would remain childless, Louis-Philippe proposed to marry his handsome son, the Duc de Montpensier, to her younger sister, Luisa. The children of their union might then level the Pyrenees which had proved such an impassable barrier even to the great Napoleon's dynastic ambitions.

In this *imbroglio*, Queen Victoria and Prince Albert had another nominee, their personable cousin Leopold of Saxe-Coburg-Kohary. However, during two meetings with the French King at Eu in 1843 and 1845, it had been tacitly agreed that Leopold's suit should not be pressed, providing Montpensier did not marry Luisa until Isabella had produced children.

When Palmerston took over the Foreign Office from Lord Aberdeen, the situation was still fluid, albeit sharply complicated by the precocious Spanish Queen's urgent desire for a mate. Palmerston favoured Don Enrique, not so much because he was the less ill-favoured of the two principal suitors, as for his connection with the pro-English Liberal party. However, probably in an attempt to smooth his return to office with the suspicious British royal pair, Palmerston sent in July 1846 a despatch to Henry

Lytton Bulwer, the British Minister in Madrid, confirming Aberdeen's instructions to refrain from advocating any particular candidate. For the record, and out of deference for Prince Albert's known views, Palmerston enumerated the three principal suitors as Prince Leopold and the Dukes Francisco and Enrique. As proof of good faith, Palmerston showed the despatch to Count Jarnac, secretary to the French Embassy in London.

The letter had included some trenchant Palmerstonian comments about the Spanish 'Moderates' ministry and its packed parliament. In August this was followed by further exhortations to Bulwer to reinforce British influence with the Liberals. Queen Victoria took exception:

> . . . The Queen has read very attentively Lord Palmerston's draft to Mr. Bulwer, which came down to her this morning [she wrote on August 17]. She cannot conceal from Lord Palmerston that its perusal has raised some apprehension in her mind,—which she thinks it right to state to Lord John Russell, whom she will desire to communicate them to Lord Palmerston . . .

> . . . Viscount Palmerston would beg to submit [the Foreign Minister wrote in reply] that they are not notes to be presented to any foreign government, nor despatches to be in any way made public, but that they are confidential instructions given to one of your Majesty's Ministers abroad, upon matters upon which your Majesty's Government have been urgently pressed to enable that Minister to give advice; and Viscount Palmerston would beg also to submit that in a case of this kind it would not be enough to communicate drily the opinion of the British Government, without stating and explaining some of the reasons upon which those opinions are founded . . .

> . . . The Queen did not object to the 'stating and explaining some of the reasons upon which the opinions given by Lord Palmerston were founded', but thought that amongst those reasons, that of counteracting French influence by means of strengthening the Liberal Party was the prominent one . . .

The damage had been done. King Louis-Philippe, who considered Palmerston 'the enemy of his house', and had never forgiven the humiliation of the Mehemet Ali affair, had seen his chance as soon as Jarnac sent his report. He used the mere mention of Prince Leopold's name by Palmerston as sufficient excuse for considering the tacit agreement of Eu with the Queen and Aberdeen as null and void, liberating him from all restraint concerning Montpensier. The criticism of the Spanish Government was forwarded gleefully to Madrid, where the French had a willing ally in the Queen Mother, Christina, who could abide neither Enrique nor Leopold. Queen Isabella was to be forced to marry her impotent cousin, and Montpensier her sister without further ado.

It was a bad miscalculation. In seeking to humiliate Palmerston, Louis Philippe's sheer bad faith outraged the British Court. On September 10, the Queen wrote to her Foreign Minister:

> The Queen has this moment received this letter from the Queen of the French,—in which she announces the unlucky marriage of Montpensier! The letter is a confidential one (the Queen of the French and the Queen are in frequent correspondence)—and similar to what the Queen generally writes when she announces any event of the family—marriage or birth. This announcement of what really is a political step, as if it was a family event like the other marriages of the princes and princesses, is completely contradictory and inconstant; it must be either one or the other.—The Queen has thought it right to answer the Queen of the French and annexes a copy of the letter she is going to write,—in which she carefully abstains from acknowledging the marriage of Montpensier,—and has spoken plainly out; it is very disagreeable to have to write to a friend and a most amiable person such an answer to an announcement of marriage, but really the French have behaved so very unhandsomely and unfairly about this—to say the least. Prevent the marriage the Queen hardly thinks we can, but delay it, she hopes we shall . . .

The following day, Palmerston had a long interview with Count de Jarnac, and in his report to the Queen was able to give his anti-French prejudices full rein:

> . . . With respect to the Montpensier marriage, the Count de Jarnac stated that it had been understood with Lord Aberdeen that the British Government would not object to the Duke of Mont-

pensier marrying the Infanta, provided the marriage should be deferred till after the marriage of the Queen of Spain should have produced a successor to the Spanish Crown; but that in February last the French Government had stated that they should withdraw that limiting condition if the Prince Leopold should ever be put forward by the British Government as a candidate; that this Prince had been so put forward in Viscount Palmerston's first despatch to Mr. Bulwer, and that consequently the French Government felt themselves released from the restriction. That Queen Christina had refused to consent to the marriage of Queen Isabella with the Duke of Cadiz unless the King of the French consented at the same time to the marriage of the Duke of Montpensier to the Infanta, and that for the reason above mentioned the French Government felt themselves at liberty to consent to that request.

Your Majesty will at once see the weakness and fallacy of this line of argument, and Viscount Palmerston did not fail to point it out to the Count de Jarnac. He said that with regard to the marriage of the Queen of Spain, he found no trace in the Foreign Office of any such agreement as Count Jarnac had claimed between Lord Aberdeen and the French Government, nor did Lord Aberdeen, when he gave Viscount Palmerston an account of the state of affairs make any mention of it . . . That even if such a verbal agreement had been made by Lord Aberdeen, it was not binding upon your Majesty's present Government. But Viscount Palmerston added that such agreement, even if it ever took place, had not been infringed; that Prince Leopold has not been put forward by the British Government as a candidate for the Queen of Spain. That Viscount Palmerston had explicitly stated to Count Jarnac, from first to last, that Prince Leopold was not an English candidate, and that all the leading members of the British Government thought, on the contrary, that a Spanish Prince would be the fittest husband for the Queen of Spain; and that consequently unless the French Government believed Viscount Palmerston to be capable of deliberate deceit and wilful falsehood, they had no ground for suspecting that the British Government had departed from the understanding asserted to have been come to with Lord Aberdeen, although they were at perfect liberty to do so if they thought fit. That in point of fact not only had England not put forward Prince Leopold as a candidate, but it was mainly owing to British influence and counsel that Prince Leopold had refrained from accepting the offer which the French Government well knew had been made to him; and that the French Government most assuredly knew the non-acceptance as well as they knew the offer. —That England has therefore behaved towards the King of the French with the most scrupulous delicacy, and with the greatest regard for feelings on his part, which they neither admitted to be just, nor acknowledged to be reasonable; and that the return which has been made by the French Government has been to *escamoter un mariage* which they well knew would be most offensive to England.

That when about the 27th August or some days sooner Count Jarnac said to Viscount Palmerston that the French Government would willingly co-operate with that of England in recommending Don Enrique, it now seems by M. Guizot's admission that, in consequence of instructions which must have been sent some time previously from Paris, M. Bresson [the French Ambassador in Madrid] was on that very day settling the marriage of the Duke of Cadiz.

Viscount Palmerston said that with regard to the marriage of the Queen of Spain, that was a matter as to which the British Government have no political objection to make. They deeply regret that a young Queen should have been compelled by moral force, and to serve the personal and political interests of other persons, to accept for husband a person whom she can neither like nor respect and with whom her future life will certainly be unhappy at home, even if it should be not characterised by circumstances which would tend to lower her in the estimation of her people. But these are matters which concern the Queen and people of Spain more than the Government and people of England. But that the projected marriage of the Duke of Montpensier is a very different matter, and must have a political bearing that must exercise a most unfortunate effect upon the relations between England and France.

That even upon Count Jarnac's own statement the King of the French has departed from a condition of his own proposing, without the intervention of that releasing circumstance which Count Jarnac says had been specified in February, but of which Viscount Palmerston never heard before. That consequently the word and promise of the King of the French given to your Majesty has been broken, and in a secret and underhand manner. That not only has this promise been so broken, but that the King of the French has virtually departed from a principle which he himself acknowledged to be just when he declined to allow one of his sons to become husband to the Queen of Spain; because, by marrying one of his sons to the heiress presumptive to the throne, he placed that son in a situation by virtue of which he might at any time arrive indirectly at the very position which it was admitted he ought not directly to fill; and that your Majesty's Government have great reason to complain that a step should have been taken without any previous communications with them.

That whatever may have passed betwen the French Government and Lord Aberdeen on this matter, your Majesty's present Ministers, being in no degree bound by such communications, consider a marriage between a French Prince and the Infanta to be under any circumstances liable to the strongest and most just and well founded political objections on the part of Great Britain. That it betokens a revival of those ambitious designs of France which disturbed the peace of Europe in the beginning of the last century, when acted upon by Louis XIV, and which, in the beginning of the present century, when again attempted by Napoleon Buonaparte, again made Spain the battlefield for England and France.—That there is but too much reason to fear that a similar attempt on the part of the present dynasty of France will sooner or later lead to similarly deplorable results; but that the responsibility of such calamities, if they should happen, must rest upon those who have chosen wantonly to become their cause.

That in the meantime Great Britain will cling as long as she can to peaceful and friendly relations with France, but that this marriage, if it shall take place, will be so manifest a proof of divergent policy, if not of the contemplation of contingent hostility on the part of France, and the whole of this transaction will so clearly show the absence of entente or cordiality on the side of France, that England must henceforward look to herself and make her own interests the exclusive guide of her conduct; or that if she shall seek alliances and intimacy with foreign powers, that intimacy and those alliances must be calculated with the view of obtaining for Great Britain a counter-balance for the accession of political, military and naval strength which is the evident object of this projected marriage to secure to France on the side of Spain. That it is for the

French Government to judge whether the friendship and confidence of England is of any and of what value to France; it is also for them to consider what, after all, the chances may be, that this marriage may fail in procuring for France all the advantages which she expects to derive from it.

Insurrections or disturbances in Spain may lead the Spanish Government to call for military assistance from France; that assistance, which without a family alliance would be declined, may in consequence of such alliance be granted. The scenes of 1808 may be revived; in addition to 100,000 men in Algiers, France may have to send 100,000 men to Spain.—A national war may again be excited, British assistance may again be asked for and granted, and another Peninsular War may terminate in the loss of all the political advantages to secure which it was begun. That no doubt can be entertained of the advantage to England and to France of a confiding and good understanding between the Governments of the two countries; that it was for the French Government to judge whether it was expedient or not for France to sacrifice the certain advantage for the chance of the uncertain one, but that Viscount Palmerston begged Count Jarnac to impress upon M. Guizot that the sentiments which he had thus explained were not to be considered as those of the present Government, or of the present moment, but that they would be shared by any men who may hereafter become Ministers of the Crown, and are more likely to be increased than weakened by future events.

That was indeed a classic Palmerstonian effusion and, for once, the Queen was entirely in agreement:

> The Queen returns this memorandum to Lord Palmerston, and quite approves the language which he held to Count Jarnac . . .

However, when Palmerston wrote to suggest that Bulwer should be promoted from Minister to Ambassador and that he had 'authorised Mr. Bulwer to draw upon secret service money to induce the Spanish newspapers to write against the Montpensier marriage', the Queen counselled caution:

> The Queen . . . entirely approves of the draft for Mr. Bulwer, as she thinks it our duty to protest against the marriage of the Duc de

Montpensier with the Infanta, as long as she is the heiress presumptive to the Crown of Spain.

The proposition to raise Mr. Bulwer to the rank of Ambassador in order to put him on a par with the Comte de Bresson, the Queen does not approve. This would be a public declaration that a fight in diplomacy and intrigue was engaged in between the two Ambassadors, which it would become a point of honour for both countries not to be beaten before the eyes of Europe.

As to money assistance, Lord Palmerston and Mr. Bulwer must know best what arms must be used in a country like Spain, but the Queen would be very sorry to be personally implicated or cognisant of the underhand dealings which in any other country could not be considered irreproachable.

The Queen is glad that Lord Palmerston means to caution Mr. Bulwer not to do anything that might encourage an insurrection. The French Government ought to be informed (in the Queen's opinion) of our having protested against the marriage.

The Queen pressed for further information, but Britain was faced by a *fait accompli*:

Viscount Palmerston presents his humble duty to your Majesty and has had no accounts from Spain later than those which your Majesty has seen. It seemed to be probable however, from Mr. Bulwer's last despatches, that the Cortes would approve the two marriages by a large majority, as the elections had been so managed that almost all the opposition had been excluded. It would seem that the French Government is determined to press forward both marriages without delay . . .

Although the British press and public opinion raged for weeks about French perfidy, by November cooler counsels prevailed at Court:

. . . The Queen thinks it would be well to check now, if possible, the violent tirades in 'The Times' on the French Government [came a note to Palmerston on November 7]; it is not dignified and will end in enraging the French nation, which fortunately till now is not ill-disposed towards us.

. . . Your Majesty's observation about 'The Times' is perfectly just and well founded [he replied], and Viscount Palmerston had so far anticipated your Majesty's wish that he had pointed out yesterday to a person who has some means of communicating with 'The Times' that it would be better to allow the subject of the Montpensier marriage to drop and he will again mention the matter to that person. But Viscount Palmerston has not himself any personal acquaintance or intercourse with anybody belonging to the management of 'The Times'. Viscount Palmerston, however, was informed yesterday by a person likely to know, that both 'The Times' and 'Chronicle' have suffered a good deal in their circulation by the competition of the 'Daily News'; and although that last mentioned paper is supposed to be on the verge of ruin, inasmuch as the proprietors are said to have spent in the last year near £60,000 more than they have received, still the existence of such a rival may render 'The Times' more likely to attend even to indirect suggestions than if it were in a career of great prosperity.

Palmerston was peppered with instructions to keep Bulwer, who was an enthusiastic plotter, on a tight rein:

> The Queen returns Mr. Bulwer's letter to Lord Palmerston which she cannot say she approves, for the notion of an English party, and of encouraging revolutionary movements, is a very injudicious one.—The Queen highly approves Lord Palmerston's intended answer to Mr. Bulwer, and he cannot too strongly forbid the encouragement of any revolutionary movement,—or the formation of any party but a purely Spanish and national one.

> ... The Queen trusts that no revolutions will ever be thought of in Spain, for they are a most unjustifiable practice most unfortunately in fashion in the Peninsula ...

To this, Palmerston could not resist a riposte in typical vein:

> ... It is unfortunately true that the Peninsula has for many years been too much the scene of revolutions and all men of all parties who know anything of the present state of Spain concur in representing the discontent great and general. The Spanish Government seem to be pursuing the same course which proved fatal to the Stuarts in this country and to Charles X in France and it is to be apprehended that it will at last produce the same kind of resistance. The Spanish Government wishes to govern despotically

44

a nation which thinks itself entitled to be governed constitutionally. As long as the army is obedient and is stronger than those who may be tempted to resist, such a system may be maintained; but the regular force may be overpowered by the insurgents, as happened in Paris in 1830; or the army, being drawn from among the population of the country, may sympathise with the general discontent, and may dislike firing at their fellow countrymen in a cause which they may think doubtful, and in either of those cases the Government would be obliged to give way . . .

All his old suspicions of the French had been reinforced. The end of the year found him exchanging memoranda for the Queen's eye with Prince Albert, in which he advocated strengthening Britain's coastal fortifications and building up a reserve army of 100,000 men in Britain and a further 40,000 in Ireland:

. . . The defenceless state of the country seems urgently to require some effective remedy, and such remedy ought to be determined upon before Parliament meets. It may confidently be affirmed that neither England nor any other first rate power ever stood in such a condition of comparative military weakness as that in which the United Kingdom (to say nothing of our foreign possessions) is now placed.

There is close to our shores a nation of 34 millions of people, the leading portion of which, it cannot be denied, is animated with a feeling of deep hatred to England as a power;—our neighbours are kind, civil and hospitable to us individually; but the French nation remembers the Nile, Trafalgar, the Peninsula, Waterloo and St. Helena; and would gladly find an opportunity of taking revenge. The two countries have in every part of the globe interests, commercial and political, which are continually clashing; and the conflict between which may at any time, on a sudden, give rise to some discussion of the most serious and embarrassing nature . . .

The Court and Palmerston had been as one on the broad issue of the Montpensier marriage, but another crisis in the Iberian peninsula at the end of 1846 was to open a breach between them which developed into guerrilla warfare lasting the best part of the next four years. The first dispute centred round British policy towards Portugal, where a revolutionary Junta based on Oporto had risen in revolt against Queen Maria. Her husband, Ferdinand, was a first cousin of both Queen Victoria and the Prince and he had taken with him an adviser, Dietz, who occupied an analogous position to Stockmar in Britain without the same disinterested abilities. Queen Maria, once the hope of the Portuguese liberals, had fallen into despotic ways under the influence of the dominant Cabral faction and refused to treat with the constitutionalists.

Queen Victoria first became uneasy when a virulent article appeared in the *Morning Chronicle*, a paper with which Palmerston's connection was notorious. The Foreign Minister had long used certain organs of the press to fly kites for him:

> The Queen had wished to have spoken to Lord Palmerston after the Council today, but she had so many other people to see and things to do that she could not; she therefore writes to call Lord Palmerston's attention to the very improper article on Portugal in to-day's 'Morning Chronicle'. If Lord Palmerston has any influence with the 'Morning Chronicle', she hopes he will use it in order to check these unjustifiable attacks on the King and Queen, which is too bad at this moment of trouble and anxiety. It is, besides, quite untrue. M. Dietz has very little political influence any more now, and there is no French leaning on the King and Queen's part. They only are as we are—on terms of great friendship and intimacy with the French royal family to whom they are nearly related,—and such attacks in the paper generally considered as the Government paper can surely not incline the Portuguese Governments towards England.

For the time being, Palmerston sent a bland reply:

> Viscount Palmerston presents his humble duty to your Majesty and entirely concurs in the remarks which your Majesty has made on the article in the 'Morning Chronicle' of yesterday on Portuguese affairs. It is of course impossible to expect that newspapers published in this country and whose profit depends upon circulation, should not make remarks on the state of affairs in foreign countries, as well as on the state of affairs at home, because readers expect to find in newspapers information as to what is passing abroad; but it seems to Viscount Palmerston to be both unjust and unwise that in discussing the affairs of constitutional countries,

where the sovereigns act by ministers who are expressly responsible for what may be done amiss, any endeavour should be made
by English newspapers to fix upon the sovereign the blame which,
if it is deserved at all belongs to the ministers and not to the sovereign;
and Viscount Palmerston is strongly impressed with the conviction
that it is the interest of England that the King and Queen of
Portugal should be popular with their subjects and that any
attempts to render them otherwise are a great disservice to British
interests.

Viscount Palmerston had already taken steps to make these
opinions known to the Editor of the 'Chronicle' and he hopes that
their justice will be felt and acknowledged.

There was not at first any serious conflict of opinion between the
Court and Palmerston over the policy to be followed. The Queen
of Portugal was to be persuaded to dismiss her reactionary ministers and restore constitutional government once the rebels had
surrendered. Communication was complicated by the fact that
Lord Howard de Walden, the British Minister in Portugal, had
just retired from his post, leaving affairs in the hands of the
legation secretary, Mr. Southern, whom Queen Victoria considered as being too favourably inclined to the rebels. On
October 21, 1846, she wrote to Palmerston:

The Queen fully feels with Lord Palmerston the necessity of
assisting the Portuguese Court from here with advice. She is very
anxious to see Lord Howard and to talk to him upon the affairs of
Portugal, which have arrived at a most critical state, where much
may be done for good or evil. The best thing to do would be to
pass to a liberal course of government by the exertions and the
honesty of a strong ministry, but not by revolutionary movements
of the democratic party . . . Mr. Southern, the Queen has no good
opinion of; he is, as Lord Palmerston must well know, an ultra
Progresista, and a most violent party man. The Queen well remembers, at the time when letters were still opened, to have seen
some of his, in which he bitterly complained of Lord Howard,
who was too moderate for him, and spoke with personal animosity against the Court.

This letter was followed in due course by an admonition to the

Foreign Secretary not to take too much the side of the constitutionalists, the first of many over the years to come, as Palmerston continued his implacable espousal of the liberal cause all over Europe:

> The Queen has just read Lord Palmerston's draft to Mr. Southern, and must observe that she does not quite approve the tone of it, as it will be likely only to irritate without producing any effect. If our advice is to be taken it must be given in a spirit of impartiality and fairness.—Lord Palmerston's despatch must give the impression that we entirely espouse the cause of the rebels, whose conduct is, to say the least, illegal and very reprehensible. Lord Palmerston likewise takes the nation and the opposition as one and the same thing. What we must insist upon is a speedy return to constitutional government, and what we may advise is a compromise with the opposition. What ministry to be formed ought to be left to the Portuguese themselves . . .

In reply Palmerston returned a soft answer:

> . . . The situation of the Queen and King of Portugal is indeed, as your Majesty says, very much to be pitied and, whichever way matters may end, the consequences must be unfortunate if the Queen's forces are defeated. The Queen will be obliged to make concessions greater than would have been sufficient before a conflict; and if the Queen and [her] forces should be completely and finally triumphant, which does not at present seem likely, the opposite party, though subdued, would long remain resentful; and some arrangement before a conflict takes place appears to be the most desirable result . . .

Suspicious of Palmerston's motives, Queen Victoria and the Prince had decided to indulge in a personal diplomatic offensive to assist their relatives. Prince Albert was in constant communication with their cousin Ferdinand, often receiving private information about affairs in Portugal before Palmerston did, much of it at variance with the official correspondence of the Foreign Office. Not blind to the Portuguese royal couple's faults, and convinced of the nefarious influence of Dietz, the British Court determined to send not only Colonel Wylde, Prince Albert's equerry, but yet another Coburg cousin, Count Alexander Mensdorff, to Lisbon. Their task was as much to persuade the Portuguese royal pair to behave reasonably as to protect them from the importunities of Palmerston and Mr. Southern. At the end of November the Queen informed Palmerston:

> . . . The Queen has just heard that her cousin Count Alexander Mensdorff (who Lord Palmerston will recollect to have seen several times in England)—has left Coburg, in consequence of her uncle Duke Ferdinand's great anxiety for the safety of his son and grandchildren, for Lisbon, and will very shortly be here on his way thither.—As Colonel Wylde is already there, this is rather too great a number of councillors, but if we can convince Count Alexander of the extreme importance of removing M. Dietz and his confederates, with Colonel Wylde, he, as a near relation and old friend of the King's, and being a very clever young man, will have much weight with the King and may in this way render essential service to the King and Queen and their country.
>
> Much of what Mr. Southern says may be true, but the Queen does not believe that the King and Queen 'have no friend in the country'; nor does she think that 'the constitutional lessons' given by the Portuguese Ministers and Cortes would be much better, if so good, as those of M. Dietz, as nobody seems to have an idea of what is constitutional there.
>
> The Queen adds a letter from her poor cousin Ferdinand, who, as well as the Queen, is much to be pitied.—This state of affairs is the more distressing as Portugal has perhaps never had more really good and virtuous sovereigns than the present Queen and King; whoever is intimate with the Queen knows how really honest, good, well meaning and courageous she is—which she fears Mr. Southern overlooks. She was not brought up for her position and that is not her fault. With a good adviser they would go on very well, the Queen feels sure . . .

Palmerston was quick to seize on this concession:

> . . . It is much to be wished, as your Majesty observes, that M. Dietz should be removed, for if he does exercise that influence which he is supposed to exert over the Queen and the King and if his views and opinions are as contrary as they are said to be to public opinion in Portugal, the Queen and the King can scarcely

be expected to take an impartial view of their position while M. Dietz remains at Lisbon and their own good sense and good feeling can scarcely have fair play. The King seems still to retain his prepossession against Lord Howard, but Viscount Palmerston would venture to submit in Lord Howard's defence that whether the present insurrection does or does not spring from the persons and the motives to which the King of Portugal ascribes it, Lord Howard did long ago foretell that the system which the Court were pursuing would lead to revolt and would endanger the Throne . . .

A new British envoy, Sir Hamilton Seymour, had also been appointed and the Queen complained of the lack of information from Portugal—an interesting sidelight on the laborious methods of diplomacy at the time:

> The Queen is much rejoiced at Sir H. Seymour's acceptance of the Portuguese mission and we hope he will soon be able to go. We are much annoyed at no news having arrived from Lisbon.—It would be really of importance that the packets should again go four times a month; could not some temporary arrangement at least be made that during the present anxious state of affairs we could hear once a week. At present the steamers cross each other and one cannot get an answer under three weeks, which at such a moment is very distressing, and really of disadvantage to public affairs. Surely a temporary arrangement might be made . . .

In December the Queen not only again had cause to complain of the tone of the *Morning Chronicle*, but took further occasion to restrain her Foreign Minister from undue pressure in Portugal:

> . . . The 'Morning Chronicle' always does us a great deal of harm in all countries by its violent abuse of the [Portuguese] Government, and unfortunately tries to make it appear that it expresses the sentiments of our Government.

> The Queen writes to Lord Palmerston to say that we have again heard this day from Ferdinand and Colonel Wylde—but the slowness of the packets is extraordinary—they take eleven and twelve days coming, whereas they might be only five or six days on their passages. By these letters the Queen's opinion—that it

Henry John Temple, 3rd Viscount Palmerston, photographed late in life as
Prime Minister

will be better now not to press the Court to negotiate, and for our part not to hold further intercourse with the rebels—is much strengthened. Colonel Wylde himself says that any compromise at this moment would lower the Queen's authority and position and not bring over the other party. Ferdinand says that summary vengeance is not thought of, but at the same time such conduct as that of the officers of the army, who have taken up arms against their sovereign, cannot be left unpunished . . .

There was an undeniable note of sarcasm in Palmerston's reply:

. . . It will no doubt be expedient, as your Majesty suggests, that the British agents in Portugal should have no unnecessary communication with the party now in arms against the Government, but Viscount Palmerston would beg to submit that it might not be advisable to interdict such communications altogether. It must be remembered that, as is stated in one of Mr. Southern's despatches, it was in consequence of communications between Mr. Southern and some of the leaders of the revolt that those leaders were induced to abstain from declaring themselves for a Regency on behalf of Pedro V [the heir to the throne] and undoubtedly that was no small advantage for the Queen, because that cry, if once raised, would probably have been more difficult to deal with then than the present cry of one set of ministers against another; and there may arise in the further stages of the contest many imaginable occasions when it may be much for the advantage of the Queen that there should be some third parties, like the British agents, able to carry on communications between the Queen's Government and the revolters, when the mutual exasperation of the contending parties would make direct communication between them difficult . . .

With regard to the 'Morning Chronicle', Viscount Palmerston begs to assure your Majesty that he has no power of exercising any detailed control over the language and opinions of that paper and though that paper gives its general support to the Government it could not and would not submit to any such interference.

A newspaper like the 'Chronicle' looks to an extensive circulation as the source of profit upon the large capital employed in such an undertaking; and the Government has nothing in its power to offer which could at all compensate for a diminution of circulation. But the circulation of a newspaper depends in a great degree upon its containing free and unreserved discussions upon all matters of public interest at home and abroad; and the writers in those newspapers follow in shaping those discussions either their own opinions for their own satisfaction and in order to propagate those opinions, or what they may imagine the opinions of the public [to be] in order to recommend the paper to its readers, and to extend its circulation. But it would not suit them in either point of view to be cramped by a strict conformance with the wishes of the Government; and as such a conformance might on many occasions of public interest end in their saying little or nothing, their paper would be divested of much of its interest, and the mass of readers would cease to take it in.

As the year drew to its close, encouraging news of the royal cause in Portugal enabled the Queen to press her relatives' case with Palmerston:

> . . . The last news from Portugal is decidedly better, and the rebels seem to be losing ground, the fact is, they hardly know what they wish for. If the King and Queen could only have reasonable and disinterested and moderate councillors, for this is in fact the great difficulty, all would go on well. However, we must hope that if the Queen is successful, good advice may be effectively given. The Queen has written to her cousins—that they should not mind the articles in the 'Morning Chronicle' for that it is in no way a Government paper, nor one which has great weight in the country . . .

Palmerston was not to be deflected from his main line of policy. Wylde had gone to Lisbon partly under his auspices and the Foreign Secretary did not hesitate to proffer advice as to his mode of conduct. Palmerston wanted him to mediate between the Portuguese Court and the insurgents, obtaining guarantees for the rebels' safety, and wrote at the end of January 1847 to say so. Prince Albert, whose part in the transaction of foreign affairs was by now indistinguishable from the Queen's, took exception. In many cases now the drafts of the Queen's letters were in the Prince's own hand, or followed closely in phraseology the voluminous memoranda he constantly deposited in the royal archives. On this occasion he wrote to Palmerston himself:

I return the copy of your letter to Colonel Wylde, which you have sent me. We could not help being very much disappointed with it.

The Queen of Portugal had addressed herself to her old ally and represented that it was prevalent opinion in Portugal that the resistance of the insurgents and consequent immense loss of lives and money in carrying on the civil war, was to a great degree owing to the current impression that England wished well to the cause of the insurgents and would at every opportunity stand up for them. The language of the 'Morning Chronicle' and the bearing of Mr. Southern amply justify such an impression. The Queen of P[ortugal] begged that before she was forced to attack Oporto and to expose that town to the horrors and the pillage consequent upon an assault, where a good deal of English property would be exposed as well, her old ally (England) should do no more than declare to the insurgents that she does not approve of their proceedings, and warn them of the consequences of further resistance.

We thought you would be entirely justified as Minister of England to comply with this request and that you would be anxious to seize this opportunity to prove that you do not sympathise entirely with the insurgents, as is believed, particularly if you could gain at the same time those objects which alone ought to be of interest to England and to you, viz. the Queen's immediate return to constitutional government, the security that the Cabrals will not be restored to power and the safety of the commercial town of Oporto.

I was very glad therefore when you agreed to send Colonel Wylde to Oporto with a declaration that 'the Queen having engaged herself towards England to return immediately after the restoration of peace and order to constitutional government and not to take the Cabrals to her councils, the only ostensible ground for which the civil war had hitherto been carried on had fallen to the ground, that if the insurgents now persisted in exposing their country to further misery, they would draw the indignation of England upon themselves'.

What is the bearing of your letter? 'That you are pleased to see at last the Court becoming tired of the unnecessary effusion of blood and waste of treasure and anxious for a negotiation with the insurgents, which England has often offered. That the Queen is to understand, that she must immediately return to constitutional government and give a pledge against restoring the Cabrals, else we would not meddle in the affair. That he was to go to Oporto charged with conditions for the insurgents of amnesties, immunities, pensions etc. etc., and to say that if this is not accepted England could do no more for them and that if they should be vanquished, England could only deplore it and pity them. That you consider that it is the fault of the Court which has brought on the insurrection'.

Our only hope is that Wylde will not show your letter at Lisbon, where it can do no good.

Then came something of a lull. Sir Hamilton Seymour made his leisurely way to Lisbon to take up his post, the military situation in Portugal remained at stalemate, the Court party maintained its position and succeeded in invoking the aid of France and Spain under the Quadruple Alliance of 1834. Britain was the fourth party and Lord John Russell, the Prime Minister, who had not entirely supported Palmerston in his tussle with the Court, devised a compromise. Britain would take action with the other two powers, providing Queen Maria would grant an amnesty to the rebels and restore constitutional government. Palmerston accepted the plan, and on March 30, 1847, faced Queen Victoria with the combined opinion of the Cabinet:

> Viscount Palmerston presents his humble duty to your Majesty and begs to state that the Cabinet, at its meeting at Lord Lansdowne's to-day, agreed to the course of proceedings in regard to Portuguese affairs of which Viscount Palmerston had the honour of stating the general outline to your Majesty yesterday; and Viscount Palmerston is to prepare for consideration a draft of an instruction to Sir Hamilton Seymour explaining and providing for its detailed execution.
>
> The general principles of the plan would be that Sir H. Seymour would state to the Portuguese Government that, in the opinion of the British Government, neither the letter nor the spirit of the Quadruple Treaty are applicable to the present condition of things in Portugal and for this reason among others, that that treaty applied to a case of disputed succession, and that the present civil war in Portugal is a contest about other matters. But that nevertheless the British Government is willing to interpose to

restore internal peace to Portugal, if it can do so upon principles that could be reconciled to the established foreign policy of Great Britain and therefore if the Queen of Portugal will authorise and empower your Majesty's Government to offer to the Junta of Oporto such reasonable terms of accommodation as the Junta, if sincere in their professions, ought to accept, your Majesty's Government would be ready in the event of such terms being refused by the Junta, to take measures in concert with Spain and France, to assist the Queen of Portugal in compelling the Junta to accept those terms. The probability however is that, either the Junta will unanimously accept the conditions to be offered, or that if some of the most violent of the party refuse them, there will be such a defection from their ranks by the submission of all moderate men, that the civil war will necessarily end from the weakness of the Junta.

The conditions which the Cabinet thought it would be right to offer are such as Viscount Palmerston mentioned to your Majesty, a general amnesty such as was published on the termination of the civil war when Don Miguel was expelled from Portugal; the revocation of the arbitrary decrees and the re-establishment of the constitution as it existed previously to the 6th October last; the appointment of a ministry to be composed of men of neither extreme, and an early convocation of the Cortes; together with the immediate departure of M. Dietz, which should take place as a private arrangement, and not as a condition to be proposed to the Oporto Junta.

The course which it may be fitting to pursue if the Queen should refuse to accede to this arrangement to be reserved as a matter for consideration if the event should happen.

The Queen still intended to exercise firm control, and replied the same day:

The Queen has just received Lord Palmerston's communication on the determination come to by the Cabinet. The Queen entirely approves of the proposed steps and only hopes that the Queen of Portugal may accept the offer we are going to make. In order to facilitate this, which is indeed of the greatest importance, the Queen hopes that Lord Palmerston will be careful that the wording of his instructions to Sir H. Seymour should be such as not to provoke any irritation or obstinacy on the part of the Queen and Government of Portugal . . .

The Queen expects to see the instructions before they are sent; by some confusion in the Foreign Office she received the last ones only yesterday evening, the ship having gone on the 27th, and she begs Lord Palmerston to let her know in time when the steamer is to go, that she may prepare her own letter for Lisbon.

APRIL 5: The Queen has received Lord Palmerston's letter and draft which she has attentively perused and quite approves. The Queen considers the draft to be very comprehensive with regard to the many possible eventualities, and so worded that the Portuguese Government must be impressed with the good will and fairness of England. The Queen trusts that it will be impossible for the Portuguese Government to refuse accepting the offer we are making, the only point which could shake the Queen's confidence in that respect is the part affecting M. Dietz. Lord Palmerston ought privately to urge Sir H. Seymour to do his best, in order not to wound the Queen of Portugal's feelings, while he takes care that the object is fully secured . . .

Then, on April 17, came a renewed reproof from the Queen, on the subject which was to cause recurrent asperity between the Court and Palmerston during the rest of his tenure of the Foreign Ministry:

The Queen has several times asked Lord Palmerston through Lord John Russell and personally, to see that the drafts to our foreign Ministers are not despatched previous to their being submitted to the Queen; notwithstanding, this is still done,—as for instance to-day with regard to the drafts for Lisbon. The Queen therefore once more repeats her desire that Lord Palmerston should prevent a recurrence of this practice.

As on many future occasions, Palmerston had his answer ready:

Viscount Palmerston presents his humble duty to your Majesty and regrets very much that the drafts of the despatches, which are to go by the packet which is to sail this afternoon, could not be submitted to your Majesty sooner; but the despatches to which these drafts were replies only arrived a day or two ago, and Viscount Palmerston was unable to give directions upon them till the night before last and the drafts were not written out fair until yesterday evening; and as they contained no instruction upon any new matter nor anything of much importance, Viscount Palmerston thought that it might not be necessary to delay sending the despatches for ten days longer. He will however take care that in future the drafts shall be sent to your Majesty in ample time before the sailing of the packet . . .

It is in vain to endeavour to shut one's eyes to the fact that the infatuation of the persons whose advice has guided the Queen, has brought her to the very verge of that ruin which was all along foretold by Lord Howard as the probable result of a course which the Queen of Portugal was pursuing . . . While almost the whole of Portugal except the ground occupied by her troops had declared against her Government, and while even her own generals were remaining in a state of inactivity, which could only be accounted for by want of zeal in her cause on their part, or want of confidence in the fidelity of their troops, the people of the metropolis were expected at any hour to rise against her, and to co-operate with the Junta. This is indeed a melancholy picture of the desperate condition to which a sovereign endowed with many good qualities has been reduced by the wrong-headedness, the prejudices, the folly and dishonesty of a set of advisers by whom she has been surrounded.

The Queen had not forgotten or forgiven Mr. Southern:

About three months ago Lord Palmerston informed the Queen that Mr. Southern was about to leave Portugal [she wrote on May 15]. Shortly afterwards he said that Mr. Southern's state of health was such that he could not well travel; the season is far advanced now, and the Queen hopes that Mr. Southern's health will now be sufficiently improved to enable him to move to Spain at least.

In reply, Palmerston pleaded pressure of business for not attending to the transfer, pointing out that Southern had been very necessary to Sir Hamilton Seymour, and suggesting that he should be made Minister at Buenos Aires. The Queen was not to be deterred:

In reply to Lord Palmerston's letter of last night, the Queen has to say that she is not very willing to grant so great a promotion to Mr. Southern as the one proposed, after the doubtful manner in which he discharged his duties at Lisbon. Now, however, if he is once fairly gone from Lisbon the Queen will consider this further.

The four-power agreement was signed. French, Spanish and British troops intervened in Portugal and, although Palmerston found himself in the invidious position of having to use British forces to coerce the rebels into acceptance, he emerged with an enhanced reputation as the arbiter of Portuguese affairs. When Queen Maria again tried to evade the conditions of the settlement, Palmerston was able to write to Queen Victoria on August 6:

. . . The Queen of Portugal cannot be unaware of these circumstances, but she clings to the present Government and she is surrounded in her private circle by adherents of the Cabrals; can it be expected that the country at large should not be thus led to believe that their Queen is again breaking her pledges, and again identifying herself with a party, instead of faithfully fulfilling her promise to the allies and to her people . . .

Another revolt founded upon a palpable breach of engagement on the part of the Queen of Portugal would (it is impossible to disguise the fact) be fatal to her possession of the Throne. No assistance could be given to her in such a case by England; and judging from the spirit displayed by the Spanish troops, and by the views of annexation disclosed by the Spaniards it may be supposed that the assistance which she might get from Madrid might not be unconnected with ulterior views by no means favourable to her independence.

If your Majesty should think that there is any weight in the foregoing considerations, there can be no doubt that a few words from your Majesty to the Queen of Portugal would have much influence upon her decision; and it would certainly be far better that whatever is to be done should appear to be her own spontaneous act, rather than that it should seem to be wrung from her by diplomatic remonstrances.

This the Queen undertook to do, but at the end of October there was a further clash, when the Queen objected to the phraseology of another draft to Sir Hamilton Seymour:

. . . The Queen has marked upon the drafts several passages which ought to be omitted. They are those which make a direct accusation against the Queen of Portugal being 'in secret understanding with the Cabrals', wholly unsupported by facts and which indeed the Queen knows to be entirely unfounded . . .

. . . Viscount Palmerston received this morning your Majesty's remarks upon his proposed drafts to Sir Hamilton Seymour; and has modified some of the expressions in those drafts; but those drafts are only private and confidential answers in his own name to private and confidential communications from Sir Hamilton Seymour, and they express only his own personal opinions, and not those of the Government.

Viscount Palmerston is sorry to say that the circumstances lately mentioned by Sir Hamilton Seymour, coupled with the course pursued at Lisbon almost ever since the successful interference of the allied powers, have brought Viscount Palmerston to the painful convictions expressed in the above-mentioned drafts, and he feels desirous, for his own sake, to place those convictions at least upon record in this Office. He will be most happy to find that he is mistaken, and will most truly and heartily rejoice if events should prove that the confidence which your Majesty reposes in the sincerity and good faith of the Queen of Portugal is well founded; but in a matter of this importance Viscount Palmerston feels that it is his bounden duty to your Majesty not to conceal his opinions, even though they should, as in the present case, unfortunately differ from those which your Majesty entertains.

The Queen acknowledges Lord Palmerston's letter of yesterday. She can have no objection to Lord Palmerston's putting on record his opinion that the Queen of Portugal is leaning towards the Chartist Party, and exposing herself, her throne and country to great danger by so doing; but the Queen would much deprecate the putting on record the grave accusation 'that the Queen of Portugal is in a secret and perfect understanding with the Cabrals' which is really not warranted by the facts of the case, and is likely to mislead both our Government and the Minister . . .

The Portuguese episode petered out as the year drew to its close, with the royal pair on the defensive. Palmerston and the Prince exchanged letters on November 1 and 2:

59

... But the King of Portugal says that the Queen is determined in no case and upon no account to make the Cabrals ministers [the Foreign Secretary wrote]. I would beg however to submit that this determination to exclude particular individuals from office, by the mere act of the royal will, may not always be practicable in a constitutional government; and that in the contingency which I am supposing, the Queen would be obliged, either to accept the Cabrals as ministers and to take the chance of the consequences, or else to dissolve the chambers, and to appeal to the free choice of the electors; the very thing which the Queen is not willing to do now; but which could be done now, with better grace and with safer results than in such a supposed case ...

The King of Portugal, Sir, if I may be allowed to say so, does not seem accurately to understand the reasons for which the appointment of the Cabrals to be ministers is objected to by the British Government, and protested against by the Portuguese nation. The Cabrals are 'much dreaded' in Portugal because the general opinion in that country seems to be, that they are unscrupulous and unprincipled men, who, having come into office as needy adventurers, have grown rich by plundering the country, and who have formed around themselves a party of adherents, by allowing their followers to imitate their example in this respect; and public opinion in Portugal seems to connect together the ideas of a Cabral ministry and of a corrupt and tyrannical rule.

I have received your letter of yesterday [the Prince replied], and cannot help agreeing entirely with your views as to the impolicy and shortsightedness of the course pursued by the Portuguese Court, but I was anxious that you should be convinced that the Queen of Portugal is sincere in thinking she can keep the Cabrals out and is trying to steer an impartial course ...

In a final flurry, Palmerston and the Queen nagged at the position each had held during the whole controversy:

Viscount Palmerston presents his humble duty to your Majesty and begs to return his thanks for the copy of the letter from the King of Portugal, which he will send on to Lord John Russell. That letter certainly contains proof of good intentions and Viscount Palmerston sincerely hopes that the Queen and the King may have formed a right judgment of the state of affairs and that things may turn out as well as they seem to expect. It is indeed true that it often happens that the result which almost everybody expects is just the very thing that does not happen; and thus it may possibly prove that a Cabral majority in the Chambers obtained by irregular means may not lead to another insurrection. But the best chance, as appears to Viscount Palmerston, against another outbreak will be found to lie in the extreme poverty and general distress which has been occasioned by the late civil war; and, as the Chambers are to meet, it is to be hoped that all parties may consent to wage their mutual war for the present in debates instead of taking to the field.

. . . It would be encouraging to Sir H. Seymour—and indeed might be so to the King of Portugal [the Queen replied], if Lord Palmerston added to one of his drafts in which he approves of Sir H. Seymour's language to the King, that the Government here were much gratified by his right and generous intentions, and trusted that he would continue to use his utmost power to carry them into execution. The poor King is often much disheartened, and his position is a very difficult one. He says in his last letter to the Queen '*nos difficultés sont énormes mais elles ne l'ont été d'avantage que pendant ces deux semaines*'.

A little encouragement may be of great use.

Nevertheless, Palmerston had overplayed his hand. For as long as he remained Foreign Secretary, neither the Queen nor the Prince really trusted him again. The Queen by now thoroughly shared her husband's predilection for foreign affairs, and as time passed it came to seem as if they regarded it as their prerogative to direct foreign policy almost as a separate department of government under their control. Such an attitude from a royal pair still in their twenties could not but be galling to an experienced and determined minister now in his sixties.

Neither side stepped outside the constitutional proprieties, but while the Queen and the Prince scrutinised Palmerston's despatches vigorously, appealing to Lord John Russell whenever they could, or requiring a full Cabinet decision on major points of conflict, their Foreign Minister continued blithely to pursue his fixed policies—the reduction of the power of monarchical despotisms and the encouragement of constitutional and liberal movements wherever he could foster them. There has surely never been a tussle like it in the whole of British history.

Before the year 1847 was out, Palmerston was already laying the foundation of three of the crises which were to exacerbate their relationship. Spain was once again in turmoil. Bulwer was fishing busily in the troubled waters, and Prince Albert, after an interview with Palmerston, was writing with foreboding in one of his memoranda:

> I argued that it was the greatest mistake to go on intriguing about this ministry and against that ministry . . . I see no fixed principle in Mr. Bulwer's conduct, but a mere longing for the excitement of walking through the labyrinth of Spanish intrigues . . .

On October 24, Palmerston was writing with some relish to the Queen:

> . . . The present position of Queen Isabella seems to be as forlorn as can well be imagined. She is surrounded by spies, traitors and enemies, a prisoner at large in her own palace, linked as it now would seem indissolubly to a husband whom she hates and despises, and whose dislike for her equals hers for him; and watched and controlled by a mother who seems only to be waiting to catch or to create an opportunity to put into her place another and a more favourite child. The tactics which will from Paris be enjoined upon Christina will no doubt be to encourage Queen Isabella in a course of conduct which will lower her in the estimation of her subjects and loosen her hold upon their affections, and thus to prepare the way for the accession of the Montpensiers, or else perhaps to cooperate with Narvaez [leader of the absolutists] in driving or persuading Queen Isabella to abdication.
>
> It is probable that the next step will be to bring the Montpensiers to Madrid and then, upon the meeting of the Cortes, some vote will be proposed and carried affirming the rights of the Montpensier succession.

The first rumble of discontent which was to lead a dozen years later to freedom was stirring in Italy. Ever far-sighted, Palmerston was proposing to send Lord Minto on a tour of southern Europe to exert British influence, and outlined his plan to the Queen:

... The objects of his mission would be first, in Switzerland, to ascertain the real views and intentions of the present rulers of the Confederation and to expect them to abstain from all violent acts and from any extreme measures which could afford either to Austria or to France any pretext for interference by force of arms.

Secondly, at Turin, to encourage the Sardinian Government to draw closer their relations, political and commercial, with Great Britain; but to abstain from any unnecessary rupture either with Austria or with France; and at the same time to continue to afford the countenance and support of Sardinia to the progressive system of internal improvement now pursuing by the Pope [*sic*].

Thirdly, at Florence, to hold the same language as at Turin and to give similar advice.

Fourthly, at Rome, to encourage the Pope to advance steadily and gradually in reforming the numerous abuses which exist in the government of his States, and to assure him of the countenance and support of Great Britain as long as he pursues the same prudent course which he has hitherto followed; to lay the grounds for diplomatic intercourse between your Majesty and the Pope and for commercial relations between the two States; and while on the one hand he holds out to the Pope the support and protection which the countenance and good offices of the British Government will afford, Lord Minto would endeavour to obtain from the Pope the exertion of his spiritual authority over the Catholic priesthood of Ireland to induce them to abstain from repeal agitation and to urge them not to embarrass but rather to assist your Majesty's Government in the measures which they may plan for the improvement and for the better government of Ireland ...

This led the Prince to commit another somewhat sour memorandum to his growing files:

... We have no hand in what is going on in Italy though we think the Italians acting wisely. We have not lent them any assistance, but we consider that every independent State has a perfect right to manage its own internal affairs and that if sovereign and people in a State are united in their determination to introduce certain reforms and another State attempts an armed invasion to stop those reforms, merely because it considers them dangerous to the maintenance of its own established system of government, we shall look upon that act as an act of aggression upon the independence of the other State, which Europe and the powers who signed the Treaty of Vienna cannot look upon with indifference . . .

The diplomatic support given to the Pope will give additional strength to the prevalent accusation against us that we are, for selfish purposes, trying to disseminate disorder and anarchy in all other States under the name of liberty, which was the course the French Jacobins pursued, and in support of which accusation our position with regard to Greece, Portugal and Spain is adduced in connection with the miseries of those countries . . .

The Prince and Palmerston were also engaged in an acrimonious correspondence about the affairs of Greece. The Court considered that the British Minister there, Sir Edmond Lyons, another Palmerstonian liberal, was too partial to the constitutional forces and too critical of King Otho. They wanted him recalled. In an enormous letter to the Prince, Palmerston fulminated against the Greek Prime Minister, Mr. Coletti, and restated his own basic principles:

> . . . Now the ill-will of the British Government towards Mr. Coletti and their bad opinions of him are founded upon the fact that he governs Greece corruptly, illegally, prodigally, unconstitutionally and tyrannically.

> England concurred with Russia and France in separating Greece from Turkey and in erecting Greece into a separate kingdom, in order that the Greek nation, who had excited the sympathy of every generous man in Europe by their heroic struggle for freedom, might by such an arrangement enjoy their freedom securely and permanently; and might thereby become prosperous and happy; and a Prince of Bavaria was chosen to be their king, because it was thought that, being then still a boy, he would by going to Greece be brought up in acquired sympathy with his future subjects; and because, as he belonged to the royal family of a constitutional monarchy, it was hoped that he would carry with him a mind imbued with those constitutional feelings which would lead him to respect the rights and to maintain the liberties of the Greek nation. When therefore the British Government sees the confidence of King Otho abused, and the just rights, civil and political, of the Greek nation trampled underfoot by Mr. Coletti,

it is impossible that the British Government should not regard with extreme displeasure a minister who thus defeats the benevolent and generous intentions with which England originally interfered and has ever since continued to interfere in the affairs of Greece . . .

I am well aware that the diplomatic agents of some of the other powers of Europe stationed at Athens either say nothing about the facts and occurrences upon which our opinions are founded, or give to their Courts reports of an opposite tendency; but unfortunately there is at present in Europe a great political schism among public men and among governments, which turns upon the question whether constitutional government or absolute monarchy is the best; and as Mr. Coletti is considered in Greece as the champion of absolute government, and as the party who oppose him are known to be the advocates of constitutional government, it is perhaps not very surprising that diplomatists in Greece who sympathise with the doctrines of which Mr. Coletti is considered to be the representative should look with indulgence if not with favour upon his general conduct . . .

A further broadside on the subjected elicited from the Prince the admission:

. . . I must disclaim all intention of being or ever becoming King Otho's champion, whose total incapacity to govern with or without a constitution, is but too evident to me . . .

Then Coletti died, but Palmerston rounded off the year with a further letter to the Prince, on December 31, in which he saw little hope of improvement:

I wish I could share your Royal Highness's anticipations of a favourable turn in the affairs of Greece, but I own that I am not sanguine on that subject. Coletti indeed is dead, but his death has not made the slightest change in the course pursued by King Otho, either in his foreign relations or in his domestic administration; and the Greek Government seems just as determined to quarrel with Turkey and England and just as much resolved to disregard the law and to violate the constitution as it could have been if Coletti had been alive; in fact, that which has passed since Coletti's death proves that we did him injustice, and that while we believed him to be the chief author and instigator of all the evil doings of King Otho, he was only the willing instrument by whom those doings were accomplished . . .

The stage was set, not only for the liberal revolutions which shook Europe, but for the bitter conflict between Palmerston and the Court which was to embroil British political life at the half-century.

CHAPTER III

The Liberal Revolution

THE LIBERAL REVOLUTIONS WHICH SWEPT EUROPE IN 1848 PROVIDED the final bone of contention between Palmerston and the Court. The Foreign Secretary could not but derive a grim satisfaction from the fulfilment of all his predictions that autocratic government must lead to revolt and that only constitutional concessions, given freely in time, would ensure tranquillity. Popular uprisings he regarded as dangerous and deplorable, to be kept within bounds before the damage spread. To the Queen and the Prince they were a catastrophe, threatening the whole European monarchical system to which they were allied. Moreover, they suspected Palmerston of giving covert support to the rebels. The proprietary rights of sovereigns were to them immutable and neither Queen nor Prince ever really understood Palmerston's flexible, pragmatic approach to the forces of change.

The first monarch to feel their effect was their near neighbour across the Channel, Louis-Philippe. His relationship with Britain strained by the Spanish marriage *imbroglio*, he had turned for support to the reactionary régimes of Austria, Prussia and Russia, which had by now spent more than thirty years extirpating the heady theories of the French Revolution. In France itself the memory had survived, and when the Paris mob rose under Lamartine in February 1848, the Orleanist monarchy crumpled overnight. The bumbling, septuagenarian King and his family were shepherded out of France in disguise through the good offices of the ingenious British Consul at Le Havre, Mr. Featherstonhaugh, and made straight for London, where the Court received them with affectionate sympathy:

> The Queen wishes to mention to Lord Palmerston that the King and Queen of the French intend to come tomorrow morning here

to visit the Queen privately. They had wished to come to-day but we thought on a Sunday there might be inconvenient crowds. The Queen wishes to know if Lord Palmerston sees there is any objection to this arrangement, or if it ought to be postponed for a day or two longer. The Queen wishes for an immediate reply.

Mr. Featherstonhaugh's accounts make one quite shudder. It is a pleasure to see how well her subjects and servants have behaved, it is only what she expected of their generous nature.

Even Palmerston could not be blamed for this calamity and at the beginning of March the Prince was noting the true cause soberly enough in one of his memoranda:

> . . . The resolution of 24th February has not only lost the Crown of Louis-Philippe, but the dynasty and the monarchy itself. France is now a Republic. The King and Queen after many vicissitudes, privations, dangers and sufferings have made their escape to England in disguise and have arrived penniless. The Duchess of Montpensier arrived by herself five days sooner in a lamentable state, the Duc de Montpensier later with the Duchesse de Nemours. They have all asked for our hospitality and protection and have received them. Guizot is likewise a fugitive in London!—M. de Lamartine, the hero of the new Republic and the soul of the new Government said to Lord Normanby [the British Ambassador]: 'To the Spanish marriages Louis-Philippe owes his downfall. I always said that selfish objects would be his ruin; it drove him into a line of politics which the country would not stand. The Government will take an early opportunity of stigmatising that policy with regard to Spain as anti-national. They desire in this country independent alliance but no exclusive influence' . . .

Palmerston himself was not certain which way events would swing. When he wrote to the Queen on March 7 he even considered the possibility of a royalist restoration:

> . . . With regard to the future, Viscount Palmerston would beg to suggest that although it seems probable that a republican form of government will for the moment be established in France, there is far greater probability of the future restoration of the Comte de Paris, than there was three weeks ago of the establishment of a Republic; and if the Comte de Paris were to become King in France, the Montpensier question would be entirely unchanged as

68

regards the interests and policy of England; and indeed even if a Republic were to be permanently established in France, the objections to the Montpensier succession might be diminished in some slight degree but they would by no means be removed.

The Queen, for her part, was not going to tolerate any unnecessary overtures to the new republican Government in France. When the first news of the revolution had percolated through, she had required Palmerston to tone down his instructions to Lord Normanby, to speak of the 'most cordial friendship' Britain felt for the new régime. A mention of the desire for 'friendly relations' seemed sufficient to the Queen. Then, on March 10, with a pathetic account of the financial situation of the French royal family, the Queen returned to the charge:

> . . . The Queen fears (indeed knows) that the poor Duc and Duchesse of Nemours are in sad want of all means; and she knows the poor Duchesse of Orleans is equally so.—It is very lamentable and the Queen feels much for them, for it is a position which, if one reflects on it, requires great courage and resignation to submit to. It would be infamous if the Republic gave them nothing. The Queen fears Lord Normanby is inclined to be on too friendly and confidential terms with M. Lamartine. Did Lord Palmerston caution him? We should do all what is right but not show any *empressement* towards what is after all a great calamity.

Palmerston's native magnanimity responded to the first circumstance, and he replied on the same day:

> . . . Viscount Palmerston deeply laments the pecuniary difficulties in which, as your Majesty states, some members of the French royal family are for the moment placed. But he has twice told Count Jarnac that whenever the Count shall tell him that such assistance would be desirable he will pay over a thousand pounds out of secret service money for the use of the royal family to any banker whom Count Jarnac may name; and upon this express condition, that the transaction shall be perfectly secret between the Count and himself, that the royal family shall not know from whence the money comes and shall therefore be under no sense of obligation to your Majesty's Government, but that the assistance shall be supposed to be furnished by some unknown well-wisher.

Fanned by events in France, the fire of revolution was sweeping the Continent. The petty German States were rocking to their flimsy, hereditary foundations. Italy was seething, and even the reactionary Government of her oppressor, Austria, trembled. In a letter to the Court, Palmerston could not resist a dig at his old adversary, soon also to be a refugee in England:

> ... The retirement of Prince Metternich is indeed for Germany what the shaking off of the old man of the mountain [sic] was for Sinbad the Sailor, it is only to be lamented that the Prince did not retire two years ago; if he had done so much of what is now happening might not have taken place; but still this retirement opens a better prospect for Germany.

London and its environs became the temporary headquarters of exiled despotism. Dispossessed or timorous royal refugees and their ministers opened *salons*, intrigued with British Tories and had many channels of communication open to a sympathetic Court. With the European opposition thus entrenched in his own backyard, Palmerston was hard pressed to master the sweep of events on the Continent. The population of the two duchies of Schleswig and Holstein, sandwiched between Denmark and the German Confederation, had caught the prevalent fever, complicated by the dynastic issues involved. The Schleswig-Holstein question, which was to complicate relations in northern Europe for nearly fifteen years, revolved round the succession to the childless new Danish king, Frederick VII. Under Danish law, the crown could devolve in the female line. This could also be applied to the attached province of Schleswig, but not to Holstein, which, while forming a union with Schleswig, was nevertheless nominally a member of the Germanic Confederation. Here the law of succession required a male heir and Prussia sponsored the candidature of the Duke of Augustenburg.

During the period 1848-52, the Prussians first endeavoured to impose their candidate by force, but were compelled to withdraw under pressure from the other European great powers. The Danes then marched into the two duchies, but were themselves obliged by the great powers to grant an increased degree of local autonomy. The succession problem was temporarily solved in 1852, when the Duke of Augustenburg surrendered his claims in exchange for a money payment, and Prince Christian of Glücksburg, a nephew by marriage of Frederick VII, was nominated as his heir. The outcome of this Protracted dispute was regarded as a setback for Prussia.

When the crisis first loomed, Palmerston made an offer to mediate. Queen Victoria felt she had been insufficiently informed and in April wrote to remonstrate, complaining at 'not having heard anything from Lord Palmerston respecting foreign affairs for so long a time'. His reply expatiated on the pressure of government business, which had been still further disrupted by the threatened march on the House of Commons of the Chartists on April 10:

> ... Although events of the greatest importance have been passing in rapid succession in almost every part of Europe, the position of your Majesty's Government has been one rather of observation than of action, it being desirable that England should keep herself as free as possible from unnecessary engagements and entanglements, in order that your Majesty may be at liberty to take such decisions as the state of things may from time to time appear to render most advisable.
>
> Your Majesty's Government indeed have intimated to the Danish and Prussian Governments a willingness to employ the good offices of Great Britain for the settlement of the Schleswig-Holstein question, if such an intervention should be asked for by both the contending parties, and Viscount Palmerston is sorry to find that the drafts of the despatches conveying that intimation were not sent to your Majesty before the despatches went off; and the only excuse that can be offered for this is the great pressure of business with which this Office has of late been overwhelmed, and the disturbance of usual arrangements, connected with the preparations made in all the offices for the possible events of Monday, the 10th, by which the regular routine business has been a good deal interrupted; but Viscount Palmerston has given strict orders that the regular course of sending drafts to your Majesty in proper time before the day for the despatches being sent off, shall be observed.

With regard to the communication itself, Viscount Palmerston trusts that your Majesty does not disapprove an overture made with a view of preventing or of stopping hostilities for which no adequate reason appears to exist; which might bring Prussia into collision with Russia and which, in consequence of the British guarantee of Schleswig in 1720, might even involve your Majesty in embarrassment.

Viscount Palmerston is sensible (although your Majesty has had the goodness not to mention it) that your Majesty must of late have observed that some of the despatches from abroad have not reached your Majesty so soon after their arrival at the Foreign Office as they ought to have done; but what with the great increase in the number of despatches received, in consequence of the state of things abroad, what with multiplied Cabinet meetings, morning sittings and long evening attendances in the House of Commons and more than usually frequent interviews with foreign Ministers, Viscount Palmerston has had in his room till within the last few days, a frightful accumulation of boxes full of despatches which he was unable to find time to read. He has now disposed of them all and trusts that the despatches will now reach your Majesty in the usual course.

In an effort to curb the revolutionary fervour of the new French Republic, Palmerston was endeavouring to harness its policies to his own more moderate ends. He wanted reform in the governmental institutions of the countries of Europe, but not an uncontrolled conflagration, and specifically no French intervention in Italy against the Austrians. He thought a little diplomatic flattery might help his influence, and wrote to the Queen at the end of April:

Viscount Palmerston . . . begs to state that M. de Tallenay, late French Minister resident at Hamburg, has arrived in London with a letter to Viscount Palmerston from M. Lamartine accrediting M. de Tallenay as provisional chargé des affaires of the French Government, but of course M. de Tallenay has no letters at present accrediting him to your Majesty; and M. de Tallenay cannot therefore be presented to your Majesty in any official capacity.

But Viscount Palmerston would beg to submit for your Majesty's consideration that it would perhaps be politic as well as courteous that M. de Tallenay as well as M. Cothe should be invited to any ball which your Majesty may give before the French Government is definitively established, and that they should be presented to your Majesty on such occasion by Viscount Palmerston as unofficial foreigners. The doing so would not, as Viscount Palmerston conceives, violate any rule of etiquette, while on the other hand the omitting them might be misunderstood or misrepresented at Paris.

The Queen thought that this might lead to 'most inconvenient precedents', and remained invincibly suspicious of French intentions:

> The Queen has been reading all Lord Normanby's despatches [she wrote on May 7], and wishes that Lord Palmerston should have the one in which Lord Normanby mentions Lamartine's speaking of 'compensation' in Italy circulated amongst her Ministers at the Italian Courts. This is an early proof of how much we can rely on the expressions of non-aggressiveness on the part of the French Government.

It was the spread of revolutionary fervour to Italy which caused the first serious rift between the Court and Palmerston. The Minto mission was beginning to bear abundant fruit. A liberal-minded Pope had been encouraged in Rome. Now the Milanese and Venetians rose against their Austrian masters in the north and King Charles Albert of Sardinia found himself the somewhat reluctant head of a loose Italian confederation bent on driving the hated white-coats under Marshal Radetzky back over the Alps into their homeland. Rather to their surprise, the Italians succeeded in their first attack. Piedmont was liberated and the Austrians withdrew to a shortened line which preserved their communications across the mountain passes.

Palmerston was unrepentantly pro-Italian. He had known the country intimately since childhood, spoke the language impeccably and ardently sought the inhabitants' independence. The Queen and Prince were pro-Austrian. Their cousin Mensdorff was now in Vienna and Albert kept up a lively correspondence with him and through Uncle Leopold in Belgium, which often ran counter to Palmerston's instructions to British Ministers abroad. Palmerston had an ally in the Ambassador in Vienna, Viscount Ponsonby, but the Queen did not like the tone of many of the Foreign Minister's despatches and a sharp interchange ensued:

MAY 21: The Queen returns this draft to Lord Palmerston which she thinks had better not be sent. It is already well known that we sympathise with the Italians against the Austrians and it would be, in the Queen's opinion, unnecessarily irritating the latter and increasing the distrust with which they view our sentiments on this question without doing any good. These accounts are sure to be much exaggerated . . .

MAY 22: Viscount Palmerston presents his humble duty to your Majesty and will, according to your Majesty's wishes, withhold the proposed despatch to Viscount Ponsonby about the cruelties committed by the Austrian troops at the village of Castelnuovo; but he has learnt since the draft was written that there is every reason to believe the account to be correct, and that the fact was that the people of the village, having by some act of hostility incurred the displeasure of Marshal Radetzsky, that general ordered the village to be destroyed, and told the troops employed on that service that he made them a present of the village and its inhabitants to deal with them as they chose; and that the Marshal boasted that the example had prevented the recurrence of any similar acts of hostility elsewhere . . .

MAY 22: In reply to Lord Palmerston's letter of this day's date, the Queen has to observe that it must be extremely difficult at a distance and from ex parte statements to decide upon acts committed during a war. The cruel part is the war itself and if a government is anxious for the sake of humanity to avoid cruelties, the only real way will be by trying to bring about peace, by making such fair and equitable propositions to the belligerent parties as will be likely to be accepted by them.

The Queen does not recollect our having protested on account of the cold-blooded murder of the Governor of Venice or any other acts of treachery on the part of the Italians, which were conspicuous throughout their revolution.

MAY 22: . . . Viscount Palmerston begs also to state that Baron Hummelauer is arrived in London, charged to request the friendly intervention of your Majesty's Government between Austria on the one hand and the King of Sardinia and the Lombards and Venetians on the other, with the view of settling the conditions upon which Austria would be willing to abandon Italy altogether; it being the intention of the Austrian Government, if your Majesty's Government should decline its interposition, or if no satisfactory arrangements on that basis can be made, then and in such case to abandon Lombardy and to take stand upon the line of defence between the Lake of Garda and the Po, consisting of Peschiera, Verona, Mantua and Legnano, and to endeavour to retain possession of the Venetian territory . . .

MAY 23: The Queen is glad to hear of Mr. Hummelauer's mission and hopes that, with such conciliatory views on the part of Austria, we may be able to negotiate successfully for the restoration of peace in Italy.

MAY 25: . . . The Cabinet however, upon a full consideration of all the circumstances of the case, were of opinion that, although if it depended upon the decision of the British Government to determine the matter, it would in many respects be most desirable that the arrangement proposed by M. de Hummelauer should be carried into execution, yet in the present state of things, viewing the weakness and embarrassments of Austria, the strong and prevalent animosity against her all over Italy, the military means at the command of the King of Sardinia, and the almost certainty that if those means should fail in compelling the Austrians to retire from the Venetian State, the French would somehow or other be brought into Italy, this arrangement now proposed by M. de Hummelauer is not one which your Majesty's Government could undertake to suggest to the Italians with any prospect of its being accepted, and with any likelihood that it would put an end to the war . . .

Viscount Palmerston ought to mention that M. de Hummelauer said in the course of conversation that, if the French troops were to enter Italy, the Austrians would not enter into any conflict with them, not intending to begin a war with France, and that in such case the Austrian army would peaceably retire and evacuate the whole of Italy without making any resistance. Viscount Palmerston observed to him that if such was the system already determined upon by Austria, it would be better for her to evacuate Italy upon conditions negotiated with the Italians, than to retreat from it without equivalent and apparently under the pressure of fear of the French army.

MAY 25: . . . The position which Austria means to take in Italy with regard to her Italian province ought to be explained and a declaration be made that Austria will, with this province, join any Italian league which the other States of Italy may wish to establish. This will be useful to Italy and much facilitate the acceptance of the Austrian proposal, as the Queen feels convinced that, as soon as the war shall be terminated, the question of the political constitution of Italy (as a whole) will have to be decided. Why Charles Albert ought to get any additional territory the Queen cannot in the least see. She thinks it will be better to proceed at once upon the revised Austrian proposal than to wait for Italian propositions which are sure to be ridiculously extravagant.

There the matter rested for the time being, with both sides in Italy jockeying for position. Hummelauer left again for Vienna, but not before Palmerston had been instructed by the Queen to tell him ' . . . to express to the Emperor and the Imperial Family her sincere wishes for their welfare and for the well being of the Austrian Empire'.

There were more shocks to come. Palmerston was dabbling gleefully in other fields, and had instructed Bulwer in Madrid to advise the Spanish Government to adopt a more legal and constitutional system. That proud nation never accepted dictation from anyone and on May 22, Palmerston had to inform the Queen that Bulwer had been given 48 hours to leave the country:

. . . The grounds upon which this serious step has been taken are stated to be Sir Henry Bulwer's alleged connection with the revolts which have lately taken place in Madrid and in other places in Spain; the disapprobation said to be felt at his general conduct by the Spanish Government and by the garrison and inhabitants of Madrid and the consequent danger of personal violence to which the Spanish Government considered him as being exposed; the condemnation pronounced upon him by the newspapers of

Madrid; by the newpapers in London; by members of the British
Parliament and by members of the British Government . . .

The Queen's cup was now filling rapidly, and her retort was the
sharpest yet:

> . . . The sending away of Sir Henry Bulwer is a serious affair which
> will add to our many embarrassments. The Queen is however not
> surprised at it, from the tenor of the last accounts from Madrid,
> and from the fact that Sir H. Bulwer has for the last three years
> been almost sporting with political intrigues. He invariably
> boasted of at least being in the confidence of every conspiracy
> 'though he was taking care not to be personally mixed up in them',
> and after their various failures generally harboured the chief actors
> in his house under the plea of humanity. At every crisis he gave us
> to understand that he had to chose between a 'revolution and a
> palace intrigue' and not long ago only he wrote to Lord Palmer-
> ston that, if the monarchy with the Montpensier succession was
> inconvenient to us, he could get up a republic. Such principles are
> sure to be known in Spain, the more so when one considers the
> extreme vanity of Sir H. Bulwer, and his probable imprudence in
> the not very creditable company which he is said to keep. Lord
> Palmerston will remember that the Queen has often addressed
> herself to him and to Lord John in fear of Sir H. Bulwer getting
> us into some scrape, and if our diplomatists are not kept in better
> order the Queen may at any moment be exposed to similar insults
> as she has received now in the person of Sir H. Bulwer, for in
> whatever way one may wish to look at it, Sir Henry still is her
> Minister.
>
> The Queen wishes Lord Palmerston to show this letter to Lord
> John Russell, and to let her know what the Government mean to
> propose with respect to this unfortunate affair . . .

In due course Palmerston attempted an explanation in which he
saw nefarious royalist influence in Spain:

> . . . Viscount Palmerston cannot but conclude from many con-
> siderations that the Duke of Glücksburg and the Montpensier
> party had much to do with the intrigues connected with this
> affair, it being obvious that the family and partisans of the Duke
> must have thought that a breach between the Spanish and British
> Governments would be a good method of preventing the Spanish

Government from making any concession in regard to the Montpensier interest, as a means of propitiating Great Britain, and of
obtaining from hence support against dangers likely to come from
republican France; and it would have been a triumph to those
parties if they could have had a pretext for asserting or insinuating
that the British Government had listened to an intrigue proposed
to it on these matters as the price of acquiescence in the sending
away of the British Minister . . .

The Queen did not disagree, but refused to be placated. Bulwer
was under no circumstances to be forced on the Spaniards again
as Minister, and Palmerston incurred a sharp rebuke:

. . . When the Queen considers the position that we had in Spain
and what it ought to have been after the constitution of the French
Republic, when we had no rival to fight and ought to have
enjoyed the entire confidence and friendship of Spain, and compares this to the state into which our relations with that country
have been brought, she cannot help being struck how much
matters must have been mismanaged.

The Queen and the Prince were now reading the Foreign Office
despatches line-by-line, and the Prince, whose hand was becoming
more and more evident in the attitude of the Court, started to
compile a special dossier on Palmerston's diplomatic misdemean-
ours. Affairs in Portugal led to the first entry on June 16:

The Queen, having found among Sir Hamilton Seymour's despatches one in which he states that he has had a long interview
with the Duke of Palmella and that the Duke is going to form a
coalition with Monsieur Magalhaes for the purpose of overthrow-
ing the present ministry and forming a new government, (Magalhaes being Sir Hamilton's great friend and chief confidant and
both he and the Duke being personally suspected by the Queen of
Portugal of conspiring against her Throne), the Queen sent this
despatch to Lord John Russell with the remark that, after what had
lately happened in Spain and considering the many embarrassments we had already, she was very anxious that we should not
get into a new one, she could not help seeing the germ for new
difficulties in ministerial intrigue in Portugal, of which our
Minister was the confidant, and thought this should be stopped at

once by Sir H. being instructed to abstain from interfering in such matters.

Lord John's answer was: 'Lord John Russell perfectly agrees with your Majesty and will write to Lord Palmerston upon the subject'.

Not having heard anything about the matter for many days, the Queen, when she saw Lord John Russell yesterday (the 15th), asked him: 'Have you written to Lord P. upon Portgual?' Lord John said: 'Yes, I have immediately, but I got no answer from him else I would have sent it to your M.—I have however had an opportunity of speaking to him in the railway train going down to Portsmouth. He struggled very hard against it, saying the Queen of Portugal had never properly fulfilled the protocol, however at last promised to write.'—I reminded Lord John of the fact that some months ago an official despatch from Lord P. had declared the protocol to be fulfilled in all respects and the matter to be finally closed, which Lord John said was quite true and he had not thought of [it].

We now find a draft to Sir H. Seymour amongst the papers sent to the Queen for approval from the Foreign Office to the following effect: 'It is quite evident that the Queen and the Government of Portugal will listen to no advice except such that agrees with their own wishes, I have to instruct you to abstain in future from giving any longer any advice to them on political matters, taking care to explain both to the Queen and the Government your reasons for doing so. You will however at the same time positively declare to the Portuguese Government that if, by the course of policy they are pursuing, they should run into any difficulty they must clearly understand that they will not have to expect any assistance from England.

This was serious enough for the Queen to feel justified in appealing to the Prime Minister, and she wrote to Lord John Russell that very day.

The Queen sends the enclosed draft and asks whether this ill-tempered note is what Lord John directed Lord Palmerston to send to Lisbon as a caution to Sir H. Seymour not to mix himself up with party intrigues to upset a particular ministry?—The Queen thinks this almost a mockery of Lord John, the Cabinet, the country and herself which can really not go on so.

Poor Lord John was caught in the first round of crossfire which was to render the next three years of his premiership a nightmare. Stronger in his staunch Whig beliefs than in personal authority, he always found it difficult to discipline the confident and politically powerful Palmerston. In any case, although he often shuddered at the tone of his colleague's despatches, there was no real disagreement between them on policy. As usual, Lord John temporised. He thought the matter should be left to Sir Hamilton's known sense of discretion. This was not enough for the Queen, who wrote again:

> The country is at this moment suffering particularly with regard to Spain, under the evil consequence of that system of diplomacy, which makes the taking up of party politics in foreign countries its principal object. This system is condemned alike by the Queen, Lord John, the Cabinet and, the Queen fully believes, the public opinion in and out of Parliament. Lord Palmerston's objection to caution our Minister in Portugal against falling into this fault brings it to an issue, whether that erroneous policy is to be maintained to the detriment of the real interests of the country or a wiser course to be followed in future.

A day later, she sent this afterthought:

> . . . Lord Palmerston has behaved about this note really like a naughty child; because he was to do what he did not like, he insisted upon doing it in a manner which he knew must be displeasing to Lord John and (the Queen cannot help suspecting) particularly to herself and this without the slightest pretext for it.

The bickering went on for more than a month, and in the end Palmerston consented to send off slightly modified instructions to Sir Hamilton, in which he emphasised again the iniquities of the Portuguese Government, but temporarily washed his hands of the consequences. However, Queen Victoria's suspicions of his conduct were now thoroughly aroused, and he found her obstinate even in matters of protocol:

> JUNE 19: . . . Viscount Palmerston would also wish to submit to your Majesty's consideration the position of M. de Tallenay, the present French Minister in London, who is an extremely well-

behaved and well-conditioned man, and whose conduct in the performance of his duty since he has been here has been all that could be desired.

Viscount Palmerston has felt anxious that if it was possible to avoid it, your Majesty should not address credentials to, nor receive them from the five persons, including Le Dru Rollin, now forming the executive committee of the French Republic; and as the permanent scheme of government is now about to be proposed to the Convention, there seems to be a fair reason for waiting until the Convention has decided upon it. But some weeks will of course elapse before the new constitution can be settled and before the new legislative assembly is elected, and the President of the Republic is chosen; and in the meantime M. de Tallenay will remain in a very mortifying position, transacting business from day to day with your Majesty's Government and doing his best to establish good understanding between the two countries upon all the pending European questions, but excluded not only from your Majesty's Court on occasions of ceremony, but also from your Majesty's presence on other occasions, when so many of your Majesty's subjects and so many foreigners have the honour of being invited. No doubt in point of strict etiquette and established rule he could not be invited to Buckingham Palace; but his case is one of (it may be hoped) singular peculiarity; and if it was possible in any way to allow it to be an exception to the established rule, such an arrangement would not only relieve a deserving man from a mortifying situation, but would diminish the contrast which might possibly be drawn at Paris, to the disadvantage of English interests, between the backwardness of the British Government in exchanging credentials, and the acquiescence of other Governments, such as those of Belgium and Prussia, in completing the form of acknowledgment . . .

JUNE 22: The Queen has maturely considered Lord Palmerston's proposition respecting M. de Tallenay. She must confess that nothing but the very strongest political reasons could induce her to depart from the established etiquette. The Queen is much afraid likewise of establishing a precedent, after which any agent of a new revolutionary government, which is not recognised, might claim admission to the Queen's Court. As M. de Tallenay does not know of Lord Palmerston's proposition, it will be better to let matters remain as they now are, unless something new should arise in the interval of time which will elapse between now and the 5th of July when the ball takes place . . .

The situation in Italy was still simmering, with Charles Albert overplaying his hand in the negotiations and Radetzky and the Austrian troops building up strength for a counter-attack. The Queen did not like the tone of some of Palmerston's despatches to Mr. Abercromby, the British Minister in Piedmont, and wrote two letters on June 28:

> The Queen returns the draft to Mr. Abercromby which she approves. She thinks however that it would be improved if, at the end of the passage which the Queen has marked with a cross, an injunction was added to encourage the Italians to agree to the plan of accommodation which Austria proposes, if they should feel themselves inclined to it.—In the Queen's opinion it does not suffice to say we have declined to make the proposition because we think the Italians will not agree to it, but in case they should be so disposed, we will not throw obstacles in the way.

> The Queen . . . did not mean Mr. Abercromby to treat with the Venetians,—but that he should encourage the Piedmontese and Milanese to agree to the Austrian proposal and not to stand out for Venice—if he should find them so inclined, and hopes that Lord Palmerston will be able to express this in a few words . . .

Palmerston's reply stated the alternatives as he saw them:

> . . . With reference to the instruction to Mr. Abercromby, Viscount Palmerston would beg to submit that it is not at present likely that the Piedmontese Government would be willing to make an arrangement with the Austrian Government by which the Venetian territory should be left to Austria, and that if the King of Sardinia should, for reasons of his own and upon a calculation of chances, not be inclined to such an arrangement, he would not be led to it by any advice to that effect from Mr. Abercromby on the part of the British Government, but the fact that such advice had been given would become known and would be made use of by parties and persons adverse to British interests, for the purpose of creating among the Italians a prejudice against England, and of thus diminishing the influence of Great Britain in Italy, and

Buckingham Palace

May — 21. 1848.

The Queen returns this draft to Lord Palmerston & she thinks had better not be sent. It is already well known that we sympathize with the Italians against the Austrians & it wd not be wise! The Queen is of opinion that unnecessarily

The Queen rebukes Palmerston. Full text on page 74.

the means of the British Government to do good. If, on the other hand, the King of Sardinia should be led by a calculation of the relative military strength of the two parties, and by a desire to bring the war at once to an end, to consent to terms by which the Venetian territory should be left to Austria, he would be reproached by the Italians for having, as they would say, betrayed their cause and sacrificed the Venetians to his own immediate interest, and it seems to Viscount Palmerston that it is very desirable that he should not be able in such a case to ascribe to the councils of England a division which would have been entirely the result of his own calculations of his own interest.

It seems therefore to Viscount Palmerston that the only safe course to take in this matter is to instruct Mr. Abercromby to give no advice or encouragement to the Piedmontese Government one way or the other, as to standing out for, or abandoning the Venetians . . .

This was digested at Buckingham Palace for a couple of days. Then Prince Albert himself composed a tremendous broadside in his own hand, which was duly copied out word for word by the Queen and sent to the erring Foreign Minister:

The Queen has not yet answered Lord Palmerston's letter of the 29th. She cannot conceal from him that she is ashamed of the policy we are pursuing in the Italian controversy, in abetting wrong, and this for the object of gaining influence in Italy. The Queen does not consider influence so gained as an advantage and, though this influence is to be acquired in order to do good, she is afraid that the fear of losing it again will always stand in the way of this.—At least in the countries where the greatest stress has been laid on that influence, and the greatest exertions made for it, the least good has been done; the Queen means in Spain, Portugal and Greece. Neither is there any kind of consistency in the line we take about Italy and that we follow in regard to Schleswig; both cases are perfectly alike (with the difference perhaps that there is a question of right mixed up in that of Schleswig); whilst we upbraid Prussia, caution her, etc.—we say nothing to Charles Albert except that if he did not wish to take all the Emperor of Austria's Italian Dominions, we would not lay any obstacles in the way of his moderation . . .

Palmerston's answer the following day took the form of one of the longest letters he ever wrote to the Queen, a dozen quarto folios in his copper-plate hand, in which he firmly justified the whole of his conduct of foreign affairs over the years:

> ... In the autumn of last year the Pope, then recently elected, entertained a strong desire to make reforms in the government in his States, the government which had long been known to be more full of practical abuses than any other in Europe; he found himself thwarted by opposing influences from within and from without, and he conveyed to your Majesty's Government by several channels, but especially through Lord Shrewsbury and Doctor Wiseman, his earnest request that he might receive countenance and support from Great Britain and that for this purpose some agent of the British Government might be sent to Rome, and that if there was any legal impediment to prevent an accredited envoy from being sent to him, he might nevertheless have the benefit of the support, assistance and advice of some person of rank, weight and, if possible, diplomatic standing, who might possess the confidence of the British Government, and whose presence at Rome might be a public manifestation of the good will of Great Britain. It appeared to your Majesty's Government that it would be proper to comply with this application and it seemed to Viscount Palmerston that the Earl of Minto, who was then going abroad for a short time with his family, exactly fulfilled the description given by the Pope of the kind of person whom he would wish to have at Rome, and was also peculiarly well qualified to carry out the views of your Majesty's Government.

> The Earl of Minto was therefore with your Majesty's approbation sent to Rome.

> But in the meantime fresh complications began to arise in other parts of Italy. The reforms begun and the further measures announced by the Pope roused the deeply-seated, though long dormant, desires of the people in the other States of Italy for improvement in their respective governments, which, though far better than that of the Papal States, were yet all founded upon the arbitrary instead of the constitutional principle. There seemed to be great chance of dangerous conflict between the sovereigns and their subjects. The sovereigns were averse to making any concessions; the subjects appeared in many places inclined to extort by force concessions unreasonably great. Your Majesty's Govern-

ment thought that the mission of the Earl of Minto to Rome might afford an opportunity to Great Britain to exert a useful influence in other parts of Italy; and accordingly the Earl of Minto was instructed to take Turin and Florence in his way to Rome. At Turin and Florence he was gladly and cordially received; and at Turin and Florence he was able to render important service both to the sovereign and the subject, by encouraging the Government to grant constitutional institutions, and by exhorting the reform party to accept and to be satisfied with the spontaneous concessions of the sovereign, and Viscount Palmerston would submit that it may safely be affirmed that the successful exertions of the Earl of Minto at Turin and at Florence were among the principal causes which have saved those capitals from serious convulsion during the last few months.

At Rome the same course of policy was pursued, and with the same good result; and although persons well acquainted with Italy still maintain that the danger of the establishment of republican governments in Italy is not yet over, Viscount Palmerston would fain hope that the reforms and improvements made and in progress, may succeed in preserving the monarchical form.

From Rome the Earl of Minto went to Naples at the invitation of the King of Naples; and at the request of that sovereign he endeavoured to negotiate a reconciliation between the King and his Sicilian subjects.

If the Neapolitan Government had adopted the Earl of Minto's advice, an arrangement would speedily have been made, by which the King of Naples would have retained on his own head the Crown of Sicily. But blind prejudice, or ill-founded hopes of assistance from other quarters, prevailed; the golden opportunity was lost; the news of the French revolution reached Palermo; and the Sicilians drew back from the conditions which, in compliance with the wishes of England, they had before been willing to agree to. Still in deference to the desire expressed by the Earl of Minto on behalf of your Majesty's Government, they consented to receive one of the sons of the King of Naples as their sovereign; but again a refusal of the King of Naples frustrated the Earl of Minto's endeavour and the Sicilians then proceeded to declare the deposal of the royal family of Naples, and to look out for some prince of some other Italian House; being impelled partly by their own preference, and partly by the exhortation of your Majesty's agents to adhere to the monarchical, instead of adopting the republican form of government.

The Earl of Minto having nothing further to detain him in Italy and being wanted in England, then returned home.

Viscount Palmerston would humbly submit that there is nothing in the course of policy pursued by your Majesty's Government in all these Italian affairs that is not honourable to Great Britain and conducive not only to the advantage of Italy, but also to the general interests of Europe and to the maintenance of its peace.

But there happened in Lombardy soon after the French revolution of February a general rising against the Austrian rule; and so determined and extensive was the insurrection that the large Austrian garrison of Milan was compelled after a long struggle to evacuate that city.

The fire of intense dislike to Austrian domination, which had long been kept by overpowering force, now burst out into a flame from one end of Italy to the other, and a general crusade was proclaimed to drive the Austrians over the Alps.—The King of Sardinia was called upon by the people of Lombardy and urged by his own ministers and subjects to take a part in the war, and to assist in endeavouring to expel the Austrian army. He was told that if he did not do so, he would run the risk of being de-throned, and that a republic might probably be declared in his dominions. To these impulses he yielded, urged on at the same time, it cannot be doubted, by his own personal ambition.

In the summer of last year when the King of Sardinia was projecting improvements in his administration, and when the movement of the Austrian force in Lombardy seemed to threaten attack in order to prevent those internal improvements, your Majesty's Government made a representation to the Government of Austria for the purpose of dissuading any such attack.

Therefore, when it seemed likely that the King of Sardinia would become the assailant against Austria, your Majesty's Minister at Turin, without waiting for instructions, which there was not time for him to ask for and to receive, stated strongly, upon his own responsibility, against the decision which he understood the Government of Turin was about to take and his conduct in so doing was approved and fresh instructions to the same effect were sent him. But the representation thus made could not be expected to outweigh the stronger motives which led to the decision, and the Piedmontese army began its march into Lombardy.

Remonstrance and argument having failed, the British Government might certainly have gone a step further, and might have intimated an intention of taking part in the war, in favour of Austria and against Piedmont. But such an active interference would have been a grave step; would not have been in unison with public opinion in this country, might probably have been disapproved by Parliament, would most likely have brought France to the assistance of Italy, and perhaps have involved the whole of Europe in war. It only remained therefore, for your Majesty's Government to remain spectators, and to watch events . . .

Your Majesty compares the case of Italy with that of Schleswig, but Viscount Palmerston would submit that there are essential differences between the two as far as Great Britain is concerned. In the case of Schleswig the British Government has been accepted by both parties as mediator, which is not the case in regard to the Italian war; and a government engaged in mediation may justly urge the contending parties to suspend the progress of the war. In the case of Schleswig too there is a treaty guarantee which has been given by the British Crown, which might if the Danish construction of it were admitted, compel Great Britain to become a party in the war, if your Majesty's Government did not succeed in its efforts at mediation.

But Mr. Abercromby was instructed to represent to the Government at Turin that the arguments by which it justified its advance into Lombardy might be turned against itself if there was an insurrection got up in Savoy and if the French came to the aid of the insurgents; and Viscount Palmerston does not recollect at the present moment that anything stronger has been addressed to the Prussian Government in regard to the affair of Schleswig . . .

Your Majesty, in adverting to the question about influence in foreign countries, observes that in those countries with regard to which the greatest stress has been laid on that influence, and the greatest exertions have been made to obtain it, the least good has been done by it, as for instance in Spain, Portugal and Greece.

But Viscount Palmerston would beg to submit that British influence in Spain was advisedly, though, as Viscount Palmerston has always ventured to think, most injudiciously surrendered by your Majesty's late Government, who gave up Spain to France, and instructed Sir Henry Bulwer to follow in all respects the lead of the French Ambassador. The Regent, the Duke of Victoria, who looked to Great Britain for support, because he is a good Spaniard and knows that England has no object in Spain except the independence and prosperity of Spain, was abandoned to the intrigues of the French Government; and the party who are willing to sacrifice the independence of their country at the shrine of personal interest were placed in power; and have retained it ever since by the same corrupt means and support by which they obtained it. This abandonment of Spain was part of the price paid for that 'Entente Cordiale' which did not prevent the dispute about Tahiti and which the recent publications in the *Revue Retrospective* sufficiently show to have been chiefly designed to deceive your Majesty and to cajole your Majesty's ministers, while the King of the French was pursuing his own schemes of family interest and political ambition.

If British influence had been maintained in Spain, such as it was in 1841 when Viscount Melbourne's administration went out, it can hardly be imagined that the two unfortunate Spanish marriages could have been brought about; and if the maintenance of British influence in Spain could have prevented those two lamentable events, it was surely worth while for the British Government to have made some effort for the purpose of maintaining that influence.

In regard to Portugal, Viscount Palmerston would beg to submit that it was the influence and action of Great Britain, co-operating as a matter of policy, but not as a matter of necessity, with France and Spain, that saved the Queen and the King of Portugal from probable dethronement, and if the influence of your Majesty's Government has not since that time been able to counteract those other influences which have led the Queen of Portugal away from a strict and faithful performance of the spirit of her engagements, that influence has at least been one among the courses which have prevented a renewal of disturbance in Portugal.

In regard to Greece, Viscount Palmerston would humbly submit that the state of that country is rather an example of the evil which may arise from the extinction or non-existence of British influence, than of the inutility of creating and maintaining it. No British Government has had any influence in Greece, or, more properly speaking, over the Government at Athens, since the majority of King Otho, or indeed it may be said, since the end of the Regency of Count Armansperg. But the reason of this circumstance lies in a narrow compass. The British Government, whoever have been the Ministers of the Crown, has always advised King Otho first to grant a constitution, and afterwards, when he had been compelled by insurrection to do so, to observe the constitution which he had agreed to. But this advice has always been unpalatable to King Otho, and his aversion to follow it has been backed and supported by the communications which he has till very lately constantly received from the Governments of France, of Austria, of Russia, of Prussia, and of Bavaria.—When five powers were advising the King of Greece to follow his own inclinations, and one power was urging him to do that which he disliked, it was not to be wondered at that the influence of the five should overpower the influence of the one. But the advice and encouragement given by the five have rendered the King hateful to his subjects, have spread insurrection and anarchy throughout the land, and have brought the State to the verge of bankruptcy, while the advice given by the one would, if it had been attended to, have bound the subject by attachment to the sovereign, have established peace and legal order in the country, and would have freed the kingdom from its financial embarrassments.

Viscount Palmerston is sensible that he has many apologies to make to your Majesty for having trespassed so much at length upon your Majesty's patience and indulgence; but the topics adverted to by your Majesty were important, and he trusts that your Majesty will forgive him for observations which have run into much greater length than he intended when he first began this paper.

To this remorseless logic the Queen could only retort somewhat defensively that although she had approved of the Minto mission at the time 'it certainly was prejudicial to the Austrians', that the danger of French interference in Italy was equally great whether Charles Albert or the Austrians possessed Venice, and that it was Palmerston's encouragement of the *Progresista* Party in Spain which had thrown Queen Christina and Louis-Philippe together, an 'unfortunate combination which cannot but be considered as the origin of all the present convulsions in Europe'.

This last charge Palmerston strenuously denied in a protracted correspondence, but although he wore the royal couple down with words he did not regain their confidence. The Queen remained invincibly suspicious of him, determined to combat the ambitions of the French Republic and to protect the rights of Austria:

> The Queen sees from Lord Normanby's last private letter [she wrote on July 22] that he is trying to come to an agreement with the French Government relative to a joint line to be taken by us and them with respect to Italy. Considering that it must be out of the question for a French Republic to take a part in any other arrangement except that of driving the Austrians out of Italy, the Queen thinks it is quite uncalled for, and would consider it very unfortunate if we were to treat with the French on this question, and thus be the first to introduce French intervention, or to enter into an 'entente cordiale' with the French Republic against Austria.

The Queen also appealed again to Lord John Russell:

> ... The Queen is afraid that Lord Palmerston has a scheme of establishing a Kingdom of Upper Italy reaching from one sea to the other and that it is for that scheme that all considerations of ancient alliance with Austria, of the peace of Europe, the regard for treaties, etc., etc. are to be sacrificed ...

This was shrewd enough, and although Palmerston was to live to see this dream largely fulfilled, it was not to be for another dozen years. Even as the Queen was writing, Marshal Radetzky had burst out of his fortified position, and inflicted a serious reverse on Charles Albert's forces at the first battle of Custozza. With Austria in the ascendant, Palmerston's enthusiasm for mediation waned. Months of stalemate and negotiations were to follow.

There was almost daily conflict between the Queen and Palmerston as the armistice talks began. Palmerston was determined to act in concert with France, if only as a means of checking the new Republic's determination to gain influence in Italy. The first step was to regularise diplomatic relations between the two countries. The French envoy had yet to be received at Court, and Normanby's position in Paris was anomalous. The Queen made her own prejudices quite clear to Palmerston:

> ... The Queen has the strongest objection against seeing an Ambassador of the Republic at her Court, at the head of the London society (who may possibly be a very awkward character). To make objections against a person selected might be very difficult and injudicious ...

The Queen's idea was that Ministers only should be exchanged in the first instance. But Palmerston wanted Normanby in Paris and could not ask him to accept a reduction in his previous rank:

> ... It could not well be expected that Lord Normanby should present credentials as Minister at a place where he has so long been acting as Ambassador, and especially when he would have thereby to descend into an inferior class of the diplomatic body, while the representatives of Spain and Belgium continued in the higher class. On the other hand, Viscount Palmerston would beg to submit that it would not be for the good of your Majesty's service to recall Lord Normanby at the present moment and to send another person to Paris to act as Minister in his room. In the first place the sudden recall of Lord Normanby just at the moment when an important negotiation has begun, in which England and France are acting together, might be looked upon by the world at large, as indicating disapprobation of, or want of confidence in Lord Normanby on the part of the Government, and would therefore be unjust by him, and in the next place the French Government and nation might think it strange if the British Government, after having for six months retained at Paris an unofficial representative with the rank of Ambassador in abeyance, should withdraw that organ and substitute a Minister at the very moment when the French Government is facing popular clamour and giving up what may be represented as the national policy of

France, in order to cooperate with the British Government, and
to follow the policy of Great Britain . . .

In the end, Palmerston and his nominee connived at converting
the matter into one involving Normanby's personal dignity, and
the Queen had no option but to agree. But she exploded in
outrage to Lord John Russell in a letter again drafted for her by
Prince Albert:

> . . . The Queen is highly indignant at Lord Palmerston's be-
> haviour, now again with respect to Lord Normanby's appoint-
> ment. He knew perfectly well that Lord Normanby could not
> accept the post of Minister and had written to the Queen before,
> that such an offer could not be made, and has made it after all,
> knowing that by wasting time and getting the matter entangled at
> Paris, he would carry his point. If the French are so anxious to
> keep Lord Normanby as to make any sacrifice for that object, it
> ought to make us cautious, as it can only be on account of the ease
> with which they can make him serve their purposes.—They of
> course like an 'entente cordiale' with us at the expense of Austria
> and as a means of propping up their Republic; but this can be
> no consideration for us, though Lord Palmerston, the Queen is
> afraid, would be glad of it, were it merely to gratify a personal
> feeling against King Louis-Philippe, M. Guizot and Lord Aber-
> deen. For vindictiveness is one of the main features in Lord
> Palmerston's character and the Queen has no doubt that he con-
> siders King Charles Albert's defeat almost as a personal one, which
> he must try to recover . . . The Queen must say she is afraid that
> she will have no peace of mind and there will be no end of troubles
> as long as Lord Palmerston is at the head of the Foreign Office.

This was serious indeed, but the Prime Minister and his Foreign
Secretary survived a further hail of complaints about their
attitude, which included another sharp dig by the Queen at
Palmerston in a letter to Lord John Russell:

> . . . Radetzky and King Charles Albert have concluded an
> armistice on a certain basis; the inducement for Charles Albert
> was to save himself and his army from destruction, that of
> Radetzky, to gain political advantage for his sovereign in return
> for his military sacrifice. Now that Charles Albert hears of the
> mediation and expects of it better things than he bargained for,

Lord Palmerston advises that the armistice should not be considered as a political one but merely as a military one. Is this
mediating between belligerents? Or merely trying to obtain
advantage for a client? What is the meaning of a *basis for an
armistice* if this is not political? The armistice would otherwise
only consist in an agreement to suspend hostilities and exchange
prisoners.—All this is very unfortunate . . .

The Queen also sent a serious injunction, again drafted in Prince
Albert's hand, to Palmerston himself:

. . . The Queen's opinion [is] that by adherence to strict right and
justice, England might have saved Europe from the chance of a
general war, but she is afraid that the deviation from those
principles of justice and international faith which we have first
made, 'in order to keep our influence in Italy', and now, to please
the French Republic, will lead us from one step to another and
will very likely bring on the very war which a nobler attitude
might have prevented.

Palmerston was by now becoming distinctly nettled at this constant supervision and reproof. Events were moving fast in Europe.
Austria had declined Britain's renewed offer of mediation and this
caused a new crisis, with France threatening to send troops into
Italy to bolster Charles Albert's position. M. de Beaumont, the
Republic's new Ambassador in London, had been particularly
pressing and in the flurry of sending new instructions to Normanby in Paris, Palmerston had omitted to tell the Queen of
the new development. She demanded information in her most
peremptory tone and received yet another evasive answer in
reply:

Viscount Palmerston presents his humble duty to your Majesty
and in reply to your Majesty's enquiry as to the communication
made by the Austrian Government to the offer of mediation,
submits the accompanying draft of a despatch which he began on
Friday but was unable to finish till Saturday afternoon in consequence of incessant interruption . . .
    Viscount Palmerston sent the despatch off by special messenger
to Lord Normanby on Saturday, without waiting to submit the

draft previously to your Majesty, because, in the state of impatience and irritation in which the French Government was about these affairs, he thought it of importance not to lose a day in placing Lord Normanby in possession of explanations which might enable him to persuade the French Government not to take any hasty decision . . .

It was now September, and the royal couple were on their way by sea to Balmoral, their newly acquired summer retreat in the Highlands, but the Queen was determined not to relinquish control of affairs and wrote from their yacht *Victoria and Albert* at Aberdeen:

> The Queen received the night before she left London (too late to write upon it) Lord Palmerston's letter and the long draft to Lord Normanby. As the draft is gone, the Queen will only remark that the passage expressing Lord Palmerston's agreement in the general argument of M. de Beaumont, 'as to the advantages which would arise from a previous concert between England and France as to any military operations which France might be compelled to undertake in Italy',—is most dangerous for the future peace of Europe, and becomes still more so from the sole objection stated: 'that the case which could require such a decision does not seem as yet to have happened'.—This clearly points out, that when it shall have happened, armed interference on the part of France and England is to take place, that is to say, a war against Austria to take from her a province which she holds by the Treaty of Vienna, to which we are a party.—This is a line of policy to which the Queen cannot give her consent. It is quite immaterial, whether French troops alone are employed for such an unjust purpose, if this is done on previous concert with England.
>
> The whole tone of the draft the Queen cannot approve.

Palmerston, in his turn, had retreated to his country seat, Broadlands, near Southampton, whence he replied:

> Viscount Palmerston presents his humble duty to your Majesty and has had the honour to receive your Majesty's communication of the 7th instant from Aberdeen; and he begs to submit that in the conversation with M. de Beaumont, of which he made a report in his despatch to Lord Normanby, his object was to calm

the extreme impatience and irritation of the French Government
who, there is good reason to believe, were on the point of sending
orders to their army of the Alps to make a forward movement
towards Italy. Viscount Palmerston made use of such arguments
as seemed to him at the moment best calculated to attain the
purpose, and whether it be owing to Viscount Palmerston's
representations, as M. de Beaumont says it is, or whether other
causes may have produced the effect, at all events Viscount
Palmerston begs to state that the French army has not moved.

Then, obviously waxing sarcastic, he went on:

Viscount Palmerston might undoubtedly have held a different
language to M. de Beaumont; he might have said that if the French
troops should enter Italy to assist the Piedmontese or the Lombards,
the British Government would have nothing to do with the matter,
and that consequently, if those troops should enter, they might
do what they liked, go as far as they liked, and settle matters as
they liked; such language would indeed have left the French
Government more free to take at once their own decision, but he
does not think that it would have had more influence in restraining
them.

If indeed he had said that in such a case England would oppose
France and join Austria in war, no doubt such a declaration might
have been effectual, but such a declaration would not have been
borne out by any intention of the British Government, nor by any
support in Parliament or in the country . . .

At all events it seems to Viscount Palmerston that it is better
that the French Government should look at a possible advance of
its army into Italy as an operation that is to be subjected to the
consent of Great Britain, rather than it should view it as a measure
to be determined upon according to the single will of France, and
with a view to its own interests and convenience . . .

There matters rested for the time being, but Palmerston's relations
with the Court had reached a point of almost hysterical exacer-
bation. The Queen picked him up on his most minor administrative actions. Just before she left on her holiday she had complained that he had opened an official letter to her from Archduke
John of Austria, who had been presiding over the meeting of the
new German Diet in Frankfurt.Wearily, Palmerston explained:

Viscount Palmerston presents his humble duty to your Majesty, and regrets very much that in the hurry of business he should inadvertently have cut open the letter addressed to your Majesty by the Archduke John, mistaking it for an official letter.—With regard to the official letters addressed to your Majesty from foreign Courts, Viscount Palmerston has always cut them open before laying them before your Majesty under an impression that it was his duty to do so, and it was always his practice to do so by such official letters during the time he had the honour of holding office under your Majesty before and also while he had the honour of serving his late Majesty; but of course if it is your Majesty's pleasure, that practice shall be discontinued. The ground upon which that practice is founded, and as Viscount Palmerston understood when first he came into the Foreign Office had been pursued by his predecessors, is, that the Secretary of State is answerable for the contents of every paper which he submits to the sovereign, to this extent at least that he is bound to inform himself of the contents of such papers, and to see that they are fit and proper to be laid before the sovereign before he becomes the channel for so submitting them; and therefore it is his duty to open letters of an official character which he may lay before the sovereign, and he would be liable to reproof, if in consequence of his omitting to do so, any communication from a foreign Court or from any other quarter should come into the hands of the sovereign, which either in its substance or in its form was not properly and suitably framed.

Viscount Palmerston must indeed confess that it sometimes happens, as it did in the case of the letter from the Archduke John, that in the pressure of business he contents himself with cutting open the cover to facilitate your Majesty in opening the letter and that, trusting to the quarter from which particular letters may come, he does not in every case read them; but wherever a doubt may exist as to whether the proper forms have been observed he not only cuts open but reads the letter.

The Queen convoked the Prime Minister to her Highland fastness and, on September 19, made the first of her demands that Palmerston should be replaced at the Foreign Office. That night she summarised their conversation in her private journal:

I said to Lord John Russell, that I must mention to him a subject, which was a serious one, one which I had delayed mentioning

for some time, but which I now felt I must speak quite openly
to him upon now, namely about Lord Palmerston; that I felt
really I could hardly go on with him, that I have no confidence in
him, and that it made me seriously anxious and uneasy for the
welfare of the country and for the peace of Europe in general, and
that I felt very uneasy from one day to another as to what might
happen. Lord John replied that he was aware of it; that he had
considered the matter already, having heard from his brother (the
Duke of Bedford) how strongly I felt about it; that he felt the
truth of all that I had said, but that, on the other hand, Lord
Palmerston was a very able man, entirely master of his office and
of affairs, and a very good colleague, never making any difficulties
about other questions, but (certainly unreasonably) complaining
of other people mixing with and interfering in the affairs of his
office. I said that he was very vindictive and that I fully believed
that that Spanish marriage question, which had been the original
cause of so many present misfortunes, would never have become so
embrouillé had it not been for Lord Palmerston. This led Lord John
to say, that though he disapproved the length of Lord Palmerston's correspondence, still that we could not have done otherwise
than object to the marriage. This is true enough. I repeated that all
that had been done in Italy last winter had also done harm, as it
was done by Lord Palmerston, who was distrusted everywhere
abroad, which Lord John regretted. I said that I thought that he
often endangered the honour of England by taking a very pre-
judiced and one-sided view of a question; that I have proofs
that he was not always straightforward in his conduct and kept
back things which he did not like should be known,—of which I
gave an instance, that his writings were always as bitter as gall
and did great harm, which Lord John entirely assented to, and
that I often felt quite ill from anxiety; that I wished Lord Clarendon
(who, I have heard, was tired of Ireland) could come over and be
Secretary of State for Foreign Affairs, and Lord Palmerston go to
Ireland as Lord-Lieutenant. Lord John said nothing would be
better, for that he was sure that Lord Palmerston would make an
admirable Lord-Lieutenant, but that another thing to be considered
was the danger of making Lord Palmerston an enemy by dis-
placing him, that Lord Minto (who was formerly a great friend
of Lord Palmerston) had told Lady John when she spoke to him
on the subject of placing Lord Palmerston in another office, that

he (Lord Palmerston) would certainly turn against the Government if displaced. I said that might be, but that sometimes there were great interests at stake which exceeded the danger of offending one man, and that this was here the case; Lord John said it was very true, but that at moments like these one of course was anxious not to do anything which could cause internal trouble. I admitted this, but repeated my anxiety, which Lord John quite understood, though he thought I a little overrated it, and said I was afraid that some day I should have to tell Lord John that I could not put up with Lord Palmerston any longer, which might be very disagreeable and awkward.

It ended by Lord John's promising to bear the subject in mind, and I must say that he took it all just as I could wish.

Viscount Palmerston begs also to state that Baron Hummelauer is arrived in London charged to request the friendly Intervention of your Majesty's Government between Austria on the one Hand and the King of Sardinia & the Lombards & Venetians on the other, with the view of settling the Conditions upon which Austria would be willing to abandon Italy altogether; It being the Intention of the Austrian Government if your Majesty's Government should decline its Interposition, or if no satisfactory arrangement on that Basis can be made, then and in such case to abandon Lombardy and to take Stand upon the Line of defence between the Lake of Garda & the Po, consisting of Peschiera, Verona Mantua & Legnano, and to endeavour to retain Possession of the Venetian Territory. Viscount Palmerston is to see Count Diedrichstein & Baron Hummelauer on this Matter Tomorrow.

Palmerston reports to the Queen. Full text on page 75.

CHAPTER IV

Conflict with the Court

LORD JOHN RUSSELL WAS TO SPEND MOST OF THE NEXT TWO YEARS buffeted between the now thoroughly aroused Queen and his forceful colleague, but although he not infrequently took the side of the Court in persuading Palmerston to modify his attitude or tone down some of his more spirited despatches, the Foreign Minister had too powerful a following in the country to be discarded or removed. This triangular conflict must be without parallel in British ministerial annals, certainly in the last two centuries, and the wonder is that it did not lead to a constitutional crisis of the first magnitude.

The bickering over Italian affairs continued in a minor key through the autumn and winter of 1848-9. Sicily was also in revolt against the despotic King of Naples. Queen Victoria had persuaded Lord John Russell to use his influence with Palmerston to permit the Neapolitan crown to reassert some of its rights. On September 25, she wrote to her Foreign Minister:

> The Queen has received the enclosed papers from Lord John Russell and sends them back to Lord Palmerston with her entire approval of the proposed line of policy to be adopted conjointly with France relative to Sicily, viz. to make the Sicilians aware that no assistance will be given them by the two powers,—but that these two powers are to stop the further progress of the war, and to mediate on the basis of the legislative and administrative independence of Sicily, under the Crown of the King of Naples, thus securing to both parties that to which they have the most undoubted right.—The same basis the Queen thinks would be best for our mediation in Upper Italy, and would at once put an end to the dangerous struggle in that part of Europe . . .

A further exhortation followed the next day:

> . . . The Queen entirely concurs in what Lord John says, and thinks
> moreover a European Congress to settle these complicated ques-
> tions highly desirable, and preferable to the settlement by the
> 'entente cordiale' with the French Republic . . .

Palmerston was extremely loth to have other powers interven-
ing and tried to dissuade the Queen:

> . . . If there was to be a general resettlement of Italy [he replied],
> or indeed any great change in the state of possession in Italy, all
> the powers who were parties to the Treaty of Vienna, by which
> the present arrangements in Italy were in a great degree deter-
> mined, might justly demand to be made parties to the new
> arrangements and indeed, if any alteration is to be made in the
> arrangements of Vienna, all the powers who signed the Treaty
> of Vienna would be entitled to have the choice of becoming parties
> to the new arrangement, by signing any treaty by which it might
> be recorded, although such powers could scarcely be entitled to
> object if the parties more immediately concerned should have
> come to an understanding on the subject.
>
> But Viscount Palmerston would submit that the essential
> matters with respect to which England and France are about to
> mediate lie in a comparatively small compass, and might probably
> be more easily settled by the joint efforts of the two powers than
> by a European Congress.

> The Queen has just received Lord Palmerston's letter of yesterday
> on Lord John Russell's memorandum. Lord Palmerston's objec-
> tion to a European Congress, on account of the claim that other
> powers would urge to be admitted to it, the Queen considers
> removed of by the precedent of 1830 with regard to Belgium.
> Lord P. was then Foreign Secretary and seems to have had none of
> the present scruples.

The Queen was determined that Austria should play her full part
in the solution of the Italian situation. When Palmerston proposed
that the British Ambassador in Paris, Lord Normanby, should
represent his country at the talks, the Queen immediately countered with a requirement that his colleague in Vienna should go
instead:

... Viscount Palmerston would beg to submit to your Majesty that Lord Normanby would on the whole be the best person to be employed by your Majesty as British representative at those conferences. He is fully master of all the questions, knows all that has passed in regard to them, understands the views of the French Government, and the state of France, and is equally well acquainted with Italian affairs.

The Queen would not wish Lord Normanby to go there. Lord Ponsonby would do much better. He knows the question in dispute equally well and the Queen is always much pleased with the frankness with which he states his opinions to Lord Palmerston.

Palmerston made one last effort to deal with all the Queen's objections:

... Viscount Palmerston would however beg to submit to your Majesty that he was not in office when the conferences on the affairs of Belgium were established and that the two first protocols of those conferences, if Viscount Palmerston remembers rightly, but certainly the first, bore the signature of the Earl of Aberdeen.

Then, after a long disquisition to prove that Belgium provided no precedent for this Italian mediation, he ended his letter by saying:

Your Majesty passes a most well deserved eulogium upon Viscount Ponsonby. Viscount Palmerston has great esteem and regard for Lord Ponsonby, who has rendered very important service to this country in most difficult and trying circumstances, and has displayed on all occasions and wherever employed an ability and zeal which fully entitle him to your Majesty's good opinion. But there are from time to time peculiar employments for which every able man is not equally well suited; and Viscount Palmerston would beg to submit that there are many considerations which would render it much better to employ Lord Normanby than Lord Ponsonby on the present occasion.

The duty to be performed is a mediation to be carried on conjointly by England and France, and much facility and advantage will accrue from employing a negotiator who is on good terms with his French colleague, who has the confidence of the French

Government as well as of his own, who is acquainted with the state of parties and opinions in France, whose advice and suggestions his French colleague may receive without distrust and may accept without jealousy, and who may be useful not only in giving effect to the views of your Majesty's Government, but also in moderating, if need be, any separate disposition of the French representative . . .

Viscount Palmerston therefore humbly trusts that your Majesty may upon these considerations be pleased to approve of Lord Normanby being employed in the conduct of this mediation.

But the Queen, her letters again carefully drafted by the Prince, was adamant:

. . . If the object of our mediation were only to drive the Austrians out of their lawful dominions in Italy by means of threatening with French intervention, Lord Normanby would be the best instrument for that purpose, as he has throughout taken a most violent Italian line from his present connection with Italy and Italians, holding even the doctrine that Lombardy belongs to the King of Sardinia as annexed to his kingdom by universal suffrage under the sovereignty of the people, but this is a policy to which the Queen cannot consent. The Queen therefore does not wish Lord N. (for whom personally the Queen has a sincere regard) to be sent. As Lord Palmerston says the time presses, the Queen hopes that he will soon submit to her another arrangement.

Palmerston had to admit defeat. The European Congress was duly held at Brussels and he had to suggest another British delegate, Sir Henry Ellis, of whom the Queen approved. During October there was another sharp exchange between Palmerston and the Court, when the Queen objected vehemently to certain expressions her Foreign Minister had used in discussing the situation in Greece with the French representative in London, M. de Beaumont. A summary of this conversation had been drafted for the information of Lord Normanby in Paris:

The Queen cannot refrain from telling Lord Palmerston what a painful impression the perusal of a draft of his to Lord Normanby referring to the affairs of Greece, has made upon her, being in so little accordance with the calm dignity she likes to see in all the proceedings of the British Government. The Queen was particularly struck by the language in which Lord Palmerston speaks of King Otho, a sovereign with whom she stands in friendly relations, and the asperity against the Government of the King of the French who is really sufficiently lowered and suffering for the mistakes he may have committed, and that of this a copy is to be placed in the hands of the foreign Ministers of the French Republic, the Queen can only see with much regret.

Viscount Palmerston presents his humble duty to your Majesty and begs to assure your Majesty that he regrets very sincerely that his despatch to Lord Normanby on the affairs of Greece should have produced on your Majesty's mind the impression stated in your Majesty's communication of the 8th instant. Viscount Palmerston undoubtedly entertained a very strong and deep feeling of the great injustice and wrong which has been committed towards the Greek nation by the King of Greece and the King of the French; and in his anxiety to persuade the present Government of France to take a fair and juster view of Greek affairs, and pursue a more equitable policy, he could not avoid observations on the personal qualities of the one, and the systematic policy of the other of those sovereigns, because those observations lay at the very root of his argument . . .

The Queen has to acknowledge Lord Palmerston's letter of the 11th respecting the draft to Lord Normanby on the affairs of Greece.—The Queen would wish Lord Palmerston to leave out those passages in it concerning the personal characters of the King of Greece, the late King of Bavaria and the King of the French . . .

But Palmerston had again sent a despatch off unaltered, and answered impenitently:

. . . He was sorry to find that by some inadvertence and mistake in the hurry of business that despatch had, contrary to the standing orders which he had given in regard to the sending off of despatches, been already transmitted to Paris . . . It is no doubt painful to have to speak of sovereigns in the terms used by Viscount Palmerston in regard to the King of Greece, the late King of Bavaria and the King of the French. But when important public interests are at stake, essential truths ought not to be withheld, and

Viscount Palmerston is firmly convinced that nothing which he has said of those three sovereigns in regard to these matters exceeds the truth. In regard to one of them he fears that what he said falls short of the truth, and that the defects of the King of Greece lie quite as much in his moral as in his intellectual qualities.

The Queen was now thoroughly incensed. Further minor brushes followed: royal doubts about the attitude of Lord Cowley, British representative at Frankfurt, over the vexed question of German unification under the Prussian King as Emperor—then, in January of the following year, Palmerston was caught in a serious imprudence.

The Sicilian rebels had approached a British manufacturer for an urgent shipment of arms. He had only recently delivered a number of guns of the type required to the British Board of Ordnance, and Palmerston had permitted him to take them out again, to be replaced as soon as possible out of later production. *The Times* got wind of the affair and published the details. In the ensuing crisis Palmerston had to back down. Britain apologised to the odious King of Naples and the Court assailed Lord John Russell again with demands for Palmerston's removal to another post. Lord John went through the motions of discussing the matter with his senior colleagues, but in the end came back with the loyal answer:

> ... Lord John Russell feels bound to say that he entirely agrees with Lord Palmerston in all the main features of his foreign policy, and meant to defend the course taken which has preserved peace in Europe during one of the most trying years ever known.

Resignedly, Prince Albert, in his bold Gothic hand, committed an account of their efforts to the royal archives:

> ... The Queen expressed herself to Lord John very strongly upon the want of ingenuousness in Lord Palmerston's conduct, the danger to which the country was at every moment exposed by it and the humiliation for her to have to sanction an apology for an act for which Lord Palmerston alone was responsible and ought to pay the penalty ...

The Queen said she did not see how Lord Palmerston could

retain his office after this, which would damage the Government exceedingly, as it was sure not to remain a secret and how could the Government defend it? Lord John replied it could not be defended, however he felt that, after the Government had approved of the whole foreign policy and considered it right in the main features, they could not abandon Lord P.—Upon my rejoining that adopting the personal mistakes of Lord P. would injure the general policy as well, which the Government had approved, he said, that both he and Lord Lansdowne felt very strongly that, after the many most unjust attacks made from all sides upon Lord Palmerston, to throw him over at the moment of the meeting of Parliament would be considered a most cowardly act on the part of his colleagues and look as if they wanted to sacrifice him in order to avoid taking that part of the responsibility which belonged to them. The Queen begged Lord John however to remember in what a painful position she was placed by having in one of the most important places as her adviser a man on whom she could not place the slightest confidence, who never dealt fairly towards her and might at any moment endanger the most vital interests of the country. Lord John saw all this and regretted it, he said that he had only a few weeks ago written to Lord P. a letter, in which he had spoken so strongly about Lord P.'s sending drafts to the Queen for her approval after he had long sent them off, that Lord John was sure Lord P. would immediately resign upon it, but that Lord P. had taken no notice of it.—I added that if Lord P. had a friend, this friend might advise him to retire, as all Lord John seemed to fear, was Lord P.'s throwing his office up in a huff.—Lord John thought Lady Palmerston the only person who could speak to him.

After this failure Queen and Prince were determined to keep Palmerston under constant restraint. When Charles Albert in Italy, apprehensive of the reconsolidation of Austrian power, decided towards the end of February on one last misguided effort to attain freedom, Prince Albert quickly drafted a letter for the Queen to Lord John Russell:

The Queen has seen a draft to Lord Normanby in answer to his despatch No. 105, in which Lord Normanby had described the consternation felt by him and the French Government at the news of the King of Sardinia having exchanged his pacific government for a war ministry and the desire of the French Government to act in perfect concert with us. The draft reciprocates this desire but immediately tries to lay the responsibility of King Charles Albert's new intentions of aggression upon the Austrian Government. The Queen cannot help recognising in this the same partial spirit for Charles Albert and against Austria which has falsified our position with reference to the original Italian quarrel. As the new acts of the King of Sardinia may lead to fresh and serious European difficulties, the Queen feels it her duty from the beginning to warn Lord John Russell to keep a watchful eye upon our foreign relations, in order to prevent any other gradual deviation from the line of justice and impartiality which alone befits the dignity of the British Government.

The situation was beyond remedy. The aged Radetzky overwhelmed the Italians. Charles Albert abdicated and the Austrians imposed crushing reparations. The new French Ambassador in London, Admiral Cecille, enquired of Palmerston if he would agree to joint action to persuade Austria to lessen her demands, a conversation which Queen Victoria quickly picked out of the despatches when Normanby reported on the favourable reaction of M. Drouyn de L'Huys, the French Foreign Minister:

> The Queen finds reference to Lord Palmerston's conference with Admiral Cecille on the terms of peace between Austria and Sardinia in Lord Normanby's Despatch No. 213, according to which M. Drouyn de L'Huys expressed himself 'much satisfied with Lord Palmerston's assurance of the moral support of England in case of necessity, etc.'
>
> As Lord Palmerston has not reported anything concerning his communication with Admiral Cecille, to the Queen, she must now ask him to supply her want of information on this point.

Palmerston tried evasion again:

> ... With reference to the conversation which Viscount Palmerston had with Vice-Admiral Cecille on the subject of the extravagant and ruinous demands made by the Austrian Government on that of Sardinia, Viscount Palmerston begs to state that Admiral Cecille enquired whether your Majesty's Government would be

willing to join with the Government of France in endeavouring to prevail upon the Austrian Government to accept more reasonable conditions and that Viscount Palmerston said he was convinced that the British Government would willingly join in, thus assisting to rescue from such oppressive terms an ancient ally whose political independence is an important element in the balance of power of Europe; the Cabinet have since authorised Viscount Palmerston to prepare an instruction on this subject to your Majesty's Chargé d'Affaires at Vienna, but Viscount Palmerston has for some days past been so pressed with urgent matters that he has not yet had time to do so.

The Court was no longer prepared to tolerate Palmerston's repeated habit of uninhibited expression of views to foreign envoys and too frequent despatch of instructions to British Ministers abroad without royal scrutiny. Prince Albert took the initiative of writing direct to Lord John Russell to require that all Foreign Office drafts should be sent first to the Prime Minister for comment and then forwarded to the Queen for approval before their despatch. Any other man but Palmerston would have resigned under the imposition of such tutelage, but he considered he could handle Lord John, and submitted. 'I will give instructions accordingly', was his total, one-line letter to his colleague, although he managed to persuade Lord John to include a tart little phrase in his answer to the Court, recommending that 'her Majesty should give every facility to the transaction of business by attending to the drafts as soon as possible after their arrival'.

Except in France, the liberal revolutions in Europe were flickering out, as the forces of reaction grimly reinstalled themselves for the second time since Napoleon. General peace had been preserved, and that, whatever the Queen might feel, was largely the result of Palmerston's often frenzied statesmanship. There were still a few outstanding problems. The confused dynastic brawl in Schleswig-Holstein continued. Palmerston's difficulty here was the passionate desire of Prince Albert for German unification. The Coburg princes, coming from their little principality of barely 300,000 souls, could afford to have large ideas on the subject, even if the more important German sovereigns proved unwilling to surrender their rights. Holstein was unquestionably a peripheral German State, by language and historical descent, even if it was nominally attached to Schleswig under the Danish Crown. British mediation had now continued ineffectually for the best part of a year, with Palmerston's covert sympathies tending towards the Danes:

> ... Viscount Palmerston may appear to your Majesty to be urging the Prussian Government somewhat too strongly on this matter [he wrote at the end of June] but he can assure your Majesty that an early termination of this disastrous conflict is of great importance, not only to the parties engaged in it, but to your Majesty's dominions. Viscount Palmerston hardly ever enters the House of Commons that he is not assailed by some member or other with representations of the great injury which this war is inflicting upon some part or other of this country; and the Chancellor of the Exchequer could inform your Majesty that he considers this unfortunate [a word missing] was one of the main causes of the falling off of the public revenue ...

The Queen responded with a small history lesson:

> ... The union of Schleswig with Holstein is not an ideal one, but complete as to constitution, finance, customs, jurisprudence, Church, universities, Poor Law, settlement, debts etc. etc. and it is not established by the Kings-Dukes, but has existed for centuries. To defend Holstein against the attack made by Denmark upon this union, Germany joined the war. It is true that it is now proposed in the new constitution for Germany to consent to the separation of Schleswig and Holstein, although last year the Frankfurt Parliament had decreed the incorporation of Schleswig into Germany with Holstein, but the question for Germany is now not to begin a war but to finish one by a lasting peace; in this she has, in the Queen's opinion, a right and a duty to see that the independence of Schleswig is secured before she abandons that country ... The Schleswig revolution was not directed against the Duke but against the King of Denmark who invaded the rights of the Duke of Schleswig-Holstein; the assistance of Prussia could therefore not be given to Denmark but to Schleswig-Holstein ...
>
> Lord Palmerston cannot be more anxious for a speedy termination of the Danish war than the Queen is, but she thinks that the

mediation will not effect this, as long as the mediating power merely watches to see which of the two parties is in the greatest difficulties for the moment, and urges it to give way, but by a careful and anxious discovery of the rights of the question and a steady adherence to the recommendation that what is right and fair ought to be done.

The cause of the war having been the unlawful attempt to incorporate Schleswig into Denmark, the peace cannot be lasting unless it contains sufficient guarantees against the resumption of that scheme.

Viscount Palmerston . . . begs to assure your Majesty that he entirely concurs in the justice of those principles which your Majesty points out as those which ought to guide a mediating power, and it has throughout this Schleswig-Holstein negotiation been his intention and desire to hold the balance as fairly between the contending parties, as the force of circumstance, and the course of events, could enable a mediator, acting only by persuasion and without any compelling authority, to do . . .

Then, when Palmerston proposed that Colonel Hodges, one of the mediation commissioners, should become a member of the provisional government of Schleswig, Prince Albert drafted another remonstrance for the Queen to copy:

The Queen . . . does not think the choice a very good one, considering the strong partiality Colonel H. has shown throughout the war, against Schleswig and for Denmark, and that, after the way in which Prussia concluded the armistice without the least reference to the Schleswigers, much of the facility of bringing them to the new arrangements will depend on their confidence in the impartiality of the English commissioner, who is to be the umpire in all cases of dispute. Prussia will find it very difficult to coerce the Schleswigers in the face of public opinion in Germany should they resist. The Archduke John seems to refuse his sanction to the armistice. It is evident therefore that for the sake of the preservation of a peace, which England has so much reason to desire, no personal consideration ought to stand in the way of doing that which will be most conducive to a speedy introduction of the new government. Lord P. may say that the prejudice these Schleswigers may have against Colonel H. is quite unfounded, but that will make no difference in the effect of such a prejudice. It can surely not be difficult for Lord Palmerston to find some other person who is wholly unconnected with these disputes.

This time Palmerston was not to be moved:

> Viscount Palmerston presents his humble duty to your Majesty, and is not aware that the people of Schleswig entertain any prejudice against Colonel Hodges, but he believes that Colonel Hodges has been on terms of much intimacy with one if not more of the leading men among that party in Schleswig which have been in revolt against the King-Duke. With regard to Colonel Hodges' own opinions, Viscount Palmerston would say from general recollection of the tenor of his despatches, that they have been pretty fairly balanced between the contending parties; but Viscount Palmerston is fully satisfied from his knowledge of the honour and integrity of Colonel Hodges' mind, that he would not allow any bias of opinion as to the merits of the general questions at issue between Denmark and Germany to sway him in deciding as arbiter on points that might be submitted to his decision, and that he would honestly and scrupulously decide according to the best of his judgment; and when it was found that his decisions were just, any unfounded prejudice that might have existed against him beforehand, would soon disappear . . .

In the end, the Queen relented, but she could not resist a last word:

> The Queen has to acknowledge Lord Palmerston's letter of yesterday. She did not expect that her objections to Colonel Hodges' appointment would alter Lord Palmerston's opinion on the subject, but she mentioned them as she has the satisfaction to recollect that she always has done, whenever she saw that a mistake was going to be made, as she thinks Colonel Hodges' appointment will be.

In Hungary, Kossuth's brave rebellion had finally been crushed by the intervention of Russian troops at Austrian invitation. This Palmerston was powerless to prevent, but when Russia demanded from Turkey the surrender of the Polish and Hungarian refugees who had fled within her border, Britain's Foreign Minister reacted vigorously. Sir Stratford Canning, his envoy at Constantinople, had already stiffened the Turks with the promise of British support if the Russians became threatening. Palmerston, in concert with the French, gave him hearty backing, and an Anglo-French fleet was moved into the vicinity of the Dardanelles to provide the necessary support.

Queen Victoria could not understand why a British Government need be exercised about the fate of a few Hungarian rebels, with all the risks involved, and tried to ensure that the able Sir Stratford Canning was not given too much liberty of action by imprecise instructions:

> The Queen returns the enclosed papers and quite agrees with Lord Palmerston that having made a demonstration in order to enable the Porte to resist the demand of extradition, it ought to remain until the Porte is safely out of her difficulties. On the other hand, Sir Stratford Canning ought to be instructed to urge the Porte to comply with the demand for the removal of the refugees, to which Russia and Austria have a clear right by treaty, if their demand should be thus modified, which appears certain from Lord Ponsonby's telegraphic despatch. Lord Palmerston's alteration of the concluding passage of the despatch makes it worse, in the Queen's opinion, by making the object of our policy more vague, which might lead Sir Stratford Canning into the mistake of supporting further resistance on the part of the Porte, and thereby bring us finally into a scrape. The Queen would like to see the policy clearly defined in the draft.

The Foreign Secretary was at Broadlands, whence he replied:

> Viscount Palmerston presents his humble duty to your Majesty and has had the honour to receive your Majesty's communication of this day proposing an addition to the despatch of Sir Stratford Canning. Viscount Palmerston has however ventured to send the despatch on as it stands, in the hope that it may yet reach London in time to be forwarded to Paris tonight in order to go by the French steamer which appears to have been kept waiting for it at Marseilles for a week; and in order to put an end to the great impatience, and the incipient doubts, of the French Government as to whether the British Government is not wishing to take some separate course in these matters.
> Viscount Palmerston felt a difficulty about the words suggested

by your Majesty; because some of the modified demands made by Russia and Austria are not warranted by treaty, but yet it may be prudent for the Porte to endeavour in some way or other to meet the views with which the two powers have made those demands; and it might not be advisable to counsel the Porte absolutely to resist all demands not founded upon treaty . . .

The final step had already been taken and the Queen could only submit with bad grace to a *fait accompli*:

. . . She is very sorry that the fleet should have entered the Dardanelles. This occurrence is a new proof to the Queen how important it is to lay down positive instructions as to the principles upon which agents abroad are to act.

The refugees were saved and, although Palmerston gained great credit with liberal elements both at home and abroad for his diplomatic triumph, his defiance of the Queen's wishes rankled. He was soon in more serious trouble. For months he had been engaged in an acrimonious correspondence with the Greek Government, over financial compensation allegedly due to certain British subjects. One of these, Don Pacifico, a Portuguese Jew born in Gibraltar, was almost certainly putting forward fraudulent claims. Undeterred, Palmerston was prepared to use him as a stick with which to beat the reactionary Greek Government. When the British fleet returned after its successful incursion into the Dardanelles, it was ordered to Greek waters, and under its guns settlement of all outstanding claims was demanded. The Greeks appealed to France and Russia to act as mediators.

This was at once the most dubious and, in its outcome, one of the most triumphant of Palmerston's diplomatic forays, and displayed him at his most headstrong. There was now the almost inevitable clash with the Court over despatches too violently worded, sent off without due approval and of covert intention. Here indeed was 'gunboat diplomacy' at its most blatant. Palmerston's excuses became increasingly disingenuous and, with the Court counselling moderation, demanding explanations and requiring an investigation of the substance of Don Pacifico's claims, the Queen decided to demand of Lord John Russell again the dismissal of his turbulent colleague. The Prince drafted on March 3, 1850, another of his meticulous memoranda:

Before leaving town yesterday we saw Lord John Russell who came to state what had passed with reference to Lord Palmerston. He premised that Lord Palmerston had at all times been a most agreeable and accommodating colleague, that he had acted with Lord John ever since 1831 and had not only never made any difficulty, but acted most boldly and in the most spirited manner on all political questions; besides he was very popular with the Radical part of the House of Commons as well as with the Protectionists so that both would be ready to receive him as their leader; he (Lord John) was therefore most anxious to do nothing which would hurt Lord Palmerston's feelings nor to bring about a disruption of the Whig Party, which at this moment of party confusion was the only one which still held together. On the other hand, the fact that the Queen distrusted Lord Palmerston was a serious impediment to the carrying on of the Government. Lord John was therefore anxious to adopt a plan by which Lord Palmerston's services could be retained with his own good will and the foreign affairs entrusted to other hands.—The only place he could think of was to give Lord Palmerston the Lead in the House of Commons—the highest position a statesman could aspire to—and to go himself to the House of Lords. He had communicated his views to Lord Lansdowne, who agreed in them and thought he could do nothing better than speak to Lord Palmerston at once. Lord Palmerston said that he could not have helped to have become aware that he had forfeited the Queen's confidence, but he thought this had not been on *personal* grounds but merely on account of his line of policy with which the Queen disagreed. —(The Queen interrupted Lord John by remarking that she distrusted him on *personal* grounds also, but I remarked that Lord Palmerston had so far at least seen rightly that he had become disagreeable to the Queen, not on account of his person but of his political doings and tricks, to which the Queen assented.) Lord Palmerston appeared to Lord John willing to enter into this agreement . . .

There then followed a discussion as to who should take over the post of Foreign Minister. Russell suggested Lord Minto, of whom the Queen did not approve and in her turn recommended that either Lord John should take it over himself or that Lord Clarendon should have it. The memorandum then went on:

> I could not help remarking that it was a serious risk to entrust Lord Palmerston with the Lead in the House of Commons, that it might be that the Government were defeated and if once in Opposition Lord Palmerston might take a different line as Leader of the Opposition from that which Lord John would like and might so easily force himself back into office as Prime Minister. Lord John however, although admitting that danger, thought Lord Palmerston too old to do much in the future (having passed his sixty-fifth year); he admitted that Sir George Grey was the natural Leader of the Commons, but expected that a little later the Lead would still fall into his hands.

Lord John could hardly suspect what a wildly inaccurate judgment this was. The Court, in the meantime, had recourse to the shadowy figure of Baron Stockmar, still functioning after a dozen years as the Prince's political adviser. That worthy delivered himself of the following pontifical judgment in a memorandum for the royal pair:

> The least the Queen has a right to require of her minister is, one: that he will distinctly state what he proposes in a given case, in order that the Queen may know as definitely to what she has to give her royal sanction and, second: having given once her sanction to a measure, the minister who, in the execution of such measure, alters or modifies it arbitrarily commits an act of dishonesty towards the Crown which the Queen has an undoubted constitutional right to visit with the dismissal of that minister.

Thus fortified, the Prince sent a private and confidential letter to Lord John, venting at length the royal spleen about their troublesome minister:

> My dear Lord John,
>
> In the quiet of the country and the leisure of the Easter holidays, I have found time more thoroughly to consider the proposition which you made to the Queen some time ago with reference to Lord Palmerston. The result of my reflection has entirely confirmed the first impression which your proposal made upon me

and which I believe to have communicated to you then: 'That it would be a most dangerous experiment to give to Lord P. the Lead of the House of Commons as a Compensation for his loss of the Foreign Office.'

Let us for a moment consider his character, the reasons why it has been found desirable to move him from the Foreign Office and their bearing upon the new position which is to be made for him—Lord Palmerston is an able politician with large views and an energetic mind, an indefatigable man of business, a good speaker; but a man of expediency, of easy temper, no very high standard of honour and not a grain of moral feeling. He is consequently quite unscrupulous as to any line of policy that he is to follow, or any means he is to use as long as they lead to his ends. Whilst he is a most easy colleague and minister with regard to other departments, never making any difficulty, he is self-willed and impatient of any control in his own. His obstinacy arises from personal conceit, which makes him almost pity those who differ from him in opinion. He carries his own points with the greatest boldness, by what is commonly called bullying, but if this fails he is equally ready to resort to any trick which may serve his purpose and is perfectly at his ease if it has succeeded. He has generally great luck, but requires success to carry him through his policy; success failing, he steers without a compass and makes one almost doubt his sagacity.

The country looks upon him as a most dangerous man, he is not respected by any party, but his boldness pleases, his dexterity amuses the public; if his case be ever so bad a one he can represent it and dress it up to his advantage and the public cries out: 'Look how he got out of this scrape again, after all he is a very clever fellow!'—This bullying tone to the weaker foreign powers is grateful to the taste of our manufacturers and small traders, who look upon other countries only as upon markets which the Governments, for selfish reasons, want to contract. The Radicals like this also and as much his intrigues with foreign revolutionists and his unscrupulous hostility to the thrones and monarchs in the different States; they are only afraid that they might one day have to pay with a war for their indulgence. If there is danger of that they join the outcry against Lord Palmerston, the danger gone they uphold him again.

The Queen has two distinct complaints to bring against Lord

Palmerston (which make it of the highest importance to her to be relieved of him at the Foreign Office), the one on account of his policy, the other on account of his personal behaviour as minister to his sovereign.

1st, without wishing to enter into details and the rights and wrongs of the various questions, his policy has generally had the effect that England at a moment and in a conjuncture in which she ought to stand highest in the esteem of the world and to possess the confidence of all powers (which should give her the greatest influence), is universally detested, mistrusted and treated with insult even by the smaller powers. There is not a sovereign or a government who do not consider Lord Palmerston as a personal enemy and would not rather prejudice their own interests than forego an opportunity to vent their spite against him; there is not a people who is not convinced that their internal dissensions and sufferings are fomented by England, in order to keep them weak and unable in consequence to compete with the English manufacturers. I need not adduce any examples as they abound. Since 1846, when Lord Palmerston returned to the Foreign Office, England has not had a single *success* except perhaps the mediation in Switzerland, which was owing to Sir Stratford Canning's possessing the confidence of the Governments with whom we differed and with whom he had had personal intercourse before setting out for Switzerland. In all European complications England's natural position made her the mediator or arbitrator and in every case Lord P.'s impossibility to take an impartial view ruined the mediation.

2ndly, as a minister the sovereign has a right to demand from him that she be made thoroughly acquainted with the whole object and tendency of the policy to which her consent is required and, having given that consent, that the policy is not arbitrarily altered from the original line, that important steps are not concealed from her and her name used without her sanction. In all these respects Lord Palmerston has failed towards her, and not from oversight or negligence, but upon principle and with astonishing pertinacity against every effort by the Queen, in which she was sometimes seconded by the Prime Minister. Besides which, Lord P. does not scruple to let it appear in public as if the sovereign's negligence in attending to the papers sent to her caused delays and complications.—

What complaints his colleagues may have to urge as to the straightforwardness of Lord P.'s proceedings I don't pretend to say.—It being pretty generally admitted that his removal from the Foreign Office is desirable, a fear has hitherto prevented the execution; that he might throw up office altogether and become a most dangerous leader of Opposition, it is anticipated that he would lead the Radicals and the high Tories and Protectionists, both parties thinking it equally likely to obtain his services!

Now it is proposed to remedy these evils by making Lord Palmerston the Leader of the House of Commons! But that would make him Prime Minister *de facto* at once and *de jure* necessarily afterwards. The Leader of the House of Commons in these days has the real power in the country and can dictate absolutely to his colleagues. So he, Lord P., would more than ever influence the foreign affairs, himself free from the responsibility of office, and which before the Prime Minister found it almost impossible to control him, he would begin to control the latter and at any difference of opinion between them keep the party with him, casting the Prime Minister in the House of Lords adrift. The Queen could never reconcile it with her duty towards the country to allow Lord Palmerston to become its ruler. The natural Leader of the House of Commons if you wish to go to the House of Lords is Sir George Grey, a man of the highest honour and integrity, of conscientious moral and religious feelings, who possesses the respect of everybody who knows him and who is equally popular with all parties in the House of Commons and is esteemed by his sovereign.

Lord Palmerston's capacity for public business might however be otherwise employed; there are other departments than the one he now presides over which are equally important and honourable; the Foreign Office is no private property of his. His love of office generally, which he has held now for nearly forty years, will in my opinion prevent his quitting the Government upon losing the Foreign Office and make him inclined to enter into such arrangements as are proposed to him in a friendly and conciliatory manner and with a view to save as much as possible the point of honour.

Palmerston, sensing his precarious position, took an almost unwarrantable risk. A compromise on Don Pacifico's claim was reached in London with the French mediator, Baron Gros, but Palmerston deliberately delayed advising Sir Henry Wyse, the British Minister in Athens, that agreement had been reached. In the meantime, final pressure was exerted on the Greek Government, which capitulated and met Palmerston's original higher demands.

The French were outraged, temporarily withdrew their Ambassador, a major political crisis ensued and Palmerston had to fight for his political life. His main defence was a brilliant five-hour speech in the House of Commons debate on foreign affairs on June 26, 1850. In a stupendous effort of inspired reasoning, he, who was normally no great orator, reviewed his whole conduct of foreign affairs over the years, ending with the famous '*Civis Romanus Sum*' reference to the right of a British subject abroad to be protected by his government. It was a parliamentary triumph of rare magnitude, which saved the Government and restored Palmerston's position to a new peak.

The Queen and Prince, who had thought to see him ousted at last, were despondent. Ten days later, the Prince took stock of the situation in another memorandum, of which he sent a copy to Lord John Russell:

> The debate in the House of Commons and its result have naturally affected the consideration whether Lord Palmerston can now safely be moved from his present post at the Foreign office. Lord John Russell considers that whole position changed, dreads the imputations which may be cast upon him if he were now to move Lord P. and the effect upon the position of parties in the House of Commons were Lord P. to throw up office altogether.
>
> There is no doubt that the result of the debate, embracing his whole foreign policy and the Greek case in particular and giving a majority of 46 in its favour, is generally considered as a triumph to Lord P.; to which may be added the admiration for his speech of five hours, which is called a masterpiece of eloquence and statesmanship etc. etc. He is more popular at this moment with the Radical Party than he has ever been and that particular faction is ready to support him through thick and thin—on the other hand, must be considered what has really brought about the majority in the division.

It will be found that the chief reason was the responsibility for Lord P.'s acts which the whole Cabinet undertook and the dread of upsetting that Government which the country cannot spare at this moment, to which may be added the natural dislike of the Commons to the dictatorial tone the House of Lords had taken without consultation with or regard for them. Whilst therefore Lord P. enjoys the triumph it is due to the merits and sacrificing friendship of his colleagues . . .

The Queen has no more confidence in Lord P. now than she had before; the debate has not shown her anything that she did not know before, though it was silent on many things that she did know . . . Foreign governments distrust and foreign nations hate Lord P. now as much as before—Lord P. himself is not likely to change his nature in his sixty-seventh year on account of a vote, which is calculated to gratify his vanity and self esteem. His colleagues are not likely to have more influence over him than they had before, as he will ascribe their opposition more than ever to intrigue . . .

It appears that Lord P. was not averse to giving up to Lord John the management of the Foreign Department against the Leadership in the House of Commons. Since that time the Queen's objections to such an arrangement seem to have satisfied Lord John and Lord Lansdowne of the inexpediency of that course. The lamentable death of Sir R. Peel has since added more weight to those objections. It has removed the man whose conciliatory voice and temperate councils had the greatest influence upon the House; parties have been set free by his removal who had all felt hitherto the control of his authority; what next session may bring nobody can tell; but in this dangerous uncertainty it would be most injurious to allow Lord John Russell to withdraw from the House also, which is more than ever wanting temperate advice and guidance . . .

Lord John temporised:

I have twice read with great attention your Royal Highness' remarks.

It must always be borne in mind that Lord Lansdowne and I concur in the position which England has held since 1848—Many of those who dislike and distrust Lord Palmerston would have had England take up a position totally different, viz. of intimate and

cordial alliance with Austria and Russia and of coldness and sullen
peace with France . . . There remain the faults of carrying a good
policy into effect by means too violent and abrupt and a demeanour
which causes undefined alarm.

Weighing all the difficulties, I think that Lord Lansdowne never
will be persuaded to take the Foreign Office, and that the appointment of Lord Clarendon, the best on many accounts that could be
made, would be particularly offensive to Lord Palmerston.

I come to the conclusion that my going to the House of Lords,
with the Foreign Office, would be the best course, leaving Sir
George Grey to lead in the House of Commons and asking Lord
Grey to yield the Colonial Office to Lord Palmerston.

However, the Court was not to be denied, and Lord John
was summoned to Buckingham Palace on July 11. The Prince's
memorandum of the interview showed that every argument was
used:

After a conference which the Queen has had with Lord John
Russell today and in which she again expressed herself about Lord
Palmerston very strongly, but in which Lord John showed
symptoms of doubt whether after all Lord P. might not have the
Lead in the House of Commons, I took an opportunity of seeing
Lord John alone and told him that as much as I disliked entering
into a matter which had been studiously kept secret hitherto and
which I could only refer to on condition that Lord John would
keep it as such when made acquainted with it, I felt it necessary
that he should know the full extent of the Queen's objections to
Lord P., which were connected with her knowledge of Lord P.'s
worthless private character.

I had often heard it stated as the nature of English Constitution
and the Royal Prerogatives that the sovereign could not interfere
with the Government in the management of Parliament, which are
left to the sole control of the responsible minister, but that he was
absolutely free in the choice of his minister. Now I differed completely from that doctrine. I held the sovereign to have immense
moral responsibility upon his shoulders with regard to his government and the duty to watch and control it and no choice almost in
in the selection of his minister if he understood his duties. The
circumstances which led to a change of ministry almost always

pointed out also the men to succeed, public opinion and parliamentary position designated the candidates and there hardly was an instance in history where the sovereign, following the best of his own inclination, had chosen another man than the one who had been brought forward by the circumstances, it had not produced the greatest difficulties to the sovereign and dangers to the country. A sagacious sovereign therefore would look forward and take his share in the preparatory arrangements of party organisation, whenever he could, in order to have those presented to his choice in times of emergency whom he had before recognised as eligible. Lord John knew, I continued, that the leader of the majority in the House of Commons would always have the strongest claim—but how could the Queen consent to take a man as her chief adviser and confidential counsellor in all matters of State, religion, society, Court, etc., etc., he who as her Secretary of State and while a guest under her roof at Windsor Castle had committed a brutal attack upon one of her ladies? Had at night by stealth introduced himself into her apartment, barricaded afterwards the door and would have consummated his fiendish scheme by violence had not the miraculous efforts of his victim and such assistance attracted by her screams saved her?

Lord John said that was very bad and made it absolutely necessary to take care to protect the Queen from Lord P.'s being thrust upon her at any time as Prime Minister. He would keep the secret, of which he felt the full importance; he unfortunately knew another lady in society upon whom he had tried the same thing!

The Prince had employed a questionable tactic. The incident he described had indeed happened, but a full ten years earlier. The lady in question was a Mrs. Brand, one of the Queen's Ladies of the Bedchamber, and subsequently Lady Dacre. To give the affair added piquancy, Palmerston had been in the habit of visiting another lady in that particular room, who was waiting vainly for him in another part of the castle. Prim as he was, Lord John's withers were not wrung, and the only satisfaction the Prince could obtain came in a letter from the Prime Minister the same evening:

Upon the whole I think it best not to make any communication to Lord Palmerston till the session has drawn nearer to its close. The

Queen will then be more at liberty to direct the arrangements which her Majesty may desire.

I have not altered my opinion that the retirement of Lord Palmerston from the ministry would make it impossible for me to hold my present position unless some disagreement in the conduct of affairs should render such a step on his part unavoidable.

Two weeks later, the Queen again returned to the attack, in what must be one of the strongest letters ever written by a British sovereign to a Prime Minister about one of his colleagues:

. . . Lord John may be sure that she fully admits the great difficulties in the way of the projected alteration, but she on the other hand feels the duty she owes to the country and to herself not to allow a man in whom she can have no confidence, who she knows has conducted himself in anything but a straightforward and proper manner to herself, to remain in the Foreign Office and thereby to expose herself to insults from other nations, and this country and to the constant risk of serious and alarming complications. The Queen considers these reasons as much graver than the other difficulties . . .

Each time that we were in a difficulty, the Government seemed to be determined to move Lord Palmerston and as soon as these difficulties were got over, those which present themselves in the carrying out of this removal appeared of so great a magnitude as to cause its relinquishment. There is no chance of Lord Palmerston reforming himself in his sixty-seventh year, and after having considered his last escape as a triumph . . . The Queen is personally convinced that Lord Palmerston at this moment is secretly planning an armed Russian intervention in Schleswig, which may produce a renewal of revolutions in Germany, and possibly a general war.

The Queen only adduces this as an instance that there is no question of delicacy and danger in which Lord Palmerston will not arbitrarily and without reference to his colleagues or sovereign engage this country.

Lord John Russell twisted this way and that, asked the Queen to receive his brother, the Duke of Bedford, to discuss the whole situation, describing him as 'very impartial, which Lord John Russell cannot pretend to be in matters concerning a colleague of fourteen years' standing', and discussed with the royal pair the whole gamut of possible Cabinet changes. Lord Clarendon, at that time Lord-Lieutenant of Ireland, would not accept the post of Foreign Secretary as Palmerston already suspected him of being in league with those whom he believed were plotting his downfall. Lord Lansdowne, nestor of the Whigs, was too old, Lord Granville, the Paymaster-General, too young and inexperienced. At one juncture, Lord John again suggested that he should go to the House of Lords, surrendering to Palmerston the honourable post of Leader of the House of Commons, but then changed his mind, as he still wanted to put through Parliament another grandiose bill for the reform of the franchise. The machinations petered out again. The idea of Palmerston being forced into Opposition was more than the Cabinet was prepared to tolerate.

To bring matters to a head, the Queen embodied Stockmar's memorandum in one of her own to Lord John Russell, laying down the manner in which she expected her Foreign Minister to conduct his duties. It was a humiliating enough rebuke, but Palmerston refused to be provoked, and asked Lord John only that he should have a couple of extra clerks to copy out the despatches for the Queen in good time. In August, the villain of the piece sought an interview with Prince Albert, who duly consigned this version of it to the archives:

> After the Council for the speech from the Throne for the proroga-
> tion of Paliament on the 14th, I saw Lord Palmerston as he had
> desired it. He was very much agitated, shook and had tears in his
> eyes, so as quite to move me, who never under any circumstances
> had known him otherwise than with a bland smile on his face.—
> He said that after what had been communicated to him by Lord
> John Russell he felt it necessary to have an explanation with me.
> That to differ from his policy or to condemn it was only condemn-
> ing his judgment and a matter of opinion upon which differences
> were natural and to be expected, but the accusation that he had
> wanted in respect to the Queen, whom he had every reason to
> respect as his sovereign and as a woman whose virtues he admired
> and to whom he was bound by every tie of duty and gratitude,
> was an imputation on his honour as a gentleman and if he could

have made himself guilty of it, he was almost no longer fit to be tolerated in society.

I purposely did not interrupt him, but when he had concluded, reminded him of the innumerable complaints and remonstrances which the Queen had to make these last years; the Queen was quite ready to make every allowance for the pressure of business in the office and his want of time and would be sure to receive his denial of any intentional want of regard, but that she had felt this could not longer go on so.—The Queen had often, I was sorry to say latterly almost invariably, differed from the line of policy pursued by Lord P. She had always openly stated her objections but, when overruled by the Cabinet, convinced that it would from political reasons be more prudent to waive her objections, she knew her constitutional position too well not to give her full support to the execution on the part of the Government. She knew that they were going to battle together and that she was going to receive the blows which were aimed at the Government and had these last years received several as no sovereign of England had before been obliged to put up with and which had been most painful to her.—But what she had a right to require in return was, that before a line of policy was adopted or brought before her for her sanction, she should be in full possession of all the facts and the motives operating. She felt that in this respect she was not dealt by as she ought, she never found a matter 'intact', nor a question in which we were not already compromised when it was submitted to her. She had no means of knowing what passed in the Cabinet, nor what passed between Lord Palmerston and the foreign Ministers in their conferences but what Lord P. chose to tell her or what she found in the newspaper, which lied ninety-nine times out of the hundred.

Lord P. interrupted me saying that his conferences took some four hours a day and it would require as much time again to make a report of them, but then he would have no time left for any part of the business of his office or the House of Commons. The documents in which the result of these conferences appeared and which came to the Queen were the drafts of despatches.

I replied that the Queen could not mean to ask for details which ought to be managed by him, but when principles were settled she ought to be informed and it could be in a few words.—She now lost much time in disputing with Lord John and Lord Palm.

about the wording of despatches, which was most unprofitable, but in the absence of any explanation of the facts which determined or the motives which guided the decisions come to, she was bound at least to watch these despatches; words might mean very little or very much according to the sense intended to be conveyed.—To this Lord P. answered that he felt the full force of this objection, but that this was the result of the arrangement represented to him as desired by the Queen by Lord John Russell: 'That all drafts should go through him to the Queen'. The Prime Minister could not be as well informed as the minister whose department was concerned. He had been ready to give explanations or to come to the Palace at any time, but could not have known beforehand whether he would be received or whether he would not appear intruding. He was ready to come to me at any time or give me any explanation I might desire.

I replied that there had been found great convenience in the drafts passing through the hands of the Prime Minister to the sovereign, but that this did not preclude Lord P.'s writing to the Queen as often and as much as he thought necessary and giving the information required. To give him an example of what the Queen wanted I would ask him a question point blanque: He was aware that the Queen had objected to the protocol about Schleswig and the grounds upon which she had done so, her opinion had been overruled, the protocol stating the desire of the great powers to see the integrity of the Danish monarchy preserved had been signed and upon this the King of Denmark had invaded Schleswig, where the war was raging; if Holstein were attacked also, which was likely, the Germans could not be restrained from flying to her assistance, Russia had menaced to interfere with arms if the Schleswigers were successful, 'what would Lord P. do when this emergency arose (provoking most likely a European war) and which would arise very probably when we should be at Balmoral and Lord John in another part of Scotland?'—The Queen expected from his foresight that he had contemplated the possibility and required a categorical answer of what he proposed to do in the event?—Lord P. entered into a long controversy about the protocol and the complicated state of the Danish question, called the contingency a very unlikely one etc., etc. After a full hour's conversation on this subject, we were however interrupted without my having been able to get a positive answer!

I spoke to Lord John Russell the following day of our interview and told him how low and agitated I had found Lord P., almost to making me pity him. Lord John answered that he thought what had passed had done a great deal of good.

Palmerston must have been shedding crocodile's tears, as the year that followed saw little amendment in his ways. During the late summer of 1850, the Queen again had occasion to upbraid Palmerston for his partiality to Denmark in the Schleswig–Holstein dispute, and sent him a memorandum she had asked the Prince to draw up on the subject. This laid down that

> England ought either to remain entirely passive with regard to the dispute between Denmark and the Duchies or, if she thinks it necessary to interfere by advice and diplomacy, she ought to be strictly impartial . . .

Palmerston retorted tersely:

> . . . It is no doubt the duty of England in her capacity of mediator to act with impartiality; but to act with impartiality means, to act according to the best judgment that can be formed of the merits of each question that comes under consideration, without being swayed by partiality to, or preference for either of the two parties. A mediator does not cease to be impartial because on any particular question he may think one party right or the other wrong and may declare his opinion in favour of the party whom he may think right. But he would cease to be impartial if, from personal or other considerations, he gave his voice in favour of the party whom he thought in the wrong.
>
> During the course of these long negotiations the British Government has endeavoured to steer according to its sense of right and wrong, and it has consequently sometimes inclined on the side of Denmark, and sometimes against her, but whether for or against Denmark, the British Government has acted upon what it thought in each case good and sufficient reasons . . .

A few weeks later Palmerston offended the royal susceptibilities again. At the beginning of September the Austrian General Haynau paid a private visit to Britain. The savage reprisals the troops under his command had inflicted on the Italian and Hungarian rebels had earned him the sobriquet of 'General Hyaena'. In London he went to inspect the premises of Barclays, the brewers, where, easily recognisable by his long moustachios, he had been set upon and manhandled by the incensed draymen. Queen Victoria thought an apology was called for and wrote to Palmerston:

> The Queen thinks that it would be proper if a draft were written to the Austrian Government expressive of the deep regret of this Government at the brutal outrage on one of the Emperor's distinguished generals and subjects—General Haynau.

Baron Koller, the Austrian envoy in London, was also pressing for a similar communication, but Palmerston, after expressing official regrets, could not resist adding a final paragraph which said, in effect, that if someone of Haynau's reputation chose to come to England, he had only received his deserts. The Court, in the meantime, had left for Balmoral, and it was not until the end of the month that the Queen caught up with her reading of the despatches. She immediately wrote to Lord John Russell, who concurred that the last paragraph was 'derogatory to the honour of the nation, as if no one could be safe in this country who was obnoxious to the public feeling'. Thus reinforced, the Queen wrote to Palmerston on October 4:

> The Queen has communicated with Lord John Russell upon the enclosed draft, of which the closing paragraph appeared very objectionable to her. Lord John entirely agreeing in this opinion, the Queen now sends the draft back to Lord Palmerston with her desire that the passage struck out should be omitted. Should Baron Koller already have taken note of the draft Lord Palmerston is requested to take care that a corrected copy may reach him without delay.

In reply, Palmerston gave his liberal feelings full vent:

> ... Viscount Palmerston had put the last paragraph into the answer because he could scarcely have reconciled it to his own feelings and to his sense of public responsibility to have put his name to a note which might be liable to be called for by Parliament without expressing in it, at least his own personal opinion,

a sense of the want of propriety evinced by General Haynau in coming to England at the present moment. The state of public feeling in this country about General Haynau and his proceedings in Italy and Hungary was perfectly well known, and his coming here so soon after those events without necessity or obligation to do so, was liable to be looked upon as a bravado, and as a challenge to an expression of public opinion. Baron Koller, indeed, told Viscount Palmerston that Prince Metternich and Baron Neuman had, at Brussels, strongly dissuaded General Haynau from coming into England and that he, Baron Koller had, after his arrival, earnestly entreated him to cut off those long moustachios which rendered him so liable to be identified.

With regard to the transaction itself there is no justifying a breach of the law, nor an attack by a large number of people upon one or two individuals who cannot resist such a superior force, and though in the present case, according to Baron Koller's account, the chief injury sustained by General Haynau consisted in the tearing of his coat, the loss of a cane and some severe bruises on his left arm, and though four of our policemen proved to be a sufficient protection, yet a mob who began by insult led each other on to outrage, and there is no saying to what extremes they might have proceeded if they had not been checked . . .

The people of this country are remarkable for their hospitable reception of foreigners, and for their forgetfulness of past animosities. Napoleon Buonaparte, though greatest enemy that England ever had, was treated with respect while at Plymouth and with consideration while at St. Helena. Marshal Soult, who has fought in many battles against the English, was received with generous acclamation when he came here as special Ambassdor. The King of the French, M. Guizot and Prince Metternich, though all of them great antagonists of English policy and English interests, were treated in this country with courtesy and kindness. But General Haynau was looked upon as a great moral criminal . . .

But Viscount Palmerston can assure your Majesty that these feelings of just and honourable indignation have not been confined to England, for he has reason to know that General Haynau's ferocious and unmanly treatment of the unfortunate inhabitants of Brescia and of other towns and places in Italy, his savage proclamation to the people of Pesth and his barbarous acts in Hungary excited almost as much disgust in Austria as in England

and that the nickname of General Haynau was given him at Vienna long before it was applied to him in London.

The Queen was totally unimpressed by such sentiments. She insisted that a substitute despatch should be sent to Vienna, omitting the offending paragraph. Palmerston appealed to Lord John Russell, saying that if an altered note was to be sent 'this must be done by another Secretary of State for Foreign Affairs, and I must in that case place my office at your disposal'. For once, his bluff was called. Lord John proved adamant. Palmerston withdrew his threat of resignation, climbed down tamely, and the altered draft was duly despatched. Lord John, who was growing increasingly weary of his rôle as arbiter, could not resist writing to the Prince:

> ... Your Royal Highness will have been somewhat amused, if not surprised, at the sudden and amiable termination of the dispute regarding the letter to Baron Koller.—The same course may be adopted with advantage if a despatch is ever again sent which has been objected to, and to which the Queen's sanction has not been given ...

By November the attempt to found a liberal federation in Germany had finally collapsed. Austria, with much connivance from other German States, had succeeded in reimposing the authority of the old Diet, and the Queen could not resist a note of sarcasm in her letter to Palmerston:

> ... Having invariably encouraged constitutional development in other countries and, in the Queen's opinion, unwisely, in such countries which from their state of civilisation were not fit for constitutional government, like Greece, Portugal, Spain, Sicily and Naples etc., etc., and having at the beginning of the great movement of 1847, which led to all the catastrophes of the following years, sent a Cabinet Minister to Italy to declare to all Italian States that England would protect them from Austria if she should attempt by threats and violence to debar them from the attainment of their constitutional development—consistency would require that we should now, when that great struggle is at an end and despotism is to be reimposed by Austrian arms upon Germany, throw our weight into the scale of constitutional Prussia and

Germany,—Germany which is surely better fitted from her state of civilisation and education to bear representative institutions.

The Queen is afraid however that all our Ministers abroad, at Berlin, Dresden, Munich, Stuttgart, Hanover, etc. (with the exception of Lord Cowley at Frankfurt) are warm partisans of the despotic league against Prussia and a German constitution and for the maintenance of the old Diet under Austrian and Russian influences. Ought not Lord Palmerston to make his agents understand that their sentiments are at variance with those of the English Government? and that they are doing serious mischief if they express them at Courts which have already every inclination to follow their despotic courses . . .

Palmerston had his answer ready:

. . . With respect to the maintenance of constitutional government in Germany, Viscount Palmerston entirely subscribes to your Majesty's opinion that a regard for consistency, as well as a sense of right and justice, ought to lead your Majesty's Government to give to the constitutional principle in Germany the same moral support which they endeavoured to afford it in Italy, Spain, Portugal and elsewhere, but though he is conscious that he may be deceived and may think better of the Austrian Government in this respect than it deserves, yet he cannot persuade himself that rational and sound constitutional government is at present in danger in Germany, or that the Austrian Government, whatever may be their inclination and wishes, can think it possible in the present day to re-establish despotic government in a nation so enlightened and so attached to free institutions as the German people now is. The danger for Germany seems to be rather in the opposite direction, arising from the rash and weak precipitation with which in 1848 and 49 those governments, which before had refused everything, resolved in a moment of alarm to grant everything and, passing from one extreme to the other, threw universal suffrage among people who had been some wholly and others very much unaccustomed to the working of representative government. The French have found universal suffrage incompatible with good order even in a republic; what must it be for a monarchy?

Viscount Palmerston would moreover beg to submit that the conflict between Austria and Prussia can scarcely be said to have

Reproduced by gracious permission of Her Majesty the Queen

e Great Exhibition opens in London in 1851, the year Palmerston fell from grace
Foreign Secretary.

turned upon principles of government so much as upon a struggle for political ascendancy in Germany. At Berlin, at Dresden and in Baden the Prussian Government has very properly no doubt employed military force to re-establish order; and in regard to the affairs of Hesse, the ground taken by Prussia was not so much a constitutional as a military one, and the objection which she made to the entrance of the troops of the Diet was that those troops might become hostile and that they ought not therefore to occupy a central position in the line of military defence of Prussia . . .

During the winter, the Queen imposed a reshuffle of British Ambassadors over Palmerston's objections, and in the spring of 1851 another almost routine attempt was made to persuade Lord John Russell to replace him with the same negative result. When the Prince's brain child, the Great Exhibition, opened in Hyde Park on May 1, Palmerston thought a little flattery might meet the occasion:

> . . . Viscount Palmerston trusts that your Majesty may not think that he is taking too great a liberty if he cannot refrain from avail-ing himself of this opportunity to tender to your Majesty his heartfelt congratulations upon the event of yesterday, a day the result of which must be no less gratifying to your Majesty, than honourable to the nation whose good fortune it is to have your Majesty for its sovereign.

Then, in the autumn, came the final rupture. The preliminary skirmish occurred over the diplomatic propriety of Palmerston receiving the exiled Hungarian resistance hero, Kossuth, who had made his way to London. The Queen was sure that this would be a breach of decorum, and wrote:

> The Queen mentioned to Lord Palmerston when he was last here at Windsor Castle that she thought it would not be advisable that he should receive M. Kossuth upon his arrival in England, as being wholly unnecessary, and likely to be misconstrued abroad. Since M. Kossuth's arrival in this country, and his violent denunciations of two sovereigns with whom we are at peace, the Queen thinks that she owes it as a mark of respect to her allies, and generally to all States at peace with this country, not to allow that a person endeavouring to excite a political agitation in this country against

her allies should be received by her Secretary of State for Foreign Affairs. Whether such a reception should take place at his official or private residence can make no difference as to the public nature of the act. The Queen must therefore demand that the reception of M. Kossuth by Lord Palmerston should not take place.

In this the Queen was firmly backed by Lord John, whose parallel request received this intemperate reply from Palmerston:

I have just received your letter of to-day and I am told, your messenger waits for an answer. My reply then is immediate and is: That there are limits to all things, that I do not choose to be dictated to as to whom I may or may not receive in my own house and that I shall use my own discretion on that matter. You will of course use yours as to the disposition of your government.—I have not detained your messenger five minutes.

A Cabinet crisis was inevitable, with the Queen urging Lord John not to submit to such intolerable behaviour. But, faced by the almost unanimous disapproval of his colleagues, Palmerston once again backed down, only to make his point by receiving ostentatiously a radical delegation which stigmatised the Emperors of Austria and Russia publicly as 'odious and detestable assassins' and 'merciless tyrants and despots'.

The Queen and the Prince seethed with indignation and written communication with Palmerston ceased. Fortunately for everyone's blood pressure, his next indiscretion went too far. In France, the future Emperor Napoleon III had seized power by a coup d'état. Palmerston was convinced that Napoleon had forestalled an attempt at restoration of the Orleans dynasty and approved privately of his action in conversation with the French Ambassador in London, Count Walewski. However, he had instructed Lord Normanby, the British Ambassador in Paris, to remain neutral and non-committal, and Normanby was greatly put out to have the London conversation reported to him by the French Foreign Minister, Turgot.

Palmerston and Normanby had not been seeing eye-to-eye for some time, and Normanby did not scruple to send to his brother, Colonel Phipps, a senior member of the royal household, detailed accounts of his complaints. Thus armed, the Queen compelled Lord John Russell to take final issue with Palmerston. This time the Prime Minister steeled himself for the break. He told Palmerston that such an expression of opinion should have had the sanction of the Cabinet. Sugaring the pill with the offer of the Lord-Lieutenancy of Ireland, with or without a British peerage, Lord John wrote that he had come to the 'painful conclusion . . . that the conduct of foreign affairs can no longer be left in your hands with advantage to the country'.—The Queen, as she confided the course of the crisis to her private journal, could hardly contain her exultation:

> OSBORNE, DECEMBER 11, 1851: Colonel Phipps met us, when we were out, with a letter from Lord Normanby about a dispute or quarrel between him and Lord Palmerston, with reference to excessively impertinent and flippant letters from the latter, in which he accuses Lord Normanby of abetting an Orléans plot (which the French Government never dreamed of and which does not exist) and of not taking sufficient part with the President in his coup d'état! And this, after Lord Normanby had been desired by the Government to remain entirely passive, in accordance with my injunctions. It seems however that Lord Palmerston told Count Walewski that the Government entirely approved Louis Napoleon's coup d'état. M. Turgot told this to Lord Normanby, who naturally was much surprised. What an extraordinary and unprincipled man Lord P. is and how devoid of every feeling of honour and consistency.

> OSBORNE, DECEMBER 19: Received a letter from Lord John Russell, saying that he had one from Lord Palmerston, explanatory of the latter's interview with Count Walewski, which was quite unsatisfactory and Lord Palmerston had been compelled to write to Count Walewski in most decisive terms, saying that the conversation would have to be submitted to me, and that he had sent a draft to Lord Normanby, which he did without Lord John's knowledge.

> WINDSOR CASTLE, DECEMBER 20: By 2 we were at Windsor, where we found a box from Lord John containing great and most unexpected news. He wrote that he sent us the correspondence

between him and Lord Palmerston, which terminated with a letter received to-day;—that Lord John had now to recommend my receiving the Seals of the Foreign Office!!—that he had summoned the Cabinet for the 22nd. It was possible they might think they could not go on,—which he did not; if they agreed with him he would recommend a successor to Lord Palmerston, and he thought Lord Granville the fittest, though others might think he had not sufficient experience.

After luncheon we saw the correspondence, beginning with a long letter from Lord Palmerston, in which he hardly touches upon his improper conduct in telling Walewski he entirely approved of the coup d'état, trying to make out that each person 'coloured highly' what the other said, and that he had merely given his opinion. He entered into a long dissertation to prove the reason why Louis Napoleon was justified in doing what he did. To this, Lord John wrote: that this explanation was quite unsatisfactory,—that he discussed questions which had no bearing on the matter Lord John had called upon him to explain; that he felt the time had come when it was best he should no longer hold the Seals of the Foreign Office, for he perceived that his indiscretion led to endless misunderstandings and breaches of decorum, which endangered our relations with other countries. He offered Lord Palmerston the Lord-Lieutenancy of Ireland, and ended by (I consider rather unnecessary and uncalled for) praises. Lord Palmerston has answered very stiffly that he will be prepared to give up the Seals as soon as his successor is appointed, but that what Lord John had laid down was impracticable viz. he could not take one thing as a minister, and another, as a private individual, for that he could not separate the two, and that he had the satisfaction of feeling that the honour, dignity, and integrity of the country had not suffered since he had been at the Foreign Office!! Just the very things it has suffered in so seriously. Our relief was great and we felt quite excited by the news, for our anxiety and worry during the last five years and a half, which was indescribable, was mainly, if not entirely, caused by him! It is a great and unexpected mercy, for I really was on the point of declaring on my part that I could no longer retain Lord Palmerston, which would have been a most disagreeable task, and not unattended with a small amount of danger, inasmuch as it would have put me too prominently forward.

WINDSOR CASTLE, DECEMBER 21: Albert, who had also written to Lord John, received an answer from him, before dinner. He said that he had felt I was becoming more and more uneasy about Lord Palmerston and that he had thought it his duty to put a stop to what was unnecessarily injuring me and the Cabinet; that he was particularly anxious to prevent my being brought prominently forward, as, were I to be attacked by Lord Palmerston's admirers, I was not in a position to defend myself, Therefore, after what had happened just before and Lord Palmerston having been specially cautioned, only on the 29th of November, Lord John felt there was no longer any hope of controlling him. Lord John added that parting from a colleague was very painful to him. He has behaved very well.

WINDSOR CASTLE, DECEMBER 24: Lord John Russell sent me a wonderful note from Lord Palmerston to him, saying he could not admit the accusation of want of decorum and prudence, for Lord John himself contradicted this by offering him the Lord-Lieutenancy of Ireland, for which office he concluded 'prudence and decorum' were required!! Really very impertinent, but at the same time it rather serves Lord John right for his weakness in offering this post.

WINDSOR CASTLE, DECEMBER 26: Very punctual luncheon on account of the Council, and not wishing to keep Lord Palmerston waiting with the other ministers when he was to deliver up the Seals. Half past 2 came, and no Lord Palmerston arrived, so we saw Lord John Russell and talked to him for half an hour, entirely about the event. He read a very short and angry note from Lord Palmerston to him in answer to one Lord John (perhaps not very wisely) had written him, telling him that this had been the most painful week he had ever had in politics and announcing when I would receive the Seals. Lord Palmerston wrote 'with regard to what you say of your feelings, I, on my part feel that just indignation which the whole transaction has produced on my mind.' We recapitulated the last proceedings which had led to Lord Palmerston's dismissal, and the unaccountable and unwarrantable delay of a week between Lord John's letter and Lord P.'s answer. Lord John said he would have to state the whole in Parliament and must say that I had asked for an explanation of the discrepancy between

Lord P.'s language and the instructions (agreed on) to Lord Normanby. I said he might add that I had frequently had to complain of similar delays. Lord John seemed to think that Lord Palmerston had certainly not now wished to bring matters to a crisis, but, to make himself master and be entirely uncontrolled. From what Walewski told Lord John, it can plainly be seen, that whatever Lord Palmerston told him, he considered as the opinion of the whole Government . . .

At 3 Lord Palmerston had still not arrived. The Seals had been sent down to Lord John, by Lord Stanley, at Lord Palmerston's desire, as Lord Stanley said Lord P. was not going through London to Windsor. We saw Lord Landsdowne,—evidently nervous,—but he said he had for some time felt that matters were coming to this pass. Half past 3 and no sign of Lord Palmerston. Lord John came in to say he thought Lord P. must not be intending to come. On my asking whether the Seals could be delivered up by another person, Lord John replied, they could, and that George III and William IV had sent for the Seals in anger, not allowing the minister to deliver them up; but it certainly always had been an understood thing that the minister ought to deliver up the Seals himself. Lord John however, at our suggestion, went to enquire about the trains, to see if any other was due and we talked a little while to Sir G. Grey. By this time it being nearly 4, Lord John returned and advised me to receive the Seals from him, which I did, and then held the Council at which Lord Granville was sworn in, and I delivered the Seals to him. After the Council we saw him and when I expressed my satisfaction at seeing him in his new office, he was so overcome as to be hardly able to speak. We talked to him generally of what had passed, the tone in which our communications with other countries had of late got into, the flippant, harsh manner in which the drafts had been written, inspiring dislike and distrust of Lord Palmerston's policy in other countries. The consequent alienation of these from England, and the slights put upon this country. We, with our internal quiet, and respect for law and liberty, ought, since '48, to have stood above all the other countries and been able to hold the grandest position and give the most conciliatory advice to them. Lord Granville seemed quite to understand everything and all he said was most discreet, giving us the impression that he was not alarmed at the task. He said he thought Lord Palmerston's faults were more easily to be avoided, than his great merits were to be copied; that he thought Lord P.'s despatches had not been written so much with the view to obtain an end as for the Blue Book. The relief of having such a good, amiable, honest man, in the place of one whom I grieve to think, I must with truth, consider an un-principled man, is not to be described, and I can hardly yet realise it.

CHAPTER V

Palmerston the Inevitable

THE ROYAL TRIUMPH OVER PALMERSTON WAS SHORT-LIVED. His downfall was ascribed, intuitively, by public opinion to Court pressure and, specifically, to the influence of Prince Albert, who found himself as unpopular as Palmerston became extravagantly popular in his misfortune. The Queen obtained the amenable courtier Lord Granville as her Foreign Minister, but his predecessor became the courted lion of political and social life.

Palmerston's strength in Parliament and the country is extremely difficult to define. For someone of such passionate and unswerving convictions, he was yet many things to many men. He never controlled a 'party', nor even a coherent group of any size in the House of Commons, yet he enjoyed an unshakable reputation in the country at large as Britain's champion. The Whigs, of whom Lord John Russell was the embodiment, accepted him, but with reserve. The Radicals in Parliament liked Palmerston's attitude to foreign liberals; the Peelites, much reduced since the death of their leader, considered him a fellow opponent of protective tariffs, and the Tories approved of his luke-warm attitude towards further parliamentary reform.

He became the most sought-after figure in political life, able to join almost any combination of forces in a leading position. Within a few weeks of his dismissal, he had brought down Lord John Russell's tottering Government, by opposing a measure for instituting a local militia.—Palmerston considered such a force should be organised on a national basis. A weak Derby-Disraeli minority administration came into power, with Palmerston giving its Foreign Minister, Lord Malmesbury—grandson of his old mentor—many a useful hint on the conduct of his office, and otherwise adorning Lady Palmerston's *salon* with his presence, his

Sligo and Broadlands estates with his proprietary zeal, and the hunting field and racecourse with his ebullient enthusiasm.

In July 1852, the *Westminster Review* published a long article entitled 'Lord Palmerston and his Policy', reviewing two books on the subject which had just been published. Baffled by the popularity of this indestructible elderly Phoenix, Prince Albert had the whole article pasted on foolscap sheets, wrote copious marginal notes all over them concerning the past iniquities of the Court's *bête-noire*, and carefully consigned his indictment to the files for posterity.

The article quoted a speech by Palmerston at the time of the French invasion of Spain in 1823 in which he said *inter alia*: 'To have brandished a sword of defiance in the hour of deliberation, and to have ended in a penful of protests on the day of battle, would have been the conduct of a cowardly bully, and would have made us the object of contempt and the laughing stock of Europe.'

> Lord Palmerston could not have uttered truer words [the Prince commented] nor have pronounced a stronger condemnation of his own later policy, when at the head of the Foreign Affairs of this country: for they describe most accurately his whole line of action, which I have never been able to understand otherwise than as that of a bully.

The article then quoted a Palmerston speech of 1829 in defence of Canning, in which he said: 'But if by interference is meant inter-meddling, and inter-meddling in every way and to every extent short of actual military force, then I must affirm that there is nothing in such interference which the laws of nations may not in certain cases permit.'

The Prince noted acidly:

> If the laws of nations permit this the laws of morality do not and these form the code under which a statesman ought to act. 'Inter-meddling in every way and every extent' short of war is the principle which on that day Lord Palmerston avowed and upon which he has acted ever since.—His own words quoted before are the best refutation of this new and dangerous principle, which

has now so long kept Europe in hot water and exposed England to the hatred of other nations. What else does this principle mean than the mixing up of the power of England with the internal dissensions, disputes and quarrels of every country, with the settled purpose, however, not to incur thereby any moral responsibility or the legitimate consequences attaching to it? How sadly are the results of this mode of action illustrated by the present state of affairs in Europe, where the people of almost all countries, after having been led to believe that they would meet with the support of England if they achieved their own liberty and having been thus encouraged to the attempt, have been allowed to be overcome without our stirring a finger on their behalf and are now abandoned to the most cruel tyranny! Can there be two codes of morality, one for nations and one for individuals? . . .

A passage in the article referring favourably to Palmerston's success in establishing the Belgian monarchy put the Prince in less censorious mood:

These negotiations reflect the very highest credit upon Lord Palmerston's dexterity, industry and patience and the result proves their wisdom. I always understood, however, from members of the then Cabinet, that Lord Grey, as long as he was Prime Minister, kept the control wholly in his own hands and revised most carefully every despatch and note written throughout the transactions. Lord Melbourne allowed Lord Palmerston to do pretty much whatever he pleased or his other colleagues would let him.

The article then described Palmerston as a very bad courtier, hated by Queen Isabella of Spain, King Otho of Greece and King Louis-Philippe. It also told an alleged story about Palmerston being snubbed by Queen Victoria at a levée. The Prince's note put part of the record straight, but still harped on Palmerston's political attitudes:

This is quite untrue. He is particularly gentlemanly and pleasing in society and has the best manners at Court. He was rather a favourite of the Queen during the first years of her reign and was treated with particular confidence by us both on his return to office in 1846. He often, however, offended both his sovereign and his colleagues by systematically setting their control at nought. The story of the levée is quite untrue. As long as he was minister, he of course never went by as he formed part of the Court, and when he came by after his dismissal we had particularly settled that no difference should be made from former times. The Queen asked him after Lady Palmerston's health and I shook hands with him.

The reason for the hatred of kings to Lord Palmerston is simply his intriguing with the parties in opposition to their respective governments and the suspicion of his encouraging revolutions against their Crowns. Those whom he was instrumental in placing upon foreign thrones must feel that, to obtain the respect and confidence of their people, they ought not to be considered as foreign nominees and dependents; they must therefore be doubly sensitive at any interference and resent all attempts at dictation, which Lord Palmerston, to show his power to the British public, often so ostentatiously assumes . . . Constitutional advice could not be party advice. The constitutional sovereign ought to be the moderator of parties. Lord Palmerston always tried to make him the partisan of that faction with which he (Lord P.) was in alliance, and as this was generally the faction which was leaning on the extreme democracy, sovereigns naturally received the advice with distrust.

The Prince's comments on Lord Minto's mission to Italy were wry and revealing:

The mission of Lord Minto arose, in fact, out of his desire to see his daughter, Lady Mary Abercromby, sister to Lady John Russell, and who was going to be confined at Turin, without having to pay for the journey. Lord Palmerston was delighted by the proposal, as it gave him as his agent the Lord Privy Seal and father-in-law to Lord John and therefore ensured to him the support of Lord John and the Cabinet if he thoroughly compromised him. The subsequent facts proved the shrewdness of this calculation, for the Cabinet were bound to support his whole later foreign policy towards Italy, even to its most extreme extravagance and immoralities.

The article then made the point that although Palmerston evinced sympathy for Hungary, he showed contempt for the Schleswigers and Holsteiners and suspected the inconstancy of the King of Prussia. This went to the heart of one of the Prince's main complaints:

> Because they had positive rights on their side and Lord Palmerston was afraid of a strong Germany which would have obtained a material and preponderating influence on the Continent. He was at no time favourable to the liberties of Germany as a whole and has by his Danish Protocol become the real cause of their extinction. This Protocol united the whole reactionary party: Russia, Austria, Denmark and France to England against constitutional Prussia and her struggle to maintain constitutionalism in Germany. My personal belief is that the Protocol was a bargain between Lord Palmerston and Baron Brunnow [the Russian Ambassador] who engaged in return for it to withdraw the hostility of Russia and Austria against Lord Palmerston personally, which was most harassing to him during his trial in Parliament on the Greek affair.

A suggestion in the article that the British Constitution requires a passive indifference on the part of the sovereign to the march of political events, but that this was impossible to expect, as the Coburg family had high interests in different parts of Europe, earned a tart comment from the Prince:

> Nowhere does the Constitution demand an indifference on the part of the sovereign to the march of political events, and nowhere would such indifference be more condemned and justly despised than in England. There was no interest of the House of Coburg involved in any of the questions upon which we quarrelled with Lord Palmerston, neither in Greece nor Italy, Sicily, Holstein, Hungary etc.
> Why are Princes alone to be denied the credit of having political opinions based upon an anxiety for the national interests and honour of their country and the welfare of mankind? Are they not more independently placed than any other politician in the State? Are their interests not most intimately bound up with those of their country? Is the sovereign not the natural guardian of the honour of his country, is he not *necessarily* a politician? Has he no duties to perform towards his country?

A reference to the delayed despatch to Sir Henry Wyse in Athens during the Don Pacifico episode, the manoeuvre by which Palmerston enabled Wyse to obtain better terms, although those proposed by French mediation had already been accepted, brought from the Prince a final summary of the Court's complaints against their Foreign Minister:

> This proceeding in itself ought to have been sufficient to have made the Queen dismiss him at once. Lord Palmerston made it a practice to write his despatches only on the day of the mail, so that it was generally rendered impossible to refer them to a Cabinet or for the Queen and Lord John to have time to consider them. On the whole there was no trick to which he did not descend towards his sovereign and his colleague in order to carry through his own plans, involving them in the responsibility . . .
>
> The sovereign is necessarily compromised by the acts of her ministers. The representation of a country with other powers is in the constitutional monarchy essentially and especially the attribute of the sovereign. The Queen's position was therefore most painful throughout Lord Palmerston's stay at the Foreign Office, as she could only be considered either as approving his acts and words or as too weak to influence them, both suppositions equally derogatory to her honour and dignity . . .
>
> Lord Palmerston has certainly taken up the liberal cause as his political cry; but that he is not actuated by a fixed principle is shown by the manner in which he has opposed or supported it at different times or in different countries. It is a curious fact that he has backed the liberal cause in all small or weak States, such as Greece, Spain, Portugal, Italy, etc., but has been found in the ranks of its opponents in the strong countries such as France and Germany.

Palmerston's career as Foreign Minister might be at an end, but the Court was not rid of him yet. The Derby ministry staggered on, survived an inconclusive election, withstood a challenge on trade protection in the House, due largely to a compromise formula suggested by Palmerston, and was then defeated on Disraeli's Budget. The only alternative was a Whig-Peelite coalition, and the awful spectre of Palmerston in office again rose before the appalled eyes of the Court. On December 28, 1852, Prince Albert contributed a sour entry to the Queen's Journal:

The delivery of the Seals of Office of the outgoing ministers and the Queen's bestowal of them upon the new Ministers took place to-day. Of the former, Mr. Disraeli seemed to feel the loss of office most . . .

We asked what Lord Palmerston had been about, during the crisis? Lord John told us in reply that Lord Palmerston had certainly been disposed to join Lord Derby's Government, but always said he could not do so alone; that if eight of them were to join, then they would have the majority in the Cabinet. Lord John also told us that he believed Lord Palmerston would have voted for some part of the Budget and against others. Lord John does not think that that large party of Lord Derby's will long keep together. Some, would vote for the Government—others, might try to raise a Protestant cry.

Lord Palmerston looked excessively ill, and had to walk with two sticks, on account of his gout.

Palmerston was far from being as decrepit as he appeared. Nevertheless, not even he could envisage another period of warfare at the Foreign Office. In the jockeying for position, Lord Aberdeen became Prime Minister, with his Peelite fellows Sir James Graham, Mr. Sidney Herbert and Mr. Gladstone, in a 'ministry of all the talents', together with Lords Lansdowne, John Russell, Clarendon and Palmerston—who accepted the post of Home Secretary.

The wary renewed relationship between Court and Palmerston at least started with an exchange of civilities. Lady Palmerston's— and the late Lord Melbourne's—brother Frederick had just died, and the Queen sent her condolences. Palmerston returned his thanks:

Viscount Palmerston presents his humble duty to your Majesty, and begs to be allowed to offer his grateful thanks for your Majesty's gracious and condescending communication which he has just received. He will immediately forward your Majesty's letter to Lady Palmerston [who] is at Brocket together with Lord and Lady Cowper.

Lady Palmerston is deeply afflicted at the loss of her last surviving brother, to whom through life she has been most warmly attached; and Lady Melbourne is entirely overwhelmed by the calamity she has sustained.

Great hopes were entertained that the illness would end in recovery, and there had been an amendment in the middle of the week; but in the night of Friday the gout flew to the head, and proved fatal at an early hour on Saturday morning.

Palmerston proved an indefatigable Home Secretary and his vigorous pen was soon being applied to a bewildering variety of subjects—prison reform, child labour, smoke abatement, sewage schemes, the licensing laws—the sheer volume of work these Victorians committed to paper in their own hand staggers the imagination. Most of his correspondence with the Queen was a throwback to the first years of their relationship—an endless exchange of proposals and approval of administrative, ecclesiastical and academic appointments took the place of the early instruction in diplomatic protocol. Most of the Queen's interventions were mild in tone:

FEBRUARY 10, 1853: Though the Queen is aware that she is to receive the Address from the Convocation at Buckingham Palace Wednesday next at one o'clock—still, as she has received no official communication on the subject from Lord Palmerston she fears there might be some mistake and she therefore writes to ask Lord Palmerston to give the necessary directions to the different officials for the reception of the Address on the Throne on Wednesday next. Lord Palmerston will naturally communicate with the Archbishop on the subject.

MAY 13: Viscount Palmerston presents his humble duty to your Majesty and begs to state that it appears to be advisable that a commission should be appointed to enquire into the present state of the Corporation of the City of London, and to suggest such reforms and improvements as might place the organisation of that Corporation more in accordance with that of the municipal institutions of other towns, as regulated by the General Municipal Corporation Act which was passed some years ago, but from the operation of which the City of London was excepted . . .

MAY 15: The Queen . . . highly approves the proposition of appointing a Commission to inquire into the present state of the Corporation of the City of London, as well as the persons whose

names Lord Palmerston has submitted to her to compose the
Commission. The Queen thinks it very wise not to have a large
number of persons for the Commission, much will now depend
on the selection of a very efficient secretary to the intended
Commission.

The name of a recent bone of contention between them, Kossuth,
came up again that spring. The Hungarian leader was implicated
in a plot involving the manufacture of explosive rockets in London
for use in renewed revolutionary activity:

> The Queen would wish to know if (as Lord Palmerston mentioned
> to her there would) a prosecution has been instituted in conse-
> quence of the papers relating to Kossuth and Mazzini which he
> sent to her? The Queen would like to know what has been done.

> Viscount Palmerston presents his humble duty to your Majesty
> and submits the reports from the police as to the proceedings
> which have been had in regard to Kossuth's manufactury of
> rockets; and he begs to state that as it appears that some rockets
> have lately been seized by the police at Berlin, he has requested the
> Foreign Office to endeavour to obtain samples of the rockets thus
> seized in order that they may be compared with those which will
> probably be seized here, for the purpose of ascertaining whether
> the rockets found at Berlin shall appear to have been made in this
> country

Palmerston sent further details to the Prince:

> Sir,
> I have to report to your Royal Highness for her Majesty's
> information that yesterday evening the police made a seizure at
> Kossuth's rocket manufactury. They seized about forty cases of
> rockets ready packed apparently for exportation, and filled with
> rockets, besides a great number of rockets in various stages of
> preparation, together with rocket composition and a considerable
> quantity of gunpowder. The police will to-day search the Chelsea
> factory also. Altogether the number of rockets made and unmade
> amounts as far as can be calculated to between six and eight
> thousand.
> The opinion of the law officers will be taken in the question

Punch version of Palmerston's fall: 'I'm very sorry, Palmerston, that you can't
[agr]e with your fellow servants, but as I don't feel inclined to part with John—you
[mus]t go, of course.'

whether these facts do not amount to proof of a conspiracy to levy war against a foreign power. It is believed that the packed up cases were intended to be sent to Rostock.

. . . Kossuth has frequently visited the Rotherhithe manufactury, had expressed great interest about it, had been present at experiments made with the rockets and had talked of the rockets been [sic] destined for the *war* which was to break out this spring.

Other exchanges often showed a sad decline in subject matter from the majestic disputes of a couple of years earlier. Mr. Bernal Osborne, the Secretary to the Admiralty, wished to exercise the right of taking his carriage through the Horse Guards Arch:

In reply to Lord Palmerston's letter of the 27th [April] relative to Mr. Bernal Osborne's request, the Queen must observe that she fears that the granting of it may be a dangerous precedent as there are so many who have been refused this permission, even the Under Secretary of State—Lord Desart—being an instance only last year of the refusal of this very privilege. If however Lord Palmerston still recommends it, the Queen would wish him to keep a record in the Home Office of its being granted to Mr. B. Osborne on the express understanding that it should make no precedent for the future.

The Queen has received Lord Palmerston's letter of the 9th [May]. She does not wish to grant the permission to Mrs. Herbert's children to ride a donkey in the Park, as she only granted this permission to Lady Salisbury as a very special favour, and if Mrs. Herbert has this privilege of course many others will apply for it and there will soon be no difference between the Park and any other public thoroughfare. Under these circumstances it would be better for Lord Palmerston to say that an exception could not be made,—he could not submit this request to the Queen . . .

The Queen's sharp eye for the slightest irregularity was in no way dimmed:

The Queen has received Lord Palmerston's letter of the 8th [November] recommending to her that Mr. R. Handyside, now Solicitor General for Scotland, be appointed a Scotch Judge in the room of the late Lord Anderson and that Mr. James Crauford should be appointed Solicitor General for Scotland.

The Queen approves these appointments, but must at the same time observe that she was much surprised to see them announced in the papers, which should not have been until her pleasure had been taken. She hopes this will not occur again.

Viscount Palmerston presents his humble duty to your Majesty and with reference to your Majesty's remarks on the announcement of the Scotch legal appointments in the newspapers before your Majesty's pleasure had been taken on them, he begs to state that this irregularity did not originate with him, and he had no communication with the persons concerned before he submitted their names to your Majesty. It must have happened in consequence of some private communications between the Lord Advocate and the gentlemen in question with a view to ascertain whether they were willing to accept the appointments if approved of by your Majesty; but Viscount Palmerston will take steps to prevent such mistakes happening in future.

All this was shadow-boxing. Palmerston's real love remained foreign policy, and a crisis surpassing anything during his previous tenures of office was in the making. The Russians, under the pretext of protecting the Holy Places in Jerusalem and Orthodox Christian subjects of the Turkish Empire, were renewing their perennial hostility to the feeble government of the Sultan in Constantinople. Aberdeen tended to be pro-Russian. Palmerston, with his eye fixed for decades past on the route to India, was sturdily pro-Turk. However, he remained amenable in the Cabinet, seeking only a suitable juncture to reverse the Government's policy. The Prince also was pro-Russian in the early stages of the dispute which was to lead to the Crimean War, and a battle for influence was joined again between the Court and Palmerston.

The situation was both complicated and simplified by Lord John Russell. The incorrigible little Whig, who had surrendered the Foreign Office to Lord Clarendon, was concentrating as Leader of the House of Commons on another cherished project for parliamentary reform. Palmerston had found Clarendon an increasingly willing pupil, and drafted long memoranda for him on foreign affairs out of his rich store of experience. Still Aberdeen —and the Prince—were not to be moved. Then Palmerston saw his opportunity. Events in Eastern Europe were moving swiftly to a climax. He therefore challenged Lord John Russell and his Cabinet colleagues on the advisability of a new reform bill, and resigned. The royal joy was unconfined, but three days later came the news that the Russian fleet had annihilated the Turks at Sinope. In the clamour of outraged public opinion, some of Palmerston's colleagues hinted that he should return to office in order to strengthen the Government. Blithely, he retracted his resignation and rejoined them.

A furious Queen scribbled the whole baffling and exasperating chronology in her private journal:

OSBORNE, DECEMBER 15, 1853: Received a letter from Lord Aberdeen, enclosing a correspondence between him and Lord Palmerston, who so entirely disagrees on the Reform Bill, that Lord Aberdeen expected to receive his resignation. The correspondence was quite amiable as concerned Lord Aberdeen, but a letter of Lord P.'s to Landsowne very abusive as concerned Lord John Russell, saying he 'would not be dragged through the dirt by John Russell'!! Lord Aberdeen has consulted with Lord John and Sir J. Graham, and neither of them could agree to the modifications Lord Palmerston wished for in the Reform Bill. Accordingly, Lord Aberdeen has written this to Lord Palmerston. Albert thought this serious, particularly as Lord Lansdowne shares the greater part of Lord Palmerston's objections.

Lord Palmerston has been eminently troublesome and mischievous and I am certain that the Government will be far better without him. He may however be dangerous as an opponent, if the Reform measure is not sure of passing. Lord Aberdeen said he hoped Lord Palmerston would not succeed in an amendment, as he had done in '52, after his expulsion. However, Lord John is very confident of success. No doubt Lord Palmerston's resignation will be attributed at first to the Eastern Question and his refusing 'to remain with such cowards, who had not the courage to make war'; but care would be taken that all should become known, and it would be well understood. Party motives and feelings would likewise be attributed to Lord Lansdowne, whom Lord Aberdeen is most anxious to try and persuade to take no rash step, intending to write to him to this same effect. The measure must and will be most carefully considered, and modifications may be made to suit Lord Lansdowne's objections, but Lord Aberdeen says 'it must not be a sham measure', for that the country would be indignant at that. He thinks it impossible for Lord John Russell and Lord Palmerston ever to act together, as their feelings against each other are so very strong.

OSBORNE, DECEMBER 16: Had much talk with Albert about Lord Palmerston's resignation and he agreed with me in thinking that Lord P. would injure himself permanently were he to go over to the Protectionists,—also that his absence would act very favourably on Lord Clarendon, who had stood in great fear of him, consulting him far too much,—as well as on Lord John, and other members of the Cabinet, who would speak out more now.

OSBORNE, DECEMBER 19: Sir J. [Graham] agreed with us to the blessing it was no longer to have Lord Palmerston in the Cabinet, but he cannot understand how the latter could be so unguarded as to send Lord Aberdeen the letter for Lord Lansdowne and to allow Lord A. to keep a copy of it. The fact was, Lord P. could not resist saying of Lord Aberdeen and Lord John Russell, to a third person, what he dared not write direct to them. Some people *wrote* guardedly and *spoke* rashly, whereas with Lord Palmerston it was just reverse.

OSBORNE, DECEMBER 20: Received a box from Lord Aberdeen which somewhat upset us. The Council at which Lord Palmerston was to have delivered up the Seals had been by his desire postponed,—as Sir George Grey, whom he had seen, was disinclined to accept office, but would wait till he had seen Lord John Russell, who was returning to town tomorrow. Meantime Lord Palmerston had given it to be understood that he would like to reconsider the step he had taken. Lord Aberdeen had not declared himself against this, as concessions would have to be made to Lord Lansdowne, which might satisfy Lord Palmerston, but that he believed a reconciliation between him and Lord John to be almost impossible. Lord Aberdeen further represented how formidable Lord Palmerston's opposition in the House of Commons would be. Feeling strongly as we did, we wrote after our dinner to Lord Aberdeen, stating my surprise and regret at the contents of his letter and giving all the reasons against Lord Palmerston being allowed to resume his place, and repeating my belief that his danger in opposition was greatly overrated.

WINDSOR CASTLE, DECEMBER 23: Lord Aberdeen then went on to say that the Cabinet had considered 'the situation of Lord Palmerston in his relations to the Government', that Lord A. fully agreed in what I had said, but that he could not personally oppose 'the general weight of the Cabinet on the question' (!!) It seems that Lord Palmerston had 'expressed himself in the strongest terms, in various quarters as being sensible of the hasty step he had taken and of having acted under a misconception'; that he was ready to reconsider this step and his objections to the Reform Bill and 'to do his best to come to an understanding with his colleagues'. 'Under the circumstances it was resolved that no concession of any important portion of the measure should be made; but that if Lord Palmerston could be satisfied by submitting certain details to fair discussion, it might be permitted. It was also resolved that the first overture for a reconciliation should come from Lord Palmerston himself. All these considerations were greatly promoted by the reluctance of Sir G. Grey to take office, as well as by the effect which, in the opinion of many members of the Cabinet, would be produced in the House of Commons by the recession of Lord Palmerston, thereby affecting the safety of the Government. Lord Aberdeen doubts very much whether this attempt can succeed, as Lord Palmerston will have to be prepared to make sacrifices of opinions, principles and consistency hardly to be expected. At all events it may be considered a matter of necessity to effect this reconciliation if possible, but it is a little like what has already been done, to secure the French alliance.' Provoking and annoying enough, but it cannot be helped.

WINDSOR CASTLE, DECEMBER 24: He [Lord Aberdeen] said he had come to inform me of the state of the negotiations with Lord Palmerston, and then read the latter's letter to him and his admirable answer, written since he got here . . . For what passed between us I will make use of a memo by Albert, the greater part of which

I will copy. Lord Aberdeen said that some of his colleagues, Sir C. Wood, the Duke of Newcastle and Mr. Gladstone, had been very anxious that Lord Palmerston should be readmitted into the Cabinet and had had interviews with him, in which he had expressed his hope to be allowed to reconsider the step he had taken. Lady Palmerston had been most urgent with her husband on this point, saying 'this *must* be arranged and settled', and working herself into a great state of excitement, to get him back again into the Government. All the people most conversant with the House of Commons stated that the Government had no chance of going on with Lord Palmerston in the Opposition and with the present temper of the public, which was greatly excited about the Oriental question, and the disaster at Sinope. Even Sir William Molesworth shared this opinion. Lord Palmerston, in his letter, puts all on a misapprehension that there could be no reconsideration of the details of the Reform Measure. After the letters (which Lord Aberdeen read) had been received, he saw Lord John Russell and Sir J. Graham, who convinced themselves that under the circumstances nothing else remained to be done. Lord Aberdeen asked Lord John whether he could tell me that it was a political necessity, to which Lord John answered: 'yes, you may'. We repeated our fear as to the harm Lord Palmerston's return might do, and the danger of taking in such a man, whom Lord Aberdeen said he believed 'not one in the Cabinet respected'. Lord Aberdeen owned that the step must damage the Government, although it ought to damage Lord Palmerston still more. Lord John answered 'yes it would ruin anyone but Palmerston'. Indeed Lord Aberdeen had thought it quite impossible that Lord Palmerston should have done what he has. He thinks that Lord P. had quarrelled with the Radicals but that he can however make no further difficulties about the Reform Bill. Lord Aberdeen Lord John and Sir J. Graham were determined to make no material alterations in the Bill. 'We shall carry that with a high hand'. Sir J. Graham is suspicious lest the wish of some of the members of the Cabinet to get Lord Palmerston in again may be an intrigue to get the measure weakened and modified. Neither Lord Aberdeen nor we believe that Lord John had much to do with it though we think that the dislike to see Lord John take the entire mastery in the Cabinet may have had some influence. We know that this autumn the Peelites were very indignant when Lord J. coolly expected Lord

Aberdeen to retire in order that he might again be Prime Minister. He must know that Lord Palmerston's presence in the Cabinet would make this now more impossible than ever.

WINDSOR CASTLE, DECEMBER 28: Lord and Lady John Russell dined, he, sitting near me. He was in very good humour and spoke of Lord Palmerston's 'escapade' as very strange, damaging and to him incomprehensible, but that he believed Lord Palmerston had not expected it to happen so soon. Lord John could not have prevented Lord P.'s returning, once he began to urge his wish to come back.

Lord John must often have meditated in hindsight that Palmerston's actions were not incomprehensible at all. Ambition is common to all politicians, whatever their age, and there is good reason to suppose that Palmerston, now nearly seventy, foresaw a combination of circumstances which might yet lead him to the Prime Ministership. The time for that was not yet. The very idea would have been anathema to the Court. Yet the old antagonists were being drawn imperceptibly together.

The beginning of 1854 saw Prince Albert subjected to a degree of public odium which reduced the royal pair to a prolonged state of shock. He was accused in the press of little less than treason for his pro-Russian attitude. All the old rumours about the royal predilection for 'despots' were ventilated again, stories of royal 'interference' in foreign affairs were rehashed, and it was even reported that the Prince had been confined to the Tower of London as a preliminary to his impeachment. The royal couple thought they detected Palmerston's hand in all this, and whether this be true or not, he reached a new summit of patriotic reputation as the one strong Minister with the right ideas.

The Crimean War broke out in desultory fashion in March. The Russians had occupied two Turkish principalities in Rumania, and France and Britain undertook to assist the Sultan's Government to throw them out.

Once hostilities had begun, the Queen and the Prince supported vigorous prosecution of the war to hasten its conclusion. In thus opposing Aberdeen, who still hoped for a compromise by negotiation through Prussian or Austrian good offices, the Court veered inevitably towards the firm line of the implacable Palmerston. Even the Prince recovered a little of his lost prestige, although he continued to be criticised for bombarding Lord Hardinge, Commander-in-Chief of the Army at the Horse Guards, with his interminable memoranda on military organisation and efficiency.

The only Minister to exhibit real administrative ability, still in his limited sphere at the Home Office, was Palmerston, and to him the Queen turned in the royal attempt to improve the military establishment:

> . . . The Queen was very glad to hear of the introduction of the new Militia Bill into the House of Commons. She hopes that the power to call out that force during time of 'war with a foreign power' will not be so worded as to deprive her of that now existing in the case of an 'imminent danger of invasion' when there is no war. It will be most useful to have the power of extending the time of training.
>
> The construction of sea defence for our principal ports is much wanted and the present moment certainly a very fit one to supply the deficiency. The Queen was therefore much pleased to hear from Lord Palmerston that they would be undertaken. She would draw his attention however, at the same time, to the importance of now obtaining and organising such local volunteer forces (artillery) as will suffice for the defence of these local works, without locking up the militia which, in case of attack, should if possible remain a moveable force . . .

Even then, there was a minor difference over method:

> . . . A regiment of militia did duty at Windsor during a great part of the last war, and if your Majesty should not object to such an arrangement at present, that would release a regiment of the line for Manchester and the manufacturing districts, where the troops would be in billets and where unavoidable communication, and in certain cases possible conflict, with the working classes would render a steady and well disciplined regiment of the line in all respects a better force than a regiment of militia . . .

> The Queen has received Lord Palmerston's letter of yesterday and quite approves of the arrangement with respect to the quartering of the embodied militia with the exception of the proposal to

place one regiment at Windsor. The duties there are so peculiar
that it requires a force a little more disciplined and trained than
any regiment of militia can be at present. The Queen would
therefore ask to have a regiment of the line stationed there which
need not prevent the question of a militia regiment relieving them
at a future time being considered hereafter, when she shall have had
a little more experience on the subject.

Viscount Palmerston presents his humble duty to your Majesty
and begs to state that in accordance with your Majesty's desire the
Windsor duty shall continue to be performed by a regiment of the
line.

In her zeal, the Queen even scrutinised the muster rolls. 'What is
to be done in a case like this when 116 are absent without cause?'
she demanded to know:

Viscount Palmerston presents his humble duty to your Majesty,
and with reference to your Majesty's communication of this
morning begs to state that it is very difficult to take any effectual
steps in regard to men absent from the training of their militia
regiments. The main difficulty lies in its being generally impossible to find the men. There was a great desire when the militia
was raised to complete the regiments as soon as possible, and the
persons employed to enrol men were not sufficiently careful to
take such men only whose places of residence were within the
county, and who were likely to remain there.—The Durham
Artillery, the report upon which accompanied your Majesty's
memorandum, affords an illustration of this. It appears that out of
166 men enrolled, only 47 belong to the county, and by a curious
coincidence 47 was the precise number of men present under
arms. The remainder were Scotch, Irish or men belonging to
other counties in England. The answer to enquiries made in cases
of this kind has generally been that the great bulk of the absentees
have enlisted into the line, have emigrated, or have left the residence at which they were when they were enrolled. It was
always indeed to be expected, from the nature of things, that a
certain proportion of the men enrolled would not always be
forthcoming at the training periods, but the whole amount of the
nominal force of 80,000 was made sufficiently large to secure the

service of a very considerable effective army ready to be called out when required, and instructions have been given to commanding officers of regiments to be more careful in future as to the character of the men whom they may enrol in their corps.

In the autumn, the Queen even unbent to the extent of granting Palmerston permission to visit an ally who had been the cause of their final estrangement three years earlier:

> ... Viscount Palmerston begs at the same time to state that he has at various times during the last eighteen months received intimations from the Emperor of the French that it would be agreeable to the Emperor that Viscount Palmerston should pay him a visit ...
>
> Viscount Palmerston has hitherto pleaded official and parliamentary engagements as obstacles to his leaving England, even for the few days which would be required for such a purpose, but he is apprehensive that if he did not avail himself of some favourable opportunity in the course of this autumn to pay his respects to the French Emperor, his abstaining from doing so would wear the appearance of want of deference and respect and create impressions which it would be desirable to avoid. Viscount Palmerston therefore trusts that your Majesty will not object to his taking advantage of some convenient opportunity in the course of this autumn to go for a few days either to Boulogne or to Paris.
>
> The Queen has received Lord Palmerston's letter of the 3rd [October] asking for permission to pay a visit to the French Court at Boulogne or Paris at a convenient opportunity and informs him in reply that she readily grants him the desired leave ...

As the year turned, Palmerston's chance to occupy the highest elective office in the land arrived. The hideously mismanaged Crimean campaign required scapegoats at home. As the stories of horror and neglect of the troops came flooding in, the House of Commons rose in its wrath. The chief target was the Peelite Duke of Newcastle, War Secretary, but the whole Cabinet stood in the pillory. Mr. Roebuck, a Radical firebrand, introduced a motion of censure. Lord John Russell, more pusillanimous under pressure than usual, thought the Government could not face it and should resign. The Government was indeed defeated. Aberdeen was discredited for his lack of resolution in the conduct of the war. Lord John Russell had disgusted his colleagues by his timidity, and Lord Derby, to whom the Queen turned to form an alternative administration, saw no chance of obtaining the necessary majority. The country was clamouring for Palmerston. The Queen fought against the inevitable for as long as she could, entering the details of her eventual capitulation every night in her journal:

> BUCKINGHAM PALACE, FEBRUARY 2, 1855: . . . What a strange state of affairs! We heard that there was a unanimous feeling against Lord John, and a very strong one amongst his own supporters. The Duke of Newcastle's admirable speech last night has greatly helped in bringing this about.
>
> We dined alone, and at half past 9 Lord Lansdowne arrived, having taken a great deal of trouble to be of use. I can however not attempt to put everything down, as it would become too lengthy and voluminous, so I shall confine myself to the strict necessary.
>
> Lord Lansdowne had nothing satisfactory to report,—on the contrary, he was all in the dark, fearing that 'he had gone back'. He had been to see Sir J. Graham, who was ill in bed, and as usual, taking a gloomy view of everything! Sir J. Graham told Lord Lansdowne that the Peelites could not possibly serve under Lord John after what had happened, and that he felt the strongest objection to serving under Lord Palmerston,—for totally different reasons,—on account of his foreign and war policy, not tending to a satisfactory peace, which he then detailed, and Lord Lansdowne could not disagree.
>
> Lord Lansdowne had been present at the meeting between Lord John and Lord Palmerston, where nothing very clear had transpired,— nothing to lead Lord Lansdowne to know whether they would serve under each other. Both seemed to wish to form a Government and he hardly knew what to advise. We then observed that the whole matter seemed to resolve itself into two alternatives,—to send either for Lord John, or for Lord Palmerston. It was very important that it should not appear as if I had

any feeling against Lord Palmerston,—on the other hand, it was Lord John who had done the mischief,—consequently he ought to be asked first. In this Lord Lansdowne entirely agreed and thought it would be far the best plan. He fully believed Lord John would fail, and the trial, the disappointment and mortification he would feel at being refused by his friends and etc. would be a wholesome and necessary lesson, in order to prevent mischief for the future. Accordingly Albert went and sketched out a letter for Lord John, in which I made the proposal that he should attempt to form a government that would give satisfaction to the country, and have some stability. By Lord Lansdowne's particular wish, so as to prevent any ill feeling, I said that I hoped Lord Palmerston would form part of such a goverment.

Just before retiring to bed, at 12, heard from Lord John that he would attempt the task, and at once communicate with Lord Palmerston and Lord Clarendon.

BUCKINGHAM PALACE, FEBRUARY 3: Lord John Russell arrived at half past 1, and reported 'some progress and some obstacles'. He had seen Lord Palmerston, who would like best to become Leader, keeping his present office, in which case Lord John would then go up to the House of Lords. Lord Palmerston had spoken very frankly about himself, saying that the voice of the country had pointed him out as Prime or War Minister, but that he was quite willing to act as Leader, under Lord John. They had talked over offices and men, agreeing that Lord Panmure should be at the War Office, and Sir F. Baring go to the Admiralty. Should Mr. Gladstone and none of the Peelites join, which Lord Palmerston considered would be a great weakness, Lord John thought Mr. Labouchere might be Chancellor of the Exchequer, (!!) though he could not be named on the same plane as Mr. Gladstone. Lord Palmerston and Lord John wished I should [see] him, as I had seen Lord Lansdowne and himself. Lord John had next seen Lord Clarendon whom, to his surprise, he had found very unwilling to remain at the Foreign Office, under Lord John, though the latter thought I might be able to persuade him to do so. Lord Clarendon considered the Peelites had behaved very handsomely to Lord John and that, if they did not join, the Government would be too weak to last. Lord John was also anxious for me to see Lord Clarendon, which I promised to do. He had seen none of his other friends, Lord Lansdowne, Sir G. Grey, Sir C. Wood, and etc., but seemed to feel certain they would join him!! he would return at 6 in the evening . . .

At 3, Lord Palmerston came and I told him that I wished to consult him about the state of affairs. He said Lord John had communicated my wishes to him,—that he was 'at my orders', and would take the Lead in the House of Commons, keeping his present office,—that no man could undertake the Lead and be Minister for War at the same time. Count Walewski [the French Ambassador] (!!) had been to him, telling him that Lord Clarendon was very unwilling to join. The Peelites would not, which was a very serious loss, and if Lord Clarendon did not join, then he should consider himself 'as off his engagement'. There was however to be a meeting at Lord John's at 5, when he hoped the difficulties might be got over though they were very great. When I asked Lord Palmerston whether he would take the Lead in any other combination, he said it would be best to dispose of one subject at a time, and that we must hope the present proposal would succeed. All, and what he said about the army, was very satisfactory.

At 4, Lord Clarendon came and certainly his condemnation of Lord John's conduct was the strongest possible. The present state of affairs was the worst he ever remembered in this country. It was not right of Lord John to put the blame of failing in forming a government upon Lord Clarendon's joining him or not;—that his opinion of Lord John was only the one universally held, which he could hear and see for himself in the papers were his eyes not absolutely blinded. Lord Clarendon certainly did feel a great disinclination to join a government which could not stand, and which would be morally wrong if it were to succeed. Besides, he did not like separating from men whose conduct had been most honourable and straightforward, and was not prepared to 'step over the dead bodies of his colleagues in order to join the man who had killed them'. The Government would be 'still-born'—'the country would tread it underfoot the very first day', composed, as it would be, of the same men who had been bankrupt in 1852, minus the two best men in it: Lord Lansdowne and Lord Grey. Were Lord Clarendon even to remain at the Foreign Office, his language towards foreign countries would lose all its weight when it was known not to be resting upon the public feeling in England;

—all this would become much worse when it became known that from the first day of Lord John's entering into Lord Aberdeen's Government he had only had the one idea viz. that of tripping him up, expelling the Peelites, and placing himself at the head of an exclusive Whig Ministry! Lord Clarendon then said that he thought, should Lord John fail, it was very important the offer to form a government should be made to Lord Palmerston, who might equally find the same difficulties, but it would do away with the idea that I had a personal dislike to him. Were this to fail, then some other combination might become possible. Lord Lansdowne had no idea of joining or going to Lord John,—Sir C. Wood said he would not go into what Lord Lansdowne did not consider it fit to go and Lord Clarendon believed Lord John had never consulted any of his other friends. He concluded by saying he thought he could not join Lord John and would neither be serving me or the country by doing so.

Lord John came at 6, much put out and disturbed at having 'nothing encouraging' to report. He had seen both Sir G. Grey and Lord Clarendon, who had strongly expressed their disinclination to taking office. Sir G. Grey had told him that he thought a government formed by him (Lord J.) would not stand and would not possess the confidence of the country;—that people expected Lord Palmerston to be either Prime or War Minister—that he considered the Peelites had behaved extremely well, and that they had been much hurt by his conduct. Lord Clarendon had also spoken very strongly.

Lord John had previously seen Mr. Gladstone and Mr. S. Herbert, who had both declined,—also Sir J. Graham, by whose bedside he had been and the latter had spoken to him fully on the subject, saying that he had been guilty of rashness, which had brought on serious difficulties and that he could not join him. Sir J. Graham, as well as the two others, had however stated that they and Lord John would have still more difficulty in joining Lord Palmerston, owing to his views respecting peace. Upon my asking what Lord Lansdowne meant to do, Lord John said that he had received a letter from him which 'was also not very pleasant' and which he then read to me. Lord Lansdowne would not even go to the meeting at Lord John's house, having heard that Lord John was trying to form a government, which it was his intention not to join. Hence, for fear of any misconstruction, Lord Lansdowne had refrained from going. Lord John added that should Sir G. Grey and Lord Clarendon, who had promised to consider the matter if they were given till tomorrow morning, finally refuse to join him, then he could not go on. Should they, on the other hand, change their minds, he would try and form a combination. Lord John seemed very much put out and to have been living hitherto in a complete delusion. It must have been very humiliating for him to have to say all this to me and I really felt it painful and wished him not to be further wounded, much as he deserves the punishment, and certainly he will not be so by us. But there is no doubt that there exists a bitter feeling in the extreme, amongst all his followers and hangers-on, who are full of indignation and fury . . .

Lord John Russell had completely underrated the degree of feeling against him and had the mortifying experience of having Whig colleagues of many years' standing refuse to serve under him. The die was cast. The Queen had no option but to turn to Lord Palmerston to form a government:

Lord John Russell having just informed the Queen that he was obliged to resign the task which the Queen confided to him, she addresses herself to Lord Palmerston to ask him whether he can undertake to form an administration which will command the confidence of Parliament and efficiently conduct public affairs in this momentous crisis? Should he think that he is able to do so, the Queen commissions him to undertake the task. She does not send for him, having fully discussed with him yesterday the state of public affairs and in order to save time. The Queen hopes to receive an answer from Lord Palmerston as soon as possible, as upon this her movements will depend.

Within 24 hours, the man whom Lord John Russell had thought six years earlier to have little active political life left in him had formed a government, which was to continue in office, with one brief interlude, for the next ten years. The Queen's journal entry for February 5 was still full of apprehension:

We got a walk after breakfast and at half past 11 started again for London, on our eternal government hunting errand!—and to hear the results of negotiations.

We saw Lord Palmerston at 1 o'clock and he told us there were circumstances which prevented him still from submitting a list of the proposed Cabinet, but he hoped to be able to do so in the afternoon. Lords Lansdowne, Clarendon, Granville, Sir G. Grey, Sir C. Wood and Sir W. Molesworth and the Lord Chancellor had consented to serve unconditionally, having withdrawn their former conditions owing to the very general opinion expressed that the country could not be left much longer without a government. He had heard that this had also made an impression on the Peelites, who had refused to join. He submitted their electioneering letters, which had been written after consultation with Sir J. Graham, but Lord Aberdeen and the Duke of Newcastle having heard of it, have since made every effort to prevail upon them to change this opinion, so that it is still possible they may do so. Lord Clarendon had suggested that if Lord Aberdeen himself were invited to form the government and could be induced to do so, all difficulty would be obviated. Lord Palmerston has, in consequence, asked Lord Lansdowne to see Lord Aberdeen on the subject, as his joining could only be agreeable to him. Many of the Peelites, not in the late Cabinet, had strongly disapproved of the decision taken by Mr. Gladstone and friends, and had offered their services, amongst others Lords Canning and Elcho and Mr. Cardwell. Lord Palmerston had been yesterday with Lord John Russell and had had a long conversation with him, in a most friendly tone. He had asked Lord John whether he would follow out his own proposal to take the lead in the House of Lords, as President of the Council. Lord John however declined, saying he preferred staying out of office and to remain in the House of Commons, which Lord Palmerston obviously much regretted. They had however gone together through all the offices, and their best distribution. Lord Palmerston would recommend Lord Panmure for the War Department, and Mr. Layard as Under Secretary!! who, having been lately at the seat of war would give confidence!!—We made an appointment with Lord Palmerston for 5 o'clock to report further progress.

Albert wrote a line to Lord Aberdeen, expressing the comfort his promise to be in the Cabinet would be to me, but received an answer which put that out of the question, though it gave us every reason to hope that by his strong advice, the Peelites would consent to join. He sent an admirable letter of his to Mr. S.

Herbert, giving the very strongest reasons for their joining, stating that not long ago he had had a satisfactory conversation on the subject with Lord Palmerston and that he thought Lord Clarendon would certainly keep matters straight in that direction, offering at the same time to go and see Lord Palmerston and obtain assurances from him of a satisfactory nature.

At 5 Lord Palmerston returned; all had been settled. He showed us a very friendly and satisfactory letter from Mr. Gladstone on the subject. Lord Aberdeen had been with Lord Palmerston and had said that if he could state to his friends that Lord A. had confidence in Lord Palmerston's views, they would join him. On this it seems that Lord P. said that, if negotiations were entered into, he would certainly not insist on the demolition of Sebastopol as a *sine qua non*, the reduction of the fleet being the chief object. Moreover, that we could not decide about Sebastopol before we had got it, and that the terms of peace must to a great extent depend upon the circumstances of the war. This Lord Aberdeen had communicated to his friends and so had placed themselves entirely in his hands and he wrote back to Lord Palmerston that he might now consider everything as satisfactorily settled.

This was an immense relief. We had some desultory conversation as to how the offices were to be disposed of. Lord Panmure would go to the War Office, or be Secretary for War, the offices of Secretary for and at War being ultimately consolidated;— Lord Granville (Lord President)—Mr. S. Herbert (Home Office) and Lord Canning possibly to come into the Cabinet. The Court appointments will all remain. We remonstrated against Mr. Layard's appointment as Under-Secretary for War, on account of his ill-conditioned abuse of Lord Raglan and Admiral Dundas,— though not against his employment. Lord Palmerston was not averse to reconsidering this. Some conversation of a general nature ensued, after which Lord Palmerston kissed hands, and at last the difficult business has been brought to a close. That so good a government has been able to be formed is entirely owing to my dear kind, excellent friend, Lord Aberdeen, but to change him for Lord Palmerston is somewhat of a trial. The latter certainly does owe us many amends for all he has done, and he is without doubt of a very different character to my dear and worthy friend. Still, as matters now stand, it was decidedly the right and wise course to take, and I think that Lord Palmerston, surrounded as he will be, will be sure to do no mischief.

Certainly we felt greatly comforted and returned to Windsor at half past 7 with very different feelings to those with which we had left it this morning.

CHAPTER VI

Victory in the Crimea

QUEEN VICTORIA AND THE PRINCE REGARDED THE COUNTRY'S NEW
first minister with distinct foreboding and they were determined
to hem him round with people they could influence. Lord Aberdeen was their chief hope, who, although out of office, should be
able to act in their interests through his Peelite colleagues who
had remained in the Cabinet—the Duke of Argyll as Lord Privy
Seal, Mr. Sidney Herbert at the Colonial Office, Sir James
Graham at the Admiralty and Mr. Gladstone at the Exchequer.
There was also the pliable Lord Granville, Lord President of the
Council and heir-apparent to the aged Lansdowne as Leader of
the House of Lords. The Queen kept sharp watch on minor
appointments. When Palmerston suggested moving Frederick
Peel, second son of the greatly lamented Sir Robert, as Under-
Secretary from the Colonial Office to the War Department, the
Queen lost no time in suggesting further nominees of her own:

> . . . She thinks Mr. Fred. Peel a very good selection for Under-
> Secretary for War. Should Mr. Peel's place have been filled by a
> peer, in order to have the Colonial Department represented in the
> House of Lords, the Queen wishes to suggest the name of Lord
> Carnarvon for Lord Palmerston's consideration, as that of a young
> man, according to general report, of great promise and because the
> Queen feels it of great advantage to the public service to seize any
> opportunity to bring forward rising talent for office. The Queen
> merely wishes to throw this out. If Lord Elgin could be taken into
> the Government (perhaps at the Duchy of Lancaster) the Queen
> feels sure it would add strength to the Government.

The royal pair also bridled when Palmerston sent a respectful
letter to Napoleon III, taking up a previous invitation from the
French Emperor to enter into correspondence on matters of
mutual interest.—'A novel and unconstitutional practice,' the

Prince commented in one of his memoranda; 'this letter gave us great uneasiness.' However, in the main matter in hand, more vigorous prosecution of the Crimean War, Palmerston's new energy gave them more satisfaction. Lord Panmure, the new War Secretary, was to prove an uninspired colleague, but for the time being Palmerston swept him along in a tide of activity. Mr. Roebuck's motion condemning the conduct of military affairs, which had brought down the previous Government, had still to be dealt with and within five days of taking office, Palmerston was outlining a sweeping plan of army reform and parliamentary tactics to the Queen:

> ... Viscount Palmerston begs to report that at the Cabinet to-day, much consideration was given to the manner in which it would be best to meet Mr. Roebuck's motion for naming the members of the committee of enquiry, the appointment of which was affirmed by the division which led to the resignation of the late Cabinet. It is felt that the actual appointment of the committee ought to be resisted, but that considering the overwhelming majority by which the resolution that such a committee should be appointed was carried, some strong reasons must be given to the House to induce them now to take a different course from that which they took on the former occasion. But the only reasons which would lead members to alter their vote would be some proof that the objects for which the enquiry would be instituted may and will be accomplished without it. Those objects are twofold, first a better arrangement of the military department at home; secondly a better arrangement and organisation of the departments connected with the service of the army in the Black Sea.
>
> With a view to this it was determined that Lord Panmure should prepare for consideration a memorandum containing a scheme for breaking up the Ordnance Office as a separate department, transferring to the commander of the forces the discipline and patronage of the Artillery and Engineers, and placing at the head of those corps an adjutant general of Artillery, to be in the same relation as the adjutant-general of the army to the commander of the forces; and placing the civil departments of the Ordnance under the direction and control of the Secretary of State for the War Department. It is conceived that if your Majesty's ministers should be able to state in Parliament that such

an arrangement is intended, such an announcement would be satisfactory to the House of Commons, seeing that it would also be stated that the office of Secretary at War has not been filled up, pending the consideration as to whether and how that office might be consolidated with that of Secretary of State for the War Department; that the management of the Commissariat Department has been transferred from the Treasury to the War Department; and that the Board of Admiralty are going to establish a separate and distinct board under their orders for arranging and managing the service of transport by sea; which service has hitherto been not very well directed by the department employed in victualling the navy, a department which had too much business of its own to do to be able properly to attend to the transport service which has now, in consequence of the war, grown into such dimensions that the expense of hiring transports for the conveyance of troops and stores will, in the year beginning in April next, amount to five millions sterling. It is conceived that these arrangements made and to be made at home ought to satisfy the desire of Parliament.

With regard to the army abroad, it must be obvious to anyone who has attended to the course of events that a large part of the sufferings and sickness of the army in the Crimea has arisen from causes which might have been prevented by better arrangements and greater activity and care on the part of the heads of the staff, and the opinion of the Cabinet seems to be that it is necessary to change the Adjutant and Quartermaster-General in the Crimea, and that it would be desirable to send out an active and intelligent officer to act as Chief of the Staff, to be intermediate between Lord Raglan [the Commander-in-Chief] and his Adjutant and Quartermaster-General, and to relieve him from many of those details which require an attention and direction which he has failed to give them.

. . . In the meantime, however, it has been determined that Lord Panmure shall send out from time to time to the Crimea some intelligent officer who shall communicate with Lord Raglan, inspect and survey the whole state of things and come back a living despatch of information to your Majesty's Government.

It has also been determined that Lord Panmure shall, either through the Admiralty or by arrangements of his own, establish a certain number of hospital ships capable of conveying five hundred sick in each, and that one of these ships shall every ten days leave Balaclava and Scutari bringing home its cargo of sick and wounded and that such ship shall immediately return to Scutari or Balaclava, loaded with hospital stores or other things required for the use of the hospitals and the army . . .

It is hoped that these arrangements may satisfy the Houses of Parliament and the public that those remedies which a committee of the House of Commons might recommend after many weeks, if not months, of enquiry will at once be applied by the action of the executive government . . .

All this pleased the Queen well enough:

. . . The determination which the Cabinet seems to have come to, with respect to Mr. Roebuck's motion appears to the Queen very judicious, as likewise the outline of the changes in the civil department of the army contained in his letter. The Queen expects, however, a more detailed exposition of the way in which the Ordnance, for instance, is to be remodelled before giving her final sanction to it; it will not be unattended with great difficulties. The decisions come to, with a view to relieve the difficulties of the army in the Crimea, appear to the Queen to be great improvements . . .

The general feeling in the House of Commons was that Mr. Roebuck's demand for a committee of enquiry could not be resisted without the defeat of the Government. Palmerston's plan was therefore to permit the enquiry, but to endeavour to limit its terms of reference. His Peelite colleagues revolted. Any committee of enquiry implied a censure on their former colleague, Newcastle, and they prepared to resign, thus removing within a fortnight of their appointment the brakes the Queen had devised for the Palmerston carriage. The Prime Minister was by no means sure that he would get out of the scrape, and wrote to the Queen:

. . . Viscount Palmerston begs to state that a Cabinet was held at half past 2, which lasted till the time when the House of Commons met. At this Cabinet Viscount Palmerston urged the necessity of coming to a decision as to the course to be pursued about the naming of Mr. Roebuck's committee. He represented that the country is unanimous and impatient for enquiry, that the House of Commons is determined to have its committee, that resistance is impossible, that defeat would be a great evil because it could not at present be followed by either of the usual consequences of defeat, dissolution or resignation.—That it being unavoidable to accept a committee, the only course was to get one composed of respectable and fitting members and not to attempt to fetter them by proposing restrictions which the House would in all probability reject . . . The majority of the Cabinet concurred in this view, but Mr. Gladstone and Sir James Graham felt difficulties which they could not at the moment get over and after much discussion, which lasted until it became necessary to go down to the House of Commons, the Cabinet agreed to meet again tomorrow at 12 . . . The objection of Mr. Gladstone and Sir James Graham seemed to turn upon an opinion that the Government, as at present constituted and by reason of its Peelite elements, does not possess the confidence of the House of Commons nor the hearty support of the Liberal Party; that the appointment of the committee would be a repetition of a vote of censure; that the committee would be dangerous both in its action and as a precedent and that it would be better that this Government should retire and that a Derbyite Government should be formed.

The answers to these objections were that the discontent of some of the Liberal Party is merely the ebullition of disappointment of some few men, who have not got appointments and will soon pass away. That the House of Commons did certainly agree to Mr. Roebuck's first resolution as a veto [sic ?vote] of no confidence in the then existing Government, but that the country has taken up the question in a different sense, and is now sincerely and honestly meaning enquiry and nothing but enquiry, and that the members of the House of Commons, even those who are most friendly to the Government, are driven on by their constituents to insist upon having the committee. That if upon the resignation of the late Government your Majesty had at once and immediately replaced it by the present one, it might have been said that it was the same Government that was reappearing, with some slight personal differences, and that the former vote of no confidence was still weighing on their heads; but that your Majesty had followed the true constitutional course, and that two heads of two great parties had successively been commanded to form an administration, and had successively failed, and that consequently the present Government presents itself under entirely different circumstances and is entitled to assume that it has the support of Parliament till the contrary is specifically affirmed . . . It was further observed that if the present Government were to resign and your Majesty were to command Lord Derby to form a government, he would be obliged to apply to your Majesty for a dissolution, that at a general election he would get a majority by a cry of Enquiry, and that the result would be an administration composed in part of incapable men, supported by a devoted majority in the House of Commons, a result very unfortunate for the country.

Viscount Palmerston hopes that Mr. Gladstone and Sir James Graham will, on reflection, concur with the rest of their colleagues, but if they do not, Viscount Palmerston will deem it his duty to submit to your Majesty the names of successors to their offices, and he proposes at all events to state in the House of Commons tomorrow afternoon the course which he is prepared to pursue on Thursday. He also intends to call a meeting of the Liberal Party on Thursday morning and to claim their support for the Government . . .

Well might the Queen reply:

The Queen thanks Lord Palmerston for his long letter received this morning in which he gives her an account of the proceedings of the Cabinet. She feels very anxious at the state of affairs. She entirely concurs in the arguments used by Lord Palmerston. Should the Peelites insist on resigning, which the Queen anxiously hopes may be avoided, she gives him full power to reconstruct the Government.

The recalcitrant Cabinet members were not to be persuaded and duly resigned. Their action shattered the Peelites as a parliamentary group, as some of their junior colleagues remained. Palmerston was thrown back for replacements on the Whigs and Radicals. In a political master-stroke, Palmerston wrote to Lord John Russell, who was expiating his desertion by acting as British delegate at preliminary truce discussions, being held under Austrian auspices in Vienna, and offered him the post of Colonial Secretary when he returned. Lord John, who still retained a devoted following among the Whig back benchers, soon accepted. —The ranks were closed, but the Queen shuddered at the thought of the renewal of this old alliance:

The Queen . . . does not expect much from the appeal to Lord John Russell which she almost regrets, as promptitude in filling up vacancies is always considered a sign of strength in a Cabinet and long delays give room to much personal intrigue and afterwards to disappointment . . .

Sir George Lewis became Chancellor of the Exchequer, Sir Charles Wood went to the Admiralty from the India Board, and was succeeded by Mr. Vernon Smith. But when Palmerston proposed to move Frederick Peel again, from the War Office to the Board of Trade, replacing him with his elder brother, the Queen objected:

. . . To have an entirely new hand, hitherto untried in any official situation (and formerly rather flighty) in a totally new office, and this the one of the greatest importance at this moment and of the greatest delicacy, when other departments are to be brought into subjection to it, does not appear to the Queen a safe arrangement. Mr. F. Peel has just begun to get acquainted with his office and is known for industry and steadiness and has succeeded well in his answers in the House of Commons. Sir R. Peel would have to begin all over again and an incautious answer to any of the thousand questions addressed with reference to the army, may cause serious embarrassment and further expose to successful attacks the already much threatened maintenance of proper authority of the Crown over the army. The Queen wishes this letter also to be shown to Lord Panmure.

However, the Queen had to give in. She and the Prince tended to regard the army almost as much a private province as the Foreign Office, but when the new committee of enquiry decided to examine N.C.O.s and privates, her protest received very little satisfaction:

. . . She would wish Lord Palmerston to consider whether this is not interfering very seriously with the discipline of the army, for it is in fact asking them to give evidence about their officers? Should Lord Palmerston agree in this, the Queen would further wish him to consider whether he may be able to prevent it, as it may cause very serious mischief . . .

Viscount Palmerston presents his humble duty to your Majesty and with reference to your Majesty's communication of yesterday, he begs to submit that it would not be possible to interfere with the discretionary exercise of the power of a committee in the House of Commons to send for and to examine any witnesses whom such committee may consider capable of giving information which would be useful for the enquiry which such committee may be making; in the case, however, to which your Majesty adverts, the evidence of the non-commissioned officer seemed to be given more as to the bad quality of the tools supplied by the Ordnance, and as to other matters affecting the physical condition of the men, than to any matters affecting the conduct of the affairs of the army . . .

At the beginning of March, Czar Nicholas of Russia died. With his successor thought to be more pacifically minded, France and Britain redoubled their efforts to bring the war to a successful conclusion. Palmerston reported to the Queen on the Cabinet's plan for the year's campaign:

. . . It seemed to be impossible to do more in the Baltic than blockade the Russian ports and fleet, for which purpose the 20 sail-of-the-line which your Majesty will send, and the five which the Emperor of the French will add to them, appear to be sufficient; but not more than sufficient, seeing that the Russians have 27 sail-of-the-line in the Baltic, and that accidents might happen in cruising to disable for a time some ships of the Allied fleets.

The Russian fleet is all concentrated at Cronstadt; there would consequently be no use in attacking Reval or Sweabourg, which are both strongly fortified. A successful attack would only knock down some stone walls which, as the bases could not be occupied or kept, would soon be rebuilt, and the attacking squadron would necessarily sustain much damage. An unsuccessful attack would of course be a disaster. Neither your Majesty nor the Emperor Napoleon could well spare or transport to the Baltic troops enough to accomplish any important operation.

It seems therefore to be good policy that England and France should direct all their efforts to the Crimea, where the real battle is to be fought and that, till success is obtained there, it would be unwise to weaken the exertions in that quarter by attempting anything of importance elsewhere. This reasoning of course does not exclude operations in the Sea of Azoff, or along the coast of Circassia if favourable opportunity should present itself . . .

The Queen scrutinised every suggestion in detail:

> . . . With regard to the expedition to the Baltic, the Queen concurs in believing it probable that we shall have to confine ourselves to a blockade, but this should be with the certainty of its being done effectively and free from any danger to the squadron from a sudden start of the Russian fleet; 20 sail-of-the-line, to which add five French ditto, would be a sufficient force if supported by the necessary complement of frigates, corvettes and gunboats. Alone they would be useless, from their draught of water, and if 20 ships only are meant (not merely sail-of-the-line) the force would seem wholly inadequate. The Queen would therefore wish, before giving her sanction to the plan of campaign, to have a complete list submitted to her of what it is intended should constitute the Baltic fleet.
>
> We ought likewise not to leave ourselves destitute of any reserve at home which the uncertain contingencies of another year's war may call upon at any moment . . .

Nevertheless, the Queen warmed to Palmerston's determined activity, and although she remained suspicious of his capacity to launch new political initiatives which she would find difficult to control, an unwonted note of approval and unanimity began to creep into their correspondence. They were at one on the proposal of Napoleon III to garner some personal glory by taking over himself the military command in the Crimea:

> Viscount Palmerston . . . has received to-day an important letter from the Emperor of the French, which he will submit to your Majesty tomorrow, in which the Emperor announces his intention of going to the Crimea for the purpose of driving the Russians from Simferopol, and then falling back to take Sebastopol. He proposes to accomplish the first operation with an army of 77,000 men, French and Sardinians, leaving 66,000 English, French and Turks to maintain the siege; the condition is that your Majesty's Government should find the means of transporting to the Crimea 10,000 French, 15,000 Sardinians and 3,000 horses. But whether the military operation be deemed practicable and

expedient or not, the Emperor's personal visit to the Crimea seems wholly unnecessary for its accomplishment, and might be attended with most lamentable consequences . .

. . . The Queen learns with much regret the proposition of the Emperor of the French. She will not express her opinion on it further now, as she will speak to Lord Palmerston on the subject when she sees him before or after the Council to-day, but she cannot but express her great doubts as to the conditions proposed by the Emperor . . .

In April, Palmerston summarised the objectives of the new campaign as being:

. . . the complete blockade of the Russian fleet and ports in the Baltic, with the possibility of some damage to Cronstadt and its fleet by bombardment; the capture of Sebastopol and the entire destruction of the Russian Black Sea fleet, and the expulsion of the Russians from Georgia and from all their posts on the coast of Circassia. These would be advantages of great military and political importance, and would put the Allies in a good position to begin the negotiations, which would of course be renewed when the next winter should have suspended active operations of war . . .

The French Emperor then paid a state visit to England, and Palmerston sought the Queen's assistance in keeping his military ardour within bounds:

. . . Viscount Palmerston would beg to submit for your Majesty's consideration that at some moment during the stay of the Emperor of the French it would be important that a consultation should be held with him as to the military and naval operations to be undertaken by the military and naval forces of your Majesty and of the Emperor in the approaching campaign, and it might be advantageous that Lord Hardinge should be present on that occasion, whenever it may be.

. . . The Queen had, as well as Lord Palmerston, thought of the importance of setting a morning aside for the consideration of our plans of campaign, and has had Lord Panmure, Lord Hardinge and Sir C. Wood invited for Tuesday evening, in order that they might be ready on Wednesday morning to attend the Emperor. As the Queen herself will not be able to join in the discussion, she wishes that the Prince should represent her on that occasion . . .

Combined pressure was successful and by April 26, the Prime Minister could write:

> . . . Viscount Palmerston congratulates your Majesty upon the decision of the Emperor of the French to give up his intended journey to the Crimea, which could only have led to embarrassments of many kinds.

During this whole period, curious and desultory talks had been going on under Austrian aegis in Vienna to discover possible terms of peace. The main point under discussion was the strength of the fleet Russia would be permitted to retain in the Black Sea. In an attempt to curry favour with both sides, Austria had proposed an involved formula which would have left Russia with very much the same power that the western allies had nominally entered the war to destroy. Drouyn de L'Huys, the French Foreign Minister, seemed disposed to accept. His Government felt itself weakened by the inconclusive stalemate in the Crimea. Lord John Russell, the British plenipotentiary, was also being unnecessarily accommodating. Only Palmerston stood firm:

> Viscount Palmerston presents his humble duty to your Majesty and begs to state that the Cabinet determined after full consideration, that the proposal recently made by Austria cannot be accepted, and that the best course to be pursued is to stand upon the plan of arrangement last proposed by your Majesty's Government and the Government of France, as settled when Mr. Drouyn de L'Huys was in London. It was felt that the terms now proposed by Austria had not the recommendation of being likely to be accepted by Russia, while, on the other hand, Austria distinctly says that she will not go to war if those terms are refused by Russia, and therefore the British and French Governments, by authorising Austria to propose them on their behalf to Russia, would only be progressively lowering their demands without obtaining any advantage by so doing . . .

During his long years as Prime Minister, Palmerston sat down every night to write in his own hand an account for the Queen of that day's sitting in the House of Commons, a feat of concentration for a weary man in his seventies, which can only excite admiration for his invariable lucidity and frequent humour. He would often incorporate other official business in these nightly reports, and this particular letter went on:

> . . . The first motion that came on in the House of Commons was a resolution proposed by Mr. Wise, recently elected and sitting on the ministerial side though below the gangway, that the recommendations of the Official Salaries Committee of 1850 respecting the Diplomatic Service should be carried fully into effect. The recommendations of that committee, which have not been carried into effect, being the reduction of all diplomatic salaries which are more than £5,000 a year, the abolition of all the missions at the smaller German Courts, leaving only a Minister at Frankfurt, and the consolidation of some of the Italian missions.
>
> It had been expected that Mr. Wise's motion would not come on and, when it did come on, he said that he should not press it to a division; many members of the Government and many supporters of the Government were therefore away.
>
> A member who has once made a motion cannot withdraw it if any one member objects to his doing so—When Mr. Wise asked leave to withdraw his motion, Mr. Baillie, the Member for Inverness, objected; a division was called for and Mr. Wise's resolution was carried by 112 to 57, after a short debate in which Viscount Palmerston stated reasons which he had hoped would have induced the House to negative the resolution. It is impossible however to give effect to such a resolution, but it will be necessary to consider in what manner it should be dealt with . . .

The Queen, in her reply, referred approvingly to Palmerston's attitude on both points:

> The Queen acknowledges Lord Palmerston's letter received yesterday. She is rejoiced to hear of the decision of the Cabinet as she feels certain that a straightforward firm course is the only one for this country to pursue.
>
> The vote in the House of Commons is very disagreeable, but must certainly not be acted upon. If ever we required agents at

all the German Courts it is now, to counteract the all powerful and baneful influence of Russia. Indeed it is to our want of skilful and active agents that our loss of all influence at the foreign Courts, particularly in Germany, is mainly attributable.

The minor point was soon settled and a fortnight later Palmerston was able to report general support for his firm attitude on the Vienna talks:

> Viscount Palmerston presents his humble duty to your Majesty and begs to state that the debate on the negotiations has ended in the most satisfactory manner. Mr. Lowe and Dr. Phillimore and Sir William Heathcote all either withdrew their amendments or allowed them to be negatived and the House then voted unanimously the latter part of Mr. Disraeli's resolution with Sir Francis Baring's beginning, which, put together, constituted a resolution which, after expressing regret that the conferences did not lead to a termination of hostilities, assures your Majesty of the support of the House for the vigorous prosecution of the war . . .

The Queen waxed positively enthusiastic in reply:

> . . . The very satisfactory termination of the debate and the brilliant and important success of the French before Sebastopol have given us the greatest pleasure and everything promises success to the right and just cause. Lord Palmerston's speech seems to have been admirable.

However, the Queen bristled immediately there was the slightest sign of any infraction of her prerogatives. Lord Dalhousie had resigned as Governor-General of India and Mr. Vernon Smith, President of the Board of Control, appointed a successor without, as the Queen thought, proper reference to her:

> . . . The Queen was much surprised to receive last night from Mr. Vernon Smith the announcement that Lord Canning was to be appointed Governor-General of India. Though the Queen has no objection to make to the choice, she is much displeased at no opportunity having been given to her of considering with her ministers this most important appointment before it had been agreed upon with the Court of Directors. The Queen has felt it her duty to write to Mr. V. Smith to point out to him the

serious inconvenience to which such a way of proceeding may lead, supposing the Queen to disapprove of the person who was to be appointed. In this, as in all appointments, the Queen's pleasure ought to be taken before any communication takes place, either with the person himself or with the public body with which he is is to be connected. The Queen, however, will readily sanction the appointment of Lord Canning, of whom she has a high opinion.

The apparent oversight was explained by reference to the statutory powers of the Directors of the East India Company to nominate a Governor-General. The Queen was sufficiently mollified to give Palmerston her support when another minister, Lord Panmure, exceeded his powers:

... Viscount Palmerston regrets to have to mention to your Majesty a matter which has caused him much embarrassment. He and the rest of his colleagues not in the House of Peers were utterly astonished at reading this morning the announcement made by Lord Panmure in the House of Lords yesterday, that it was his intention to double the pay of the army in the Crimea. It is a standing rule of all the administrative departments that no addition can be made to any establishment of office and that no new regulation involving increased expense can be promulgated without the previous sanction of the Treasury; and it is also a standing rule that no head of a department should take any important step without first consulting the Cabinet, or, at all events, without the concurrence of the head of the Government. But here is Lord Panmure announcing publicly an intended measure which would add little less than a million a year to the public expenditure, without having said one syllable on the subject either to the Cabinet or to the head of the Government. Indeed he came to Viscount Palmerston yesterday morning on his way to the Palace, conversed with Viscount Palmerston for more than a quarter of an hour upon the state of the army in the Crimea, the arrangements to be made as to staff commands, and other military matters, and never uttered one syllable which could lead Viscount Palmerston to imagine that any such plan as that which he announced in the afternoon was in the remotest degree in his contemplation.

The matter is one of the utmost gravity. As an administrative act it is entirely incompatible with the fundamental principles on which the government of this country is carried on, and no man could continue responsible for the conduct of affairs as head of your Majesty's Government if Ministers presiding over departments were to assume such independent powers of action. The administration would become an anarchy, and the affairs of the State would fall into confusion . . .

The Queen has just received Lord Palmerston's letter, and is grieved to see the embarrassment in which the Government has been placed by Lord Panmure's announcement of the increased pay for her troops in the Crimea of which she likewise knows nothing.

When Lord Panmure came to the Palace on Thursday, the Queen spoke to him about the slowness of recruiting, and what could be done to improve it. She then mentioned to him that the Duke of Cambridge had spoken of a plan of giving 'Batta' [a special field allowance in the Indian army] to our troops while serving in the Crimea, which was a notion of Lord Ellenborough's, as one which might be worthy of consideration, as the difficulty of getting men for the army is greatly increased by the large pay given to those corps like the land transport, the navies, etc., while our men receive so much less. Lord Panmure, however, though not altogether rejecting this plan, did not give us any reason to think that it would be considered by the Government, much less that he would make any announcement without first submitting it to her. The Prince, who met him afterwards at the Wellington Barracks to look at some new tents, found him conversing with Lord Hardinge, but heard nothing from him whatever, which could lead him to think the matter was at all settled. Our astonishment therefore at seeing Lord Panmure's announcement in the House of Lords, though the Queen was glad to see that (as she believed it) the Government had adopted a measure which would very rapidly fill our ranks, was very great. This is all that the Queen knows of the subject. She trusts however that this great embarrassment may be satisfactorily arranged.

The Queen entirely concurs with Lord Palmerston in the importance of not losing the unity of action of our Government by allowing its different departments to act for themselves, to ensure which, a strict adherence to what is now slightingly termed 'official routine' is absolutely necessary.

That crisis was solved by a sharp rebuke from Palmerston to the erring Minister, Panmure's apology, and a compromise proposal in the Cabinet to give the men in the Crimea sixpence a day field pay.—Palmerston's tactful handling of his colleague was not the least factor in the gradual consolidation of his position and the survival of a government which owed its tenuous majorities largely to his own personality and the public confidence reposed in him.

One of the great sources of strength of this indefatigable, confident, humorous old man lay in the temperament which enabled him to rise above even the worst crisis. Sheer experience counted for much of this ability to remain unflurried. Before the decade was out he would complete a half century in the House of Commons.

The man who, as a young Secretary at War in the days of Napoleon, had held his own against the Duke of Wellington and the Duke of York, who had defied Europe and, latterly, his own sovereign during more than fifteen years as Foreign Minister and had then been called by public opinion to fill the highest office in the land, could afford an air of authority and superiority. But it was also inherent in his sanguine character. Even during the worst periods of stress he avoided nervous prostration by leading a normal life. He graced his wife's frequent receptions, maintained a formidable appetite for food and drink and could always recuperate his strength in the country pursuits he loved. In the midst of running a major war, he nevertheless found time to let his mind run on lesser subjects:

JUNE 14: . . . Viscount Palmerston has turned his thoughts to those considerations connected with Westminster School to which your Majesty and his Royal Highness the Prince Albert recently directed his attention, and although he is not prepared to submit for your Majesty's consideration any definite arrangement, he would nevertheless beg leave to state his present impressions.

It seems to him that Westminster School, having at present large endowments connected with the education of boys, either the sons of the upper classes, or destined for the liberal professions, and the school having for those purposes beneficial appointments for young students at Oxford and Cambridge, there would seem to be reasons for continuing to apply the instruction given at the school to the same purposes as hitherto.—Moreover, the wealthy classes who would naturally wish to give to their sons the kind of education, in classics, languages and mathematics, now given at a public school, are progressively increasing in number, while on the other hand the supply of such education has not proportionately increased. Eton can educate about 800, but if that number were much increased it is probable that the inconveniences of undue augmentation would be felt. Harrow can accommodate 400, but would not receive a much larger number. Winchester has a comparatively small number and Rugby is not altogether conducted on a footing to place it in the same class as Eton and Harrow. There can be little doubt that if Westminster were made more attractive, there would be ample demand for all the means of liberal education which it could supply; and that it might receive four or five hundred boys without interfering injuriously with Eton or Harrow. But while Westminster remains where it is, such an increase of numbers is impossible. The school was a few years ago reduced to about 60, and even now, with all the advantages of the high qualities of its late headmaster, it has only about 120 boys. To make Westminster what it ought to be and is capable of being, it ought to be removed into the country.—Dr. Liddell [who had just become Dean of Christ Church] has suggested some place in the neighbourhood of Henley-on-Thames, where it might be possible to procure a site, healthy in itself, surrounded by an open country for the exercise of the boys, and near the Thames for rowing and for bathing and swimming.

Such a removal could not be accomplished without an Act of Parliament; but if it was effected, the 12 acres which are now occupied by the school and buildings and houses connected with it, might probably by a different arrangement be converted into the site of a great and striking improvement of the town in connection with Westminster Abbey, the Houses of Parliament, the parks and Palace; and that district which is now a reproach to London might be rendered one of its distinguishing ornaments.

JULY 4: Viscount Palmerston presents his humble duty to your Majesty and begs to state that in consequence of some communications which passed between himself and Sir Benjamin Hall

[President of the Board of Health] as to the present state of the water in the lake in the garden of Buckingham Palace, he directed some enquiries to be made to ascertain what department is charged with the liability to keep that piece of water in good order . . . If the lake should be found to require cleaning out, the process of cleaning would best be performed in the autumn. With regard to the suggestion that the lake should be drained, and be converted into a flower garden, Viscount Palmerston would be glad to know your Majesty's wishes . . .

On this point he found the Queen less co-operative:

The Queen returns these papers to Lord Palmerston. She upon no account wishes the lake in the garden here to be done away with; it is its chief ornament and a source of great amusement to ourselves and the children. All that is required is a constant supply of water all the year round, the cleaning out does little or no good.

In July, Lord John Russell returned to face a parliamentary storm. The Vienna negotiations had broken down, but several members felt he had been not only too pliant but disingenuous in his accounts of the attitude he had adopted. One of Palmerston's parliamentary reports apprised the Queen of this new crisis:

Viscount Palmerston presents his humble duty to your Majesty and begs to state that this evening in the House of Commons has not been an agreeable one . . . Mr. Milner Gibson, according to notice, in a speech of some acrimony, called upon Lord John Russell to explain the degree of assent which he had given to the Austrian proposal which he and M. Drouyn de l'Huys had undertaken to recommend to their Governments; and also to say how that assent was to be reconciled with his remaining in office to carry on the war. Lord John Russell made a clear statement, but stated rather more strongly than necessary that he had thought that the Austrian proposal might have and ought to have put an end to the war and to have led to a safe and honourable peace; and he added that he still retained that opinion, but remained in office from a sense of the public inconvenience which, in the present state of affairs, must ensue from repeated and frequent changes in ministerial arrangements. Mr. Cobden then followed and pretended to be astonished at what he called Lord John's revelations and inveighed against him for having remained in office to carry on a war when he thought that a sufficient peace might have been made . . .

Then followed an account of the dilemma in which these two old Cabinet colleagues found themselves:

> . . . Viscount Palmerston had a long conversation this morning with Lord John Russell, the result of which is that Lord John is ready on the first opportunity, which however is not likely to present itself before the Committee of Supply on Friday, to say that what he said last Friday was misunderstood. That he did not mean to say that he thinks the Austrian proposal could now be accepted, and that he still thinks now that it might have been accepted at the time when it was made. That the whole state of things has changed since the middle of April when that proposal was made. That at that time the honour of the two countries had not been so committed to the capture of Sebastopol, as it has been since, by the assaults, some successful, some unsuccessful, which have been made. That our military position is so much im-proved since that time that we are entitled to demand better terms than we might then have accepted . . . He will say that having found the English and French Governments, each for reasons of their own, unwilling to adopt the Austrian proposal, he had acquiesced in its rejection, and having done so, had con-curred without reserve in the vigorous prosecution of the war. An explanation of this kind, if given, will remove the notion that there is a division in the Cabinet on the question of the war.
>
> Lord John Russell said to Viscount Palmerston that when the offer of the Colonial Office was made to him, he accepted it from a desire to contribute to strengthen the present Government, but that if Viscount Palmerston and his colleagues now thought that his retirement would be advantageous to the Government, he was ready at once to retire. Viscount Palmerston said he fully appre-ciated the handsomeness of that offer, but so far from thinking Lord John's retirement an advantage to the Government, he should consider it as a great blow, and as seriously weakening the Government, and that he hoped and trusted that Lord John would not think of any such step.
>
> There is for the moment a great and general feeling among the supporters of the Government adverse to Lord John and distrustful

of the Cabinet, but it is to be hoped that a few days' reflection and explanations that will be given and the papers that will be laid, will set matters right again.

This was over-optimistic and the advice to Lord John unsound to the point of directly endangering the Government. The House of Commons refused to be assuaged, and Lord John was obliged to resign as the only means of saving the administration from an adverse vote:

> Viscount Palmerston presents his humble duty to your Majesty and begs to state that Lord John Russell made to-day at the meeting of the House a further explanation of his conduct in regard to his negotiation, and a statement of the reasons which led him to resign, and this explanation and statement were well received by the House . . . Viscount Palmerston begs to submit for your Majesty's consideration the arrangements which he thinks would be the best for the interests of the Government and for your Majesty's service in consequence of the retirement of Lord John Russell.
>
> He would propose that Sir William Molesworth should be removed to the Colonial Department; that Sir Benjamin Hall should succeed Sir William Molesworth at the Board of Works, but not in the Cabinet; that Mr. Bouverie should be President of the Board of Health instead of Sir Benjamin Hall, and that Mr. Lowe should succeed Mr. Bouverie as Vice-President of the Board of Trade . . .
>
> There is always an advantage in making a move of promotion in a party when it can be done; it encourages the subordinates and infuses a good spirit among the adherents of a government . . .

The Queen gave Palmerston her full support and approved with unusual warmth of his proposals to reconstruct the Cabinet:

> . . . The Queen thinks the proposed new appointments . . . extremely good, and likely to strengthen the Government, as well as to ensure the efficient discharge of the various offices. The Queen therefore readily authorises Lord Palmerston to communicate with these gentlemen. She wishes Lord John Russell to deliver up the Seals in person, which is the right way of proceeding and which practice she wishes adhered to.

The military situation in the Crimea had improved, with the

repulse by the French at the river Tchernaya of a Russian attempt to relieve Sebastopol. Palmerston's letter to the Queen just before she paid her return state visit to France in August was almost embarrassingly fulsome:

> ... Viscount Palmerston begs to congratulate your Majesty upon being preceded at Paris by the news of a victory in the Crimea, in which the French army bore the chief part, and which will therefore be more peculiarly gratifying to the feelings of the French nation.
>
> Viscount Palmerston is rejoiced that your Majesty should have for your voyage and journey that which is now from your Majesty's good fortune in that, as well as in more important matters, proverbially called 'the Queen's weather'; but indeed, if Viscount Palmerston might be allowed to take the great liberty of saying so, if the possession of all the virtues and highest qualities which adorn human nature, and the ardent prayers and constant wishes of a devoted and worthy nation can draw down the favour and protection of Providence your Majesty and your Majesty's royal family must surely enjoy them ...

Even better news came a month later:

> Viscount Palmerston presents his humble duty to your Majesty and begs to tender to your Majesty his cordial congratulations on the evacuation of the town of Sebastopol by the Russians, and upon the destruction by them of the remainder of the Russian fleet in the harbour of that place. However strongly fortified the Russian position on the northern side of the harbour may be, it is not unreasonable to expect that before the winter sets in they will be obliged to retire also from that position, and that thus the Allied armies will have quiet winter quarters in the Crimea ...

> The Queen has received Lord Palmerston's letter of the 10th [September]. The glorious news of the fall of Sebastopol, which certainly came unexpectedly upon us, gave us the greatest satisfaction. It is a most important event, which will produce great results, both as regards the comfort and relief of our army, as well as on the Continent, where success on our part would long ago have caused a feeling in our favour instead of the bitter enmity which has existed ...

Then, in October, came a splendid exchange about the iniquities of the country's leading newspaper and its editor, Mr. Delane. The Queen's complaint was more than usually peppered with her emphatic underlinings:

> The Queen has been as much disgusted with the late *extraordinary* articles in 'The Times' on the army in the Crimea, the King of Prussia, the late promotions etc. etc., as she understands the Cabinet to have been in London. Lord Panmure even speaks of the desire evinced in different quarters to establish an 'Anti-Times League'. The Queen believes that would but aggravate the evil like any repressive laws, but she would put it to Lord Palmerston whether it is *right* that the editor, the proprietor and the writers of these *execrable* publications *ought to be* the *honoured and constant* guests of the ministers of the Crown? Their introduction into our higher society and political 'reunions' to the extent to which it is now carried, and the *attention* which is publicly shown to them *there* is the most direct *encouragement* they could receive, adding both to their importance and power to do mischief. Their *exclusion* from these circles would, on the other hand, without being a direct attack, mark fitly the *disapproval* of the *acts* and operate as a check on the *reckless* exercise of that anomalous power, the danger of which to the best *interests* of the country is universally admitted.
> Lord Palmerston would perhaps show this letter to his colleagues.

> . . . Viscount Palmerston was as disgusted as your Majesty was at the articles in 'The Times' to which your Majesty adverts, and he has shown to his colleagues in London your Majesty's letter. With regard however to any practical remedy, there is much difficulty in finding any that would be immediately effectual. There is no doubt some inconvenience in the admission of editors and writers of newspapers into general society, but if they happen to be in a position in life which would naturally lead to their being invited, it would not be easy to exclude them merely on account of their connection with a newspaper; and if they were not to be excluded entirely, it is obvious that it would not be advisable to make their admission or exclusion depend upon the character of the last article in the papers with which they may be understood or known to be connected.

With regard moreover to 'The Times', it is further to be considered that there is no one person who writes or is answerable for all the leading articles in that paper. There are many hands employed in writing articles, and those only who are in the confidence of the editors can know who any given article was written by. The person connected with 'The Times' who is the most frequently seen in general society is Mr. Delane, but Viscount Palmerston has been informed within the last two days that Mr. Delane is at present abroad, and could not therefore have been the writer of the articles on which your Majesty so justly animadverts. But though 'The Times' both does and intends to do much mischief, yet that mischief is often very temporary and much limited. That paper often takes a line in hopes of being followed by public opinion, but when it finds that public opinion goes another way, it changes its course and follows public opinion.

What the managers aim at above all is to get a great circulation for their paper, and that is not to be obtained by running long against the feelings and opinions of the mass of the nation. Thus it was that 'The Times', having begun by taking the part of Russia, has now become one of the most violent antagonists of Russia; and there have been many other instances of similar changes of language, as to men and things. Viscount Palmerston has had as much reason as most persons to complain of 'The Times', for from the time when he first went to the Foreign Office, for some reason or other which he never could discover, 'The Times' has been animated by undeviating hostility, personal and political, towards him, and he has never known from whom or from whence that hostility proceeded.—Within the last fortnight 'The Times' has in some degree changed its tone, with apologies for doing so, merely because the capture of Sebastopol has turned public opinion strongly in favour of the existing government; but before long the paper will probably revert more or less to its former course . . .

Christmas found the Court and the Palmerstons on distinctly easy terms:

. . . The Queen and Prince wish Lord and Lady Palmerston many happy returns of the Season.

Viscount Palmerston presents his humble duty to your Majesty and begs to tender the best thanks of Lady Palmerston and himself for your Majesty's gracious communication of the day before yesterday and they write in the fervent hope that the approaching year may bring with it to your Majesty and to his Royal Highness the Prince as much prosperity and happiness as have attended those which have gone before it, and that the British may for many and many years to come continue to enjoy the good fortune of seeing in your Majesty and in his Royal Highness the objects of their devoted attachment and a security for their permanent welfare.

With the western allies now holding a much stronger position in the Crimea, Austria plucked up sufficient courage to emerge from her timid neutrality and send an ultimatum to Russia to make certain concessions, including the surrender of a portion of Bessarabia, as a preliminary to peace. The conference was to be convened in Paris and the Queen struck a note of warning to Palmerston as the new year opened:

JANUARY 26: The Queen thinks it of the utmost importance that while the consideration of the measures respecting the possible and probable peace are engrossing the attention of the Government,— the Council of War, and the Emperor's proposal in consequence of its deliberations, should not be neglected, but a decision come to respecting it. We may have to refer to it very speedily and not a moment should therefore be lost in considering it. The best way would be for Lord Palmerston to see Lord Hardinge and all the officers who were members of that Council and to receive from them an oral report of what has passed, according to which the Government could come to some decision which they could sub-mit to the Queen. This ought to be done before the meeting of Parliament adds to the multitude of affairs, which already press upon the Government.

JANUARY 27: The Queen thanks Lord Palmerston for his letter received last night. The possibility of agreeing with the French Government,—and thus starting with them is a great object attained, whatever may be our own feelings as to the course itself. The Queen is equally rejoiced with Lord Palmerston at our having made the first offer of having the negotiations at Paris . . .

Lord Clarendon, the Foreign Secretary, went to Paris to represent Britain. The Russian plenipotentiary, Count Orloff, proved a wily negotiator, and was soon demanding an alteration in Russia's favour to the Bessarabian frontier as a condition of surrendering the fortress of Kars to the Turks. There was a very mild echo of an old complaint in the Queen's letter to Palmerston on the subject, but in the main she gave him unequivocal support:

> The Queen has received the telegram sent by Lord Clarendon last night and those sent in answer. The Queen quite feels the importance of sending these replies with as little delay as possible, but she hopes that, when they contain directions as to the line to be taken in conference on the points upon which peace and war will depend, he will give her an opportunity of seeing them before they are sent. The Queen will see Lord Palmerston before the Council to-day and therefore will say nothing upon the subject itself, except that she concurs with him that the want of exhibiting firmness from the beginning would very likely weaken our position throughout the conference; and the reparation clause having been the work of Austria, if we are to risk the peace on its account, we ought clearly to receive an engagement in return from Austria that she will make war for it.

> . . . With regard to the question about the Bessarabian cession, Viscount Palmerston would beg to observe that unless the Russian Government had accepted the conditions of the Austrian ultimatum purely and simply and without any reservation, the present conferences at Paris would not have been held, and that to admit now that any of the matters settled by the ultimatum should be reopened for discussion and negotiation would be to unsettle all that has been settled, and to throw great discredit upon your Majesty's Government.—Moreover, as a matter of policy it would be very unadvisable . . .

> It is very easy to argue in a case of this kind that each separate condition, taking the conditions one by one, is not of sufficient importance to justify a continuance of the war for that particular condition; but such a mode of arguing would lead step by step to an abandonment of every condition essential to future security. The conditions demanded must be taken as a whole, it is only as a whole that they can be judged of, and it is only as a whole that they can be recommended to the acceptance of the nation.

The Queen then suggested:

> ... Would it not answer to take this line: to say to Russia, 'you have accepted the ultimatum *pur et simple* and have now again recognised its stipulations as preliminaries of peace. You will therefore first of all have to execute them; you may then come to the question of Kars and say you mean to keep it, then you will see that Europe, bound to maintain the integrity of Turkey, will be obliged to go on with the war, and it will be for you to consider whether you mean to go on fighting for Kars; but at present this is not in question, as you are only called upon to fulfil the engagements to which you have solemnly pledged yourself?' . . .

Palmerston remained unruffled:

> ... Notwithstanding all apparent difficulties and the bluster of the Russian plenipotentiaries, Viscount Palmerston is not without hope and expectation that by steady firmness all that the allies have asked may finally be obtained . . .

The French were not proving as firm as might be wished and the Queen was quick to realise that some concession might be necessary:

> ... Lord Clarendon gives it as his opinion that, for the sake of the alliance, we ought to be prepared ultimately to give up the reparation frontier. This is a very serious and important question, the answer to which ought to be very fully considered. It may be that the Russians will finally give way before the united attitude of the allies,—but should they not, the Queen thinks that Lord Clarendon should not be left without the power to do what may appear to him the best, on a full appreciation of the peculiar circumstances of which he alone will be able to judge at the time . . .

Palmerston was inclined to agree, but still hoped that a united front would prevail:

> ... If it should turn out that the British plenipotentiaries should be left alone in the conference, all the others siding with Russia, that would be a very awkward state of things and would require very serious consideration. But that does not at present appear to be likely, and it is much more probable that the Russians will give way.

They will not perhaps do so at once, they will suspend the conference and say that they must refer to Petersburg and in the meantime will try the effect of intrigue, cajolery and menace; but if the allies are firm, being as they are clearly and indisputably in the right . . . Russia . . . will and must give way. Count Orloff's manner and language vary according to times, places and persons, and no particular importance can be attached to what he says at any particular moment. He is, like most of the Russians, a very accomplished actor . . .

Nevertheless, Napoleon III began to waver and Palmerston had to be checked by the Queen when he tried to inject a little backbone:

The Queen has received the enclosed draft and whilst admitting the propriety of making the Emperor of the French aware of the feelings of this country—thinks it important that we should not commit ourselves too strongly, if it should end by our having to give way. The expression in the fourth page 'that we could never be a consenting party' to what the Emperor proposes, appears to the Queen therefore too strong. The Queen hopes also that the position of Lord Clarendon will be borne in mind, who has immense difficulties to consider, and if the opinion of the Government is placed on record in too positive a form he may be placed in a very awkward situation as regards this country, if upon him alone the responsibility for disregarding this opinion were made to rest.

Lord Palmerston will probably find no difficulty in guarding against this danger in the draft.

Palmerston acquiesced:

Viscount Palmerston presents his humble duty to your Majesty and has altered 'willing and consenting party' into 'willingly consenting party', which only implies that the British Government would consider but unwillingly.

But he could not resist adding this rider in a second note later the same day:

Viscount Palmerston presents his humble duty to your Majesty and is glad to find that as far as the proceedings of the conference are concerned the progress of the negotiation, though not all that could be wished, is however not unsatisfactory. If the Emperor of the French would but have held firm, all the reasonable demands of the allies would beyond doubt have been carried . . .

In fact, both of them were now resigned to the inevitable:

With reference to Lord Clarendon's letter, the Queen must say that she, though very reluctantly, shares his opinion that we have no choice now but to accept the peace, even if it is not all we could desire and though another campaign might have got us better terms, she feels certain that the bad accounts of the French army in the Crimea, which appears to suffer now all the misery which ours suffered last year at the worst time of the siege, will more than ever indispose the Emperor from wishing a renewal of hostilities. It is affirmed that the French have beyond 20,000 men in hospital! . . .

Viscount Palmerston presents his humble duty to your Majesty and in transmitting the accompanying despatches and private letter from Lord Clarendon would beg to submit that Lord Clarendon seems to have exercised a sound discretion in consenting to the alteration proposed by the Emperor in the Bessarabian boundary line.

The Russians went on niggling with minor demands about the size of ships their reduced fleet would be allowed to maintain in the Black Sea, but by the end of March, two years after the war had started, the terms of peace were agreed and the treaty signed. In offering her congratulations, the Queen nevertheless expressed some forebodings for the future:

. . . She rejoices with Lord Palmerston at having succeeded in obtaining terms, which though they are not all what we could wish or what we might have obtained if France had behaved as she ought, still are very important ones. What reconciles the Queen to the peace, which is not tasteful to her feelings—is the conviction that France would not have gone on with us, and that thus hampered, we could have obtained none of those successes which we had so much cause to hope for. The Queen is convinced that war would no longer have been carried on by France, and therefore we must be glad that we have obtained such a peace.

But let us not for a moment rely on many years of peace, inasmuch as our army and our defences are concerned. Let them be kept up in so organised and efficient a state that the next war finds us in a very different state to what we were in two years ago. Lord Palmerston will find the Queen very determined in reminding him and the whole Government of the paramount necessity of keeping up our naval and military establishments. She hopes he will lose no opportunity of impressing this necessity on the House of Commons. Only four years ago, the whole country was wild with the invasion fever; the Emperor may die and the Regent for his child, or any other successor, may not be a friend to this country.—Where should we then be if we allowed our army and our other establishments to be let down to what they were before the war? . . .

For some months, relations between Britain and America had been severely strained by side-effects of the Crimean War. The United States was endeavouring to apply the Monroe Doctrine to a British attempt to annex some islands north of Honduras, but the chief bone of contention concerned the distinctly dubious activities of the British Minister in Washington in endeavouring to recruit American nationals for the British armies. Mr. Buchanan, the American envoy in London, and subsequently President of his country, had made forceful protests on both counts.

However, Palmerston bore him no ill-will:

. . . Viscount Palmerston begs to state that he has heard that Mr. Buchanan, the American Minister, has observed to some of his friends that if, on his return to the United States, the President should ask him any question about Windsor Castle, he should be obliged to say that he never saw it, as he never happened to be honoured by an invitation from your Majesty to Windsor. Mr. Buchanan has certainly no particular claim as regards himself to any marked attention from your Majesty, for though his individual bearing has been always courteous to all and friendly towards this country, his foolish objection to Court dress, and the discussion he has raised about Central America expose him to just observations. Nevertheless, he is a man of much influence in his own country, of considerable personal vanity (like most Democrats), not a little artful and very likely when at home to represent any slight which he may think to have been offered to him, as indicating unfriendly feelings towards his country. In the present state of the relations between the two Governments anything of this kind would perhaps better be avoided and it is therefore for your Majesty to consider whether it might be worth while notwithstanding that Mr. Buchanan has had his formal audience of leave, that he should be invited to dine and sleep at Windsor either tomorrow or Tuesday and that he should on the following morning before returning to town be shown over the Castle. He has fixed his departure for Paris for Tuesday, but if your Majesty should determine to invite him, and should prefer doing so for Tuesday rather than for tomorrow, he would probably have no difficulty in putting off his journey till Wednesday.

The Queen was not agreeable:

. . . With respect to Mr. Buchanan, as he has taken leave of the Queen, as she knew for some time that he was going away and had therefore invited him to dinner a short while ago, and as the Queen is going down to Windsor to spend the Passion Week in perfect quiet and to devote that time to the Princess Royal's Confirmation, inviting Mr. Buchanan there, when no one else is asked, would be so evidently done for the purpose of stopping his mantle that the Queen thinks it would do more harm than good.

With regard to his never having seen Windsor, that is his own fault, and as to his not having been invited there, many of the foreign Ministers have never been there, as it is not our habit to invite the Corps Diplomatique down there, except for some special reason and with a few exceptions only. The Queen believes that neither of Mr. Buchanan's immediate predecessors have been invited to Windsor.

However, Queen and Minister were agreed on a distinctly less propitiatory gesture:

. . . Viscount Palmerston begs to state that while questions of great importance in their possible results though of apparently small importance in themselves, are pending between the Government

Queen Victoria, photographed at Osborne by Mayall on July 28, 1855, in her thirty-seventh year.

of the United States and that of your Majesty, it seems inexpedient to leave your Majesty's North American provinces with the very small number of regular troops now in them, and Viscount Palmerston would beg to recommend that a force not much short of 5,000 infantry should be sent direct from the Crimea to your Majesty's North American provinces to be ready to defend them against any attack, authorised or unauthorised, which may be made upon them from the United States . . .

. . . The Queen readily gives her consent to a division of her troops being sent direct from the Crimea to her North American provinces, but she wishes no arrangement to be made without its being first submitted to her. The Queen wishes an entire division to go—with its proper complement of Artillery and Transport, so that it should be ready to take the field if it should be required, otherwise if a few regiments of infantry without any organisation is sent out piecemeal—and they should take the field—they would inevitably miserably perish, as so many did from the same causes in the Crimea during the first winter.

The Queen will write to Lord Panmure upon the subject . . . The Queen thinks it would do good, if even before she writes to Lord Panmure, Lord Palmerston were to speak to him on the subject and also to consider whether this would not be an excellent opportunity of sending some battalions of the German Legion there, where they might perhaps be induced to settle or become the nucleus of a local organisation for defence.

During this period, there had been a scene in the House of Commons, when, as Palmerston reported: 'Sir Charles Napier, with his usual want of judgment, moved for a committee to enquire into the proceedings of the fleet in the Baltic in 1854 while he was in command. His object was to state his grievances against Sir James Graham and Admiral Berkeley.' The reactions of the Queen and her Prime Minister offered an interesting contrast:

The debate in the House of Commons was indeed, as Lord Palmerston terms it, a very painful one—and she quite agrees with him that such recriminations cannot tend to raise the national character and promote the public interest. It is indeed most painful to see our representative bodies and our peers do all they can to lower this great and prosperous country and unfortunately this is the effect produced on the Continent. Can nothing be done to check such unseemly exhibitions?—Could not members be made to feel the disgrace they inflict upon their country and its institutions by bringing forward such motions?—But to be sure with two such men as Sir de Lacy Evans [who had served as a colonel in the Carlist wars and as a general in the Crimea] and Sir C. Napier—one cannot expect any right feeling or high tone.

Viscount Palmerston presents his humble duty to your Majesty and with reference to your Majesty's communication of this morning, he fears with your Majesty that such wrong-headed men as Sir Charles Napier and Sir de Lacy Evans can never be prevented from exposing themselves and to a certain degree bringing discredit upon their country. These evils are inevitable attendants upon parliamentary institutions, but are more than counterbalanced by the great advantages which those institutions confer ...

The end of the Crimean War provided the Queen with an opportunity of signalising the remarkable change which had taken place in a year in the temper of her relationship with Palmerston:

Now that the moment for the ratification of the Treaty of Peace is near at hand, the Queen wishes to delay no longer the expressions of her satisfaction as to the manner in which both the war has been brought to a conclusion, and the honour and the interest of this country have been maintained, by the zealous and able guidance of Lord Palmerston. She wishes as a public token of her approval, to bestow the Order of the Garter upon him. Should the two vacant Ribbons already have been promised to the peers whose names Lord Palmerston has on a former occasion submitted to the Queen, there could be no difficulty in his being named an Extra Knight, not filling up the next vacancy which may occur. This course was followed when Lord Grey received the Garter from the hands of King William.

Viscount Palmerston presents his humble duty to your Majesty and is unable to express in words the gratification and thankfulness which he feels upon the receipt of your Majesty's gracious and unexpected communication of this morning. The utmost of his ambition has been so to perform the duties of the high position in which your Majesty has been pleased to place him, as to prove himself not unworthy of the confidence with which your Majesty has honoured him, and the knowledge that your Majesty has found no reason to be dissatisfied with your choice and that his endeavour properly to discharge his duties to your Majesty and to the country have met with your Majesty's approval, would of itself be an ample reward for any labours or anxiety with which the performance of those duties may have been attended; and therefore the gracious communication which he has this morning received from your Majesty will be reserved by him, as in his eyes still more valuable even than the high honour which it announces your Majesty's intention to confer upon him. That high and distinguished honour Viscount Palmerston will receive with the greatest pride as a public mark of your Majesty's gracious approbation, but he begs to be allowed to say that the task which he and his colleagues have had to perform has been rendered comparatively easy by the enlightened views which your Majesty has taken of all the great affairs in which your Majesty's Empire has been engaged, and by the firm and steady support which in all these important transactions your Majesty's servants have received from the Crown.

The personal cordiality of nearly twenty years earlier seemed to have been restored. When Palmerston's step-son died, the Queen's commiserations were heartfelt:

> The Queen has just heard of the awfully sudden death of poor Lord Cowper,—and will not delay an instant in asking Lord Palmerston to convey to Lady Palmerston the expression of our very sincere and heartfelt sympathy upon the loss of her excellent son,—and in a manner so dreadfully sudden as to add considerably to her grief. The Queen fears the shock to Lady Palmerston and her two daughters (not to mention poor Lady Cowper herself) must be very great—and she sincerely hopes that none of their healths will suffer. The Queen will write to Lady Palmerston bye-and-bye herself—but in the meantime she begs Lord Palmerston to convey all their expressions to her, Lady Cowper and all the bereaved family.

Palmerston had indeed reached a second peak of esteem in his relations with his sovereign, although he was never accorded the personal friendship and regard in which Sir Robert Peel and Lord Aberdeen had been held. For the time being mutual confidence had been restored, but there were still many years to come.

CHAPTER VII

The Indian Mutiny

NO SOONER HAD THE CRIMEAN PEACE TREATY BEEN DRAFTED, THAN the Queen returned insistently to the problem of maintaining Britain's armed strength against all eventualities. Although personal cordiality existed between the British and French Courts, the Queen refused to allow the fact that the two countries had just won a war together to allay her suspicions of the turbulent neighbour across the Channel:

> ... The Queen believes that the Cabinet are going to consider to-day the amount of retrenchments which may be necessary for the army and navy [she wrote in April 1856]. She trusts and expects that this will be done with great moderation and very gradually—and that the difficulties we have had and the sufferings which we have endured may not be forgotten; for, to the miserable reductions of the last 30 years are entirely owing our state of helplessness when the war began and it would be unpardonable if we were to be found in a similar condition when another war—and who can tell how soon there may be one—breaks out! We must never for a moment forget the peculiar state of France and how entirely all there depends upon one man's life! We ought and must be prepared for every eventuality, and we have splendid material in that magnificent little army in the Crimea ...

There was much agitation in Parliament and in the press for wholesale economies in the armed services and Palmerston, with recalcitrant legislators to control, had to temporise. In May he wrote to the Queen:

> ... Viscount Palmerston would beg to submit that the numerical amount of a peace establishment is not so important a matter as its organisation and accompanying arrangements. It is, of course, not to be expected that Parliament will provide funds in time of peace

for an army as numerous as would be wanted in time of war, and the practical question between the Government and the Parliament will eventually be reduced to a choice between 10 or 15,000 men more or that number less; in either case leaving the numerical amount inferior to what would be required for an actual war. But the value of either the larger or the smaller number will mainly depend upon its organisation and efficiency, and it will be of more importance to obtain from Parliament the means of making the army in time of peace a well organised, a well equipped and a well practised force, than to add a few thousand men to its numbers . . .

Another point of great importance as an object of expenditure in time of peace, and preferable to mere numbers of men, is the completion of the defences of vulnerable places, such as the dockyards, and of points connected with the protection of the metropolis, such as Dover; and also the finishing of works bearing upon the command of the Channel, such as Alderney and Portland. Money laid out in permanent works of defence renders the country stronger after the expiration of the year in which the expense is incurred; money expended in maintaining men leaves the country in no degree stronger after the expiration of the year in which the expense is incurred, unless the same expense is incurred again year after year; and it would seem therefore to be better management to strain a point to get from Parliament the means of completing defensive works rather than to press for any very large amount of numerical force . . .

On a general view, however, of the state of the country, it may safely be affirmed that the United Kingdom never was in better condition of defence than it will be at the commencement of the present peace, whether with reference to the land or the sea. The fleet never consisted of so great a number of vessels peculiarly adapted to defensive as well as to offensive operations. The defences of the Channel, of the coasts and of the dockyards never were so well arranged and armed. The regular army never was so well ordered and equipped and armed, and the militia never was in time of peace so well officered and organised; and it is further to be borne in mind that the lively interest which your Majesty takes in all that concerns the welfare, the comfort and the efficiency of your Majesty's army and navy infuses a spirit throughout the whole of both those services which greatly enhances the military and naval value of any given number of either force.

A further exchange in July found the Queen still persisting:

> . . . The Cabinet at its meeting to-day were of opinion that, in consequence of the reports received from the Cape of Good Hope that attacks were apprehended from some of the native tribes, one or two regiments ought to be sent thither if the despatches which will arrive on Monday should confirm the accounts recently received, and it might in such case be advisable to send off at once to the Cape the German battalions which are to be settled there as colonists . . .

> The Queen . . . is sorry to hear of the accounts from the Cape, and thinks it would be most important that the German Legion should be sent out there as soon as possible. This is only another proof of how very necessary it is not to reduce our army rapidly. The House of Commons do not ask for it, and therefore we should not forestall their economical humour, but keep up the present splendid army as much as we can. The state of France and of the Emperor's health ought to give additional weight to what the Queen has above stated; for, to increase our army suddenly in case of any event in France would be invidious and calculated to provoke the very suspicions which we would wish to avoid . . .

Not all their correspondence during this period dealt with such weighty matters. There had been public disturbances in Hyde Park the previous year and, in an attempt to provide people with wholesome entertainment, the Queen had agreed with marked approval to a plan for military bands to play on Sunday afternoons in Kensington Gardens. A strong body of opinion resented this shattering of Britain's puritanical Sunday calm and a proposal in Parliament to open the museums produced a violent reaction:

> . . . Sir Joshua Walmsley then made his motion for the purpose of having the National Gallery and the British Museum opened on Sunday afternoon, a long debate ensued in which 15 speakers took part. There was great exaggeration on both sides. Those who were for the motion attributing undue effects to the proposed measure as likely to produce great moral and intellectual improvement in the lower classes; while those who opposed it represented it as the first step towards the utter demoralisation of the people . . . Sir

Joshua's motion was negatived by 376 to 48. Viscount Palmerston and the other members of the Government voting against it.

. . . The Queen regrets the debate on Sir J. Walmsley's motion, which she thinks is going backwards. She really thought that the disgraceful scenes in Hyde Park last year would have opened the eyes of those who act most injudiciously in thinking, by depriving the poor people from all intellectual and innocent amusement on Sunday, they make them religious! ! It is very well for those people who have no hard work during the week to go two or three times to church on Sunday and to remain quiet for the rest of the day, but as regards the working classes the practice is a perfect cruelty . . .

The agitation against the bands in the Parks reached a point where the Archbishop of Canterbury intervened with Palmerston, who had to report to the Queen:

. . . This agitation is likely to produce very inconvenient consequences in the House of Commons. The Scotch members and the Dissenters are violent upon the subject . . .

It is a source of regret to find feelings so nearly approaching to fanaticism so widely prevailing, but the matter is in itself not of sufficient importance to be worth the risk of a defeat in Parliament with widespread irritation among influential electors in most of the boroughs in the kingdom. The bands might perhaps play on Saturday afternoon instead of Sunday.

The Queen's views on the matter were strong, and not by any means in concordance with the reputation she left to posterity of Victorian gloom:

The Queen . . . cannot sufficiently express her regret at the incomprehensible blindness and mistaken piety of the so-called 'Evangelical Saints'.—The national character positively suffers from want of that innocent recreation which Lord Palmerston so properly describes. The Sunday is really a day of fast for the poor people, and the Queen fears a repetition of the scenes of last year in the Parks. Lord Palmerston could not help doing what he has done, but is not the loss regrettable? Perhaps more sensible and enlightened and less fanatical views may in the course of time prevail.

Perhaps there may have been a little want of tact and management in the manner in which the bands were first directed to play in the Parks on Sundays. At Windsor they have done so on the terrace from time immemorial and in all garrison towns they play on Sundays. If it could be managed to have them play on Saturdays— but she fears this will not answer the purpose, as the poor people are being at market and remain there up to a late hour on Saturday.

Palmerston had to bother the Queen again about another House of Commons agitation for wheeled access to St. James's Park:

... Viscount Palmerston fears that the House of Commons will be unmanageable on this matter, and he would submit as a question for your Majesty's consideration whether the best course might not be to open the two iron gates between St. James's Palace and Marlborough House and to straighten the road . . . The expense of such an arrangement would be small and if it would not materially contract the garden at St. James's Palace, the equivalent that might be added to the garden of Marlborough House might be deemed a compensation . . .

The Queen, as in anything affecting Crown property, was extremely touchy on the subject:

... The House of Commons have shown themselves really too unreasonable and thoughtless. They are however purposely misled by 'The Times' agitators and it will require more than usual care and attention on the part of the Government to set them right.—The gates by the German Chapel never were open, notwithstanding Mr. Stafford's and 'The Times' assertion, nor were hackney carriages and cabs allowed passage through Stable Yard in 1851, which they also assert. In that year that indulgence, now permanently enjoyed, viz. the passage of private carriages, was asked as a temporary boon, with the promise that it should not be drawn into a precedent nor lead to an application for hackney carriages. The permanent privilege was however asked and ceded in 1852. The objection to Stable Yard is its narrowness, which would render the traffic, if increased, both dangerous and intolerable for the inmates of St. James's Palace and Clarence House.

The Queen has given permission for hackney carriages going

through the Park provided a safe and proper passage was made for them and that they were confined to a direct route so as not to straggle all over the Park and lead to further difficulties. This principle is so fair and so simple that there ought to be no difficulty in carrying it out, if properly explained to Parliament . . .

There were distinct eighteenth-century undertones to one letter Palmerston wrote to the Queen in July. Only his indifference to further parliamentary reform can account for his complacent acceptance of the situation he described:

. . . Viscount Palmerston will take the necessary steps for calling Lord Shelburne up to the House of Peers in accordance with the arrangement which Lord Clarendon informed him your Majesty had approved. Lord Lansdowne will bring in for Calne, in the room of Lord Shelburne, Sir W. Williams . . . whose duties at Woolwich, Lord Panmure states, will not be inconveniently interfered with by occasional attendance in the House of Commons. Lord Lansdowne's command of Calne is founded entirely on personal influence, as he has no property in the town, although his property lies near and around it. He says that he can always secure the election of a member of his own family, or of a person distinguished in any way; he has no relation to bring in, and he chose Sir William Williams as a man whose return he could secure, and who would not try to establish in the borough any personal interest at variance with that of Lord Lansdowne's family.

Parliamentary affairs provided much of the subject matter of the correspondence between the Queen and Palmerston during 1856. Every evening, no matter what the hour, the Prime Minister sat down to pen his private *Hansard*, often including other matters of moment of the day. Each report is a model of lucid and straightforward prose, the mirror of the clear-thinking man who wrote them. On July 24, the Queen was moved to comment:

The Queen has to thank Lord Palmerston for three long and very interesting letters with full accounts of the proceeding of Parliament, which no one gives so clearly as Lord Palmerston . . .

The Queen was a great stickler for protocol in all matters concerning the royal prerogative. When Lord Hardinge, the army commander-in-chief, had a stroke and had to retire, the Queen was quick to suggest her cousin, the Duke of Cambridge, for the post. The Duke had good qualifications after his Crimean service, and was generally regarded as the best man, but the Queen was insistent on the manner of his appointment:

> The Queen was glad to receive the announcement of the agreement of the Cabinet with her that the Duke of Cambridge will be the fittest successor to Lord Hardinge. As to the mode of his appointment, the Queen thinks that it does not rest with the Secretary of State to take her pleasure, but that the Prime Minister ought to communicate the appointment to the Duke, to whom she would also write herself. The office is not a subordinate one, of the class of those appointed to by the head of a department, and has at all times been recommended for by the Prime Minister. Lord Derby wrote to Lord Hardinge and the Queen knows this to have been in strict accordance with former precedents, which the Queen wishes to have adhered to. She would wish to have an immediate answer from Lord Palmerston to this letter, as she will regulate her own proceedings accordingly.

One of the consequences of building the royal summer seat at Balmoral was the necessity of designating a Minister-in-Waiting to keep the Queen in touch with affairs. All of them loathed the duty, but the Queen would brook no refusal:

> ... As the different ministers (including Lord Palmerston himself) will probably be leaving town for the summer, the Queen would wish him to ascertain which of them could go to Scotland with her, and relieve each other during our stay at Balmoral. We shall not start before the 27th or 28th of August and would be there about six weeks. Would it suit Lord Palmerston himself to come there for any time? Would Sir G. Grey or Lord Panmure or the Duke of Argyll be able to come? Would Lord Clarendon perhaps—who has never been in Scotland and ought to have some rest—like to come for a few days?

Palmerston was careful to ensconce himself at Broadlands. However, the Queen took no umbrage and, when Palmerston lost his brother, William, long a distinguished diplomatic representative, her condolences were heartfelt:

Both the Prince and the Queen have seen with deep concern in to-day's papers that Lord Palmerston has lost his brother. Though Lady Palmerston told the Queen that they were extremely uneasy about him, she did not seem to anticipate this sad result so soon. Knowing Lord Palmerston's warm attachment to his poor brother we can easily imagine how much he must feel his loss— and we beg him to accept our very sincere expressions of condolence.

Viscount Palmerston presents his humble duty to your Majesty and begs to return his sincere thanks to your Majesty and to His Royal Highness the Prince Albert for the very kind and condescending communication which he has had the honour of receiving from your Majesty on the occasion of his recent affliction. Viscount Palmerston had indeed for some little time entertained great apprehensions as to the probable result of his poor brother's illness, but he had not expected so early a termination. But the discomfort and distress which that illness occasioned was so great that if recovery was impossible the release was a mercy, though nothing could exceed the calmness and patience with which the malady was born . . .

So the end of the year was reached, with the Russians contesting ineffectively every clause of the peace settlement and the quarrel with America over the recruitment of men still simmering. However, both sides were ready to make conciliatory gestures and Palmerston wrote to the Queen at Osborne, her residence in the Isle of Wight:

DECEMBER 12: . . . Viscount Palmerston begs to state that the *Resolute*, one of your Majesty's Arctic discovery ships, which, having been abandoned in the ice afterwards floated out and was taken into an American port by an American ship, and which has been sent over to this country by a vote of the Congress to be offered to your Majesty as a mark of respect by the United States, has arrived at Portsmouth. She is commanded by a very distinguished officer in the service of the United States, and is manned by a picked crew. Viscount Palmerston would beg to suggest that which has no doubt already occurred to your Majesty, that it would be a very gracious act on the part of your Majesty if

Admiral Martin at Portsmouth were desired to bring the American captain to Osborne to have the honour of being presented to your Majesty, and if afterwards your Majesty should find it not inconvenient to visit the ship which has thus been sent over for your Majesty's acceptance . . .

DECEMBER 13: . . . The Queen had already heard of the arrival of the *Resolute* at Spithead and she will with pleasure receive the captain who commands her here. She is doubtful whether on such an occasion some one on the part of the Government ought not also to be present. It will hardly be possible for the Queen to visit the vessel, but the Prince could do so if the weather, which has been tempestuous and uncertain beyond all beliefs, will admit of his doing so . . .

DECEMBER 16: . . . The Arctic ship *Resolute* was small enough to be brought along the Trinity Wharf in Cowes Harbour, so that the Queen with the Prince and the three eldest children were able to step aboard her quite easily—and we went there this morning and were much interested by what we saw. The captain, whom Sir G. Seymour presented, made a very complimentary speech to the Queen and he is to dine here tonight, so that the Queen hopes that the Americans will be pleased and satisfied.

The exchange of New Year messages between the Queen and Palmerston included a further mark of royal approval:

. . . The Queen thanks Lord Palmerston in the Prince's name as well as her own for his very kind expressions and wishes for the New Year and we both wish him and Lady Palmerston *many* happy New Years.

. . . The Office of Warden of the Cinque Ports is also vacant and the Queen would have much pleasure in offering it to Lord Palmerston if it should suit him.

Palmerston, a little ungraciously, thought the sinecure should be abolished altogether, although later he accepted it.—But the old gentleman was suffering from a crippling attack of gout and the Queen, although commiserating with him, was anxious to get down to public business:

The Queen is very sorry not to see Lord and Lady Palmerston here
to-day and to hear of his indisposition, which she trusts will not be
of long duration. Perhaps Lord Palmerston would be so good as to
inform her when he is well enough to come, as she is anxious to
see him to talk over with him the many important subjects which
the approaching session of Parliament will naturally call forth.

There had been a desultory correspondence on the subject of
instituting the new post of Director-General of Army Education.
The Queen wished the plan to be discussed exhaustively between
the Prince, the Duke of Cambridge, Panmure and Palmerston,
who acquiesced with almost fulsome praise of the Prince:

... Viscount Palmerston will be very glad to have the meeting on
this subject which your Majesty proposes between His Royal
Highness the Prince Albert, the Commander-in-Chief, Lord
Panmure and himself. He will take steps for this purpose as soon
as he returns to town. Viscount Palmerston has always derived so
much advantage from all the communications with which His
Royal Highness the Prince has honoured him on public affairs,
that he will be most desirous to have the benefit of His Royal
Highness' views on this important subject.

In the latter half of January Palmerston's health improved:

... Viscount Palmerston begs to tender to your Majesty his best
thanks for your Majesty's enquiries about his health. He is very
much better and is going to London tomorrow, though he has not
quite got rid of the remains of gout.

There was a heavy parliamentary session ahead and, with the
unifying effect of the Crimean War wearing off, Palmerston was
finding his supporters and opponents—especially the unnatural
alliance of Gladstone and Disraeli—increasingly difficult to handle.
But during the debate in February on Sir George Lewis's Budget,
Palmerston had the Queen's full support:

FEBRUARY 4: ... Mr. Disraeli ... gave notice of his intention to
move for a repeal of the war income tax and expressed a wish that
other members, who in the early part of the evening had given
notices to the same effect, would leave the matter in his hands. To
this however those members did not seem inclined to consent.

Mr. Disraeli, however, appeared to admit that Parliament ought in the first place to determine what amount of expenditure is required for the public service, and that then would be the proper time to fix the means of providing the requisite income, an admission at variance with the notice he had given, inasmuch as the tendency of that notice was to cut off revenue before the expenditure could be settled. Mr. Gladstone followed, and . . . directed his attack against the continuance of the war income tax and contended for the maintenance of the arrangement which he had made in 1853 by which the income tax would diminish by successive gradations, and wholly cease in 1860.

Mr. Gladstone, however, assumed that the estimates for the army and navy would amount to 24 or 25 millions and comparing that amount with the highest amount before the war, which he put at 16 or 17 millions, he argued that the proposed estimates would be greatly too high and must be materially reduced.—The intended amount of army and navy charge, as your Majesty is aware, would range from 21 million to 21,600,000 and if the amount can be brought down to 21 million, Mr. Gladstone would logically be led to admit the amount not to be unreasonable; but there seems to be an understanding established between the Peelites and the Derbyites and it is probable that the two parties will unite in their votes, though retaining their separate positions in the House, and will endeavour to embarrass the Government on questions of finance . . .

It is manifest that to maintain the war income tax would be utterly impossible. Some good judges of the disposition of the House doubt whether a reduction from sixteen pence to eight pence will be accepted and whether the House will not insist upon reducing the tax to seven pence, yielding to the pressure of constituents. Viscount Palmerston, however, is still inclined to think that eight pence will be accepted for the ensuing year at all events, and he is not without hopes that this amount may be continued for the two following years . . .:

FEBRUARY 4: The Queen thanks Lord Palmerston for his full and interesting report of last night's proceedings in the House of Commons. The object of reducing the income tax seems to be a favourite one with the Derbyites and Peelites, but the Queen would most strongly deprecate further reduction of the Army and

Navy Estimates as positively dangerous to the security of the country and as likely to lead to serious mischief. The Queen thinks that it should be fairly and clearly stated to Parliament that the great expenditure of this last war, as well as the great sufferings of the army, arose in a great measure, if not entirely, owing to the state of inefficiency in which we were during the long time of peace preceding this last war, that the Government and the country (which last has done nothing but complain of these very evils) would be guilty of great improvidence and of real want of foresight, as well as of economy, if they were not to enable the Government to keep up the necessary protection of the country by which alone war could be avoided. This should be put in strong terms before the House of Commons and the Queen cannot really believe them to be so reckless of former sufferings and so devoid of true patriotism as to aid in reducing the defences of this great nation to so low an ebb as, in fact, to invite insult and thereby produce the very consequences which they wish to avoid.

FEBRUARY 16: . . . Mr. Disraeli gave notice that he should move a resolution affirming that the Chancellor of the Exchequer would, according to his own statement, have a deficient income in the years beginning in April 1858 and in April 1859, and that it is desirable to make arrangements for the entire cessation of the income tax in 1860. Sir George Lewis invited Mr. Disraeli to go into the discussion at once and this evening, but this was declined and the discussion was fixed for Friday. It was the general wish of the House that the Navy Estimates should be put off till after that discussion and they were accordingly postponed. Sir George Lewis is confident that Mr. Disraeli and Mr. Gladstone are labouring under some great mistake in imagining that his statement would leave a deficit for the two years mentioned by them . . .

FEBRUARY 16: The Queen has just received Lord Palmerston's letter with the account of this evening's proceedings, which surprise her. What does Lord Palmerston think is the cause of this proceeding on the part of Mr. Disraeli, which is strange considering that we have just heard that Mr. Gladstone meant to make a great speech relative to the next two years deficit? She would wish also to know what Sir G. Lewis really thinks of this prospect for these two years. Has Mr. Disraeli, in Lord Palmerston's

Punch saw in Palmerston the champion who would resolve the initial disasters suffered
in the Crimean War.

opinion, made his throw in conjunction with Mr. Gladstone, or in order to keep the attack in his own hands? . . .

FEBRUARY 17: Viscount Palmerston presents his humble duty to your Majesty and in reply to your Majesty's enquiries of yesterday evening begs to state that Mr. Disraeli's intended motion of yesterday was evidently a surprise intended to be practised on the Government, and combined between Mr. Disraeli and his party on the one hand, and Mr. Gladstone and about twelve of the Peelite party on the other . . . The intention of the allies evidently was to make unexpectedly yesterday evening a motion of the same nature as that which was announced by Mr. Disraeli yesterday for Friday next . . . But they were prevented by the forms of the House, which prevent such a motion from being made in a Committee of Supply, and render it proper only for a Committee of Ways and Means . . . Now yesterday was the first day of the Committee of Supply, and the Committee of Ways and Means cannot begin till the report of yesterday's proceeding in regard to supply has been received by the House this afternoon. Friday therefore is the earliest day on which the House can resolve itself into a Committee of Ways and Means, and as Mr. Disraeli's intended motion can be made only in Ways and Means, he was obliged to forego his intended surprise last night and to put off his motion to Friday next. Sir G. Lewis challenged him to a discussion, but a discussion without a division was not what he wanted, and he declined the invitation, and so did Mr. Gladstone . . .

FEBRUARY 19: The Queen returns these papers and thanks Lord Palmerston for his letter explaining the unexpected course of the Opposition on Monday. She thinks that everything promises well for tomorrow, that there is no cause for alarm and that Lord Palmerston feels satisfied that the calculations of Mr. Gladstone and Mr. Disraeli are at fault?

Will the debate last beyond tomorrow? As regards the Estimates there must be no giving way, as the Queen fears we have already cut them down terribly and indeed quite as much as the safety of this country will admit of . . .

FEBRUARY 23: Viscount Palmerston presents his humble duty to your Majesty and begs to state that Mr. Disraeli's motion was negatived this evening by 286 to 206, all the Peelites voting for the motion, and several of the Conservatives voting with the Government . . .

FEBRUARY 24: The Queen is most truly rejoiced at the most satisfactory debate of last night and at the large majority which the Government had on this important question. She trusts now that the Estimates will be firmly defended and their object explained. She feels in what a doubtful state of peace Europe is and how paramount the necessity is of being prepared, though alas! we have already reduced our forces to that extent that it makes the Queen very anxious for the future. She relies therefore on Lord Palmerston doing all he can to stand by the present state of our Estimates. Mr. C. Villiers told her the other day that there was no wish to see them reduced, quite the contrary, provided people lost the additional 9d. which they now have . . .

The triumph was short-lived.—There was trouble in China, where the Emperor's Government was failing to meet its treaty obligations to admit foreign merchants into Canton. Palmerston had been urging 'gunboat diplomacy' and, when the Chinese seized a coasting vessel called the *Arrow* flying the British flag—albeit illegally, as its licence to do so had run out—the Prime Minister proposed armed intervention to bring the Chinese to heel. In the House of Commons, Cobden, the great Radical free-trader, introduced a motion condemning Palmerston's China policy and a tired and fractious House suddenly coalesced behind it. Faced by a combination of Russell, Disraeli, Gladstone and the Radicals, the Government was defeated by 16 votes. The Queen was incensed, writing to Palmerston on March 4:

Though prepared for an unfavourable result, the Queen is not the less grieved at the success of evil party motives, spite and a total absence of patriotism.

The Queen would be glad if Lord Palmerston would let her know by telegraph at what hour she may expect him this afternoon, in order that she may be home at the right time, and if he will remain here the night?

That night she made a note of their conversation in her Journal:

... Lord Palmerston came at 6 and our anxiety was soon relieved by hearing that the Cabinet unanimously agreed that it would not be right, in this peculiar instance, to resign, but on the contrary the country should be appealed to, which he had every reason to think had still more confidence in this Government than in any other that could be formed. No doubt this might be factiously opposed, but he hardly thought this extreme measure would be resorted to, at any rate the Government with its supporters would be able to defeat such a proceeding. They intended only to ask for the Meeting Act to be passed for three months and the other arrangements for the income tax and tea duties, only for a year. They would probably dissolve just at the beginning of April and meet again at the beginning of May. I asked if none of the Cabinet were opposed to this, to which he replied, only Sir C. Wood, who had observed that 'it would be a good political move to resign!' All the others had exclaimed that it would be a very bad move. 'It was the old Whig notion', Lord P. said, 'to resign in order to come in stronger!' not thinking that in the meantime one was leaving the fortress to be occupied by one's enemies and that it would have to be retaken. He further said that they felt that the state of affairs with China was very critical, and that they proposed sending 5,000 men from here to take the direction of affairs, mentioning either Lord Elgin or Sir G. Clark, who had been formerly at Bombay. We spoke of the wretched cant and humbug displayed in the debates, Mr. Gladstone holding doctrines and displaying principles, relative to the conduct of our merchants etc., which while he was minister [Secretary for the Colonies] he never attempted to remedy ... Lord Palmerston, who sat next to me ... was looking ill and suffering from a return of the gout, but was in excellent pluck. He thought Lord Derby was prepared to form a Government and Mr. Gladstone ready to join him. Speaking of Lord Russell, Lord P. said that his present position must be very humiliating to him. He sat behind the Treasury benches with only two or three followers, (who voted against him and for the Government yesterday) having so tangled the Party, in and out of office, that it would be far the best thing to get him to go to the House of Lords. That he had always been very vain and cried up, really much beyond his merits, also he had a wonderful notion of the importance of the Russell family!

The Cabinet decided firmly to call new elections and, on the 6th, Palmerston could report better news to the Queen:

> ... Viscount Palmerston hears ... the most encouraging accounts for all parts of the country, and he believes that the Coalition has unintentionally rendered a good service to the Government, and that the Government is more likely to gain strength by a general election brought about as the approaching election will be, than if the session had gone on in the usual way and if the dissolution had taken place without any particular event out of which a distinction between opposing parties could have been drawn ...

> The Queen thanks Lord Palmerston for his two letters and is truly rejoiced to see how well (with the exception of Mr. Gladstone and Lord J. Russell) his announcement has been received last night—and how much reason there is to anticipate that the country will show that good and sound feeling which the House of Commons so signally failed in displaying in the vote come to on Tuesday. The country seems—by what has already shown itself—highly to disapprove the combination (so loudly disclaimed) which led to the defeat of the Government last Tuesday. The Queen trusts therefore that the result of the dissolution will be decidedly favourable to the Government.

The campaign proved a personal triumph for Palmerston, who returned with a substantially increased majority, while many of his Radical tormentors lost their seats. The Queen followed the voting with avidity and, as soon as Palmerston was returned for Tiverton at the end of the month, wrote to congratulate him:

> The Queen is glad to see that everything went off so well at Tiverton and that the elections are going on so famously ... That Messrs. Bright, M. Gibson, Cobden and Layard, Sir J. Walmsley etc. should be turned out, is excellent, and very striking. On the other hand, the Queen believes that one of the worst men, and one who will be troublesome and mischievous in every way, has come in for Brighton, Mr. Conningham ...

> Viscount Palmerston presents his humble duty to your Majesty and has had the honour to receive your Majesty's communication of yesterday. The result of the elections as far as they have gone is

indeed highly satisfactory and the calculation is that on the whole
the Government will gain 40 seats, which would make a difference
of 80 in a division. The rejection of Mr. Bright, Cobden, Milner
Gibson and Sir Joshua Walmsley is a strong indication of the
right feeling of the country and more especially in the case of Mr.
Cobden, who, having been told that he would not be re-elected
for the West Riding, was refused admittance at Salford and
beaten at Huddersfield . . .

This parliamentary upheaval had come at the time when the
Queen was bearing her last child, Princess Beatrice, and at the
end of April Palmerston was able to greet the happy event with
further reassuring news:

> Viscount Palmerston presents his humble duty to your Majesty and
> begs in the first place to tender to your Majesty his heartfelt con-
> gratulations upon your Majesty's rapid recovery, which is not only
> most gratifying to all your Majesty's subjects with reference to the
> present moment, but is a happy evidence of a strength of con-
> stitution which promises to the nation a long continuance of that
> reign which has contributed so much to the happiness and content-
> ment of the Empire.
>
> The results of the general election have in the aggregate been
> most satisfactory. Many objectionable members of the last House
> of Commons have been thrown out, and though a few men have
> now been elected who would have been better away, yet on the
> whole the composition of the new members is good and there are
> in the present House of Commons more gentlemen and more
> men of character and substance than has usually been the case.
>
> The Government however has sustained some losses among its
> subordinate members. Mr. Fred. Peel, Lord Monck and Mr. Ball
> have lost their seats . . .

> The Queen received Lord Palmerston's communication last night
> and has much pleasure in being able to answer him herself and to
> thank him for his congratulations on her rapid and complete
> recovery which has this time (if possible) been even speedier than
> usual. She cannot be sufficiently grateful to Providence for this,
> as well as for the health and strength of our little girl.
>
> The Queen is happy to hear of the excellent result of the elections
> which (with the exception of some losses which Lord Palmerston

has enumerated) is most satisfactory . . . Most readily will the
Queen make Mr. F. Peel a Privy Councillor, but the Queen hopes
that Lord Palmerston will take an early opportunity of employing
Mr. F. Peel again whenever any vacancy occurs, as he is a very
clever and hard working young man.

The Queen concludes with expressing a hope that Lord Palmerston will be very firm and hold a high tone on the already so much
reduced Estimates, which with his very large majority he can
easily do. The state of Europe and indeed of the whole world
demands our not being left in an unprotected and unprepared
condition.

Everything appeared to go well during the first few weeks of the
new Government, and the Queen's letters were notably cordial:

The Queen . . . is much obliged for the useful little book giving a
classification of the new House of Commons . . .

The Queen was much pleased to see the good spirit shown upon
the Navy Estimates being voted and hopes that an equally good
one may be exhibited when the Army Estimates are proposed,
though she fears this will hardly be the case, but she trusts that a
high tone will be held, upon the extreme necessity of being duly
prepared in case of war and averting similar disasters (which
would inevitably occur) to those which caused such clamour on
the part of the House of Commons and the public at large during
the late war.

The Queen hopes that Lord Palmerston's leg is quite well again
and that he will be prudent and not over-fatigue himself.

Then, at the end of June, the administration was faced by its first
major challenge—the Indian Mutiny. Reports of restlessness and
indiscipline in the East India Company's troops had been trickling
in for some time and, for once, Palmerston did not seem alive to
an imminent danger. When the insurrection and massacres became
serious, Palmerston wrote to the Queen recommending the despatch of reinforcements. His sovereign had taken a much more
serious view of the situation:

The Queen has just received Lord Palmerston's letter and is likewise much alarmed at the news from India. She has for some time
been very apprehensive of the state of affairs in the army there,

216

and her fears are now fully realised. She trusts that Lord Palmerston and Lord Panmure will consult with the Duke of Cambridge without delay as to what measures should be taken to meet this great danger and that no time will be lost in carrying them out.

Palmerston was stung to action. The septuagenarian could still move swiftly in a crisis:

> Viscount Palmerston presents his humble duty to your Majesty and begs to state that the Cabinet took into consideration to-day the disagreeable news announced by telegraph from India. It was determined that the four regiments and the detachments for your Majesty's forces and for the India Company's troops now under order for India should proceed to their destination immediately. Mr. Vernon Smith informed the Cabinet that the India Company are about to ask immediately for a further reinforcement of four regiments of your Majesty's infantry and it was resolved that as soon as that requisition is received, the necessary steps shall be taken to put the regiments under orders and to provide shipping for this conveyance. It remains to be considered whether the additional four regiments shall proceed direct to India, or whether they should go to the Cape, four regiments from thence being sent on to India ... All persons acquainted with India agree that a regiment accustomed to the Cape climate and service would be more useful in India than a regiment direct from England ...

Within a fortnight there was worse news. The mutiny was spreading inexorably throughout Bengal and the Cabinet hastened to send out the one officer who had emerged from the Crimean War with an enhanced reputation:

> Viscount Palmerston presents his humble duty to your Majesty and begs to state that the Cabinet, having taken into consideration the bad news received this morning by telegraph from India, have requested the assistance of His Royal Highness the Commander-in-Chief, who is now with them and that the first measure which they beg to submit for your Majesty's approval is that Sir Colin Campbell should be sent out immediately to India to take the vacant appointment of commander-in-chief.
>
> Lord Panmure and the Commander-in-Chief, who had communicated on these matters this morning, have ascertained that

Sir Colin would be ready to start tomorrow evening and it will be possible by telegraph to stop the Indian Mail at Marseilles so as that it shall wait for his arrival and take him on at once to India. He says that he can get at Calcutta everything that he may want for outfit. It is also proposed that General Mansfield, now at Warsaw, whom Sir Colin wishes to have as chief of his staff, should be brought home and sent out after Sir Colin . . .

The Queen has just received Lord Palmerston's letter and highly approves the proposed appointment of Sir Colin Campbell as commander-in-chief in India and thinks it very handsome of this distinguished, loyal and gallant general to be ready to start at once on so important and arduous a mission. The Queen likewise approves of General Mansfield's appointment and of the intention of sending out more troops forthwith.

The Prime Minister was full of activity now and reported again on July 15:

Viscount Palmerston presents his humble duty to your Majesty and begs to state that the Cabinet took into consideration this afternoon various matters connected with the affairs of India and of China.

With regard to India, the result would be that in accordance with the opinion come to by the War Committee yesterday, in concert with the Commander-in-Chief who was there, the total addition which will be made to your Majesty's forces in India by November next in regiments and corps, including two troops of horse artillery and six companies of foot artillery, will be between 17 and 18,000 men, and including drafts for regiments now there it will amount to upwards of 20,000.

Steps will be taken to purchase horses for cavalry and artillery at the Cape and in Asia Minor. It is proposed that as part of the force originally intended for China will be diverted to India, one of the brigadiers with General Ashburnham shall go to India and, in order to provide for casualties among general officers in India, it is proposed to send from hence two or three young officers of distinction to be at the disposal of the Governor-General for staff commands . . . A regiment which can be spared from the Cape will be sent to Ceylon, where the military force has been reduced to a handful of men by the sending of a regiment to India. With a view to fill up the gap in the home force occasioned by these reinforcements to India, it is proposed that all regiments on the home station shall immediately be raised by recruiting to a thousand men each . . . The Commander-in-Chief recommends the formation of second battalions in order to provide the means of periodical reliefs, but it is said that not more than 200 men a week could at this season of the year and till the harvest is quite over be raised . . .

Parliament was also keen to see vigorous measures taken and when Palmerston reported that his critics were contending 'that the Government was not doing enough to reorganise a defensive force for home service', the Queen could not resist the opening:

The Queen has just received Lord Palmerston's letter of yesterday and must say that if she had been in the House she would have joined in saying that the Government were not doing enough to 'reorganise a defensive force for home service'. The Queen will write a memorandum on the subject when she gets to Osborne, but in the meantime she must observe that she thinks the moment a most critical one, and that it is not a question of a little more or less being done, but of doing all we can to avoid serious disasters! Let European complications arise (and God knows how soon they may, for the state of Europe is very bad) and we may find ourselves in an awful position of helplessness! The Queen must repeat that the Government must do all they can to keep up the army at home while they spare no means to send out a really efficient force to India.

Viscount Palmerston presents his humble duty to your Majesty and has had the honour to receive your Majesty's communication of yesterday, stating what your Majesty would have said if your Majesty had been in the House of Commons. Viscount Palmerston may perhaps be permitted to take the liberty of saying that it is fortunate for those from whose opinions your Majesty differs that your Majesty is not in the House of Commons, for they would have had to encounter a formidable antagonist in argument, although on the other hand those who[se] opinions your Majesty approves would have had the support of a powerful ally in debate.
  But with regard to the arrangements in connection with the

state of affairs in India, Viscount Palmerston can assure your Majesty that the Government are taking and will not fail to continue to take every measure which may appear well adapted to the emergency, but measures are sometimes best calculated to succeed which follow each other step by step . . .

The Queen's memorandum was quickly forthcoming. Her chief fear, and one that Palmerston to some extent shared, was that the European powers might take some intiative now that Britain's military reserves were engaged elsewhere. There were disturbing signs that Napoleon III was contemplating some new adventure in Italy, and the development of rifled guns and armoured ships in France was causing consternation in England. The Queen did not mince her words:

> The Queen is anxious to impress in the most earnest manner upon her Government the necessity of taking a comprehensive view of our military position at the present momentous crisis, instead of going on without a plan, living from hand to mouth and taking small isolated measures without reference to each other. Contrary to the Queen's hopes and expectations, immediately after the late war the army was cut down to a state even below the peace establishment recognised by the Government and Parliament in their own Estimates, to meet the parliamentary purpose of economy, and this in spite of the fearful lesson just taught by the late war and with two wars on hand, one with Persia and the other with China! And of this materially reduced peace establishment already drawn upon for the service in China, we are now to meet the exigencies of the Indian crisis, and the Government, as it always has done on such occasions, has contented itself with sending out the few regiments left at home, putting off the day of reorganising its forces.
>
> When the regiments ordered out shall have gone, we shall be left with 18 battalions out of 105 of which the army is composed, to meet all home duty, to protect our own shores, to act as the reserves and reliefs for the regiments abroad and to meet all possible emergencies! ! The regiments in India are allowed one company, raised by the last decision of the Cabinet to 100 men, as their depot and reserve! !
>
> A serious contemplation of such a state of things must strike

everybody with the conviction that some comprehensive and immediate measure must be taken by the Government, its principles settled by the Cabinet, but its details left to the unfettered execution of the military authorities, instead of which the Cabinet have as yet agreed only upon recruiting certain battalions up to a certain strength, to get back some of the men recently discharged and have measured the extent of their plans by a probable estimate of the amount of recruits to be obtained in a given time, declaring at the same time to Parliament that the militia will not be called out, which would have probably given the force required.

The Commander-in-Chief has laid a plan before the Government which the Queen thinks upon the whole very moderate, inexpensive and efficient.

The principle which the Queen thinks ought to be adopted is this: That the force which has been absorbed by the Indian demand is to be replaced to its full extent and in the same kind, not whole battalions by a mere handful of recruits added to the remaining ones. This will not only cost the Government nothing, because the East India Company will pay the battalions transferred, and the money voted for them by Parliament will be transferred to the new ones, but it will give a considerable saving as all the officers reduced from the war establishment and receiving half pay will be thus absorbed and no longer be a burden upon the Exchequer. Keeping these new battalions on a low establishment, which will naturally be the case at first, the depots and reserves should be raised in men, the Indian depots keeping at least two companies of 100 men each. The Crimean battalions of eight companies had eight others in reserve, which, with the aid of the militia even, could not keep up the strength of the service companies; in India there are eleven to be kept up by one reserve. No possible objections can be urged against this plan except two—

(1) That we shall not get the men. This is a hypothesis and not an argument. Try, and you will see; if you don't succeed, and the measure is necessary, you will have to adopt means to make it succeed. If you conjure up the difficulties yourself you cannot of course succeed.

(2) That the East India Company will demur to keeping permanently so large an addition to the Queen's army in India. The Company is empowered, it is true, to refuse taking any Queen's troops whom it has not asked for, and to send back any it

may no longer want. But the Company has asked for the troops, now sent at a great inconvenience to the Home Government, and the commonest foresight will show that for at least three years to come this force cannot possibly be dispensed with, if at all. Should the time however arise, the Government will simply have to reduce the additional battalions and the officers will return to the half pay list from which they were taken, the country having had the advantage of the saving in the meantime.

But the Queen thinks it next to impossible that the European force could again be decreased in India after the present fearful experience. The Company could only send back Queen's regiments in order to raise European ones of their own. This they cannot do without the Queen's sanction, and she must at once make her most solemn protest against such a measure. It would be dangerous and unconstitutional to allow private individuals to raise an army of Queen's subjects larger than her own in any part of the British Dominions; the force would be inferior to one continually renewed by reliefs from the mother country and would form no link in the general military system of England all over the globe, of which the largest force will always be in India; the raising of new troops for the company in England would most naturally interfere with the recruiting of the Queen's army, which meets already with such great difficulties. The Company could not complain that it was put to expense by the Home Government in having to keep so many more Queen's regiments, for, as it cannot be so insane as to risk to reform the old Bengal Army of Sepoys, for every two of these regiments now disbanded and one of the Queen's substituted, it would save £4,000 (a regiment of Sepoys costing £27,000 and a Queen's regiment £50,000). The ten battalions to be transferred to the Company for twenty Sepoy regiments disbanded would therefore save £40,000 instead of costing anything; but in reality the saving to the Company would be greater because the half pay superannuation of the officers, and therefore the whole dead weight, would fall upon the mother country. The only motive which could therefore actuate the Company could but be a culpable love of power and patronage, to which the most sacred interests of the Company ought not to be sacrificed.

The present position of the Queen's army is a pitiable one. The Queen has just seen in the camps at Aldershot, regiments which, after eighteen years' foreign service in most trying climates, had come back to England to be sent out after seven months to the Crimea; having passed through this destructive campaign, they have not been home for a year before they are to go to India for perhaps twenty years! This is most cruel and unfair to the gallant men who devote their services and lives to their country and the Government is in duty and humanity bound to alleviate their position.

The Queen wishes Lord Palmerston to communicate this memorandum to the Cabinet.

There followed, during August, a constant stream of exhortations from the Queen demanding immediate and vigorous measures. The Government tabled a Bill to embody the militia—the Queen considered it inadequate. She demanded a return of naval strength and found it deplorably weak. Palmerston tried to defend himself:

... With regard to the general question as to the naval and military establishment of the country, Viscount Palmerston would beg to submit that they are somewhat larger than they have been at any former period of peace, and Viscount Palmerston believes them to be sufficient for the security of the country. But the Government had not the choice of fixing them at a higher amount. All establishments must be limited by the amount of means to pay for them. It was impossible to persuade Parliament to continue the war income tax, or to try on any new taxes equal in amount to the war portion of the income tax. It therefore became a matter of inevitable necessity that the expenses of the country should be so reduced as to be brought within the income of the country, and to do this it was necessary to make great reductions in the army and navy establishments and charges, these being the great heads of expenditure upon which reductions could be made.

The royal bombardment continued unabated:

AUGUST 24: The Queen returns Sir Charles Wood's memorandum, which she has read with much interest. She felt sure that the Admiralty would prefer sending her a general argumentative statement, instead of the simple return of the responsible officers which the Queen had asked for, Such a statement is usually made in answer to any interpolation in the House of Commons and very good for that purpose, but as the Queen does not wish to make any attack upon the Admiralty, but merely to receive the data upon which to form an opinion whether we are really prepared or not, she must repeat what she wrote in her letter of the 4th 'that she wishes a report sent to her as to the force of screw ships-of-the-line and other classes, which can be got ready at the different dock-yards and the time required to get them to sea for active service and also the time required to launch and get ready the gunboats; not a mere formal answer from the Admiralty, but for detailed reports from the admirals commanding at the different ports and particularly the captains in command of the Steam Reserve'. Three weeks have elapsed since the Queen made this request and she hopes that more time will not be lost now in satisfying her.

SEPTEMBER 3: . . . We are in great anxiety at the bad and alarming news from India, and deeply grieved at the horrible details. The Queen is glad to see that the Government has increased the battalions, though she thinks not yet sufficiently and that other means are being taken to increase and make more efficient our forces to be sent out, as well as to provide for an ample reserve at home, but all this will ill suffice what will ultimately be required . . .

SEPTEMBER 18: . . . The Indian news upon every further development justifies less the opinion that it is rather favourable than otherwise and leading to the hope that affairs will soon take a favourable turn in India.

It is evident from a comparison of the news with the map, that whilst the seat of the Mutiny was Oudh, Delhi and the Upper Ganges,—to which localities all troops have been despatched, it has now broken out in their rear, cutting them off from the base of operations, viz. Calcutta, and that it has reached the gates of the seat of Government itself. On the other hand, it has moved down from Delhi in a south-westerly direction towards Bombay, and the defection of the first of the Bombay regiments gives serious cause for apprehension, as to the future of that army! The Queen cannot understand how a single Bengal regiment can be left undisarmed and undisbanded, but from the news of new mutinies in the rear of our forces on the Ganges it is quite clear that this must be so. Our troops are sure to remain victorious against the Sepoys in the open field, if numbers be not too disproportionate, they be not badly led or physically reduced by weakness and fatigue; the latter being however much to be apprehended. But the difficulty will be to get a proper *ensemble* into the military movements and this will hardly be the case unless an army be formed at Calcutta strong enough to operate from thence with certainty upon the parts of country in revolt and serving as a *point d'appui* for the scattered forces. Our reinforcements dropping in one by one run the risk of being used up by being sent on to relieve the different stray columns in distress.

When Lord Palmerston speaks of the reinforcements arriving which are to give a favourable turn to affairs, has he considered that the first which were dispatched by the Government to India (exclusive of the Chinese expedition of 5,000 men diverted to it and now there) will arrive only in October? The time lost in the arrangements, in taking up shipping etc. brought their departure to July. There will therefore be two whole months, August and September, when the Indian Government will get no relief whatever, while fighting, marching etc. lose to them often as much as 500 men a day!

These are the considerations which make the Queen so anxious about early decisions and immediate steps at home; for, while we are putting off decisions in the vain hope that matters will mend, and in discussing the objections to different measures, the mischief is rapidly progressing and the time difficult to catch up again.

The Queen sees in the decision of the Cabinet to attempt the raising of a black regiment in Canada and of a Maltese regiment, the first indication of their desire to exert themselves to meet an extraordinary emergency by extraordinary means, and she would like a Corfu regiment to be tried as well. All these decisions are being taken however rather late, the subject was discussed already at Osborne during the visit of the Emperor, and so likewise did the Duke of Cambridge urge the sending of two companies to Aden before the Queen's leaving town three weeks ago . . .

The Queen would wish Lord Palmerston to show this letter to the Cabinet.

On October 2, Palmerston attempted to mollify his royal taskmistress:

Viscount Palmerston presents his humble duty to your Majesty and begs to state that the Cabinet, having been occupied yesterday and to-day in considering various matters connected with the present state of India and the memorandum which your Majesty sent to Viscount Palmerston some little time ago to be communicated to his colleagues, have come to the following conclusions: That the standard for recruits should be lowered from 5' 5" to 5' 4" and that the limit of age should be extended from the range between 18 and 25 to the range between 18 and 30. The recruiting is going on very well and latterly at the rate of 1,200 a week, but time is of great importance and one man raised in the next three months is for Indian purposes worth two raised at a later period. The cavalry standard is also to be lowered from 5' 6" to 5' 5".

Secondly, immediate steps are to be taken for raising a fourth West India regiment from the negro refugees in Canada, such regiment, when formed, to be sent to the West Indies to relieve one of the black regiments now there, which would go on to India, and if another black regiment could afterwards be raised in Canada that would be done. Steps will also be taken by communication with the Governor-General of Canada to raise, if he thinks it an advisable measure, a white regiment in the North American provinces . . .

Thirdly, it is proposed to embody 10,000 more militia, making in the whole 25,000 militia embodied.

Viscount Palmerston is not without some apprehension that unless there be a sufficient military force stationed in Ireland, there may in the course of the winter be some attempts at disturbance in that country, and the militia would be a good force for preventing or repressing any such attempts. That portion of the Irish militia which may be embodied, which belongs to the south and the more Catholic part of the country, would be brought over to England, and part of the English militia would be sent to Ireland. Many symptoms have shown themselves indicating that the Ultra Catholic Party and remnants of the revolutionary Irish Party are not without intentions of taking advantage of what they expect to be the reduction of military force in Ireland during the winter; but they will be mistaken, and the spirit of the mass of the Irish people is fond and good . . .

The Queen has received Lord Palmerston's letter of the 2nd, giving an account of the decisions of the Cabinet. She thinks them all judicious and tending to the right object, though they would have been still more useful if taken two months earlier.

Time is the only thing which no money or exertion can make up for. The Queen quite feels with Lord Palmerston the objections to accepting foreign aid in any shape so long as we can take care of our own interests ourselves, but foregoing such aid renders vigorous exertion in providing means ourselves doubly necessary. The Queen is relieved however at seeing the Government now becoming anxious.

The Irish symptoms are very bad and only show that we dare not be militarily weak, for any reverse or difficulty will bring up enemies whom we may take to be staunch friends in times of prosperity . . .

Nevertheless, affairs in India had taken a radical turn for the better. Delhi had been recaptured, Lucknow relieved and sufficient troops were on hand to quell the Mutiny. In Europe, Palmerston had been even more successful. Neither Russia nor France had dared, under his stern eye and remonstrances, to fish in the troubled waters of Italy or the Middle East, where there was a conflict for influence in Persia. The French Government, in fact, had offered to allow British reinforcements for India to travel across France to Marseilles. By the middle of October, Palmerston's fertile and sanguine brain had had time to dwell on two major long-term objectives: a radical change in the pattern of government in India and the necessity for further parliamentary reform in Britain:

. . . The Cabinet on Friday had little to do but to hear and read the accounts, on the whole satisfactory, received by the last mails from India, but one little incident occurred tending to show the inconvenience of administering the government of a vast country on the other side of the globe by means of two Cabinets, the one responsible to your Majesty and to Parliament, the other responsible only to a mob of holders of Indian stock assembled for three or four hours three or four times a year. The Cabinet were informed that the Court of Directors object to sending any more troops to India and specially to the sending thither of any black troops. Both these objections, however, will probably be overruled.

But it being the strong personal opinion of Viscount Palmerston that the present double government of India ought not to continue, and it being his belief that the nation at large are prepared for a change, he has requested Mr. Vernon Smith, Sir Charles Wood and Sir G. Lewis to prepare for the consideration of the Cabinet when they meet for business in the beginning of November, the heads of a measure for abolishing the Board of Control, the Court of Directors and the Court of Proprietors, and for empowering your Majesty to appoint a Secretary of State for India, to be assisted by one or two Under-Secretaries, who should be capable of sitting in either House of Parliament and should be political officers changing with the Government, and also to be assisted by a Council of non-political men, possibly four in number, who should not sit in Parliament and should not change with changes of Government, but should be in the position of the Permanent Under-Secretaries of the four Secretaries of State, with the condition that no one should be so appointed who has not served for a certain number of years in India in a civil or military capacity.

There would be other arrangements as to the debt of the Company and the revenues of India, their collection, their expenditure and their audit, which would require much consideration. Viscount Palmerston conceives that the best way of bringing before the Cabinet the great and general question whether India shall continue to be governed by a Company of India stockholders, no longer even merchants or traders in their corporate capacity, or whether it shall henceforward be governed in your Majesty's name and under your Majesty's direct authority, like every other part of your Majesty's Dominions, would be to show by some prepared plan how the changes could be effected. There will of course be much opposition on the part of all persons connected with the India Company, and the Opposition in Parliament might take up their cause and the matter therefore will require to be well weighed before any recommendation on the subject can be submitted for your Majesty's consideration.

There is another matter of very great importance which the Cabinet will have to consider in November, and that is the measure of Parliamentary reform which the Government stands pledged to propose to Parliament next session, unless other more urgent and important matters should justify them in abstaining from doing so. Viscount Palmerston has requested Sir George Grey to prepare materials for consideration on this subject. Viscount Palmerston's own personal wishes and opinion are that any disfranchisement, and any lowering of the borough franchise should be avoided. If the chapter of disfranchisement is opened, a struggle of interests will be excited, and it will be hard to know where to stop, and the ten pounds franchise for boroughs goes quite as low as intelligence and independence reach.

What Viscount Palmerston would like to do, would be to admit to the franchise large numbers of well educated and independent men, who are now shut out by the technical test of a ten pound house in a borough or a forty shilling freehold on a farm in a county. He would give a right of voting to all officers of the army and navy on full or half pay above the ranks of ensign or mate, or perhaps including them and including also the militia; to all graduates of any university, to all barristers and attorneys, to all physicians, surgeons and apothecaries, to all rectors, vicars and curates, to all clerks of merchants, bankers and manufacturers, and to any other class who might be found to come within the same principle.

He would lower the county franchise as dependent upon tenure from a fifty pound holding to a twenty pound holding, which is the qualification to serve on a jury, and he would like much to discover some qualification which would admit some of the best and most intelligent of the working classes, without touching the ten pound franchise. It has been suggested that this might be accomplished by giving a vote to any man who has for a certain time, say three years, had a certain sum, say a hundred pounds, in a savings bank, or who for a certain time has been in the receipt of yearly wages of a given amount. But all these matters will require great consideration before any scheme can be submitted to your Majesty. Such a scheme as the foregoing would greatly disappoint the Radicals and greatly satisfy all reasonable men both in and out of Parliament, but many a man in the House of Commons, when his heart might think such a measure of change quite sufficient, would be compelled by pledges unguardedly and needlessly made to some few radicals in his borough or county, to cry out that it fell far short of what justice and propriety demand.

By the end of the year the situation in India had been so much restored that the victorious generals could be decorated and the Prime Minister felt free to suggest a new order of knighthood for those who had contributed to the reimposition of British rule:

... Viscount Palmerston would wish to submit for the consideration of your Majesty whether it might not be advantageous that your Majesty should establish an Order of Knighthood for India, similar to the Order of St. Michael and St. George, which has been established for the Mediterranean. Such an Order divided into classes might afford your Majesty more ample means of rewarding services performed by your Majesty's British and Indian subjects, and the highest class of the Order might be made use of as the means of acknowledging the friendly conduct of native princes in alliance with your Majesty. There is reason to believe that the native princes and your Majesty's native subjects would be proud of such a distinction, and that it might have a very useful political effect.

The Queen has received Lord Palmerston's letter of yesterday. The idea of instituting an Order for India to be bestowed on native princes and natives who have well deserved of the Queen and who have stood by us at a time when their loyalty was of the utmost importance and required great courage and forbearance on their part, strikes the Queen as a very good one. It seems too soon to institute it yet, before our power is established, and it will require careful consideration and what its relative value and position will be with regard to the Bath ...

The Queen had a further suggestion:

The Queen thinks that a medal ought to be conferred upon the brave troops in India and that this intention should soon be made public, as the unfortunate part of the campaign may now, she hopes, be considered to have closed. Usually the East India Company has awarded such medals, but as the Government is soon to be assumed by the Crown, this act of grace ought, in the Queen's opinion, in this instance to emanate from her. The medal might be given for 'Bengal' to all who were or are engaged in the campaign with clasps for 'Delhi', 'Cawnpore' and 'Lucknow'. Cawnpore to include all the actions of General Havelock in taking that place and fighting his way into Lucknow. Lucknow to include the defence and relief of the place. These four names might then be inscribed on the colours of the regiments which were severally engaged. If Lord Palmerston should concur with the Queen he would perhaps communicate with Mr. Vernon Smith and Lord Panmure on the subject.

The Government might well consider it could rest on its laurels. Palmerston's reputation seemed to have reached a new height and he embarked on the new year's legislation with confidence. Nevertheless, there was an undercurrent of hostility. His apparent overwhelming majority was one cause—the House felt that the Prime Minister was becoming somewhat high-handed. On February 18, he obtained a vote of 318 to 173 on the first reading of his Bill to reorganise the Government of India, and could report to the Queen:

> . . . The majority was even greater than had been expected and proves how little credit is to be given to reports which circulate in clubs and drawing rooms as to the probable results of parliamentary proceedings.

There was another Bill before the House which, a few days earlier, had received a majority on its first reading of more than 200. This was a measure designed to increase from a misdemeanour to a felony, with heavy penalties, the crime of conspiracy in Britain to procure the murder of any person, whether sovereign or subject, in any foreign country. The necessity for it had arisen out of a recent attempt on the life of Napoleon III by one Orsini, the preparations for which had been made by refugees in England. French public opinion was incensed and, although the Emperor himself maintained an anglophile attitude, his own position at home was none too strong and he had to countenance some of the protests.

Between the first and second readings of the Conspiracy Bill, a particularly offensive series of addresses appeared in France, and Walewski, the Foreign Minister, sent a sharply worded despatch to Lord Clarendon demanding that the subversive activities of refugees be curbed. This caused immense resentment in Britain, where Palmerston had long since taught his fellow citizens never to truckle to foreigners. This time he was hoist with his own petard. The French note was more or less an agreed formality, but the parliamentary Opposition in the House of Commons

forged it into just the right weapon to defeat Palmerston, who
found himself in a minority of 19 in a snap vote, by the same
combination which had ousted him a year earlier.

The next day, writing in her Journal, the Queen could still
hardly believe the report, but had no option but to send for Lord
Derby to form an alternative government:

> FEBRUARY 20: ... Were much vexed and thunderstruck at finding
> that the Government had been beaten by 19 upon the Conspiracy
> Bill, on which they had but a few nights ago had a majority of 200!
> Much put out and uncertain as to what the Government will do.—
> We walked in the garden for a short while.—At 5 were startled by
> hearing that Lord Palmerston had come. We saw him and he at
> once said he had to communicate what I must have expected, the
> resignation of the Government! The Cabinet was unanimous. To
> remain in would be against their honour and not for the good of
> my service or that of the country! The two parties had combined
> and voted for Mr. M. Gibson's amendment, which was not
> against the measure, but censuring the Government for not having
> answered Count Walewski's despatch. Lord Derby's party had
> voted as a body,—Lord John Russell and the Peelites, all against
> the Government! ! Nothing to be done, but to accept the resig-
> nation. Lord Derby and Lord John Russell, the two possible
> candidates, the one, having no party, and the other in a minority!
> Lord Palmerston thanked me for my kindness. It is a sad result of
> total want of patriotism, and like last year, placing me and the
> country in the greatest difficulty. Albert and I reflected, and
> decided to write and ask Lord Derby to come immediately. He
> expressed great surprise at what had happened, the more so, as he
> had done all he could to further the Bill.

A Derby Government was indeed the only alternative, although
its support in Parliament would at best be haphazard. Only a
formal and rather baffled exchange of letters the next day sig-
nalised the parting between the Queen and the old Minister whom
she had accepted so unwillingly and who had served her so well:

> ... The Queen sent for Lord Derby immediately after Lord
> Palmerston had left her, and saw him shortly afterwards. She
> charged him with the formation of a government: he begged her

to consider the subject more fully before she finally charged him with this commission. She has done so and can come—under the circumstances—to no other conclusion and has therefore this morning written to him finally charging him to undertake to form a government, which she knows he will comply with . . .

Viscount Palmerston presents his humble duty to your Majesty and begs to return his best thanks for your Majesty's gracious communications. Viscount Palmerston quite concurs with your Majesty in thinking that under the circumstances of the case by far the best course, and indeed almost the only one which could lead to a result, was that which your Majesty has adopted, namely to charge Lord Derby with the formation of a government.

CHAPTER VIII

Prince Consort

DURING THESE HALCYON YEARS OF ROYAL APPROVAL, PALMERSTON had earned the additional gratitude of his sovereign by twice engaging in negotiations of great delicacy on behalf of the Court —over the granting of an appropriate British title to Prince Albert, and on the question of providing a dowry and allowance for the Princess Royal, the first of the growing family of royal children to approach marriageable age.

Parliament proved recalcitrant on both issues, although the initial flurry of congratulation when the Queen first informed Palmerston confidentially in September 1855 that the young Princess Royal, at that time barely fifteen years old, was to become betrothed to Prince Frederick William, heir to the throne of Prussia, gave little hint of the difficulties to come:

> . . . Viscount Palmerston trusts that the event, when it takes place, will contribute as much to the happiness of those more immediately concerned, and to the comfort of your Majesty and of the royal family, as it undoubtedly will to the interests of the two countries, and of Europe in general . . .

The Queen thanks Lord Palmerston for his letter received this morning and for the kind congratulations contained in it, on a subject so near and dear to her heart.

The young Prince Frederick William is so charming, amiable and elegant a young man that the Queen feels truly thankful and happy at the thought of the future life of our dear child being confided to him, as she feels perfect confidence in her happiness being thereby assured. The Queen entirely agrees with Lord Palmerston in the great political importance for this country and Europe of this alliance . . .

By the spring of 1856 the rigid protocol of the Prussian Court
was causing a problem:

MARCH 24: Lord Palmerston will remember that when, on our
return from Scotland, we spoke to Lord Palmerston about the
Princess Royal's intended marriage with Prince Frederick William
of Prussia, we told him that till after her Confirmation we did not
wish the subject to be considered as settled, and that we consulted
him as to whether at that period a Declaration in Council ought
to take place.—Lord Palmerston thereafter consulted with several
of his colleagues and informed the Queen through Lord Clarendon that it was thought better not to do this, as the Declaration
in Council generally preceded the demand to Parliament for a
provision for the Princess, which could not well be made till three
or four months before the marriage actually took place. We
therefore then agreed that though the event might be privately
communicated to our relations and friends, no public announcement need take place, unless the Prussian family felt obliged to
make one in Prussia.

In consequence of this agreement, we wrote to the Prince and
Princess of Prussia informing them of this proposed course of
proceeding and asking them if they would pursue the same. This
very morning we have received their answers, by which it appears
that, according to the established rule in Prussia, no such private
family agreement can take place, without being officially announced as 'a betrothal' to the members of the royal family, and
published in the *Gazette* there. Now the difficulty arises—if this is
done in Prussia and it seems it must be, according to the customs
of the country, which in the case of the heir presumptive to the
House could naturally not be omitted—can we avoid making an
announcement here? The only other alternative would be to leave
the thing unknown, which would place us all in a very false
position towards all our relations, would deprive the young people
seeing each other, which would be very hard upon them, and
moreover be an encouragement to the enemies of this marriage
to throw (as many already do) doubt on its reality . . .

MARCH 25: . . . At present not even our other children are acquainted with it, which puts the Princess to great trials. The young
people long to see each other again and ought not to be prevented

235

from doing so, and yet their meeting again and their deportment before the world will be most embarrassing if it is not to be known that they are engaged to each other. Surely a course ought to be devised which would accord with the real position of the affair and the proper feelings of all parties concerned in it, and this will in the end be politically the wisest, whether precedents exist for it or not.

The Prince will write to the Prince of Prussia and ask him to consider the German part of the question, whilst the Queen asks Lord Palmerston to consider our own.

The Queen also reacted very sharply to any suggestion that this was an arranged, dynastic marriage: . .

MARCH 26: . . . The Chancellor speaks of people being inclined to make remarks as to its being wrong that the Princess Royal should be at so young an age bound to contract a marriage a year and a half hence, which would tend to fetter her future direction while she ought to be left a free agent.

He is however probably unaware that the Princess' choice, although made with the sanction and approval of her parents, has been one entirely of her own heart, and that she is as solemnly engaged by her own free will and wish to Prince Frederick William of Prussia, as anyone can be, and that before God she has pledged her word. Therefore, whether it will be publicly announced or not, she could not break this solemn engagement. The Princess is now confirmed and old enough to know her own feelings and wishes, though she may not be old enough to consummate the marriage and leave her parents' roof.

Lastly, the Queen could cite many instances even in this country, where young people have been engaged for two or three and even six years before they married, and in royal and princely families, where the choice must naturally be so very limited, this is of more frequent occurrence.

Palmerston succeeded in winning over his Cabinet colleagues and reported to the Queen:

. . . The various difficulties adverted to by your Majesty were fully appreciated as well as those pointed out by the Lord Chancellor. With regard to the time at which the marriage should take place, and whether it should be put off until after the Princess has completed her seventeenth year, or whether it might take place in the spring of next year, your Majesty will best be able to judge, but there are very many instances of young ladies married at sixteen, and the Princess' mind and understanding are so formed already that any person who conversed with Her Royal Highness would readily believe her to be two years older than she really is. The ceremony of betrothal was, it seems, abolished by law in this country in comparatively early times, owing to abuses which occasionally took place in regard to it with reference to fortunes; and upon consulting the Royal Marriage Act it appears that there is not any necessity for any communication from the sovereign with regard to the marriage of a member of the royal family, other than a signification of consent which may be made at any time before the marriage actually takes place. No communication to Parliament would be required until a provision was proposed . . .

There the matter rested for the time being, but the Queen's mind was exercised by another project even closer to her heart. She had long been brooding over her husband's official position and the problem of his title and precedence clearly occupied their minds from the moment of their marriage. The subject was first broached in inconclusive fashion with Sir Robert Peel back in 1841. Then, in 1846 the Queen carefully copied out the decree of Queen Isabella of Spain granting her husband the honorary title of King, and various memoranda crossed between Queen Victoria and Baron Stockmar on the constitutional proprieties of some similar action on her part. However, the Palmerstonian years of abuse of the Iberian kingdom hardly provided a propitious period for further action, and the Queen only felt free to make a political issue of the proposal to grant the Prince some official status in a conversation with Lord Aberdeen in 1854.

Nothing came of the initiative at that stage, but in the spring of 1856, when the Prince's public reputation had recovered somewhat from the nadir of press vilification at the outbreak of the Crimean War, the Queen returned to the subject again. Although Palmerston had by then been Prime Minister for more than a year, the Queen broached her plan to have the title of Prince Consort conferred on her husband in a letter to Lord Aberdeen, who, although out of office, had remained a royal favourite and confidant. Aberdeen thought that Parliament might now be better inclined to the project and the Queen, thus encouraged, drew up a lengthy memorandum on the subject for his detailed comments. This exchange took place in May 1856 and it was only then that the Queen sent a copy of the memorandum to Palmerston, with a covering letter dated June 5. Both letter and enclosure are so prodigal in the underlined words to which the Queen was addicted that this emphatic form of punctuation is retained:

> The Queen sends Lord Palmerston a confidential memorandum on a subject which she has *much at heart*, and which she considers of the *greatest importance* to herself and her family as well as for posterity. It speaks for itself so that the Queen need not further explain it, beyond saying that she cannot anticipate any real difficulty, as it is only *settling* and *defining* by law what exists already, more or less by *suffrance*.
>
> Lord Palmerston will in the first instance *perhaps*, *only* consult the Lord Chancellor, who has already been consulted by Lord Aberdeen upon it, when he was Prime Minister, and he will then communicate again with the Queen.
>
> When afterwards, Lord Palmerston will have considered the subject with his colleagues (in strict confidence) and have agreed as to the best mode of proceeding—the Queen would wish before any measure was proposed to mention it *herself* to Lord Derby and Lord Russell—as such a measure personally touching herself and the Crown must not appear in the light of a party one, or be proposed to Parliament unless passed with unanimity.

> *Memorandum:* It is a strange omission in our Constitution that while the *wife* of a *King* has the highest rank and dignity in the realm after her husband assigned to her by law, the *husband* of a *Queen Regnant* is entirely ignored by the law.—This is the more extraordinary as a husband has in this country such particular rights and such great power over his wife, and as the Queen is married just as every other woman is, and swears to 'obey' her lord and master as such, while by law, he has no rank or defined position! This is a strange anomaly.—No doubt, as is the case *now*, the *Queen can* give her husband the highest *place* by *placing* him

always *near her person*, and the *nation* would give it him as a *matter of course*. Still, when I first married we had much difficulty on this subject; much bad feeling was shown, and several members of the royal family showed bad grace in giving precedence to the Prince, and the late King of Hanover positively resisted doing so. I gave the Prince precedence by issuing Letters Patent, but these gave no rank in Parliament or at the Council Board,—and it would be far better to put this question beyond *all doubt*, and to secure its settlement for *all future Consorts* of *Queens* and thus have this omission in the Constitution rectified. *Naturally my own* feeling would be to give the Prince the same title and rank as *I have*, but a *titular King* is a complete novelty in this country and might be productive of more inconvenience than advantages to the individual who bears it. Therefore, upon mature reflection, and after considering the question for nearly *sixteen years*, I have come to the conclusion that the *title*, which is *now* by universal *consent* given to him, '*Prince Consort*' with the *highest rank in* and *out of Parliament immediately after* the Queen and *before every other Prince* of the *Royal Family*, should be the one assigned to the *husband* of the *Queen Regnant once* and *for all*. This ought to be done before our children grow up, and it seems particularly easy to do so *now*, that none of the old branches of the royal family are still alive.

The present position is this:—that while every British subject *down* to the Knights *Bachelor*, *Doctor* and *Esquire* has a rank and position *by law*, the *Queen's husband alone* has one by *favour*,—and by his *wife's favour*, who may grant it or not! When granted, as in the present case, it does not extend to Parliament and the Council, and the *children may deny* the position which *their mother* has given to *their father* as a *usurpation* over them, having the law on their side; or, if they waive their rights in his favour *he* will hold a *position* granted *by* the *forbearance* of *his* children! In both cases this is a position most derogatory to the Queen as well as to her husband, and most dangerous to the peace and well being of her family.—If the *children resist*, the Queen will have her *husband* pushed away from her side by *her children* and *they* will take *precedence* over the *man* whom *she is bound to obey*; if *they* are *dutiful, she* will *owe* her peace of mind to *their* continued *generosity* ! !

With relation to *foreign Courts*, the Queen's position is equally humiliating in this respect. Some sovereigns (crowned heads) address her husband as 'brother', some as 'brother and cousin' and some merely as 'cousin.'—When the Queen has been abroad *her husband's* position has always been a subject of negotiation and vexation; the position which has been accorded to him, the Queen has always had to *acknowledge* as a *grace* and *favour* bestowed on her *by* the sovereign whom she visited! While, last year, the Emperor of the French treated the Prince as a royal personage, his uncle declined to come to Paris, avowedly because he would not give precedence to the Prince, and on the Rhine in 1845 the King of Prussia could *not* give the place to the Queen's husband which common civility required, because of the *presence* of an *Archduke*, the third son of an uncle of the then reigning Emperor of Austria, who would not give the *pas* and whom the King would not offend.

The only *legal* position in *Europe*, according to international law, which the *husband* of the *Queen of England* enjoys, is that of a *younger brother* of the *Duke of Saxe-Coburg*, and this *merely* because the English Law does *not know* of *him*! This is *derogatory* to the dignity of the Crown of England.

But *nationally* also, it is an injury to the position of the Crown that the Queen's husband should have *no* other *title* than that of *Prince of Saxe-Coburg*, and thus be *perpetually* represented to the country as a *foreigner*—'the Queen and *her foreign husband*, the Prince Albert of Saxe-Coburg and Gotha!'

The Queen has a right to *claim* that her husband should be an Englishman, bearing an English title, and enjoying a *legal position* which she has not to defend with a wife's anxiety, as a usurpation against her own children, her subjects and foreign Courts.

The question has often been discussed by the Queen with different Prime Ministers and Lord Chancellors, who have invariably entirely agreed with her, but the wish to wait for a good moment to bring the matter before Parliament has caused one year after another to elapse without anything being done. If I become *now* more anxious to have it settled, it is in order that it should be so before our children are so far grown up that it might not appear to be done in order to *guard their father's* position *against them personally*, which could not fail to produce a painful impression upon their minds.

If properly explained to Parliament and the country, I cannot foresee the slightest difficulty in getting such a necessary measure passed, particularly if it be made *quite clear* to the House of

Commons that it is in no way connected with a desire to obtain an increased grant for the Prince.

Palmerston consulted with Lord Cranworth, the Lord Chancellor, who saw little difficulty from the legal point of view, but thought it essential to test privately the likely reaction of the various factions in Parliament. Palmerston reported this to the Queen and proposed to bring the matter before the Cabinet:

> The Queen has received Lord Palmerston's letter and the Lord Chancellor's enclosure, which is very satisfactory.
>
> The Queen would now wish the subject to be brought before the Cabinet and begs Lord Palmerston to read her memorandum to his colleagues. She hopes however that he will give them strict injunctions of secrecy, as it is of the greatest importance that the subject should be properly brought before the public and properly understood and not ooze out, so that misapprehensions might arise about it in the public mind or be created by the press—before it is explained. As Lord Palmerston has not given his opinion on the subject to the Queen, she concludes that he shares her views, but it would be satisfactory for her to hear this from him.
>
> With regard to ascertaining the views of the different parties, to which the Lord Chancellor refers, the Queen thinks it would be best to be done by her personally, so as to avoid the appearance of a mere government measure.

Palmerston acquiesced:

> . . . The Cabinet entered fully into your Majesty's view of the matter, but thought that before any step is taken about it in Parliament, it would be desirable to ascertain, as your Majesty proposes to do, what course would be taken about it by the leaders of political parties; and, with a view to furnish your Majesty with the best means of doing so, it was agreed that the Chancellor should prepare and give to Viscount Palmerston for submission to your Majesty a short memorandum of the heads of such a Bill as might appear to him fitted for the purpose . . .

These exchanges continued during the second half of June. The other parliamentary leaders were benevolently disposed, although even Aberdeen warned against an ambiguity in the wording of the proposed Bill, which might result in the Prince acquiring the title of 'King Consort'. His right to sit in the House of Lords and the Privy Council was also questioned. Lord Derby, in conjunction with his former Lord Chancellor, Lord Lyndhurst, presented the powerful argument that there was little likelihood of passing the Bill through both Houses before the end of the closing session's heavy pressure of business and that the long recess would give undue opportunity for unfavourable discussion of the measure in the press. The Queen was obliged to agree:

> The Queen received yesterday the accompanying letters from Lord Derby and Lord Aberdeen with the enclosures, which she sends to Lord Palmerston and which she would wish him to show to his colleagues, but perhaps first to the Lord Chancellor, as there are various points in them which he should consider. They are very satisfactory to the Queen. There is no doubt much force in Lord Derby's opinion respecting the time of the introduction of the measure, and it might therefore be better not to bring it forward now in the face of such an opinion. The Queen has doubts, however, about the prudence of mentioning it in the Speech.
>
> When Lord Palmerston has communicated with his colleagues, she would naturally wish to have their final opinion and she would also then wish to see the Lord Chancellor, who could after that communicate confidentially as to the framing and wording of the Bill with Lord Lyndhurst, who seems to be most favourably inclined to the measure. The only thing which makes the Queen anxious about the delay till next year is the fear of its becoming in any way known and then misrepresented! It would therefore be most important to repeat the injunctions of secrecy.
>
> Lord Palmerston will be so good as to return all these letters to the Queen when he has done with them.

Palmerston concurred with Derby and the project remained in abeyance until December. By then, Aberdeen had advised the Queen that the subject could properly be mentioned in the Speech from the Throne. The Cabinet disagreed:

> . . . Viscount Palmerston duly consulted with his colleagues as to the course which it will be best to pursue in regard to the matter to which Lord Aberdeen's memorandum relates, and the opinion

come to is that it would not be advisable to mention the subject in your Majesty's Speech from the Throne, but that soon after the beginning of the session your Majesty might send a message to both Houses of Parliament recommending the matter for their consideration. If the subject were mentioned in the Speech from the Throne it would be mixed up with the many other topics of discussion and could not be accompanied with proper explanation, whereas if it were made the subject of a separate message full explanation would at once accompany the announcement . . .

In the meantime, the question of the Princess Royal's dowry was threatening to cause difficulties in Parliament which might well increase opposition to the granting of a title to a Prince who, in nearly twenty years, had yet to win the unreserved confidence of the British public. The Queen was asking for a substantial sum for her daughter and, in order to justify this, had asked Palmerston to look into the annuity granted to George III's daughters:

. . . The paper made out at the Treasury does not appear to the Queen as complete as it ought to be. She knows for instance, and it can be seen by the Annual Register, that the Princess Royal had £5,000 a year granted her on her marriage, on the Irish Revenue. This, with the fifth part of £30,000 granted to the daughters of George III in 1778 made her income £11,000 a year. The Queen hopes that further researches will be made, as it is most important that the information should be complete. It is not stated in the paper which of these grants were additional to former ones, and which in lieu of former ones. If, in the case of Princess Elizabeth, the £6,000 granted in 1778 went on, and the two new grants of £9,000 and £4,000 are added, she received £19,000 a year. Was that so? All this has a material bearing on our case . . .

Both matters dragged on. Lord Derby required more time to prepare his supporters for the Prince Consort Bill, and Palmerston wanted to get his Budget out of the way first. The Queen was becoming impatient and wrote again to the Prime Minister at the end of February 1857:

The Debate on the Budget being now over and the time having elapsed which Lord Palmerston wished should, before 'The Prince Consort Bill' was proposed, she writes to him to say that we are

R   243

going to Windsor on the 2nd March (Monday next) to return here on the 11th and that she thinks it would be of importance that the Government should so far have agreed as to the mode of proceeding, the wording of the message, and the Bill itself (which she has not yet seen and which she hopes the Chancellor has, as he promised her to do, communicated upon with Lord Lyndhurst and Lord Aberdeen) that she could confidentially communicate with the Duke of Cambridge and the Duchess of Gloucester before she went out of town on the 2nd, as also to be able to inform Lord Derby and Lord Aberdeen that it is the intention of the Government to bring it in on such and such a day. It should not be delayed so long as to come near any arrangement to be proposed respecting the Princess Royal and the other royal children, but should appear to be entirely unconnected with it.

It would therefore seem to be advisable that it should be got well over before Easter, indeed for many reasons the Queen would much wish that all difficulties respecting the measure could be got over before the end of March. The Queen trusts that she shall soon hear from Lord Palmerston on this subject, which she has so much at heart to see properly settled.

Palmerston replied the same day:

Viscount Palmerston presents his humble duty to your Majesty and begs to state that he brought before the Cabinet this afternoon the question of the proposed Bill for defining the rank and position of the Prince Consort, with reference to the time at which it might be advisable to bring the matter forward. The Cabinet gave great attention to the subject, but were strongly of opinion that the present moment would not be favourable for the purpose and that, notwithstanding the influence and exertions of the heads of parties, the measure might fail to pass through Parliament. It was however thought best that the view taken of this matter should be stated in a minute to be submitted for your Majesty's consideration and as soon as it has been drawn up Viscount Palmerston will have the honour of laying it before your Majesty.

Ten days later, the Queen wrote again:

Without wishing to appear impatient or indeed troublesome at a moment when so much business of importance presses upon Lord Palmerston, the Queen must nevertheless recall to his recollection that ten days have now elapsed since the minute of the Cabinet of the 'Prince Consort Bill' was to have been submitted to her.

The Cabinet, when it came to formal consideration of the proposal, had proved recalcitrant and on March 11 Palmerston was obliged to reply:

> ... The accompanying draft was drawn up and has been circulated to and concurred in by several members of the Cabinet, but the announcement of an intended dissolution of Parliament having rendered any measure on this matter impossible for the present, the draft has not been passed on as rapidly as it otherwise would have been to all the remaining members of the Cabinet.
>
> Your Majesty will see that the great objection which it is apprehended might be urged against the proposed measure would be founded upon the circumstance that it would interpose the Prince Consort between the sovereign and the heir to the throne. There might be less liability to objection if the rank proposed to be given to the Prince Consort were to be confined to precedence over all the other members of the royal family, assuming that the advantages to be obtained by such a Bill would be such as to make it worth while to incur the inconvenience which might arise from the discussion which it would create ...:

The minute itself was nothing if not explicit:

> Your Majesty's confidential servants have had under their careful consideration the draft of a Bill prepared by the Lord Chancellor, entitled 'an Act for settling the Rank of the Husband of the reigning Queen', which it is contemplated to introduce into Parliament, upon the responsibility of the Government, after the attention of both Houses shall have been called to the subject by a message from your Majesty.
>
> In expressing to your Majesty with great deference and respect, the opinion which they have formed upon this matter, they need scarcely say that in their deliberations upon it, they have been actuated by the warmest attachment to your Majesty's Throne and person, and by a sincere wish to adopt such a course as shall not only promote the real interests of the Crown, but shall conduce to

the domestic happiness and comfort of your Majesty and of H.R.H. Prince Albert.

The object of the Bill in question is declared to be, with reference to H.R.H. Prince Albert and to all future husbands of a reigning Queen of England, to put the husband of the reigning Queen in a position corresponding with that of the wife of a king, which is not now, and never has been the case. The measure proceeds on the assumption that the difference is accidental, or exceptional, and contrary to analogy and ought therefore to be removed.

It is however certain that the difference is the result of no accident or exception, that it is founded on a distinctly understood policy, and that it is in accordance with the general law of the country.

According to the law and usage of England, the wife of a peer, though by birth a commoner, receives her husband's rank. The wife of a duke, born a commoner, would legally take precedence of a duchess in her own right. By the law and usage of England a man, having an hereditary title, communicates that title, together with its incidence in respects of honours, rank and precedence to his wife.

But the converse of this rule does not hold good. A peeress in her own right confers no title, rank or precedence on her husband. The same remark applies to those more common honorary titles of women, which are conferred by courtesy. By the ancient law and usage of this realm, a woman having an hereditary title, is incapable of communicating that title, or any incident or advantage flowing from that title, to her husband. A man ennobles his wife, a woman does not ennoble her husband.

These are the rules which have hitherto been applied to the Crown, not through error, or inattention, but deliberately, knowingly and designedly, as being the highest and indeed most illustrious of hereditary titles, but nevertheless surrounded by those limitations which the Constitution of this country, jealous of the communication of hereditary honours, and anxious by their close restriction to preserve their value, has guarded the distinctions of the peerage.

Precisely similar rules and distinctions apply to the other members of the royal family. Even after the Royal Marriage Act, the marriage of an English Prince or Princess with a subject, provided that the consent of the sovereign is obtained, or other conditions are fulfilled, is valid. If the Duke of Cambridge were now to contract legal marriage with a commoner, he would communicate to her all the incidents and advantages of his rank, as the Duke of York, the brother of Charles II, did to Anne Hyde; whereas, if his sister, the Princess Mary, were to contract a similar marriage, her husband would derive no rank from her, but would remain a commoner. These distinctions are of no recent origin, but pervade the entire history of the country. Catherine (of France) the Queen of King Henry V, married after his death a private Welsh gentleman, Sir Owen Tudor. She imparted to him no royal rank, and she bore him two sons, who inherited no title, but were created Earl of Richmond and Earl of Pembroke. Again, after the death of Henry VIII, Catherine Parr married Lord Seymour, the Lord High Admiral, whose rank was not affected by his royal marriage, but remained subordinate to that of his powerful elder brother, the Protector Somerset.

If this fundamental principle, hitherto invariably maintained, is to be departed from, and if the husband of a Queen Regnant is to be placed in a legal position analogous to that of the wife of a king, the change contemplated would appear too confined and not co-extensive with the policy indicated in the preamble. It would follow by a necessary and inevitable consequence, that the husband of the Queen Regnant ought, by Act of Parliament, to be constituted King Consort, and to receive that legal designation, as the wife of a King is denominated Queen Consort. So closely is this conclusion connected with the declaration of the preamble, that the present measure would unquestionably be represented, as probably believed, to be a precursor of a Bill for making that ulterior change.

It cannot be said that the question to which this Bill refers has been overlooked. When the Bill for the naturalization of H.R.H. Prince Albert was introduced, it was proposed to enable your Majesty to confer rank on H.R.H., and Lord Cottenham, the Lord Chancellor, stated that it was intended to recommend that he should have rank next after the heir apparent. The proposition was however objected to and subsequently abandoned.

It should be further borne in mind that in virtue of the rule already mentioned, a Prince Consort, surviving a Queen Regnant, would under the measure in question, in the event of his contracting a second marriage, communicate to his wife, who might be altogether a stranger to England, his own rights and precedence over the royal family of this country. It will be observed that a Prince Consort is in no way subject to the restraint of the Royal Marriage Act, and would therefore be wholly independent of the sovereign for the time being.

Your Majesty's servants do not understand that any practical inconvenience has hitherto arisen in this country with respect to the rank of H.R.H. Prince Albert. His rank next to your Majesty has never, so far as they are aware, been contested on any public or private occasion. The esteem and respect with which H.R.H. is universally regarded, and the persuasion that he has invariably observed the bounds which define the position of the consort of a constitutional Queen, lead them to anticipate that his rank will continue, as heretofore, to be admitted without dispute or question. The legal and constitutional power of your Majesty to confer any rank upon H.R.H. subject only to the limitations imposed by the Act of Henry VIII, has never been denied by any lawyer. They therefore seriously doubt the propriety of disturbing any priority which the law and Constitution of this country may at present assign to the Prince of Wales, in the Parliament chamber or at the Council table. The Regency debates of 1788 show what was the view taken by constitutional lawyers, of all parties, respecting the practical position and moral rights of the heir apparent to the Crown, and a shock might be given to the feelings of the people, feelings based upon their loyalty and affection to the Throne, and upon their respect for the hereditary principle of succession, if rights of a public nature, which place the Prince of Wales next to the sovereign, now actually possessed by him, were proposed to be taken out of him by Act of Parliament, and if another person, however entitled to his veneration and affection on domestic grounds, were visibly interposed, in great constitutional solemnity, between him and the Throne.

Even apart from the unfavourable impression which might be produced upon public opinion, and considering the question upon domestic grounds, your Majesty's servants cannot but fear that a Bill depriving the Prince of Wales of a precedence and a legal position in the Parliament chamber and at the Council table, which the heir apparent to the Crown has hitherto enjoyed, would be represented as an invasion of his rights and might, by this perversion, be made the means of engendering dissatisfaction and jealousy in the precise quarter where it is desired to prevent their growth.

The Queen, her hopes of achieving this long-sought position for her husband dashed, was mortified, but determined to find some way out of the *impasse*:

> The Queen has to acknowledge the receipt of the minute of Cabinet upon 'The Prince Consort Bill'. Lord Palmerston will not be astonished when she tells him that the perusal of this document has caused her much surprise, so totally at variance is it with what had been expressed to her up to this moment as the opinion of the Cabinet on this question.
>
> The arguments now brought forward against the measure at the moment when it was to be introduced must have occurred to the Queen's advisers before and, if so, they ought not to have allowed her to communicate with Lords Derby, Aberdeen and Lyndhurst and John Russell to obtain their adhesion to the measure which the Government had decided to bring into Parliament and which they would have done last year, had Lord Derby not recommended its postponement to the opening of this session.
>
> It is not the Queen's intention at this moment to enter into a discussion upon the arguments set forth in the minute further than to say that she feels the difficulty which the constitutional position of the Prince of Wales may cause, but the analogy sought to be drawn between the Queen's case and that of private individuals is surely beside the question. It is nothing peculiar to the English law that wives do not give rank to their husbands, while husbands do so to their wives, but is the case all over the world, and has always been so. If it were to rule the Queen's case, her husband could have no rank and precedence at all, as he is not known to the Act of Henry VIII.
>
> The Queen quite admits the impolicy if not the impossibility of bringing forward the measure under the present political circumstances. But having now waited 17 years without approaching any nearer the solution of what she considers a most important question to her and her family, and every new political juncture having brought new difficulties with it, she is inclined to think that it will be better for her, instead of attempting an Enactment by Parliament with its attendant discussions, to do merely as much as her prerogative will enable her, which prerogative is strongly

maintained in the minute, to leave for the present all question of precedence out of consideration, and to content herself with simply giving her husband by Letters Patent the title of 'Prince Consort', which can injure no one, while it will give him an English title consistent with his position, and avoid his being treated by foreign Courts as a junior member of the House of Saxe-Coburg.

If the Cabinet, to whom the Queen wishes this letter to be shown, should agree with her, she thinks it right to communicate this change in her intentions to those leaders of political parties with whom she has previously communicated.

The proper time for issuing the Letters Patent may be left for consideration; the Queen is inclined to think the latter end of the ensuing session.

Lord Palmerston knowing how anxious the Queen is upon this subject, [she] trusts he will give it his best consideration and not leave her long without an answer.

Palmerston doubtless felt that something had to be done to placate his exasperated sovereign:

... It is quite true as your Majesty states that the Cabinet, last year, being most anxious in all matters to give effect to your Majesty's wishes, contemplated the introduction of a Bill in this session of Parliament and the Chancellor had accordingly prepared the draft of a Bill and of a preliminary message. But when they came to discuss more minutely the details of the proposed arrangement, objections and difficulties connected with it presented themselves more forcibly than they had done before, and the Cabinet, without any diminution of their anxious desire to consult your Majesty's wishes, were led more strongly to doubt the advisability of the proposed measure.

With regard to the course which your Majesty now suggests, namely that your Majesty should by Letters Patent confer upon H.R.H. the Prince Albert the title of Prince Consort, there does not seem at first sight to be any objection to such an exercise of the royal prerogative, but on a question of this kind the Chancellor would be glad to be allowed to give it a little more consideration than could be given to it offhand, and Viscount Palmerston will have the honour of communicating to your Majesty such observations, if any, as may occur to the Chancellor thereupon . . .

Cranworth was still inclined to niggle and was summoned to the royal presence:

> ... The Queen showed the Chancellor a copy of the original Letters Patent giving the Prince the precedence he now enjoys, granted March 1840, and which he had never seen. He said they simplified the question so much as to remove all difficulty in the way of the execution of the Queen's wishes as regards the title of 'Prince Consort', which is all that the Queen would propose now to do, as leaving the question of precedence untouched. The Chancellor's doubts seemed to have arisen from his imagining that the Queen expected to do more by Letters Patent than is the case.
>
> The Queen now only waits to hear from Lord Palmerston whether she can communicate her altered intentions to Lords Derby, Aberdeen etc. etc., which she is anxious to do either to-day or tomorrow.

Even then, Cranworth tried to find a way out of declaring an opinion without consulting the other law officers of the Crown. Palmerston, exasperated in his turn, asked him bluntly whether his own opinion as Chancellor was not sufficient. The ultimatum worked, Cranworth capitulated and Palmerston was able to write to the Queen at the end of March:

> ... Viscount Palmerston submits the Chancellor's answer, which will enable your Majesty to communicate at once with Lord Derby and Lord Aberdeen.
>
> Viscount Palmerston begs to assure your Majesty that the course this whole affair has taken has been the cause of great annoyance to him. When the matter was brought last year before the Cabinet there appeared to be an almost unanimous opinion in favour of the proposed Bill and that opinion seemed to prevail until lately, but when, at the beginning of this session of Parliament, the matter was again considered with a view to immediate action, doubts were started and difficulties were suggested and after much discussion the opinion of the Cabinet entirely changed, and although that of Viscount Palmerston was not altered, he felt that in a matter that so deeply concerned your Majesty's personal feelings it would be improper to run any risks of results which might be disagreeable and which the greater part of the Cabinet considered as not improbable.

The announcement had to be further delayed as the amount of the Princess Royal's dowry was causing heated public discussion. The Queen was asking for an annuity of £8,000 a year and a dower of £40,000. Lord Derby wanted the allowance limited to £6,000 a year, although he was prepared to be reasonable about the initial capital grant. There were other suggestions that the money should come out of the revenues of the Duchy of Cornwall, reserved to the Prince of Wales, and the Queen would have preferred to have the whole question of the financial needs of her fast maturing family considered *en bloc*. However, she resigned herself to abandoning this proposal, provided the full requirements of the Princess Royal were met.

This proposal was duly passed and by June the Queen could see more clearly on her other project:

> . . . The Queen thinks that the time has now arrived when the Letters Patent conferring on the Prince the title of 'Prince Consort' might be issued. The Princess Royal's dotation has passed and no suspicion as to any ulterior measures entailing an increased allowance for the Prince could be created. The wording of the document will however be of some importance, so as to explain clearly the object had in view in conferring this title, viz. more in accordance with the Prince's position. Perhaps the best and simplest course would be for Lord Palmerston to desire the Chancellor to draw up a form and to send it to the Queen for consideration. The Chancellor possesses a copy of the original Letters Patent, conferring precedence on the Prince issued March 5, 1840. When this has taken place there will remain nothing more to be done, than to have a Council to alter the name in the Liturgy, and after that the Queen thinks a circular should be sent to the Queen's Ambassadors and Ministers abroad, to inform foreign Governments of the title the Queen has conferred on her husband.

The Queen had reached the end of her long battle to obtain formal recognition of the place the Prince occupied as her guide and counsellor, but the triumph could not be enacted in Parliament and took the final form of a modest paragraph in the *Gazette*:

> On the 25th June a Council was held at Buckingham Palace, at

which Letters Patent were approved conferring upon His Royal Highness Prince Albert the title and dignity of Prince Consort and granting him, except where otherwise provided by Act of Parliament, place, pre-eminence and precedence next to Her Majesty. Prayer books were altered accordingly. Alterations in the Liturgy consequent on the Letters Patent were made. The words 'Prince Consort' were inserted in the prayers instead of the words 'Prince Albert'.

CHAPTER IX

Napoleon III in Italy

PARLIAMENTARY DEFEAT IS A SERIOUS MATTER TO A MAN IN HIS seventy-fourth year, but Palmerston's long career was far from over yet. Lord Derby's second ministry proved even shakier than his first and after fifteen precarious months of life succumbed in 1859 to a hostile vote in the House of Commons on a muddled attempt to put through a measure of parliamentary reform. Fresh elections were called, which gave the Conservatives a solid block of 300 seats. Every other faction combined mustered 350.

During most of his period out of office, Palmerston had looked a spent force. Whigs, Liberals and Radicals were riven by personal antipathies. Palmerston and Lord John Russell, the two living Whig Prime Ministers, were at loggerheads, and the leadership of the Party devolved on Lord Granville in the House of Lords. The remaining Peelites still leaned towards Derby and Disraeli, whose survival had been due largely to the chaos in the Opposition. But Palmerston, his vitality and debating skill unimpaired, gradually re-established his position. Not for the first time, events abroad played into his hands.

After a dozen years, agitation in Italy to throw off the Austrian yoke had built up to explosion heat again. This time, the Sardinian king, Victor Emmanuel, had the services of a Minister of genius, Cavour, who had succeeded in winning the support of Napoleon III. In April 1859, the French Emperor attempted to emulate his great predecessor and namesake and crossed the Alps with his army.

Palmerston found himself in the happy position of emerging again as the champion of those who favoured the Italian cause. These, of course, did not include the Queen, but they had come to include Gladstone, who had returned from a visit to Italy incensed at the excesses of monarchical despotism. They also included Lord John Russell, who agreed to sink his personal differences and political disagreement over Reform with Palmerston. The election period saw, in effect, the formation of the Liberal Party out of a genuine Whig-Liberal-Radical coalition, which knew it could attract the Peelites behind the defecting Gladstone.

The Queen had hoped to the last, either that the country would prefer the pro-Austrian Conservatives, or that some parliamentary combination would be achieved to spare her the awful spectre of either Palmerston or Russell determining foreign policy. The manœuvres were labyrinthine. At one point, Disraeli had tried to tempt Palmerston to join forces with the Conservatives on a platform of moderate reform. When Derby finally lost hope of reconstructing his administration, the Queen tried to stave off the inevitable by a somewhat disingenuous attempt to persuade both Palmerston and Russell to serve under the pliant Granville. Her Journal for June 11–13 told the story:

> JUNE 11: . . . Lord Derby came at about 12, most grateful and pleased at his Garter, and seemed altogether much agitated. Talked of Mr. Disraeli's having only a few days ago still been perfectly confident of success, which we could not understand. Lord Derby said, whoever I might send for, I might be sure of his readiness to support the new Government, provided no extreme measures of reform were proposed. The Party had never been more united and were well satisfied, thinking they had been most fairly dealt by, and would therefore be powerful. We impressed upon him the great importance of a really strong Conservative Party, as a check upon the Liberals and not, as it had been now to a certain extent, competing with the Liberal Party. He was profuse in expressions of thanks for our kindness etc. Wrote to Lord Granville, asking him to come at 4 . . .
> At 4 came Lord Granville, who stayed more than an hour. Told him that this was a very serious moment, that considering the equal positions of Lord Palmerston and Lord J. Russell, both having been Prime Ministers, I thought it would be less invidious to choose neither; that therefore I called upon him (Lord G.), as head of the Liberal Party in the House of Lords, to form a government.

Another reason for my wishing this being the bad effect Lord Palmerston's name would have in Europe, after the speeches he had made. Lord Granville replied that he had sometimes thought of this possibility, and knew that combinations of this kind were often better under a third person, but that he doubted this being the case now. Lord Palmerston and Lord John had agreed to serve under one another [sic] and he believed were agreed upon Reform. The Peelites would join. Lord Granville believed my best course would be to send for one or the other, to which I objected, preferring the attempt to be made. Stated my strong opinion that Lord Clarendon should be at the Foreign Office, without which there could be no security. Lord G. felt and agreed in this, but feared there might be a difficulty with Lord Palmerston and Lord J. Russell. With Lord P. less, indeed hardly any, if, as I wished, the Lead of the House of Commons should be given him. Lord Granville thought Lord Palmerston would consent to serve under him, but feared Lord J. Russell might not, and though a government might be formed without him, it would not be a strong one. I promised to write and did so to both, stating my reasons for calling on Lord Granville to form a government, as less invidious to both and calling on them to join and assist Lord Granville. I also wrote a line to Lord Clarendon, asking him to assist Lord Granville. The latter left with the letters, intending to go first to Lord Palmerston and then to Lord J. Russell . . .

JUNE 12: On waking, received a letter from Lord Palmerston, very proper, ready to join with Lord Granville and sit under him, but only if he could form a strong government—and one from Lord Granville, saying Lord Palmerston had behaved very handsomely. Lord J. Russell had likewise expressed no objection to serving under Lord Granville, but thought he could not give effect to his views unless he were Prime Minister or Leader of the House of Commons, the latter Lord Granville told him he could not be. Lord Granville again saw Lord Palmerston, who maintained that he must keep the lead. Lord Granville saw Lord Clarendon, who 'acted up' to the spirit of my letter, but both he and Sir G. Grey would strongly deprecate any government without Lord J. Russell. Sir G. Lewis, Mr. Gladstone and Mr. S. Herbert, are anxious Lord J. Russell should be comprised, but thought government might be formed without him. Mr. M. Gibson (Radical) said Lord John's being in the government was a *sine qua non* of support of Liberals below the gangway (extreme Liberals). Lord Granville had written to ask Lord J. Russell for final answer . . .

After luncheon saw Lord Granville, who stayed till past 4. He said he had nothing satisfactory to report and gave me a letter from Lord J. Russell, in which the latter says he could not serve under Lord Granville, as under him he would be third while under Lord Palmerston second, for he should expect Lord Palmerston to give him the choice of every office except his own! Dreadful personal feelings again! Lord Granville says Lord John certainly looks to the Foreign Office! It is most trying and annoying in every way, for we can have no confidence in him and we would have felt so sure with Lord Clarendon. Lord Granville felt sure he would never be able to form a government without Lord John since this last letter; if things had rested where they were yesterday, he thinks he might. Under the circumstances, we decided to send for Lord Palmerston. Lord Granville thought that Lord P. could more easily than he form a government without Lord John. Lord Granville talked of many things. No one could have behaved better than he has. Wrote to Lord Palmerston to ask him to come . . .

We went in at 6 to see Lord Palmerston and told him that in consequence of Lord Granville's having relinquished the task of forming a government, I asked him to do so. He accepted, saying his first object would be to secure Lord J. Russell. He had asked Lord John if he would come to a meeting a week ago and if so, if he would enable him to say that he would act with and under Lord Palmerston, and vice versa. Lord John had agreed upon the Reform Bill, but since had again disagreed upon Reform. From what Lord P. had heard, however, he said Lord John might make conditions, which he could not agree to, viz. Lord P.'s going to the House of Lords and Lord John having the Lead. This Lord P. could not agree to, having the largest following and thinking he could be of more use to me in the House of Commons, that he thought India would be the best post for Lord John, but that if the latter insisted on the Foreign Office, he, Lord P., could not refuse it or break off on that account, whereas he could on the Leadership. He would have much liked to see Lord Clarendon at the F.O. and knew how I had wished for it. I felt this was a sad truth, but secretly hoped it might yet be averted. Spoke of the great importance of strict neutrality being adhered to, which he agreed in, though he seemed to think Germany had nothing to do with Austrian dominions in Italy. We explained to him how likely it was that, should France be victorious, she would attack Germany and then us, each in turn, once she had finished with Austria. He said that might possibly be. He was all for being well armed and prepared, and talked sensibly about arming the people in the sea coast towns. He hoped to have the assistance of the Duke of Newcastle, Mr. Gladstone, Mr. S. Herbert, Mr. Cardwell, Lord Elgin, Sir G. Grey, Lords Granville and Clarendon, Sir G. C. Lewis, and thought Mr. M. Gibson or Mr. Cobden should be taken into the Government. Mr. Herbert for War; Sir C. Wood for the Admiralty and Sir B. Hall in his old place. Lord Palmerston, however, in answer to a question of mine, said that even if Lord John did not join, he would undertake to form a government. Lord P. behaved very properly . . .

JUNE 13: A fine morning.—Received a letter from Lord Palmerston, saying his conversation with Lord John had been satisfactory, but he was sorry to say Lord John laid claim to the Foreign Office 'in such a manner as to oblige Lord Palmerston to consent to it'. This is most vexatious. Enough cause for annoyance, God knows . . . Heard again from Lord Palmerston, with a sort of sketch of proposed Cabinet, though no offices had really yet been offered . . . At 3 Lord Palmerston came and we chiefly talked over the arrangements for the new Cabinet. Lord John's wish for the Foreign Office was merely a little feeling of his own dignity, which he wished to keep up. Lord Palmerston heard that Lord John gave out 'he meant to settle Europe and then give up'. Observed that I took this opportunity of once more pointing out the great importance of perfect neutrality, as he and Lord John were credited with being very anti-Austrian. Lord Palmerston agreed in this, saying he felt its great importance, equally of our armaments being at least as large as had been proposed. That he (Lord P.) was all for Austria being a strong power in the middle of Europe and of our being prepared to stand by Germany and Belgium should they be attacked. I told him he would see, when he once knew all that had passed, that it was France, not Austria, who would not keep to their bases.—Talked of names, which

The triumphant entry of Queen Victoria into Paris, August 18, 1855, marked the turn of the tide in the Crimean War

Water colour by Googen, reproduced by gracious permission of Her Majesty the Queen

were not yet settled. Lord Clarendon seemed to feel not being Foreign Secretary and was disinclined to take any other office. Lord Palmerston begged I would see Lord Clarendon and speak to him. He could have any other office, his support in the Cabinet and in the House of Lords being most important, there being some people of very advanced opinions, whom Lord P. would like Lord Clarendon to counteract. Mr. Cobden (an honest man) was to be offered a seat in the Cabinet. We strongly urged Sir C. Wood being Indian Secretary as he understood it so well and Lord P. agreed. Sir R. Bethell he considered, on the whole, as the best for Lord Chancellor.—Wrote to Lord Clarendon asking him to come as soon as he could, and he appeared before 6. After a little general talk, during which he observed he thought the Government would do well,—Lord John would be found moderate and anti-French and both he and Lord Palmerston would be obliged to be so; they might be able to do more than those who were in fact (like the late Government) more impartial—I lamented over his (Lord C.) not being Foreign Secretary and urged him to join the Government in some other office. But I found him immovable, saying there was nothing he would not do for me, but that he had been much attacked, when and after being at the F.O. This he did not mind, but were he to take any other office it would be admitting the truth of the attacks, and besides he had never given any other office much of his attention. He could do neither me, or the Government, any good and it would be injurious to himself. I could not after this press him any further. We talked of Lord J. Russell's conduct, which we blamed, but Lord Clarendon said he had expected, but he did not think he would last long. If Lord John made difficulties and was troublesome in the Cabinet (which he very likely would be), then he would most likely be ejected and set at defiance. That I could not have opposed his having the F.O., as that would have exposed me to blame. I had acted absolutely rightly, in first calling on Lord Granville to form a government, but that it was better he had failed, he never could have worked well with Lord John and Lord Palmerston under him, that it would have been 'like driving two wild horses'. As late as two days ago, Lord John had told Mr. S. Herbert he did not feel sure whether he could join Lord Palmerston!! on account of Reform!! We took Lord Clarendon for a little while with us into the garden, and talked over the same things, and the war—the dreadful dangers to Europe whatever happened. Lord Clarendon repeated his determination not to join the Government, but expressed his readiness to do so as Foreign Secretary, should there be a vacancy. We think him right, and wished we could see him in his old place ere long!— . . .

Palmerston's Cabinet, one of the strongest and most gifted of the century, included the Peelites, Gladstone, Sidney Herbert and Cardwell, as Chancellor of the Exchequer, War Secretary and Irish Secretary respectively. In a gesture of reconciliation, an overture was made to the great Radical, Cobden, to take the Board of Trade. He declined, but the post went to his colleague Milner Gibson, and the Poor Law Board to another Radical, Villiers. With great Whigs like Russell, Sir George Lewis and Sir Charles Wood at the Foreign, Home and India Offices, the pattern of coalition for a half-century to come was set.

Even so, strong Cabinets are often less easy to control than weak ones, and there were to be several issues which strained its new-found cohesion to the limit. Palmerston's masterly handling of these conflicting elements probably provide him with his best claim to be remembered as a major statesman. The first crisis—Italy—inevitably embroiled him with the Court as well.

Palmerston, Russell and Gladstone wanted a free and independent Italy, embracing the whole country south of the Alps. Queen Victoria and the Prince Consort resisted any encroachment on the rights of Austria in the Italian principalities which had formed part of the post-Napoleonic peace settlement of 1815, to which Britain was a party. The other Cabinet ministers felt less committed either way. The position as they took office was that Napoleon III and the Sardinians, with the victory of Solferino, had overrun again the territory won a dozen years earlier by King Charles Albert in the first attempt to liberate Italy. The Austrians had retreated once more to their central redoubt, and held Venetia and Modena in the east. But the French had suffered unexpectedly severe losses and Napoleon III, realising he must incur more if he was to conquer northern Italy and always fearful of his position at home, prepared to treat with the Austrian Emperor on the basis of each holding his position. This would mean the retention by Austria of Venetia, with an Archduke as its ruler and dominating membership of any Italian confederation. This eventuality Palmerston hoped to forestall by interested mediation. Here lay the seeds of nearly a year's renewed conflict with his own Court. His first letter to the Queen on the subject, on July 4, aroused her worst suspicions:

> . . . It is clear that Austria will have to submit in the end to the loss of her Italian provinces, but possibly some arrangement may be made by which those provinces may take upon themselves some portion of the Austrian debt, although it cannot but be felt that such an arrangement would be more difficult after a decisive campaign than before it.
>
> It is much to be feared that the discontent created in Hungary by the bad Government which has there prevailed may break out into revolt, which would be a great misfortune, as the maintenance of Austria as a great German power is essential for the general interests of Europe.

Two days later he informed her of an approach that had been made by the French Ambassador:

> . . . The Cabinet also considered the communication from Count Persigny, suggesting that your Majesty should propose an armistice to the contending parties, to last a fortnight, in order that they might consider a proposal to negotiate for peace upon the basis that Italy should be restored to the Italians, that is to say evacuated by the Austrians; Lombardy, Parma, Massa and Carrara to be given to Piedmont; Venice and Modena to an Austrian Archduke as an independent State; Tuscany to the Duchess of Parma; the legations to a Lay Viceroy and the rest of the Roman States to the Pope. As Count Persigny was waiting for an answer, Lord John Russell informed him that no proposal could be made to Austria for an armistice with a view to negotiate on the basis of the surrender by Austria of all her Italian territories without first ascertaining privately that Austria would be willing to treat on such a basis. It is however highly improbable that in the present state of things she would agree to such terms . . .

The last thing the Queen wanted was for Napoleon III to have his backbone stiffened by her two incorrigible old Whigs. She had been through all this before in 1849 and, although they had now exchanged posts, she still distrusted the combination. Lord John received a peremptory letter instructing him to maintain strict neutrality and to bring its contents before the Cabinet. Palmerston refused to be hemmed in and answered for him:

> . . . With respect however to your Majesty's communication to Lord John Russell, which was read to the Cabinet, Viscount Palmerston would beg to submit that neutrality between belligerents means, in its proper sense, abstinence from giving to either party assistance in carrying on the war, but it does not preclude good offices or mediation with a view to the restoration of peace, and that in fact it is only a neutral power that can advantageously perform those functions. But a mediator, to be useful, must not merely be content with transmitting from one party to the other propositions and answers, but should accompany those communications with such opinions, recommendations and advice, as may conduce to an amicable arrangement, according to the best judgment which the mediating power may form.
>
> There is therefore nothing in your Majesty's position of neutrality which should prevent advice being given either to the allies or to Austria, to accept any proposals that your Majesty's Government might at the request of the one party transmit to the other; and if it be thought, as seems pretty clear, that a continuation of the war would lead to a state of things in which Austria would not get conditions of peace as little disadvantageous as those which have now been offered, it would be a friendly office towards Austria, and in no degree whatever inconsistent with the character of neutrality, to advise Austria to accept those conditions.
>
> But, moreover, it seems generally admitted that to the treaty of peace which is to conclude this war, and to the arrangements of that treaty, Great Britain with other powers not parties to the war, ought to be parties. But Great Britain cannot be a party to a treaty simply to register arrangements made by other powers. If Great Britain is to be a party to a treaty, the British Crown and Government must be a party to the negotiations by which that treaty is to be settled and must approve of the arrangements which such treaty is to sanction; and it is therefore perfectly in accordance with the double character in which your Majesty stands of neutral in the war, and of future party to the treaty of

peace, that your Majesty's Government should have an opinion and should express an opinion as to any proposals tending to establish a basis on which negotiations for peace should be founded; and the more especially when invited by the proposing party to do so . . .

If Austria had consented to go into Congress she would have saved her Italian provinces by the sacrifice of her undue and illegitimate authority beyond her own limits, and if she were to consent to the conditions now offered to her, she might retain that connection with Venetia which the placing an Austrian Archduke as its ruler would give. Such an arrangement would be liable to much objection on the part of the Italians, and might in spite of all precautions lay the foundation for a renewal of war, but, nevertheless, if Austria would consent to it, it might secure peace for a considerable time to come.

To the Prime Minister's chagrin, Napoleon III, who lacked his great uncle's final audacity, had met the Austrian Emperor at Villafranca and concluded peace on terms so favourable to Austria that they included the reinstallation of the puppet Italian rulers of Modena and Tuscany. The moment the news arrived, the Prince Consort drafted in his own hand a tart note for the Queen to copy and send to Palmerston:

> The Queen has received Lord Palmerston's letter on the question of neutrality and active diplomatic interference. She is glad to be relieved by the happy news of the concluded Peace, from the necessity of answering it.

Palmerston was not finished yet. He protested formally to Persigny that the treaty would hand over an Italian confederation bound hand and foot to Austria, and sent a copy of this to the Queen. Again, the Prince Consort drafted a stiff reply for her:

> The Queen returns to Lord Palmerston the copy of his letter to Count Persigny. The effect of placing Austria in an Italian confederation will certainly be to legalise that influence for the future, the supposed illegal exercise of which was put forward as one of the reasons for the late war; yet it is one of the conditions of peace bought by much blood and the loss of a rich province by Austria. We did not protest against the war and Lord Palmerston personally

wished France success in it; we can hardly now protest against the peace, and Lord Palmerston will, the Queen is sure, see the disadvantage which would accrue to this country should he make it appear as if to persecute Austria was a personal object with the first Minister of the Crown.

The Queen is less disappointed with the peace than Lord Palmerston appears to be, as she never could share his sanguine hopes that the 'coup d'état' and the 'Empire' could be made subservient to the establishment of independent nationalities and the diffusion of liberty and constitutional government on the Continent. The Emperor follows the dictates of his personal interests and is ready to play the highest stakes for them, himself entirely uncontrolled in his actions; we are cautious, bound by considerations of constitutional responsibility, morality, legality, etc.—our attempts therefore to use him for our views must prove a failure (as the Russian peace has shown before) and exposes us rather to be made his dupes. This should be kept steadily in mind, when the question of the Congress comes to be considered, in which we are probably intended to supply the Emperor's shortcomings.

Palmerston sent a temporising answer:

... Viscount Palmerston has had the honour of receiving this evening your Majesty's observations on his private letter to Count Persigny. Viscount Palmerston would beg to submit that as far as at present appears, the only points definitely settled by the two Emperors at Villafranca were that Venetia shall remain to Austria, and that Lombardy shall be attached to Piedmont. But it would seem that all that was agreed about an Italian confederation was that the two Emperors would encourage or recommend it. In fact, such a confederation could not be created without the previous consent of the States that would compose it; and Viscount Palmerston would be much inclined to doubt the consent of the King of Sardinia to belong to a confederation constituted in the manner proposed. This however, as well as other matters, would naturally be for discussion in any Congress or conference which may be held.

That was written on July 18. There then followed a furious five weeks, during which the Queen stubbornly refused to approve a series of drafts by Lord John Russell, in which he proposed to inform the French Government that Britain would support her denunciation at the peace conference to be held in Zurich, of the clauses giving Austria entry into the Italian confederation and the rulers of Tuscany and Modena the right to return home. In the meantime, Palmerston did not fail in his duties as a parliamentary reporter:

> ... Mr. Vincent Scully made a speech which the House thought amusing, though there was not much wit or humour in it, complaining that no Irishman is in the present Cabinet and enough had not been in former Cabinets, but his motion for returns was negatived without a division. It is said that Mr. Scully, who is an Irish barrister and was in Parliament for some years before 1857, when he lost his seat, observed to a friend that the House of Commons is a strange assembly; that when first he came into it he talked sense, and nobody listened to him, but that since he had taken to talk nonsense he had become a favourite with the House ...

> The Queen thanks Lord Palmerston for giving her so regularly such full accounts of the debates in the House of Commons; the one received to-day relating Mr. V. Scully's opinion of the House of Commons, amused us very much ...

There was also a more serious incident, indicative of Palmerston's curious combination of liberal sentiments abroad and distinctly more peremptory attitude to some aspects of social advance at home:

> ... The meeting of the people concerned in the builders' strike met this afternoon in Hyde Park to the number, according to the police estimate, of 25,000, but conducted themselves peaceably and separated without disorder. There were troops and police in readiness if it had been necessary to make use of them.
>
> It might be legally possible to forbid such meetings being held in Hyde Park, but they could be prevented only by shutting all the gates and stopping everybody from entering Hyde Park, which would be a great inconvenience to the inhabitants of London and would not prevent meetings, because they could be held elsewhere; and if the meeting was allowed to take place it might be

dispersed by force, after a warning given that it would not be
allowed to be held, but the meeting could not be dispersed without some employment of force, which might lead to serious
consequences and so long as the people assembled behaved peaceably it would be best to allow them to assemble.

The cause of this strike is that the trade union of the builders
workmen have resolved to have ten hours a day wages for nine
hours a day work. They began by attacking one employer, order-
ing all his workmen to strike work.

The other builders, foreseeing that if the workmen carried their
point against this one firm, they would perform the same operation afterwards on all the others in succession, resolved to act
vigorously in their own defence. They therefore turned off all
their workmen, saying they would not take the men back again
into employment until the interdict against the one builder,
against whom the edict of the workmen had been issued, should
be rescinded.

This is the present state of the matter. It is said the workmen
have a fund of £20,000 for their support during the strike, but if
they have not more they will soon be reduced to distress, which
will bring them to terms.

But there was no keeping Napoleon III out of the forefront of
events, and Palmerston could give vent to his general exasperation
in a somewhat brutal hint he passed to the Emperor's cousin,
which he could not resist reporting to the Queen:

> ... Viscount Palmerston submits a letter which he received a
> few days ago from Mr. Sidney Herbert. He recommended Mr.
> Herbert to advise the gun-maker to inform Prince Napoleon that
> there is no shooting *chasse* worth having in Ireland, and that the
> only *chasse* in that country is fox-hunting, which is very dangerous
> and has broken several necks of men of high rank.

However, the Queen's quarrel with the Foreign Secretary was no
laughing matter, and her insistence on the right of the rulers of
Modena and Tuscany to return to their duchies brought this
defiant homily from Palmerston:

> ... Viscount Palmerston would beg to submit that your Majesty's
> Government would incur a heavy responsibility from which

they would be unable to relieve themselves, if force should be used to coerce the people of those States to take back their former dynasties, and it would be alleged that the British Government, foreseeing that such employment of force was possible, had not employed the moral influence of Great Britain to prevent it by a timely remonstrance and protest.

The real question at issue is whether a nation belongs to its ruler, or whether the ruler belongs to the nation. The first position is maintained by the despotic sovereigns of Europe, and was the doctrine of the House of Stuart and of their adherents. The latter position is the foundation on which the thrones of Great Britain, of France and of Belgium rest—and with regard to any reversionary rights which Austria may claim upon any of those duchies, if it be admitted that the people of those States are entitled to set aside the existing dynasties on account of their subservience to Austrian influence and of their participation with Austria in hostilities against Italian freedom, they must surely be equally entitled to set aside the contingent and reversionary rights of Austria herself.

When the British nation declared the abdication of James II, and called William III to the throne, they set aside not only the existing rights of James, but also the contingent and reversionary rights of any person who might claim through him. It seems very difficult to foretell how these Italian complications will be cleared up, but the hasty and vaguely worded agreements of Villafranca appear to contain the seeds of much difficulty and conflict of opinion . . .

The Queen proved adamant. No official encouragement was to be given to the French to renounce the Villafranca agreement, and in this she received the support of the majority of the Cabinet when the matter was put to them. Palmerston had one last resort, one he had used at his peril before. He exchanged 'private' letters with Persigny, the anglophile French Ambassador, recommending unofficially that the disputed duchies should be attached to Piedmont. Although they wrote on August 23/24, copies of their correspondence were not forwarded to the Queen until September 4, by which time she had left for Balmoral. The battlemented towers beside the Dee seethed for two days, and then the Prince Consort drafted a curt remonstrance:

The Queen returns to Lord Palmerston his correspondence with M. de Persigny . . . She has nothing to add but to repeat her conviction of the great danger and inconvenience arising out of such private communications and the apprehension she must naturally feel that the attempt to convince the Emperor Napoleon that it would be for his interest to break his word to the Emperor of Austria should reflect upon the honour of the Queen's Government. She must insist upon this being distinctly guarded against.

In the meantime, Palmerston had thought it advisable to send a detailed justification of his step:

> . . . With regard to Viscount Palmerston's letter to Count Persigny, that letter, together with the Count's answer, has already been laid before your Majesty, and your Majesty will have seen that the first part of Viscount Palmerston's letter, which relates to the memorandum of Villafranca, is in strict conformity with that protest against military interference in the duchies, which was agreed to by the Cabinet, sanctioned by your Majesty, and officially communicated both to the French and to the Austrian Governments; and as to the opinion contained in the latter part of the letter, that is an opinion that Viscount Palmerston sincerely entertains, which he thinks is well-founded, and by which he is prepared to abide.
>
> But he would humbly submit that some misconception appears to prevail as to what took place at Villafranca in regard to the duchies, and he wishes to state what he understands and believes to have passed. He understands the Emperor of Austria to have asked that the Archdukes should be restored; that the Emperor of the French consented, provided no force should be used for the purpose, and that the Emperor of Austria agreed to that condition. In pursuance of what passed verbally in the interview between the sovereigns, the Emperor Napoleon sent to the Emperor of Austria a memorandum of the substance of what they had agreed upon, and that memorandum contained the condition that no force should be employed against the duchies.
>
> The Emperor of Austria objected to the insertion of that condition in a document which was to be made public, because it would encourage the duchies to reject their former dynasties, and would deprive those dynasties of their chance of being recalled, a sufficient indication, it may be observed in passing, of the opinion

entertained by the Emperor of Austria of the feelings of the people of the duchies towards their former dynasties. To this omission the Emperor of the French consented for the reason given by the Emperor of Austria, but he still held the Emperor of Austria to the verbal agreement.

If this be a correct version of what took place, which Viscount Palmerston believes it to be, the Emperor of Austria is as much bound in honour not to endeavour to restore the Archdukes by force, as the Emperor of the French would have been to have acknowledged their restoration if it had been accomplished by the good will of their former subjects.

But the people of the duchies have elected representative assemblies, and these assemblies have unanimously and by vote by ballot, declared the deposal of the former dynasties, and a determination of a union with Piedmont. The two Emperors, being the principal belligerent parties, might claim for themselves the right of disposing of the territories which were the seat and the prize of war—Piedmont, Lombardy and Venetia—but they had no right to dispose of the future destiny of other parts of Italy, and accordingly Count Walewski repeatedly admits, as stated by Lord Cowley in the despatches of the 31st August, that the future destiny of the duchies and of central Italy is a matter for the consideration of Europe.

Now England is one of the great powers of Europe, and must take a part in European deliberations; and it must rest with the British Government to determine when and in what manner its opinions upon a European question can best and most usefully be expressed. The British Government may withhold its opinions till a general Congress shall have been assembled; but if it thinks that by expressing them without waiting for a Congress its views and policy would be better forwarded, it is perfectly entitled to do so.

Now Viscount Palmerston would beg to submit that there are two systems of policy which might be followed in regard to the present state of things in Italy. The one an Austrian, the other an Italian system of policy.

The Austrian policy would lead to the restoration, and if possible the augmentation of Austrian supremacy in Italy. But this supremacy is not really advantageous to Austria herself; it exhausts her resources, adds nothing to her real strength as a great European power, and makes her odious to all liberal and enlightened men throughout the world. On the other hand, this supremacy and domination of Austria has for a long course of years been the cause of infinite misery, social, civil and political, to the nations of Italy. This is a system of policy which Viscount Palmerston never could advise.

The Italian system of policy, on the contrary, would tend to free the people of Italy from the thraldom of foreign control and to leave them at full liberty to decide for themselves what should be their internal organisation and their condition of political existence. This is the policy most consistent with the principles of generosity and justice, most in accordance with the honour and dignity of England and most conducive to the welfare and happiness of the 20 millions of men who inhabit the Italian peninsula.

This is the system of policy which for a long course of years has guided the British Government and which may almost be said to be the stereotyped policy of England. This is the system of policy which under various administrations was pursued towards Greece, towards Belgium, towards Spain, towards Portugal, towards France since 1815, and towards the Spanish republics of America; and this is the only system of policy which Viscount Palmerston would humbly and respectfully submit he could in any capacity, whether in or out of office, ever make himself responsible for . . .

Your Majesty is perfectly right in observing that a Secretary of State or First Lord, when communicating with a foreign Minister, ought always to make that Minister understand whether what is said to him is the personal opinion of the British minister talking to him, or is the official opinion of the Government which he represents. But this is a distinction always observed and practised by ministers and members of the Government of all countries. International relations could not be carried on with advantage if no conversations or communications were to take place except of a strictly official character; and not a single day passes in Europe without many conversations of an easy unofficial character between members of Governments and ministers accredited to their Courts.

So also Viscount Palmerston would submit in regard to despatches, a Minister for Foreign Affairs ought not to enter upon a new and important course of action without the consent of the Cabinet and the sanction of the Crown; but when any system of policy has been entered upon, the Secretary of State must be free to deal with it in the detailed application without summoning a Cabinet during the recess for the consideration of each despatch.

Now Viscount Palmerston would beg humbly to submit that the despatch of the 25th July to Lord Cowley, and the protest against armed interference in the duchies, both of which policies were agreed to by the Cabinet and sanctioned by your Majesty, lay down leading principles of policy in regard to Italy, and Viscount Palmerston would beg to submit that the two proposed drafts by Lord John Russell contain nothing at variance with these leading principles. If the Secretary of State were to confine himself during the dispersion of the Cabinet to simply acknowledging the receipt of despatches, without dealing with their contents, the action of the British Government would for a time be paralysed, and England would for a period cease to occupy the position which belongs to her as a European power.

When the Queen's letter of the 6th arrived, Palmerston was stung to another sharp response in which he questioned the good faith of Count Walewski, the French Foreign Minister:

Viscount Palmerston presents his humble duty to your Majesty and has had the honour to receive your Majesty's communication of the 6th of this month; and although he had the honour of addressing your Majesty yesterday afternoon, he deems it his duty to submit some observations upon this communication.

Your Majesty states that Viscount Palmerston in his letter to Count Persigny endeavoured to persuade the Emperor of the French to break his word to the Emperor of Austria, but Viscount Palmerston must beg very respectfully but entirely to deny that accusation. The circumstances were as follows:

It was well-known that the engagement at Villafranca was that the Archdukes should return if they could do so without the employment of force, either French or Austrian, though that latter part of the agreement had been kept out of the written and published memorandum in order to give them a better chance.

It was well-known that Count Walewski, by his connections and those of the Countess, was much in the interest of the Grand Ducal family; that by his agents at Florence he had been threatening foreign interference and compulsion, while the Emperor of the French had been giving assurances of a contrary character to the Tuscan and Modenese deputations.

In this state of things, Count Walewski said to Lord Cowley that it was probable that the treaty to be signed at Zurich would be word for word the memorandum of Villafranca. Now it is evident that to put into a formal treaty at Zurich, in the greatly altered state of things in central Italy, those words of the memorandum of Villafranca which expressed only a part of the agreement there come to, would be tantamount to entering into a new and different engagement, leading in its consequences to that employment of force which had been repudiated at Villafranca, and against which the British Government had protested. This it was which Viscount Palmerston pointed out to Count Persigny, and Count Persigny in his reply fully admits the justice of the remark, and says that if the passage in the memorandum about the Archduke is inserted in the Zurich treaty, it ought to be accompanied by a record of the verbal agreement that no force was to be used—so far then from trying to persuade the French Emperor to break his word, Viscount Palmerston only suggested that he should adhere to his engagements.

Viscount Palmerston also urged in his letter to Count Persigny that it would be for the advantage of France that the duchies should be united to Piedmont and your Majesty seems to think that this was an inducement to the Emperor of the French to break his word.

Now the engagement taken at Villafranca was that the Archdukes should return if they could do so without force. But the events which have happened in central Italy since the meeting at Villafranca must have demonstrably shown that the return of the Archdukes without the employment of overwhelming force has become utterly impossible; and the only questions latterly discused have been what other arrangement should be made for the duchies. The alternatives suggested have been union with Piedmont, unanimously voted for by the representative assemblies of the duchies; sovereignty of a Prince of the House of Savoy; sovereignty of Prince Napoleon; Republic under the guidance of Mazzini. The last would be a calamity; the last but one is repudiated by the people of the duchies; the second would perpetuate the weakness of fractional division; the first is recommended by every consideration connected with the welfare of Italy. But Count Walewski says to Lord Cowley that the union of Tuscany with Piedmont is an impossibility, though he did not explain the grounds upon which that opinion rested; and whether it was impossible with reference to French interests or to Italian considerations. He did, however, say to Lord Cowley that France would be jealous of any greater accession of territory to Piedmont. Viscount Palmerston therefore, deeming the restoration of the Archdukes wholly out of the question, gave reasons why, in his opinion, a union of the duchies with Piedmont would be advantageous instead of being injurious to the interests of France and he does not conceive that in stating this opinion he was trying to persuade the Emperor of the French to break any engagement he had entered into.

Your Majesty is pleased to observe upon the danger and inconvenience of private communications with foreign Ministers, and to add that your Majesty must insist upon this being distinctly guarded against. Viscount [Palmerston] would be very desirous of knowing the precise meaning of those last words. If your Majesty means what is to be guarded against is any attempt to induce a foreign sovereign to break his word, Viscount Palmerston cordially subscribes to that opinion, and maintains that he has not done so in the past, and declares that he has no intention of doing so in the future. But if your Majesty's meaning is that Viscount Palmerston is to be debarred from communicating with foreign Ministers, except for the purpose of informing them officially of formal decisions of the British Government, Viscount Palmerston would beg humbly and respectfully to represent to your Majesty that such a curtailment of the proper and constitutional functions of the office which he holds would render it impossible for him to serve your Majesty consistently with his own honour or with advantage to the public interest.

Wearily, the Queen stood her ground:

Lord Palmerston has written (on the 8th) a long letter to the Queen, which, besides giving his private opinions on the politics of Italy, which were not disputed, purports to show that when a principle of policy had been adopted by the Cabinet and sanctioned by the sovereign, the Foreign Secretary ought not to be impeded in carrying out the details, either by objections raised to them by the sovereign, or by making them dependent on the meetings of Cabinets, difficult to obtain at this time of year. Now the question raised by the Queen was just the reverse. The principle adopted by the Cabinet and sanctioned by the Queen was: not to interfere by active advice with the peace to be made at Zurich. The Foreign Secretary had submitted a draft which had appeared to the Queen to be in contradiction to this principle, which, upon the sovereign's objection, he withdrew; the Cabinet was summoned and rejected a similar draft submitted to them, and the Queen then complained that the very same advice should have been given by the Prime Minister in an indirect way, to which the sovereign and Cabinet could not agree openly. Lord Palmerston's letter was not communicated to the Queen until it had been alluded to in a public despatch, and Count Walewski had insinuated to our Ambassador that, rather than be a party to a line of conduct which he would look upon as dishonourable for his master, he would resign office. What the Queen has asked for is: an intimation to the French Government that private communications like that of Lord Palmerston to M. de Persigny must not be looked upon as the official expression of the opinion of Her Majesty's Government, and that we disclaim ever having intended to induce the Emperor to break his engagements made at Villafranca, whatever they may have been. The Queen does not conceive that Lord Palmerston can object to this course, nor does he attempt to do so in his letter.

P.S. Since writing the above the Queen has received Lord Palmerston's letter of the 9th. As she has just written at length, she does not conceive that it would be necessary to make any further observations in reply, except to a distinct question put by him in the latter part of his letter, viz. what the Queen wishes to have 'distinctly guarded against'.

It is the danger and inconvenience of private communications with foreign Ministers, without a distinct understanding that they are strictly private, and not to be treated as conveying the opinions of Her Majesty's Government, where the sanction of the Crown and adhesion on the Cabinet have not been obtained. Lord John Russell has now expressed this in a paragraph in one of his drafts to Lord Cowley, which he will send to Lord Palmerston.

As a proof of the necessity of such caution, the Queen has only to refer to the public use made of Lord Palmerston's private letter to Count Persigny, and the use made to our prejudice by the Emperor Napoleon at the time of the armistice at Villafranca of a private communication with Count Persigny, which was represented to imply assent to certain conditions of peace by England, with a desire of pressing them on Austria, when no opinion had been expressed by the Government to justify such an inference.

During November the Treaty of Zurich was signed. In spite of Palmerston's efforts, it contained most of the provisions of the Villafranca agreement, but proposed the calling of a Congress to settle Italian affairs. Palmerston was quick to repeat in guarded fashion to Lord Cowley, the British Ambassador in Paris, all his old arguments for submission to the assembled powers, and prodded the willing Persigny with another private letter. The Queen roused herself to protest:

> The Queen returns to Lord Palmerston his letter to Count Persigny, which she had read with unmixed regret. He will not be at a loss to understand the reason if he will call to mind the former correspondence on an exactly similar communication and the instructions to Lord Cowley detailing the views of the Queen's Government so recently settled in Cabinet and sanctioned by the Queen.

Palmerston was unrepentant:

> Viscount Palmerston presents his humble duty to your Majesty and has had the honour of receiving your Majesty's communication of this morning, and he much regrets that your Majesty should not have approved of his private letter to Count Persigny; but he would beg humbly to submit that the substance of that letter and the previous conversation with Count Persigny, of which the letter was a summary, were entirely in accordance with the recent despatch to Lord Cowley which was sanctioned by your Majesty.
>
> That despatch stated that the arrangement of Italian affairs which your Majesty's Government would prefer and which they think would be the best for Italy, for France, for Austria and for Europe would be the annexation of Central Italy to Piedmont and Viscount Palmerston, in his conversation and letter, endeavoured to argue in support of that arrangement. He argued, and he ventures to think conclusively, that the principle once admitted that no force shall be used to coerce the peoples of central Italy— the measure of annexation to Piedmont ought to follow as a

necessary consequence provided that the people of central Italy
continue to desire that union; for it would be a mere play upon
words to say that no compulsion shall be put upon the people of
Central Italy directly, but that indirectly and through the Sardinian Government threatened with force, compulsion shall be
put upon them to prevent them from obtaining what they desire
to have.

Viscount Palmerston would beg to submit that the policy which
your Majesty's Government are urging in regard to Italy is
precisely the same in principle as that which he laboriously,
perseveringly and successfully acted upon throughout the long
negotiations upon the affairs of Belgium. There was then in this
country a Dutch party and there is now an Austrian party desirous
of compelling a people to submit again to a domination which
had been irksome, and which they had shaken off. But there is this
difference between the two cases, that the Dutch party was
numerous, whereas your Majesty may depend upon it, the
Austrian party as regards the resubjection of Italy to the Austrian
yoke is extremely small, and in no respect represents the public
opinions of this country.

Your Majesty in your letter to Lord John Russell, remarked
upon Viscount Palmerston having said in his letter to Count
Persigny that Piedmont, even with the addition of central Italy,
would have to lean on France for support, though it would not
have so often to apply for aid as if it were a smaller and weaker
State.

The statement seems to be well founded and was intended to
meet the objection which some persons about the Emperor are
understood to have made to the union, namely that Piedmont so
enlarged would become hostile or at least dangerous as a neighbour to France. It is self-evident that the more Piedmont is
strengthened by enlargement, the less dependent on France she
will be, but it is also clear that enlarged as she may be, she must
always, from being in geographical contiguity with the larger
power France, and also in contact with a hostile neighbour in
Austria, be obliged to look to France for support.

With regard to the annexation of central Italy to Piedmont,
your Majesty will have seen by a recent despatch from Berlin that
the Prussian Government take a similar view of that matter to that
which Viscount Palmerston has urged, and are of opinion that if

the Archdukes cannot be restored, (and it is impossible now to suppose that they can be) the annexation of central Italy to Piedmont would be a much better arrangement than the creation of a separate State . . .

That Christmas the Queen's greetings were strictly formal:

The Queen wishes Lord and Lady Palmerston many happy returns of the Season . . .

and a chagrined Prince Consort marked the last day of the year with a sharp-tempered memorandum for the record:

All his [Palmerston's] old tricks of 1848 and the previous period are revived again. Having Lord John Russell at the Foreign Office, whose inefficiency in the office, love for Italy and fear of Lord Palmerston makes him a ready tool and convenient ally, he tries to carry on a policy of revenge against Austria and to bind us to the Emperor Napoleon more than ever, regardless of all the interests of England or Europe, and if impeded by the Cabinet or the Queen he is violent and overbearing, and if this be of no avail, cheats and tricks. He has taken towards the Crown quite his old position of 1851 before he was dismissed by Lord John, has again pamphlets written against me and the 'Coburg Influence' in order to bear down all opposition, etc., etc.

When Parliament reassembled there was an exchange on a relatively minor matter, which illustrated well the difference in approach between the Queen and Palmerston to questions of legislative and constitutional competence:

FEBRUARY 2: Viscount Palmerston presents his humble duty to your Majesty and begs to state that Mr. Wise moved this afternoon a resolution that a committee of the House of Commons ought to be appointed every session to examine the Civil Service estimates and those of the Office of Woods and Forests . . . and on a division the motion was carried by 121 to 93 . . .

FEBRUARY 3: The Queen has seen with much regret the success of Mr. Wise's motion. She was surprised that Lord Palmerston did not make personally a bold stand against what must be considered a practical subversion of responsible government and that he should not have been supported in it by the leader of the Conservative Party. From Lord Palmerston's letter she surmises, however, that Lord Palmerston means to defeat the measure in its next stages. Two executive governments, one under the Crown and the other appointed by the House of Commons can hardly be expected to work long together.

After fifty years in the House, Palmerston was far too wise in its ways to be similarly alarmed, and he replied the same day:

... Viscount Palmerston submits an analysis of the division by which it appears that the two sides of the House were each much divided in the vote. The fact is that the miscellaneous estimates have of late years immensely increased from many unavoidable causes, and it is probable that many members who voted for the motion thought it a good opportunity to give an economical vote to please their constituents. As the matter stands, however, the vote is of little consequence, for the resolution is that it is desirable that every year a committee should be appointed, not to examine the estimates of the year, but to enquire into the expenditure of the year preceding and as that expenditure cannot be ascertained till the accounts have been received and made up, which cannot well be done till some months after the 1st April, the committee would not begin to sit till about the time when Parliament was going to be prorogued. Mr. Wise obtained the committee in 1858 on the consular service, and the result was that his committee recommended an increase of expenditure ...

More serious matters were pending. Emboldened by Palmerston and Russell, the French Emperor summoned up sufficient courage to inform the Austrians that neither an Italian confederation nor the return of the rulers of the two duchies were practicable, and his adversary acquiesced. But Napoleon III's next step brought the British Court and its two chief ministers together again. The French had undertaken to clear the Austrians from Italy in return for the cession by Sardinia of Savoy and Nice. This *pourboire* had not been earned, but was offered again for French assistance in annexing the Papal States in central Italy. Palmerston and Russell were caught between two fires. They sympathised with Sardinia's liberalising evangelism, but French territorial aggrandisement was a high price to pay and they fully shared the British public's suspicion of worse to come.

In endeavouring to justify the further liberation of Italy, Lord John Russell overstepped the mark in a letter to the Queen, as disrespectful as it was waspish:

> ... Lord John Russell unfortunately does not partake your Majesty's opinions in regard to Italy, and he is unwilling to obtrude on your Majesty unnecessary statements of his views ... Whatever may be the consequence, the liberation of the Italian people from a foreign yoke is, in the eyes of Lord Palmerston and Lord John Russell, an increase of freedom and happiness at which, as well-wishers of mankind, they cannot but rejoice.

This was too much for the Queen, and the Prince Consort drafted a resounding complaint for her to send to the Prime Minister:

> The Queen sends a letter to Lord Palmerston which she has received yesterday evening from Lord John Russell. She is induced to do so from a feeling that it is to Lord Palmerston, as head of the Government, that she has to look, when she may have reason to take exception to the tone of communications she may receive from members of his Cabinet. Lord Palmerston will not fail to perceive that the enclosed is not the kind of communication which the Foreign Secretary ought to make when asked by his sovereign to explain the views of the Cabinet upon a question so important and momentous as the annexation of Savoy to France, and the steps which they propose to take with regard to it. She need not remind Lord Palmerston that in her letter communicated to the Cabinet, she had given no opinion whatever upon Italian liberation from a foreign yoke, nor need she protest against a covert insinuation, such as is contained in Lord John's letter, that she is no well-wisher of mankind and indifferent to its freedom and happiness. But she must refer to the constitutional position of her ministers towards herself. They are responsible for the advice they give her, but they are bound fully, respectfully and openly to place before her the grounds and reasons upon which their advice may be founded, to enable her to judge whether she can give her assent to that advice or not.—The Government must come to a standstill if the Minister meets a demand for explanation with an answer like the following: 'I was asked by the Cabinet to give an

answer but as I do not agree with you, I think it useless to explain my views'.

The Queen must demand that respect which is due from a minister to his sovereign.

As the Queen must consider the enclosed letter as deficient in it, she thinks Lord John Russell might probably wish to reconsider it and asks Lord Palmerston to return it to him with that view . . .

Palmerston, beset by the general sense of outrage at Napoleon's manœuvres, had to climb down:

Viscount Palmerston presents his humble duty to your Majesty and has had the honour of receiving your Majesty's communication of to-day upon the subject of Lord John Russell's letter of yesterday to your Majesty. Viscount Palmerston and Lord John Russell, with whom Viscount Palmerston has communicated, very deeply regret that Lord John Russell's communication of the 9th should have been deemed by your Majesty deficient in that respect towards your Majesty which is so justly due by your Majesty's servants, and which is so sincerely felt by Lord John Russell, and Lord John Russell has gladly taken back a letter which has appeared to your Majesty to bear a character so different from that which he intended to give it.

If Viscount Palmerston might be allowed to make an explanatory observation on the matter, he would say that the impression produced on your Majesty's mind seems to him to have in a great measure originated from the incompleteness of a sentence in Lord John Russell's letter, the sentence namely in which he says that after he had read to the Cabinet your Majesty's letter 'it was agreed that Lord John Russell prepare an answer, which he was engaged in writing when he received your Majesty's letter.'— Your Majesty seems to understand that which is the apparent meaning of that sentence, that the answer which the Cabinet agreed that Lord John Russell should prepare was an answer to your Majesty's letter, and your Majesty was naturally surprised at finding no such answer in Lord John's communication. But the fact is that Lord John, probably in the hurry of writing, omitted to explain that the answer which the Cabinet agreed that he should prepare, was an answer to the French communication about Savoy to which your Majesty's letter related; and it was conceived by the

Cabinet that the draft of such answer, when submitted for your Majesty's approval, would be the best and most satisfactory answer to your Majesty's letter, because it would show that the Cabinet entirely concurred with your Majesty in condemning and objecting to the scheme for annexation of Savoy and Nice to the French Empire.

Your Majesty has, since the date of your Majesty's letter of this day, received the draft of the proposed answer to the French despatch and Viscount Palmerston trusts that your Majesty will have been of opinion that your Majesty's sentiments and those of the Cabinet upon the Savoy and Nice annexation scheme are expressed in that draft as strongly as is consistent with international courtesy.

Viscount Palmerston cannot but hope that this communication together with the unanimous expression of opinion in the debate in the House of Lords, may have a salutory effect upon the decision of the Emperor of the French on this matter.

This satisfied the Queen, whose humour was finally restored when Palmerston agreed to her proposal that Austria, Prussia and Russia should be requested to exert pressure with Britain on the French. The Swiss Confederation was worried about the effect of French possession of that part of Savoy which bordered on its territories, and Palmerston, by now exasperated by Napoleon's obstinacy, sent him a sharp message through Count Flahault, an old friend, who had often acted as an unofficial channel of communication between the two Governments:

. . . Viscount Palmerston may mention to your Majesty the substance of a short conversation he had with Count Flahault on Tuesday. The Count came to him just as he was going down to the House, wishing to have some talk before he went to Paris yesterday morning, and Viscount Palmerston, unable to wait, took the Count down in his brougham to the House. Count Flahault said he should see the Emperor and wished to know what he might say to him, as from Lord Palmerston, on the unpleasant state of affairs.

Lord P. said he could only refer Count F. to what Lord John Russell had said on Monday in the House of Commons. Count F. hoped not, as what had been then said was personally offensive to the Emperor. Lord P. did not see in what way it could be so considered. Count F. said that Lord John had expressed distrust, but admitted that no objection could be taken to the latter part of his speech as to the political course which England might follow. Lord P. said distrust may be founded upon either or both of two grounds. Either upon the supposition of intentional deceit, or when such frequent changes of purpose and of conduct as to show that no reliance could be placed upon the continuance of the intentions or policy of the moment and Count F. must admit that without imputing the first, there is ample ground for a feeling founded on the second consideration.

Count F. said his great object was to prevent war between the two countries. Lord P. said that he feared the Emperor and Thouvenel had schemes and views which tended to bring about that result and might array Europe against France. Count F. did not fear that, but was apprehensive that irritation on both sides might bring on war between England and France. Lord P. said that he was most anxious to prevent such a war, but if it was forced upon England, England would fearlessly accept it, whether in conjunction with a confederated alliance or singly and by herself; that the nation would rise and rally as one man and that though speaking to a Frenchman he ought perhaps not to say so, yet he could not refrain from observing that the examples of history led him to conclude that the result of a conflict between England and France upon anything like equal terms would not be unsatisfactory to the former.

Count F. said that he had been in the Battle of Waterloo and knew what English troops were, but that the French army now is far superior to that which fought on that day. Lord P. said no doubt it was, and so is the present English army, but with regard to the excellence of the French army, he would remind Count F. of what passed between Marshal Tallard and the Duke of Marlborough when the former was taken prisoner at the Battle of Blenheim, *'vous venez Milord'*, said the Marshal, *'de battre les meilleur troupes de l'Europe'*. *'Excepté toujours'*, replied Marlborough, *'celles qui les ont battues.'*

But, said the Count, what I fear is an invasion of this country for which steam affords such facilities and which would be disastrous to England. Lord P. replied that steam tells both ways, for defence as well as for attack, and that as for invasion, though it would no doubt be a temporary evil, we were under no apprehension as to the results. That a war between England and France would doubtless be disastrous to both countries, but it is by no means certain which of the two would suffer the most. Arrived at the House, they took leave of each other, Count Flahault saying he should not say anything to the Emperor calculated to increase the irritation which he expected to find, but should endeavour to calm. Viscount Palmerston said that of course the Count would judge for himself what he should say, but that he, the Count, must have observed what was the state of public feeling and opinion in this country.

The conversation was carried on in the most friendly manner and Viscount Palmerston has mentioned it only to Lord John Russell and one or two of his colleagues, and he reports it to your Majesty only because he wishes while it is fresh in his memory to state it to your Majesty, in case it should be mentioned by Count Flahault at Paris and should be reported to London in any way distorted and misrepresented by those through whom it might pass.

For once, Palmerston's sabre-rattling had the Queen's whole-hearted approval:

... The account of his conversation with Count Flahault has interested us extremely and gives us great pleasure. It is most important that the French should be aware of the united action of England with the other powers, the knowledge of it will have a most wholesome influence on the French Government. She trusts therefore that the Cabinet tomorrow will not urge any further delay.

The Queen will naturally not mention to any one what Lord Palmerston has reported to her of his conversation with Count Flahault.

When the Prime Minister's strictures were embodied in a formal despatch, the Queen positively glowed:

... The Queen read with much pleasure Lord Palmerston's letter to M. de Persigny; nothing but a firm, high, fearless tone! now will be of any use, and the Queen much wishes she could see

something of the same in Lord Cowley's letters and despatches—
the tone of which grieves her much.

The French Emperor succeeded in the end in exacting the price
for his assistance to the Sardinians, at the cost of international
distrust which was to last the rest of his reign. As for Palmerston,
his basic suspicion of French motives, which had now lasted for
nearly half a century, was reinforced and during his remaining
years in office he devoted much time to containing French ambitions and building up Britain's own defences. In this he was to
enjoy the Queen's unstinting support.

CHAPTER X

Gladstone and Lord John Russell

THE PARLIAMENTARY SESSIONS OF 1860 WERE BEING ENLIVENED by debates on two perennial subjects—the state of Britain's defences and the need for further electoral reform. The former involved Palmerston in the first of many arguments of principle with his formidably gifted, but tortuous-minded Chancellor of the Exchequer. Reform was still the occupational obsession of Lord John Russell, who preferred juggling with paper schemes for adjusting the franchise qualifications to his duties at the Foreign Office. In May, the Prime Minister reported to the Queen on his colleagues' hobby horses:

... In the Cabinet in the morning Viscount Palmerston pointed out that the Reform Bill as it stands cannot be expected to pass; that if the Government could agree to raise the £6 for boroughs to £8 and to raise the £10 proposed for counties to some higher amount, two of the main objections to the Bill would be removed, and that if, after the passing of the English Bill, the Scotch and Irish Reform Bills were put off, as in fact they must be, till next session, and the dissolution were thereby postponed till the end of 1861, possibly the third objection to the measure might be diminished and the English Bill might pass this session. Lord John Russell seemed not disinclined to such an arrangement and will say something generally to this effect on moving the next stage of the Bill on Monday, 4th June. There is however on the part of a large number of members a fixed intention to prevent the Bill from passing this session, if they can do so.

Mr. Sidney Herbert brought before the Cabinet the report of the Commission on the Fortifications, and the scheme for providing the money by a loan of about 8 millions and a half to be repaid in 20 years. Mr. Gladstone read a long memorandum which he had prepared, stating a series of objections to the measure, written

285

with his usual ability as to style, but sadly deficient in good sense and statesmanlike views. He objected that it would be unconstitutional that the Crown should possess so many fortified places, but to this Mr. Herbert replied that almost all these places have been fortified for a century and a half, though their defences require now additions and improvements . . .

The Queen found her Prime Minister's attitude highly satisfactory:

> The Queen has received Lord Palmerston's letter giving an account of the decision of the Cabinet and of the proceedings in Parliament and is very glad Lord John Russell should have consented to the modification of the clause in the Reform Bill, substituting £8 for £6. She is very sorry to hear that Mr. Gladstone cannot raise himself to a statesmanlike view, but relieved that Lord Palmerston is determined to place the safety of the country above all other considerations.
>
> The Queen was not aware of its being constitutional that the dockyards should be fortified!

The defence of the realm continued to preoccupy the royal mind and Palmerston was being badgered to draw up a Cabinet minute on the whole subject of containing French ambitions:

> The Queen is anxious to remind Lord Palmerston of the minute which has been promised her; during the Whitsuntide holidays the Queen trusts Lord Palmerston will be able to draw it up.— Every day tends to show the schemes of France and the Queen feels sure that we must soon take further steps to agree with the other powers . . .
>
> The reports which Lord Palmerston mentions to the Queen, of the determination of France to proceed in her line of annexation— and the necessity for putting a stop to such proceedings, becomes therefore daily more obvious. Nothing short of agreement with the other powers can effect this. France is most active in trying to divide Europe by lies—and intrigues and proposals of all kinds— and we should not let her enjoy this advantage too long with impunity.

Palmerston duly drafted a long retrospective survey of Napoleon III's policies which, while acknowledging his assistance in the Crimean War and the facilities he offered during the Indian Mutiny for the transportation of British troops across France and across Egypt, nevertheless contended that at the beginning of 1859, particularly in a speech he made on 1st January, the Emperor had embarked on a policy of territorial expansion. He had encouraged the Carlists in Spain with the hope of obtaining the Balearic Islands for France, demanded Nice and Savoy as the price of his assistance to the Italian States against Austria and generally allowed it to be supposed that he would not be content with less than the whole of the left bank of the Rhine and the annexation of Belgium. The Cabinet proposed that joint notes be sent to the Austrian, Prussian and Russian Governments, informing them that Britain intended to oppose these adventures and calling for the support of the three Governments concerned. However, Palmerston was obliged to advise the Queen that his colleagues were opposed to the idea of adopting the draft as an official document:

> ... Viscount Palmerston read to the Cabinet his proposed draft of minute. This gave rise to much discussion. Some thought the historical part dwelt too much on vague reports for a document to be submitted by the Cabinet to your Majesty, others thought that it did not begin early enough to point of time in its enumeration of the symptoms of a change in the policy of the Emperor, others were of opinion that as the Cabinet had adopted your Majesty's views ... there would not be any sufficient reason for a Cabinet minute, which is only required on very special occasions...

This did not appeal to the Prince Consort's tidy mind and he drafted a further exhortation for the Queen to copy:

> The Queen has received Lord Palmerston's letter stating that the Cabinet, having objected to the minute which he had prepared, on account of its basing the policy to be pursued upon mere rumour and hearsay, they consider the case hardly one requiring so formal a step as the drawing up of a Cabinet minute, particularly as they are in principle agreed, as well amongst themselves, as with the Queen, and have approved a despatch to Lord Bloomfield [British envoy in Berlin] embodying those principles. All that they think now necessary (should the Queen consider that

despatch sufficient) would be the sending of a similar one to Vienna.

After the Cabinet had empowered Lord Palmerston at a former meeting to inform her that such a Cabinet minute should be drawn up and had charged him with it, the Queen was naturally surprised at the present announcement and regrets it, not because of any difference of opinion, which Lord Palmerston says does not exist; but because, at a moment of such gravity as the present, a fixed line of policy laid down, considered and approved by all parties, would have given great security that the different steps to be taken from day to day will be in conformity with a general principle.

The Queen crossed out the next paragraph of the Prince Consort's draft, which read: 'That principle the Queen understands to be to protect ourselves and Europe from underhand plots and complications possibly producing war, by dissipating doubts and suspicions between the powers of Europe.' The letter then went on:

The French alliance was established for the purpose of preventing the disturbance of the territorial arrangements of Europe, threatened by Russia in the east. It has been maintained until lately, but France has under its cover produced the very result against which it had been directed and is supposed to contemplate still further disturbances, in which all symptoms indicate a connivance on the part of Russia. England, Austria and Prussia are vaguely alarmed not only as to a French scheme, but as to the course which each may pursue with regard to them. This alarm and uncertainty weakens their action, whilst it powerfully aids any scheme of aggression.

What is required, and is now attainable for their security, is a mutual agreement between the three powers 'that each should make known to the other two any overture or proposition, direct or indirect, which either of the three may receive from France, tending to any change of the existing state of territorial possession in Europe and that no answer should be given to such overture or proposal, until the Government to which it may have been made shall have had an answer from the other two to the communication so made'. Anything short of this will not effect the object of giving absolute confidence. The despatch to Lord Bloomfield is written in that sense, but in its shortness and form (not even directing it to be laid before the Prussian Government or a copy of it to be furnished), it rather nears the character of a civil message without any binding force.

It ought not to be difficult to find a form in which the desired object may be secured.

The Cabinet, doubtless under Palmerston's guidance, was unwilling to be pinned down to a directive on foreign policy, even if they had drafted it themselves, and the matter was dropped.—So was the project for parliamentary reform, which even Lord John Russell realised he would never get through the House. Palmerston must have heaved a sigh of relief. He had never been convinced of the necessity for it, and it was to be the last time his oldest colleague was to trouble him with his pet obsession:

JUNE 4: Viscount Palmerston presents his humble duty to your Majesty and begs to state that this being the day for the House to go into committee on the Reform Bill, several motions had been announced of instructions to the committee, but the Speaker decided that only one of them could regularly be moved, that mainly by Mr. Bentinck, that the Committee should have power to add to the Bill clauses against bribery and corruption. Lord John Russell disappointed Mr. Bentinck by agreeing to the motion and thus avoiding a debate. Lord John then moved that the Speaker should have the Chair, and in doing so stated that the Scotch and Irish Bills must stand over until next year, by which it follows that there would not be a dissolution till the end of 1861. He also said that the Government would be willing to consider any proposal for raising the borough and county franchise above the amounts proposed by the Bill. This proposal did not seem to please Mr. Disraeli, who tried to show it was inconsistent and would be delusive.

Mr. Mackinnon then moved his resolution that the Reform Bill should be put off till after the census of 1861, which would practically be to put it off till 1863, because the result of the census would not be known till the spring of 1862, and it would be too late then to begin a Reform Bill . . .

JUNE 9: Viscount Palmerston presents his humble duty to your Majesty and begs to state that Lord John Russell proposed to the Cabinet that under the evident impossibility of passing the Reform Bill this year, he should announce on Monday, when the Order of the Day is moved, that the Bill will not be persevered in this session, but saying nothing one way or the other about the future. This course, after much discussion as to the best manner and time of making the announcement, was agreed to, but it was felt to be important that this intention should not be known, lest it should get into 'The Times', and thus offend the supporters of the Government at its premature publication . . .

JUNE 11: Viscount Palmerston presents his humble duty to your Majesty and begs to say that Lord John Russell this afternoon withdrew his Reform Bill, alleging as reason for so doing, the late period of the session, the number of amendments given notice of for the Committee on the Bill, and the mass of other important business to be disposed of before the prorogation. The announcement was received almost in silence. Everybody expected something of the kind, it being clear that the Bill would not pass even the House of Commons this session. The Opposition were glad to be freed from the Bill, but there was a mixture of disappointment in their feelings. They had rather expected that Lord John Russell would resign on losing his Bill. They also looked for the retirement of Mr. Gladstone and Mr. Milner Gibson, and to a coalition Government to be formed by a junction between them and the remainder of the present Government. They overlooked all the great difficulties of accomplishing such a change, and the dislike and suspicion with which such arrangements are viewed by the nation . . .

Gladstone was proving an even more difficult colleague. He had inherited from the great Sir Robert Peel a real understanding of public finance and was able to conduct virtuoso performances with his figures for political ends. He disagreed fundamentally with Palmerston and his own Peelite colleague, Sidney Herbert, over the necessity for increasing armaments, and tried to gain his ends by proving that he could not provide the money. He wanted to reduce the tax on paper so that newspapers—and the dissemination of knowledge—would be cheaper. The House of Lords,

he State Butler gets up another batch of fine old smoke! *Punch* thought the Queen's
peech at the opening of Parliament in 1857 singularly ungrammatical, full of hard
almerston's false concords and hard Panmure's rum relatives.

appalled at the prospect of a flood of radical propaganda, threw out the clause, whereupon Gladstone proposed to send the entire Bill up to them again, with an increase in the spirit duties to compensate for the loss of revenue. When it appeared that he would not obtain the full support of the Cabinet, he threatened to resign,—as he did with increasing frequency. Palmerston reported on the weary struggle in some exasperation to the Queen:

JULY 2: . . . When all the other members had left the room, Mr. Gladstone requested Viscount Palmerston to submit to your Majesty that he could no longer continue to carry on the business of his department. His opinion strongly was that action and not a resolution was required, that one of three courses ought to be pursued: either that the Paper Duty Repeal Bill should again be sent up to the Lords; or that a Bill should be sent up for suspending the paper duties for a year; or that a Bill should be sent up reducing those duties gradually year by year; or, fourthly, that with the repeal of the paper duties should be coupled the imposition of spirit duties. Viscount Palmerston said he really could not undertake the communication which Mr. Gladstone wished to be submitted to your Majesty, and earnestly entreated Mr. Gladstone to reconsider the matter; he urged in detail all the reasons which ought to dissuade such a step, and he thought that he had produced some impression on Mr. Gladstone. It was agreed between them that Viscount Palmerston, instead of giving notice this afternoon of a Motion tomorrow, and laying the resolution on the table this evening, should give notice this afternoon of a Motion for Thursday, and promise to lay the resolution on the table tomorrow. This gives Mr. Gladstone more time to think, and more room to turn round in. Mr. Milner Gibson has no intention of going out, and has so told Mr. Gladstone, strongly advising him to stay in; and Viscount Palmerston's impression is that Mr. Gladstone, having failed to become master of the Cabinet by a threat of resignation, will in the end yield to the almost unanimous decision of his colleagues, The only person who supported Mr. Gladstone's views, except Mr. Milner Gibson, was the Duke of Argyll, who, however, like Mr. Gibson, had no intention whatever of accompanying Mr. Gladstone in resignation . . .

JULY 11: . . . Viscount Palmerston is inclined to think that Mr.

Gladstone means to resign on the fortification question. If he should do so, it will be in a few days time and Viscount Palmerston would beg to submit for your Majesty's gracious approval that in such case the office of Chancellor of the Exchequer may be offered to Sir George Lewis, and that Secretary of State for the Home Department may be offered to Lord Clarendon. Viscount Palmerston would then have to consider whom he should propose to your Majesty for the office of Post-Master-General . . .

JULY 22: . . . The Cabinet also considered the accompanying draft of Bill for Fortifications. The Duke of Argyll read a letter from Mr. Gladstone, who had left the Cabinet to go to Cliveden, saying that he is willing, though with much reluctance, to agree to the plan of fortifications, and to the mode of raising the money by terminable annuities, but his condition is that, whereas the Bill gives power extending over four years, that power being to be renewed each year in company with the annual vote. This is a childish condition, but it does not make any essential difference in the arrangement, and although Mr. Gladstone's wayward conduct might render his colleagues glad to be freed from so uncommodating [*sic*] a companion, yet in the whole it has been thought better to keep him, as he has yielded upon the main principle of the arrangement.

JULY 24: . . . Viscount Palmerston submits the draft of the Bill for the fortifications, but some alterations are yet to be made in it which will not however alter its substance. Mr. Gladstone told Viscount Palmerston this evening that he wished it to be understood that though acquiescing in the step now taken about the fortifications, he kept himself free to take such course as he may think fit upon that subject next year, to which Viscount Palmerston entirely assented. That course will probably be the same which Mr. Gladstone has taken this year, namely ineffectual opposition and ultimate acquiescence.

The session had been long delayed.—The Queen retired to Osborne and during August Palmerston kept her informed in more humorous vein of the endless debates:

AUGUST 13: . . . the House then adjourned. The prospect of the end of the session does not improve and the prorogation can scarcely be till quite the end of the present month.

Members however are leaving town, but the tiresome ones who have no occupation of their own and no chance of seeing their names in the newspapers when Parliament is up, remain to obstruct and delay by talking. The Speaker, who has not been quite well, grows as impatient as any official man who has hired a grousing moor and cannot get to it, and a few nights ago, when a tiresome orator got up to speak just as an end to the debate had been expected, the Speaker cried 'Oh, Oh,' in chorus with the rest of the House.

August 18: . . . There were some votes to-day discussed and objected to. The vote for the collection of historical portraits was objected to by Mr. Spooner, one of whose arguments was that morality was not sufficiently attended to in the selection, inasmuch as the collection contains a portrait of Nell Gwynn. Some persons were tempted to suggest that his objections might be removed if that portrait were withdrawn and his own put in its place, but the answer to him was that the portrait had been given and not bought.

August 21: . . . next came the Bill for placing certain Roman Catholic charities under the control of the Charity Commissioners, without danger of forfeiture on account of some conditions imposed by the founders that masses should be said for the souls of the dead, which is considered by English law to be a superstitious use, rendering invalid and liable to forfeiture the whole of the bequest. The first clause of this Bill, which contains almost the whole enactment, had given rise to great discussion and difficulty. As it was originally framed by Sir George Bowyer, who brought in the Bill, or rather by his Catholic advisers, it would have left the charities too much at the disposal of Cardinal Wiseman. Sir George Bowyer and the whole House had acquiesced in a different clause proposed by Mr. Selwyn, Member for the University of Cambridge, but taken from a Bill on the same subject brought in by Sir George Lewis last year. Cardinal Wiseman however, on examining that clause, found that it would tie him up too closely and he reproached Sir George Bowyer for not having opposed it and urged him to try to get it rejected. Sir

George was thereby wrought into a state of irritation and excitement hardly ever before witnessed in the House of Commons, and tried to throw upon everybody else, on the Attorney-General and the Government, the blame which the Cardinal had cast upon him. He made a violent personal attack on the Attorney-General, who replied with that quiet cutting and sneering sarcasm in which he greatly excels. Sir George afterwards made an onslaught on the Government in general, which Viscount Palmerston was obliged to repel. The disputed clause had however been carried by 70 to 13 before this discussion began, so that the House on this occasion practised the often proposed system of voting first, and debating afterwards . . .

AUGUST 23: Viscount Palmerston presents his humble duty to your Majesty and has to apologise for not having reported the proceedings in the House of Commons yesterday morning, but they were wholly unimportant. The only thing out of routine having been that Sir George Bowyer made excuses for his rudeness and violence the night before, and that Viscount Palmerston and the Attorney-General courteously informed him that it was much the same to them whether he was rude or civil . . . The House adjourned early in order that the members of the Government might go to Greenwich for their Fish Dinner, and, as there has been so much speaking during the session, it had been agreed that the bantering toasts and speeches formerly usual at those dinners should not take place, and that the attention of the parties should be concentrated on the real business of the evening . . .

The traditional whitebait dinner at the "Cutty Sark" inn normally marked the end of the session, which was not long delayed. The Queen, by now at Balmoral, had been greatly diverted by Palmerston's reports and had no intention of allowing her holiday to be unduly interrupted:

The Queen has to thank Lord Palmerston again for many interesting and some very amusing reports of the really puerile and absurd conduct of many members of the House of Commons. The Queen would be ready to hold the Council on Monday 27th —but thinks it would suit us all best if it could be at 11 o'clock, as it would enable us to get out for the day should it be fine, which in this very uncertain weather would be a great object . . .

As the year drew to a close, the Queen had further family news to impart—her second daughter, Princess Alice, had met her future husband.—Their eldest daughter married into the Battenberg–Mountbatten line, which was not only to play such an important part in British history during the following century, but was to provide the Consort of Queen Elizabeth II, Prince Philip:

> The Queen mentioned to Lord Palmerston the other day—in a cursory manner (as the Prince also did) that the reports respecting a marriage between our daughter Alice and of Prince Louis of Hesse-Darmstadt were premature, but not unlikely in a little time to become true. We then said we expected to see the young Prince again shortly, to enable him and Princess Alice to become more intimately acquainted with one another before the final agreement took place, though we know that during his short visit here in June both parties made a favourable and lasting impression on one another.
>
> We have now just heard that Prince Louis will arrive here on a visit to us on the 24th inst. He is, as the Queen already mentioned, the eldest son of Prince Charles of Hesse and heir presumptive to the Grand-Duke of Hesse-Darmstadt, who has no children. His mother is the daughter of the late Prince William of Prussia, a distinguished soldier—and sister to Prince Adalbert and the late Prince Waldemar, who took so noble a part in Lord Hardinge's campaign in the Punjab. Prince Louis himself is only 23 and possesses all the qualities of head and heart which we could desire for our dear child's happiness; but as both parties are young no marriage would yet take place until Princess Alice has attained her 19th year—consequently not till the spring of '62 . . .

Palmerston found time during the recess to attend to more constructive plans than his two main colleagues' hobby-horses:

> . . . Viscount Palmerston then proposed to the Cabinet the plan recommended for the erection of new courts of law by the commissioners who reported on that subject in August last, and it was agreed that some further information is required which will be obtained before the Cabinet meets again at 3 o'clock on Thursday. The proposal is that a large block of buildings between Lincolns Inn Fields and the Strand should be bought and pulled down and

that all courts of law now scattered inconveniently over the town should be brought together upon that site. The expense of the arrangement, which would be about a million and a half, would be defrayed out of money in the Suitors Funds applicable to such a purpose. The convenience to all the members of the legal profession would be great and the advantage to parties engaged in law suits would be still more considerable. The public might be required to contribute £16,000 a year for a limited period of time.

The metropolis would be improved by the substitution of handsome law courts for a mass of filthy, unhealthy and discreditable habitations and narrow courts and alleys . . .

The new year found Sovereign and Prime Minister exchanging greetings and statements of intention of almost fully restored harmony. Palmerston may have been suffering from one of his winter attacks of gout, but for the first time his usually impeccable handwriting started to exhibit the uncertain squiggles of an old man:

> Viscount Palmerston presents his humble duty to your Majesty and begs to be allowed to wish your Majesty and His Royal Highness the Prince Consort many prosperous returns of New Years' day with increasing happiness to your Majesty and the royal family, and progressive advantage to the nation who have the good fortune to have your Majesty for their sovereign; and to adopt the language of Pope, he would say
>
> > 'May day improve on day, and year on year
> > 'Without a pain, a trouble, or a fear.'

This autumn and winter, however, have been productive of events in three of the four quarters of the globe which future years are not likely to repeat. The capture of Peking in Asia by British and French troops; the union in Europe of nearly the whole of Italy into one monarchy; and the approaching and virtually accomplished dissolution in America of the great northern Confederation [by the secession of the southern States of the Union], are events full of importance for the future, as well as being remarkable in times present.

Viscount Palmerston submits two letters which your Majesty may feel an interest in seeing. With regard to that from Lord John Russell, stating a half-formed wish to go to the House of Lords, Viscount Palmerston does not expect that the desire will be repeated when the session begins, although Lord John said last year that he felt attendance in the House of Commons in addition to the labour of his office more than he could well get through. He would be a loss to Viscount Palmerston in the House of Commons, especially after the removal of Mr. Sidney Herbert to the House of Lords and, speaking confidentially to your Majesty with regard to the future, Viscount Palmerston would think himself doing better service by recommending the House of Lords for Mr. Gladstone than for Lord John Russell . . .

The Queen thanks Lord Palmerston much for his kind good wishes for the New Year, which we both return sincerely to himself and Lady Palmerston. The Queen has much to be thankful for, both publicly and privately, amongst the latter nothing has been a greater source of joy and satisfaction than to see her beloved second daughter's future settled in so happy a manner.

The peace in China and the prosperity of this country are great public sources of happiness and thankfulness. But turning towards the Continent, there is nothing but clouds and causes of deep anxiety. The Queen wishes she could join with Lord Palmerston in rejoicing at the unity of Italy. In that place this does not, as yet, exist and she much fears we shall only have seen the disruption of existing things, without the certainty of the construction of the new order of things. The Queen must also remind Lord Palmerston of his own admission in the summer, that it would not at all be for the interests of this country to see the south of Italy in the hands of a power so entirely under the command and mixed up with the intrigues of France as, unfortunately, Sardinia now is! The one danger in Europe is France and the Queen feels that all that is now going on will add to her strength, while it will weaken all the other powers, so essential to keep her in check.

Though no doubt Lord John Russell's and Mr. Herbert's both leaving the House of Commons would be a loss, Lord Palmerston is a host of strength in himself and has many able men,—Mr. Gladstone, Sir G. Grey, Sir C. Wood and Sir C. Lewis to support him. The Queen cannot but think that if Lord John wishes himself to go to the House of Lords he ought not to be prevented from doing so . . .

That January also saw an odd political plot, which was to bring the Conservative Opposition behind Palmerston in an attempt to thwart Gladstone's penny-pinching defence Budgets. The Radicals, led by Cobden, who had been in Paris negotiating a trade treaty, were supporting the Chancellor and when Disraeli suggested at Court that the Tories were prepared to assist Palmerston to counter this trend, the Prince Consort was quick to write on the Queen's behalf to the Prime Minister:

> Yesterday after dinner I had some conversation with Mr. Disraeli and happened to touch upon our armaments and the round robin sent to the Radical M.P.s to induce the Government to reduce our military and naval force. He lamented the circumstance very much, which he attributed to intrigues emanating from the Tuileries and Mr. Cobden, but which he did not fear so long as the ministers remained firm. He said he had taken great pains to ascertain the views of his party and he could promise that they would to a man support the Government in resisting retrenchment in this important crisis for the country and Europe; he had sent out summonses to more than 300 M.P.s at their own request, who formed a compact and formidable party but a most useful one, to the Crown and the Government, as they were contented, wanted nothing, did not wish for office but thought solely of strengthening the hands of the Government in a patriotic sense. The only thing they required in return from the Government was that it should distinctly declare its principles and not enter into a line of what he termed 'democratic finance'. What he said was deliberately said, it was not an offer to a minister to urge him on in order to trip him up afterwards, but was said to me and to the Queen with the full consciousness of the responsibility which attached to it. Mr. Disraeli said no minister since Mr. Pitt had been so powerful as you might be; the Conservative Party was ready not only to give general support to a steady and patriotic policy, but even to help the minister out of scrapes if he got into any.
>
> This conversation I thought too important not at once confidentially to communicate it to you. It is evident that there exists great fear of the peace party and a full knowledge that the Emperor

desires a 'Gladstone-Cobden' Government to disarm this country, in order to domineer over it, if not to attack it.

The Conservatives were also working on Palmerston direct, but the old gentleman reported to the Queen that he felt quite capable of handling the problems of the coming session:

> . . . Viscount Palmerston saw Lord Malmesbury on Friday before the Cabinet. They both came up in the same train, though not in the same carriage, and Lord Malmesbury came to Viscount Palmerston's in Piccadilly at 3 o'clock.
>
> He said that he was charged by Lord Derby and Mr. Disraeli with a message similar to that which he had conveyed last year, namely, that if Mr. Gladstone were to propose a democratic Budget, making a great transfer of burthens from indirect to direct taxation, and if, the Cabinet refusing its concurrence, Mr. Gladstone were to retire, the Conservative Party would give the Government substantial support, except in the case of the Government wishing to take an active part in war against Austria. That this did not of course mean an abstinence from usual attacks and criticisms in debate, but that no step would in such case be taken tending to produce a change of Government. In fact, said Lord Malmesbury, neither the Conservative leaders nor the Party wish at present to come into office, and have no intention of taking any step to turn the present Government out. Mr. Bright had indeed proposed to Mr. Disraeli to join together with the Radical Party, the Conservatives, for the purpose of turning out the present Government; and especially to get rid of Viscount Palmerston and Lord John Russell. Mr. Bright said he would in that case give the Conservative Government a two years' existence, and by the end of that time the country, it might be hoped, would be prepared for a good and real Reform Bill and then a proper Government might be formed.
>
> This proposal, which it must be owned was not very tempting, Lord Malmesbury said had been declined. He also said that Count Persigny, on returning from one of his trips to Paris, had brought a similar proposal from Mr. Cobden for a co-operation of Radicals and Conservatives to overthrow the present Government; but that also had been declined. Viscount Palmerston requested Lord Malmesbury to convey his thanks to Lord Derby

and Mr. Disraeli for the handsome communication which they had thus made to him, and to assure them that he fully appreciated the honourable and patriotic motives by which it had been prompted...

The Queen commented tersely in reply: 'The scheme of Count Persigny (and his master) and Messrs. Cobden and Bright would be amusing if they did not reveal a very evil spirit . . .'

The year 1861 was to prove somewhat quieter than its predecessor. The Queen persuaded Palmerston to prevent Lord John Russell from sending too friendly a letter to Garibaldi, who was threatening further trouble for Austria in Italy. Then, in February, after the British Ambassador in Paris had reported an alarming increase in French naval construction plans, especially of new ironclads, she urged her Prime Minister to look into the strength of Britain's navy and the efficiency of the Admiralty:

> FEBRUARY 22: The perusal of that most important confidential memorandum from Lord Cowley (February 18th) makes the Queen very anxious to have an exact report of our state of preparations with regard to iron-cased ships and the steps to meet our deficiency. We must be superior in numbers to the French and greatly superior from our general position, if we are not to expose ourselves to disasters.

> FEBRUARY 22: Viscount Palmerston presents his humble duty to your Majesty and has received your Majesty's communication of this morning upon the very important question of iron-cased ships treated on in Lord Cowley's memorandum. The Duke of Somerset three days ago sent Viscount Palmerston a confidential memorandum, drawn up and signed by all the Naval Lords of the Admiralty, calling the attention of the Government to the extensive preparations making by the French Government for a powerful fleet of iron-cased ships and to the very backward state of your Majesty's navy in this respect; and recommending that contracts should immediately be entered into for the construction of ten iron-cased ships of the size and force of the *Warrior*, and that ten 80-gun wooden ships-of-the-line should be cut down to single-decked ships and be cased with iron. Viscount Palmerston is going to see the Duke of Somerset upon this matter this morning . . .

This arrangement would give your Majesty 27 iron-cased ships as against the 26 which the Emperor of the French will have when all his orders are completed.

FEBRUARY 22: The Queen is very glad to see that the Government is seriously taking up the question of iron-cased ships and looks forward with much interest to the result of Lord Palmerston's conference with the Duke of Somerset. The number wanted appears large, but the Queen must add that she does not consider one ship a sufficient preponderance over the French navy for this country. 27-26 would give this.

FEBRUARY 28: ... Sir James Elphinstone then began a discussion about the constitution of the Board of Admiralty and moved some resolutions developing his scheme for a reconstitution of the department. He explained at much length his notions of the defects of the present organisation of the naval department, and his plan for improving it; but said that as tomorrow a committee is to be appointed to consider the subject he should not press the resolutions to a division, but should wish them to be considered by the committee ...

MARCH 2: The Queen has received Lord Palmerston's report on the debate on Thursday night. She trusts Lord Palmerston will consider with his colleagues the advantage of substituting for the present clumsy Board of Admiralty an administration analagous to that of the army. No real improvement will be made, particularly in the organisation of the forces, until they be placed under single and permanent command. Has Lord Palmerston ever had time to cast his eye over a little book called 'Admiralty Faults and Defaults'? It will well repay its perusal and give the whole case in a clear and compressed form. The Queen believes that public opinion is very much made up on the subject, but she thinks committees of the House of Commons hardly the right instrument for carrying out a grave change in the administration of the country. The Cabinet ought to consider them and, if time and knowledge should fail them, a Royal Commission would be a more constitutional instrument than a committee appointed by the House of Commons.

Later in March Palmerston felt free to ask the Queen for a small acknowledgement of his services:

> Viscount Palmerston presents his humble duty to your Majesty and would not intrude upon your Majesty upon any subject not immediately connected with the performance of his duties, if it were not for the pressure of time.
>
> Your Majesty was graciously [pleased] on the death of the late Lord Dalhousie to express a disposition to appoint Lord Viscount Palmerston to the vacant office of Lord Warden of the Cinque Ports, and Viscount Palmerston, in expressing his thankfulness to your Majesty, stated that as the salary of the office had been abolished, and the remaining duties attached to it might be transferred, the preferable arrangement would be that the office itself should be abolished. Since that time, however, he has had several representations from the Cinque Ports against the abolition of the office, it being, as they state, an essential part of their ancient organisation, so that its abolition would involve other changes which they would not wish to see made. Under these circumstances and considering that no saving would arise to the public from the abolition of the office, while it would be at variance with traditional feelings in the Cinque Port towns, which are entitled to a certain degree of respect, Viscount Palmerston has come to the conclusion that it would be advisable that the office should be continued and should be filled up. If therefore it should still be your Majesty's pleasure that he should be appointed to it, Viscount Palmerston would feel gratified and proud of an honorary appointment which would be a mark of your Majesty's gracious and condescending approval. But as there are some small local advantages attached at present to the office, it is one, the acceptance of which would vacate a seat in the House of Commons and render a re-election necessary. This is a process, which in the middle of a session, would have been very inconvenient to Viscount Palmerston and would have interfered perhaps with the public service, but as the Easter holidays are approaching, his re-election might take place during the recess, so that he could take his seat again on the meeting of the House when the recess is over.
>
> On such a supposition, if his appointment to the office by your Majesty were to be declared to him by your Majesty on Friday morning, his seat having by that means become vacant, his writ

would be moved for on Friday, the day on which the House is to adjourn for the recess and his re-election, of which he entertains no doubt, would take place at Tiverton on the Wednesday or Thursday of next week.

Palmerston's chief service during the first six months of the year was to obtain an adequate grant from the Cabinet and Parliament for Princess Alice on her betrothal to Prince Louis of Hesse. The Queen had been very firm in her demands.

She pointed out that during the 24 years of her reign she had never asked for a penny from the country for herself, but that while eight members of the royal family had died and nine had been born, the yearly allowances to them had diminished by £189,000. With the younger royal children still growing up, the Queen would have preferred some general settlement. 'It is a most unpleasant feeling for the Queen to have continually to come, as it were as a beggar, to Parliament and to be exposed to every variety of remark . . . The only way in which the Queen could remedy the evil would be to prevent her daughters marrying as George III did . . .'

The Cabinet, and particularly the parsimonious Gladstone, jibbed at this, and although Parliament finally voted Princess Alice an annuity of £6,000 a year and a dower of £30,000, it took them, to the Queen's expressed annoyance, until after the Easter recess to do so. However, Palmerston had laboured mightily on the Queen's behalf, and in her letter of May 6, in which she referred to the death of her mother, the Duchess of Kent, only two months earlier, she expressed her appreciation:

> The Queen has just received Lord Palmerston's letter from the House of Commons with the very gratifying intelligence of the vote for Princess Alice's pension having been passed without one dissentient voice. It is most satisfying to our feelings and to those of our dear child and will be equally so to Prince Louis. The kind and loyal feeling shown to the Queen by the country and Parliament on this and on the late heavy affliction which befell her, and the universal sympathy for her overwhelming grief, have touched her deeply, and the Queen only wishes it could be known how much she felt it.

Lord Palmerston has not mentioned anything with regard to Lord John Russell.

Lord John, his zeal for Reform blunted by an indifferent House of Commons, had at last made up his mind to accept a peerage and seek quieter pastures, while still retaining his ministerial post. He had written to his old colleague:

> . . . Forty-five years in the House of Commons and about twenty spent in the service of the Crown, including five-and-a-half years as First Lord of the Treasury, seem to entitle me to an easier seat and a position in a more quiet assembly.
>
> It would be for the Queen to say whether she would be pleased to give me a higher rank in the peerage than that of Baron. Cowley and Canning have been raised to earldoms.
>
> In conclusion I can only say that I should be delighted to go on fighting by your side in the Commons if I felt myself equal to it.
>
> I should wish, after the Queen's pleasure is made known to me, to keep my seat in the Commons for a short time, say till Whitsun-tide, in order to prepare my friends in the City for a new election.

In forwarding the request to the Queen, Palmerston could not refrain from a mischievous comment:

> . . . Lord John Russell will, of course, expect to be the Leader in the House of Lords, and will probably before long become a zealous champion of the rights and privileges of that House.
>
> Viscount Palmerston will however endeavour to persuade Lord John not to press his request on your Majesty at all events till the end of the session.

In this the Prime Minister was successful. He also persuaded Lord John not to disturb Lord Granville as Leader of the Upper House, and proposed to the Queen that the new Earl Russell should also receive the Garter. The Queen thought otherwise:

> The Queen . . . is quite ready to confer an earldom upon Lord John Russell . . . and glad at the same time that he does not pro-pose to interfere with Lord Granville as Leader of the House of Lords. She thinks that an earldom and the Garter would be too much to confer at once on the same person and would therefore

wish Lord Palmerston to submit some other name instead for that distinction. She thinks it moreover useful to keep something in hand, to be able to mark services which may be rendered here-after . . .

Palmerston now required an additional Foreign Office spokesman in the House of Commons:

> . . . Lord John Russell concurs with Viscount Palmerston in thinking that Mr. Layard would be very useful as Under-Secretary for the Foreign Department. He held that office under Lord Granville, who speaks very highly of his efficiency; and he would be useful to Viscount Palmerston for questions and debates on foreign affairs in the House of Commons . . .

The Queen objected. Mr. Layard, an archaeologist and former diplomat, had in the past been a vocal critic of foreign policies in the House and the Queen wished for someone more amenable. Her exchanges with Palmerston on the subject brought a renewed note of acrimony:

> JULY 22: . . . Lord Palmerston knows his defects as well as the Queen and she is sure that on further reflection he will agree with her that they would make his appointment to that particular office not conducive to the public good. In the contact with foreign countries we should be represented by a thorough gentleman.

> JULY 23: Viscount Palmerston presents his humble duty to your Majesty and is sorry that your Majesty should object to the appointment of Mr. Layard as Under-Secretary of State for the Foreign Department, but he still hopes that your Majesty may upon full consideration be led to sanction it.
>
> The removal of Lord Herbert and of Lord John Russell to the House of Lords has deprived the Treasury Bench in the House of Commons of two able and powerful debaters, and it is of great importance for the strength and stability of your Majesty's Government that this loss should if possible be supplied. This can only be done by taking into the ranks some persons on the Liberal side who have shown aptitude and capacity for debate . . .
>
> With regard to Mr. Layard, about whom alone it is necessary

for Viscount Palmerston to speak, it is to be observed that he is a very able and active-minded man, has shown himself when Under-Secretary to Lord Granville at the Foreign Office to be a very good man of departmental business, is very efficient as a speaker and debater in the House of Commons, and is very conversant with all the affairs of Europe of late years. Lord John Russell wishes to have his assistance in the office, and Viscount Palmerston is desirous of having his help in the House of Commons. As to his communication with foreign Ministers, which, however, would be infrequent, except during the occasional absence of Lord John Russell, his manners in personal intercourse are conciliatory and agreeable and Viscount Palmerston is quite sure that no foreign Minister, even though he might differ on the subjects talked about and might take a view of the matter different from that of your Majesty's Government, would have any complaint to make of Mr. Layard's manner towards him. Viscount Palmerston therefore hopes that your Majesty will consent to this appointment . . .

JULY 24: The Queen acknowledges Lord Palmerston's letter of yesterday. She is sorry that she cannot alter her determination about Mr. Layard. She fully recognises the importance of the parliamentary exigencies, but the Queen cannot sacrifice to them the higher interests of the country. Neither Mr. Layard nor Mr. Osborne ought to be proposed to the Queen as representatives of the Foreign Office in the House of Commons and therefore of the Crown to foreign countries. If Lord Palmerston can bring Mr. Layard into office in some other place to get his assistance in the House of Commons she will not object.

Palmerston wrote another long justificatory letter to the Queen on the subject of Mr. Layard, and even pleaded his cause with the Prince. The Queen made a grudging concession:

The Prince has reported to the Queen all that Lord Palmerston said to him on the subject of Mr. Layard; this has not had the effect of altering her opinion as to this disqualification of that gentleman for that particular office for which Lord Palmerston proposes him. This appointment would, in the Queen's opinion, be a serious evil. If Lord Palmerston, on sincere self-examination,

m (the Veteran Shop Walker): 'Now then, Mr. Russell! What have we got to put the window?'

r. Russell: 'Well, sir, there's some Reform Checks, Foreign Ties, Berlin Worsted, der Quiltings, Russian Towelling, French Designs, lots of Remnants and any antity of Red Tape.'—*Punch* on the Prime Minister's dilemmas during his last tering year of office.

should consider that without it the difficulties of carrying on his Government are such as to endanger the continuance of its success, the Queen will, of course, have to admit one evil for the country in order to avert a greater. She still trusts however that knowing the nature of the Queen's objection, he will not place her in this dilemma.

Palmerston took advantage of the opening with a little too much alacrity. He praised fulsomely the Queen's 'soundness of judgment' and thanked her for her 'gracious and condescending acquiescence' in Mr. Layard's appointment. The royal couple were furious, and the Prince was moved to complain to Lord Granville:

> I send you the two letters which close the correspondence between the Queen and Lord Palmerston on the Layard question. You will not fail to perceive with how little candour Lord P. meets that of the Q. and how little real consideration he shows to her, which is rendered still more offensive to delicate feelings by the uncalled for flattery which accompanies it.

However, by September, relations had been sufficiently restored for sovereign and Prime Minister to exchange more amicable letters:

> . . . Viscount and Viscountess Palmerston came to town on Saturday from Walmer Castle, where they have been staying on and off for near a month, and they are full of thankfulness to your Majesty for the gracious gift of that residence. It is undoubtedly one of the healthiest spots in the kingdom and full of interest. It has been of great service to Lady Palmerston's health . . .

> . . . The Queen is much pleased to hear that Walmer has been so beneficial to Lady Palmerston's health and conducive to their comfort. It is certainly a very healthy place.
> The Queen finds herself much the better for the pure bracing air and the fine scenery and complete quiet of the Highlands.

But in foreign affairs a new danger now loomed. With the outbreak of the American Civil War in April 1861, British public opinion at first sided with the South, and although the Government maintained a lukewarm neutrality, relations with the North were far from cordial. In May and June the Queen and Palmerston had already referred to possible trouble ahead:

> The Queen . . . thinks it of great importance that we should be strong in Canada, and thinks an increase in Artillery as important as the sending of two more battalions, as that arm cannot be supplied at all by the Colony. The naval forces would, however, require strengthening even more. It is less likely that the remnant of the United States could send expeditions by land to the North while quarrelling with the South, than that they should commit acts of violence at sea.

> Viscount Palmerston presents his humble duty to your Majesty and begs to state that the Cabinet at its meeting to-day considered the proposal made by the United States Government to that of France and communicated by the French Government to that of your Majesty, that privateering should be abolished and its abolition enforced upon the Southern Confederacy; and that private property should be exempt from capture on the sea.
>
> The Cabinet were of opinion that the abandonment of privateering offered by the Northern States should be accepted, but that such an abandonment could not be imposed by force on the Southern States, as to do so would be a departure from that neutrality which both England and France have determined to observe, and that it would be unadvisable for a great maritime power like England to forego an effective mode of employing its naval strength, and that consequently an agreement that private property should be exempted from capture on the sea cannot be entered into by Great Britain . . .

By November 13, Palmerston had more specific cause for concern:

> . . . There was reason to suspect that an American federal steamer of war of 8-guns, which had lately arrived at Falmouth, and from thence at Southampton, was intended to intercept the mail packet coming home with the West Indian mail, in order to take out of her Messrs. Mason and Slidell, the two envoys from the Southern Confederacy, supposed to be coming in her . . .
>
> According to the Law of Nations, as laid down by Lord Stowell, and practised and enforced by England in the war with France,

the Northern Union, being a belligerent, is entitled by its ships of war to stop and search any neutral merchantmen, and the West India packet is such; to search her if there is reasonable suspicion that she is carrying enemy's despatches, and if such are found on board to take her to a port of the belligerent, and there to proceed against her for condemnation. Such being ruled to be the law, the only thing that could be done was to order the *Phaeton* frigate to drop down to Yarmouth Roads from Portsmouth, and to watch the American steamer, and to see that she did not exercise this belligerent right within the three-mile limit of British jurisdiction, and this was done.

But Viscount Palmerston sent yesterday for Mr. Adams [the American Minister] to ask him about this matter, and to represent to him how unwise it would be to create irritation in this country merely for the sake of preventing the landing of Mr. Slidell, whose presence here would have no more effect on the policy of your Majesty with regard to America than the presence of the three other Southern Deputies who have been here for many months. Mr. Adams assured Viscount Palmerston that the American steamer had orders not to meddle with any vessel under any foreign flag; that it came to intercept the *Nashville*, the Confederate ship in which it was thought the Southern envoys might be coming; and not having met with her was going back to the American coast to watch some merchantmen supposed to be taking arms to the Southern ports . . .

The assurances proved insufficient. The two Southern envoys were seized off the British packet, and the danger of war between Britain and the United States suddenly flared. On November 29 Palmerston wrote:

Viscount Palmerston presents his humble duty to your Majesty and begs to state that the Cabinet at its meeting this afternoon resumed the consideration of the forcible capture of the Southern envoys from on board the *Trent* steamer, upon which the law officers had yesterday given the opinion contained in the accompanying report. The law officers and Doctor Phillimore, Counsel to the Admiralty, were in attendance. The result was that it appeared to the Cabinet that a gross outrage and violation of international law has been committed, and that your Majesty should be advised to demand reparation and redress. The Cabinet is to meet again tomorrow at 2, by which time Lord Russell will have prepared an instruction to Lord Lyons [British Minister in Washington] for the consideration of the Cabinet, and for submission afterwards to your Majesty. The general outline and tenor which appeared to meet the opinions of the Cabinet would be, that the Washington Government should be told that what has been done is a violation of international law, and of the rights of Great Britain, and that your Majesty's Government trust that the act will be disavowed and the prisoners set free and restored to British protection; and that Lord Lyons should be instructed that if this demand is refused he should retire from the United States . . .

Shocked at the imminent possibility of open conflict, the royal couple were anxious to avoid war if any formula could be found. In returning the draft despatches to Earl Russell, the Queen wrote:

The Queen returns these important drafts, which upon the whole she approves, but she cannot help feeling that the main draft, that for communication to the American Government, is somewhat meagre. She should have liked to have seen the expression of a hope that the American captain did not act under instructions, or, if he did, that he misapprehended them—that the United States Government must be fully aware that the British Government could not allow its flag to be insulted, and the security of her mail communications to be placed in jeopardy, and her Majesty's Government are unwilling to believe that the United States Government intended wantonly to put an insult upon this country, and to add to their many distressing complications for forcing a question of dispute upon us, and that we are therefore glad to believe that upon a full consideration of the circumstances, and of the undoubted breach of international law committed, they would spontaneously offer such redress as alone could satisfy this country, viz. the restoration of the unfortunate passengers and a suitable apology.

On the draft of the letter in the royal archives the Queen was soon to write:

This draft was the last the beloved Prince ever wrote; he was very unwell at the time, and when he brought it into the Queen he said: 'I could hardly hold my pen.'

With the long delay in mail communication keeping the question of peace or war seething for weeks, Palmerston wrote jauntily to the Queen on December 5:

> Viscount Palmerston presents his humble duty to your Majesty and submits for your Majesty's information a memorandum from the Duke of Somerset on the subject of the proposed naval arrangements with reference to the possibility of war with the United States. A War Committee will meet tomorrow at 2 o'clock at the War Department to consider generally the precautionary measures the best to be adopted . . .
>
> Nobody can form any reasonable guess as to the answer which the Federal Government will make to the British demands, because that Government is not guided by reasonable men; but Viscount Palmerston was told this afternoon that Mr. Wood (Viscount Palmerston believes that to be his name), a great friend and adviser of Mr. Seward [the American Secretary of State], and who came to Europe with General Scott and arrived in London a few days ago, said yesterday to a person who told Viscount Palmerston's informant, that he, Mr. Wood, had been so much struck with the intensity and unanimity of feeling in this country that he had written to Mr. Seward to advise him to yield to the British demands absolutely and immediately. Your Majesty's position is anyhow a good one. If the Federal Government comply with the demands it will be honourable for England and humiliating for the United States. If the Federal Government refuse compliance, Great Britain is in a better state than at any former time to inflict a severe blow upon, and to read a lesson to the United States which will not soon be forgotten . . .

No such lesson proved necessary. The Prince's formula was to prove acceptable to the American Government. Instead, a more personal tragedy was about to strike the royal household.

CHAPTER XI

The Desolate Queen

THE PRINCE WAS MORTALLY ILL. NEVER A ROBUST MAN, IN SPITE of his imposing appearance, the formidable domestic and political duties he had taken upon himself over the years had lowered his physical resistance. The month of November had brought new mental distress. Three members of the closely related Portuguese royal family, including the young King Pedro, had died of typhoid fever. The Prince of Wales, to his parents' chagrin, had become involved in an amorous escapade. Shortly after travelling down to Madingley Hall, Cambridge, to remonstrate with the heir to the throne, the Prince Consort had in some unexplained fashion contracted a typhoid infection. Debilitated by the low fever, he had continued his public duties, but on the day after suggesting alterations to the Foreign Office draft on the *Trent* incident, he retired finally to his sick-bed.

The illness was lightly diagnosed at first—as a feverish cold, rheumatism, influenza. The royal physicians were not remarkable for their competence. Their doyen, Sir James Clark, was seventy-three, and Sir Henry Holland, physician-in-ordinary to the Prince, was another septuagenarian. Even the gifted Dr. William Jenner, the pathologist who first recognised the typhoid germ, was slow to determine the true nature of the ailment.

Palmerston happened to pass the night at Windsor when the Prince was first taken seriously ill. His opinion of the resident physicians was low, and he entreated the Queen to obtain further medical advice. She was herself in a condition of such anxiety and distress that the letter was answered by Sir Charles Phipps, Keeper of the Queen's Privy Purse. For the time being he became, in effect, her private secretary, an office he performed for several months during the period of desolation which followed the

Prince's death. This burden was gradually taken over by his colleague, General the Hon. Charles Grey, the Prince's Private Secretary, and between them they introduced a new component into the relationship between sovereign and ministers. Phipps' first news of the Prince's condition, on December 3, was distinctly reassuring, but the situation deteriorated fast:

> The Queen is very much obliged to you for the kind interest displayed in your letter received this day. The Prince has had a feverish cold the last few days, which disturbs his rest at night, but Her Majesty has seen His Royal Highness before similarly affected and hopes that in a few days it will pass off.
>
> In addition to Sir James Clark the Queen has had the advantage of the constant advice of Dr. Jenner, a most skilful physician, and Her Majesty would be unwilling to cause unnecessary alarm where no cause exists for it, by calling in a medical man who does not upon ordinary occasions attend at the Palace.
>
> Nothing, I believe, would annoy the Queen more than any alarm in London with regard to the Prince's health.

> DECEMBER 6: The Prince is, I hope, decidedly better to-day—and has taken more food since last night than he had before done since Sunday.
>
> After your letter I thought it my duty to keep you informed, upon my own responsibility, of the state of His Highness' health, but everything connected with the subject required much management.
>
> The Prince himself, when ill, is extremely depressed and low, and the Queen becomes so nervous—and so easily alarmed, that the greatest caution is necessary. The suggestion that it could be desirable to call in another medical man could, I think, frighten the Queen very much, and the Prince already is annoyed with the visits of the three who attend him. Sir J. Clark is here daily—Dr. Jenner remains here permanently, and Mr. Brown, the Windsor apothecary, who knows the Prince's constitution better than anybody, also sees him.
>
> Dr. Jenner does not think that there is any doubt as to the nature and cause of the illness—and it is one in which no active treatment is admissable.
>
> If any further advice were sought, it would be necessary first to

send for Sir H. Holland, and I do not think any advantage would be gained.

You will easily believe with how much diffidence I hesitate to act upon any suggestion of yours—but I sincerely believe that to ask to call in another Doctor would do more harm than good. The mere suggestion the other night upset the Queen and agitated her dreadfully, and it is very essential to keep up the spirits both of her and the Prince . . .

DECEMBER 7: After the favourable report that I was able, with the greatest truth, to send you last night, I am sure that you will be very much disappointed and grieved to hear that the Prince's illness is to-day declared to be a gastric fever.—The symptoms are all favourable, and there are not, at this time, any appearances of any kind that give cause for present anxiety.

The illness however must have its course, and it always lasts a month.—Supposing therefore, as it is now thought, that the Prince has been under the influence of this particular disease for a fortnight, there is a fortnight of illness still to be watched, and to get through.

The Queen is at present perfectly composed and prepared to watch through this long prospect of constant anxiety with calmness and hope—but I must tell you, most confidentially, that it requires no little management to prevent her from breaking down altogether. The least thing would alarm her to a degree that would unfit her for the discharge of any duties.

It would be well that she should have as little to shake her nerves as possible, and what would particularly try her would be any public alarm about the Prince, which, coming back to her through the public prints, would make her fancy that the truth was concealed from her.

Her Majesty is not up to much writing, but would not, if it were necessary, object to see any of her ministers. Were this requisite it would be desirable that whilst the kindest sympathy were expressed to her, as cheerful a view as possible shoud be taken to her of the state of the Prince . . .

DECEMBER 8: . . . Sir James Clark and Dr. Jenner have decided, not from any opinion in the least less favourable, but from the rank and station of the patient, to call in further advice—and tomorrow

Sir H. Holland, and Dr. Watson will be asked to come down to Windsor. The former is physician-in-ordinary to the Prince and could not be passed over—and Dr. Watson, one of the physicians-extraordinary to the Queen, has a very high reputation.

This measure has been made very difficult first by the Queen's being disinclined to it, and secondly by the fear of alarming the Prince himself. He is extremely low about himself—there is no doubt that the death of the King of Portugal, not only grieved him very deeply, but would make him exceedingly nervous if he had any idea that his illness bore any similarity to that of which the King died . . .

DECEMBER 9: I think I should have done an injustice to the medical men who have been attending the Prince, if I conveyed to you the idea that they had been treating him for a malady different from that with which he was really afflicted.

Although it was only yesterday morning that the disorder distinctly declared itself, they were perfectly aware that the symptoms exhibited were such as might precede the more distinct characterisation of gastric or bowel fever, and they had throughout treated H.R.H. with this view . . .

Dr. Watson has just seen the Prince. He thinks him *very ill*, not that there are at present any unfavourable symptoms, but that the malady is very grave and serious in itself—and that even the Prince's present weakness is very great—in short he says that it is impossible not to be very anxious.

DECEMBER 12: I am able to report another very good night, and that the Prince is not worse than yesterday. Watson told me last night that the Prince 'held his ground well'.

There never has been the slightest divergence of opinion as to the treatment of the case between Watson and Jenner.

The Prime Minister was by now seriously alarmed. His worst suspicions had been confirmed, and the prospect of the Prince's illness becoming fatal perturbed him greatly. The two men had always been poles apart in temperament, but Palmerston had come to recognise the Prince's enormous competence in the conduct of royal business, and realised that he enjoyed great prestige in the European Courts, which had frequently been of great advantage. Moreover, in the many altercations about policy with the Queen over the years, the Prince had often served as a personal buffer. Palmerston was growing old and sentimental, and many of the political battles of the past were becoming softened in retrospect. If the Prince were to disappear from the scene, a distraught sovereign might again become difficult to deal with direct, and Palmerston's vehemently chivalrous nature recoiled at the prospect. In the meantime, he vented his spleen on the principal physician in an outburst to Phipps:

> DECEMBER 12: I am glad to hear by your letter to-day that the Prince is not worse, but his illness is, as everybody knows, of a formidable character, and liable to take a sudden and unfavourable turn from day to day.—I do hope and trust therefore that Dr. Watson will remain at Windsor to watch the case from day to day till all danger is over. Sir James Clark has already incurred a heavy responsibility by delaying so long to call in additional advice; and I must officially request that the advice at last called in may be retained for constant attendance during the course of the malady. I feel that as Head of the Government and charged with a responsibility of my own, I have reason to complain that Sir James Clark did not at once inform me of the true nature of the attack, instead of leaving me to find out by my own conclusions that it was of a much more serious nature than was represented to me by him at Windsor last week. Pray show this letter to Sir James.

The Prince was beyond help. Sir Charles Phipps' letters over the next 48 hours could only tell of his tragic end:

> DECEMBER 13: . . . The Queen keeps well, and very hopeful—but I feel confident that, in spite of her determination not to contemplate any misfortune, she must be aware of the serious nature of the disorder.
>
> Dr. Jenner, in whose skill she has the most implicit confidence,— and I am sure deservedly—has, without creating alarm that would upset her altogether, told her from time to time sincerely the progress of the symptoms. His attention, watchfulness and care— day and night—are beyond all praise . . .

> DECEMBER 13: I am deeply grieved to say that the Prince's disease

has taken a very unfavourable turn, and that the doctors are in the *greatest anxiety*—they have even fears for the night.

DECEMBER 13 [*telegram*]: I grieve to say the Prince is much worse. The doctors in great anxiety. I send a messenger by next train.

DECEMBER 14: . . . I took an opportunity of asking Watson, when by himself, whether he thought that anything could have been changed in the treatment.

He said that nothing could have been done different and he added that, in the profession, Jenner would be considered *the* man to have the management of the case, and that his experience in fevers, coupled with Clark's intimate knowledge of the Prince's constitution, formed an unusually fortunate combination of medical requirements . . .

DECEMBER 14: Alas! the hopes of this morning are fading away. The improvement has not been maintained and though the physicians can still keep up the pulse, by stimulants, the quickness of breathing, from the congested state of the lungs, increases. A bulletin is about to be issued saying that the Prince Consort continues in a very critical state.

The Queen is wonderfully composed and says that she is prepared for the worst.

[DECEMBER 14]: I hope that I had sufficiently prepared you for the dreadful event which took place at ten minutes before eleven this night.

The Prince, who had been gradually becoming worse during the afternoon, at about 10 o'clock broke out into a profuse perspiration—and then rapidly sank, until ten minutes before 11, when he expired, without pain, or the slightest movement. He was surrounded by the Queen, the Prince of Wales, and the Princesses, and also the Prince and Princess of Leiningen.

The Queen, though in an agony of grief, is perfectly collected, and shows a self-control that is quite extraordinary.

Alas, she has not realised her loss, and when the full consciousness comes upon her—I tremble—but only for the depth of grief —What will happen?—Where can she look for that support and

317

assistance upon which she has leaned in the greatest and the least questions of her life?

I cannot write more and I am sure you will forgive me, for I hardly know what I write.

DECEMBER 15: The Queen's calmness and submissive resignation to the Will of God in view of this stunning affliction is wonderful. Except in the paroxysms of her grief she is perfectly composed . . .

The Queen is determined to do her duty to the country, and I am sure will most fully, thinking always that he is looking down and approving her—but at present she is quite unable to think upon any subject but one. Her health has not suffered.

I think a letter from you of condolence and comfort would be acceptable.

Then, on December 19, Sir Charles broached a proposal for carrying on the essential business of State:

. . . The Queen is quite aware that the support and assistance which Her Majesty has heretofore received is gone for ever, the mind that conceived, the head that judged it is gone, and Her Majesty must strive as best she can to perform those high functions that Providence has imposed upon her.

I come now to a question which of all men in the world it is most difficult for me to touch—but I act under orders sacred to me and I must act, putting self on one side, as if I were writing of a third person.

The Queen has daily and hourly need of assistance, and she naturally turns for it to those in whom many years of experience have given her confidence. The title under which this assistance is given is of little consequence, so long as the agency is not surreptitious but unacknowledged. The Queen wishes to be assisted by General Grey and myself. I have served Her Majesty now confidentially for 12 years, General Grey has been Private Secretary to the Prince for the same time.

My own impression is that it would be more open and straightforward if either we were to be called 'Joint Private Secretaries' or I were to be called 'Private Secretary', and some other title implying confidential employment found for General Grey.

But the Queen's only wish is that she should have us two acknowledged as persons authorised to assist Her Majesty in the conduct of business to which she must be unequal alone. Her Majesty would not attach much importance to my designation being altered—and, to point out to his more constant and intimate employment, General Grey might be styled 'Resident Equerry'.

With regard to ourselves, I can confidently say that we have neither of us any personal feeling. We are only anxious to devote ourselves to the assistance and service of the Queen, to whom we promised, at the deathbed of the Prince, her beloved husband, an unfailing devotion, which we intend to carry on to our lives' end.

The Queen feels sure that your wish is only to facilitate this arrangement in the manner that, whilst it gives Her Majesty most assistance, may least offend the constitutional forms, or even the prejudices which exist upon this subject.

On the 26th, Sir Charles was able to give a slightly better account of his sovereign's condition:

The Queen, though weak and indisposed to any physical exertion, is not ill in health. She sleeps several hours every night and continues perfectly calm and composed in her grief.

She walks out a little daily, and takes an interest in everything which he took under his own management here. She has directed to steward of the property always to attend her, and gives her own orders . . .

Her wish and determination to do her duty is most touching. I hope that the Prince of Wales may every day be a greater assistance to her. He seems most willing to be useful to her.

On that day the Queen roused herself to write to Palmerston in her own hand:

. . . Business she can as yet hardly think of, for her whole soul, bruised and crushed as it is, and her utterly broken heart lives but in that future World which is now nearer than ever to her, as it contains he who was the life of her life, the sunshine of her existence, her guide, support,—her all, and who was too pure, too perfect for this world. The Queen feels her life ended, in a worldly point of view; her own wish is to leave it very soon to join him for whom she would have given hers a hundred times over, would have followed bare foot over the world! If she must drag on a pleasureless and a dreary life, it will be to follow in everything his blessed example, his wishes, great and small, and then she knows that she will be doing right! Above all as regards his poor children, she has but one object in view and that is to follow his views, his plans for their future and for their good without swerving. His wishes will be her law, and this must and will be her object, her sacred duty! Duty and self sacrifice were his principles and he himself shortened his precious life by overexertion for the good of his country and for mankind in general!' May this country, who never possessed so great, so pure and so perfect a prince, ever prove itself worthy of him.

She hears with satisfaction of the universal and just feeling of millions and feels sure it will be an everlasting one. The sympathy for herself touches her much, but she feels she deserves it, for there never perhaps was woman's loving and devoted heart so cruelly pierced as hers! But God will support her, and the gentle pure spirit of her blessed, precious husband will be near her, and inspire her to do what is right. The Queen is very weak and shattered . . .

At the end of the month Palmerston was obliged to send the Queen a few official papers and certain recommendations for the New Year's honours list, and expressed his heartfelt concern:

> Viscount Palmerston presents his humble duty to your Majesty, and has read with deep emotion your Majesty's letter of the 26th, every word of which went straight to the heart. Viscount Palmerston would, however, humbly express a hope that the intensity of your Majesty's grief may not lead your Majesty to neglect your health, the preservation of which is so important for the welfare of your Majesty's children, and for that of your Majesty's devotedly attached and affectionate subjects; and which is so essentially necessary to enable your Majesty to perform those duties which it will be the object of your Majesty's life to fulfil . . .

For weeks it proved difficult to bring the Queen's mind to bear on public affairs. At the beginning of January, Phipps was forced to write again:

> I am sorry to say that the point raised in Sir George Lewis's letter with regard to filling up the post of Grand Master of the Order of the Bath, has brought on so painful and depressing a paroxysm of

grief that Her Majesty is quite unable to write in answer to your letter.

All these occasions, of proposing to place anybody in the positions which the Prince held, will be most trying to the Queen, and unless there were any objection to it, I know it would be more agreeable to Her Majesty's feelings, if I were allowed to take an opportunity of mentioning any such proposal instead of her opening a box and suddenly finding such a proposition laid before her. It is the sudden revulsion which does her so much harm . . .

However, the Queen could still respond to State business which had involved her late beloved Consort. On January 9, Palmerston wrote to inform her:

Viscount Palmerston presents his humble duty to your Majesty and begs to state that the Cabinet, at its meeting this afternoon, had read to it Mr. Seward's long note announcing the determination of the Federal Government to release Messrs. Slidell and Mason; and the Cabinet considered what answer it would be proper to give. There are in that long answer many doctrines of international law laid down, which your Majesty's Government could not agree to, and it was thought best to refer those parts of the note to your Majesty's Law Officers for their suggestions as to the answer to be given. But in the meantime Lord Russell will prepare a despatch to Lord Lyons accepting the release of the prisoners, and the declaration in Mr. Seward's note, that Captain Wilkes acted without any orders or authority, as a full satisfaction of the demands of the British Government; but he will add that there are many doctrines laid down in Mr. Seward's note to which your Majesty's Government cannot assent, but upon which observations will by another occasion be sent. Lord Russell will at the same time express a confident expectation that the persons taken out of the *Eugenia* will be released upon the same principle upon which the release of Messrs. Mason and Slidell has been granted . . .

The Queen replied in her own hand:

The Queen has received Lord Palmerston's letter and approves entirely of the course proposed to be pursued by the Government in accepting the release of the prisoners, and Mr. Seward's declaration that Captain Wilkes acted without orders, as a sufficient satisfaction; and in reserving for a future occasion the expression of their opinion on some of the doctrines advanced by Mr. Seward.

The Queen is sure that it will not have escaped Lord Palmerston's observation that, in addition to the assertion of doctrines to which the Government thinks it right to discuss, Mr. Seward seems to assume, in the last paragraph of his letter, that by now yielding to the British demands, he is setting at rest on American principles a question on which the two Governments have been at issue...

Later the same day she had an afterthought:

The Queen, being much fatigued with many affairs of a private nature and being so weak and exhausted from her utter misery and desolation, makes use of General Grey's pen.

She cannot but look upon this peaceful issue of the American quarrel as much owing to her beloved Prince, who wrote the observations upon the draft to Lord Lyons which Lord Palmerston so entirely concurred in! It was the last thing he ever wrote!

Palmerston's response was magnanimous:

... Viscount Palmerston is glad that your Majesty has some assistance in the writing of your Majesty's communications. The peaceful settlement of the difference with the Federal Government is indeed a happy event, for although there can be no doubt that your Majesty's arms would have been most successful in a war with the Northern States, yet even success in war must be purchased by a large expenditure of money, by much embarrassment to commerce and by painful sacrifices of the lives and blood of brave men. There can be no doubt that, as your Majesty observes, the alteration made in the despatch to Lord Lyons contributed essentially to the satisfactory settlement of the dispute. But those alterations were only one of innumerable instances of the tact, the judgment and the power of nice discrimination which excited Viscount Palmerston's constant and unbounded admiration...

The Queen's grief seriously curtailed public business. Essential meetings of the Privy Council were kept to the minimum attendance of three of its members, the details of the Royal Speech at the opening of Parliament were settled by correspondence. It even required the intervention of King Leopold of the Belgians, who had come to London to comfort his niece, and Lord Granville, Lord President of the Council, and ever her favourite in the House of Lords, to persuade her to grant the first audience of her widowhood to the Prime Minister. She dreaded meeting the forceful old man, but he made his way down to Osborne and their encounter went well. The problem of the Prince of Wales, whose errant disposition, it was hoped, might be cured by marriage to Princess Alexandra of Denmark, provided common ground. 'I would hardly have given Lord Palmerston credit for entering so entirely into my anxieties,' the Queen noted in her Journal on January 29.

Palmerston endeavoured to arouse his sovereign's interest with little commentaries on developments abroad:

> . . . Viscount Palmerston is sorry to learn by the telegram from Turin that Baron Ricasoli [the Italian Prime Minister] and his colleagues have resigned, and that Signor Ratazzi will probably form a new government. This change seems to indicate some change in the policy of the Italian Government and that change is not likely to be for the better. It has been known for some time that the King did not like Ricasoli and that persons who have influence with the King were bent upon substituting Ratazzi for Ricasoli. The danger is that Ratazzi should be too subservient to the Emperor Napoleon, but it may be hoped that, when he becomes charged with responsibility and obliged to lean for support upon the Italian parliament, he may find it necessary to be more honest than people in general give him credit for being.

In America a new general named Ulysses Grant was starting to distinguish himself in the western theatre of the Civil War:

> MARCH 6: . . . The late success of the Federal troops in the neighbourhood of the Ohio was no doubt important, if they took 15,000 prisoners as stated by them, but in the opinion of persons who are competent judges of the matter, that victory does not tend materially to decide the result of the Civil War.

Palmerston's own health was not too robust that winter. The annual attack of gout had been particularly severe and for the first time he was unable to pen his parliamentary reports in person:

> Viscount Palmerston presents his humble duty to your Majesty
> and, being prevented from attending the House of Commons this
> evening, has asked Sir George Grey to send your Majesty a report
> of the proceedings of the evening. Viscount Palmerston's right
> hand being still disabled by a slight attack of gout he trusts your
> Majesty will excuse him for employing another person's hand for
> this communication.

Palmerston's gout was an old enemy and it had been conquered
before. He was more worried about the Queen's health:

> ... Your Majesty mentioned to Viscount Palmerston yesterday
> that the food which your Majesty takes does not sufficiently
> afford nourishment. Might Viscount Palmerston presume to ask
> whether your Majesty has cold or hot meat? It is well known that
> for chemical reasons hot meat is more digestible than cold and
> therefore more easily and effectually assimilates itself, as nourish-
> ment, to the system.

He received a not very encouraging reply from Lady Augusta
Bruce, the Queen's Lady-in-Waiting:

> The Queen commands me to thank you very much for your
> kind interest in her health and to answer your question respecting
> the food Her Majesty takes. The fact is that it is not the food
> itself which affords no nourishment, but that the Queen takes it
> without the slightest appetite whether it be cold or hot; that the
> physicians say that the Queen's constant grief, which is so very
> deep-seated, and which no exertion or occupation or outward
> circumstance can at all allay (and which can perhaps be best
> expressed by the word pining), causes a depression which prevents
> Nature's deriving the refreshment and sustenance from sleep and
> food which it would under different circumstances.
>
> The Queen finds it necessary, in order to eat at all, to consult
> her taste at the moment—to take what is least unpalatable, and
> has been obliged to discard general rules. Her Majesty, however,
> both as regards attention to health, occupation and exertion, does
> indeed everything that can be wished and that is advised by her
> medical attendants, whom H.M. sees constantly ...

However, a perennial subject succeeded in rousing the Queen from her lethargy—the condition of the country's defences. A paper by a young engineer officer attracted her attention and she forwarded it to Palmerston, with the now inevitable rider about her feeling of helplessness:

> The Queen sends Lord Palmerston in strict confidence a memorandum relative to the fortifications which she thinks so sensible that she wishes him to read it . . . The Queen feels naturally doubly nervous and anxious [about] all these very important subjects, now that the great head and mind who directed all, who understood all, and who had the safety and welfare of this country so intensely at heart, is no longer with us in this world. She feels that he has left all these important subjects to her to watch over,— alas! she can do so but very imperfectly, but while she lives she will devote her whole time and strength to that she knows he wished and pray that his beloved spirit may guide and assist her in her anxious, arduous task! Her sad, pleasureless life is now solely devoted to duty.

Parliament had been discussing the same subject, particularly in view of the inconclusive engagement in the American Civil War during March of the first two ironclads with armoured gun turrets. It seemed as if every naval vessel—and coastal fort—had at one blow become obsolete, and Palmerston was compelled to report:

> . . . Mr. Osborne then moved that the works on the Spithead forts should be suspended for a time in order that the relative efficiency of floating defences might be considered . . . This seemed to satisfy the House, which has run wild about iron-cased floating batteries in consequence of the action in America between the *Merrimac* and *Monitor* . . .

Sir Charles Phipps answered for the Queen, who felt understandably perturbed about her safety at Osborne, just up the Solent from the Spithead forts:

> The Queen directs me, in thanking your for your report of Friday night's debate, to add that Her Majesty understands the difficulty

in which the Government were placed on that night, and the necessity of a compromise.

At the same time their immediate abandonment of a well-considered system of defence upon the first experiments of a new system of warfare makes Her Majesty very anxious, particularly under her present sad circumstances, and viewing the subject with reference to her position in the Isle of Wight.

The Queen feels more deeply than ever the loss of that opinion and advice upon which, on this subject, as on all others, she knew that she could implicitly rely . . .

The Prime Minister tried to calm her fears:

. . . Viscount Palmerston will pay due attention to the communication he has received from your Majesty through Sir Charles Phipps. He hopes that the result may be that, without giving up the Spithead forts, the House may be induced to allot a portion of the loan to the construction of some iron-cased floating batteries.

A minor administrative matter next produced a spark of the Queen's old fire:

The Queen feels it necessary to call the attention of Lord Palmerston to the enclosed published memorandum from the Admiralty.

Lord Palmerston will see that the Lords of the Admiralty state that they have caused additions to be made to the Queen's Regulations. There is no mention of the Queen's sanction having been sought or obtained. The Queen is sure that the power thus assumed, of altering regulations issued under her authority, is one that Lord Palmerston will feel, equally with herself, cannot belong to any subject whatever office he may hold.

Palmerston duly explained that although alterations to the Queen's Regulations could indeed only be made by an Order in Council, Admiralty Instructions, which formed part of the same publication, were issued by the Board in circular letters. The Queen was partly satisfied, but returned a tart comment through General Grey:

. . . But considering that these regulations are called 'The Queen's Regulations' it would be more satisfactory to Her Majesty that it should appear that any change in them was made with her previous sanction.

There is no doubt that the authority of the sovereign in naval matters has been deputed to a Board of Commissioners by whom it is legally exercised, without any necessary reference to the sovereign. But the Queen cannot help feeling, and the Prince entertained the same feeling very strongly, that it is too much the tendency of all Admiralty administrations to set the Crown entirely on one side.

At the beginning of May, the Queen had returned to Balmoral, the sight of which induced a further *cri de cœur* to Palmerston:

> . . . She can give but a very bad report of herself; the journey was no fatigue, but this place—this country and everything indoors and out-of-doors are perfectly overwhelming to the Queen and she feels herself still weaker and her nerves especially more shaken even than before. Her handwriting will show this. She feels as if she could not bear the torture of this existence without the idol of her poor life!
>
> No one knows what her bitter anguish and sufferings are—or how that poor heart is pierced and bleeding. She always told everyone: 'The Prince's life is the Queen's life' and so it will be forever! But as long as life remains in this shattered frame it will be devoted to her children and her country—as her adored Lord's was!

Another letter from Phipps to the Prime Minister also gave an early indication of the determined position the Queen was to adopt in the matter of the Prince of Wales' position in the kingdom:

> In a letter which I have received from the Queen this morning, Her Majesty directs me to answer for her one which she had received from you, relative to the office of Master of the Trinity House, and Her Majesty directs me to say that she, as well as the Prince of Wales himself, has a great objection to H.R.H. being put, for some years, into any position lately held by the Prince Consort, in which either there are any important functions to be performed, or in which H.R.H. would be prominently brought forward to make speeches or to take on a responsible part. In the letter which I wrote to Lord Russell, by the Queen's command, and which he probably communicated to the Deputy Master of

the Trinity House, the objection of Her Majesty was not therefore limited to the period of the Prince's coming of age, which would involve only an interval of a few months, but was dependent upon the Prince of Wales becoming sufficiently matured to make his appointment not appear merely a tribute to rank, without consideration of other qualifications.

This office was last filled, in succession, by the Duke of Wellington and the Prince Consort, and some of the most important speeches of the latter were made, as you are aware, at the annual dinners of this corporation.

The Prince of Wales was most anxious that he should not at his age be selected for posts that would induce such comparisons, and spoke to me frequently and earnestly before he went abroad upon the subject . . .

Fortunately, the parliamentary session contained little of consequence. The debates were counted out at night on more than a score of occasions, due to the absence of the necessary quorum of 40 members. Palmerston kept up his daily summaries, eliciting from the Queen during July her thanks 'for giving her so regularly and fully the parliamentary reports. She hopes the session is rapidly drawing to a close.' The American Civil War still provided the chief topic of concern abroad—allied with the effect on the Lancashire mills due to the cessation of cotton shipments. Palmerston reported:

JULY 14: . . . Your Majesty's Government think it would not be seemly that Parliament should be prorogued without passing some precautionary measure to meet the distress which the increasing scarcity of cotton is too likely to create in the manufacturing districts in the ensuing autumn and winter; and in order to render unnecessary a meeting of Parliament in October or November to do that which might be done now.

The simplest measure which has been suggested for the purpose and which is under consideration, could be to give a power to boards of guardians in cases in which the Poor Rates leviable in parishes should prove insufficient to provide for the destitute, to raise money by loan by a mortgage on the Poor Rates of such parishes.

JULY 15: . . . Mr. Lindsey moved his resolution recommending an offer of mediation between the belligerents in North America, and the acknowledgement of the Southern Confederacy, Mr. Lindsey being entirely in favour of the Southern States. Mr. Taylor, who is strongly for the Northern States made a vehement speech against all interference of any kind; declared himself adverse to the Southern States on account of their being slave owners, contended that the question of slavery was the real cause of the war, and blamed the Northern States for having, as he alleged, yielded too much to the South about slavery, before the election of Mr. Lincoln. Lord Adolphus Vane was in favour of the South. Mr. Forster, who is a partisan of the North, was more moderate than heretofore in his championship; he was against interference of any kind at present, but was for an offer of mediation whenever a proper moment might arrive. Mr. Whiteside made a good speech in favour of acknowledging the South and making an offer of mediation. Mr. Gregory made also a strong and well-argued speech in favour of the South, and urging acknowledgement and mediation. It was indeed manifest that the feeling of the majority of the House is decidedly in favour of the South, on the ground that they are now fighting for their independence on the very same principles on which both North and South acted in their separation from England.

Viscount Palmerston regretted the discussion, because many violent things had been said against both the belligerents; he defended the course of non-interference and neutrality hitherto pursued by your Majesty's Government, declined to say anything as to the relative merits or rights of the two belligerents, or as to the course which it may be advisable for Great Britain to pursue in future contingencies which cannot be foreseen, and urged the House to negative Mr. Lindsey's resolution and thus to leave it to the judgment and responsibility of the Government to regulate its conduct according to future circumstances, and to leave it free to determine what to do, and when, and how to act if any step towards the restoration of peace in America should appear likely to be attended with success . . .

The Queen seemed to be seeking solace in frequent journeys. She had returned to Osborne during June, but by July was back in the Highlands again, taking a little more interest in public affairs, but still shattered.

The Queen has to thank Lord Palmerston for many interesting reports of the proceedings in Parliament. She hears to-day that it is likely to be up early next week.

The Queen bore the journey down here less well than the preceding one, from being weaker and her nerves generally worse than they were. She is now much the same, but certainly no stronger . . .

The autumn found the Queen on a pilgrimage to Brussels and Coburg, a journey which should have been rendered happy by the Prince of Wales' engagement to his Danish Princess. Palmerston's first intimation of the betrothal came from Sir Charles Phipps, whom the Queen had left at Brussels to make a confidential report on the Prince's proposal, which took place at the royal palace of Laeken:

> I have just received a note by messenger from the Prince of Wales, from Laeken, informing me that he has made his proposal to Princess Alexandra of Denmark, and has been accepted; and I am sending off a telegram in cypher to the Queen. According to my promise I write at once to you.
>
> We have been all charmed by the young Princess, who is far prettier than we had been led to expect—features, complexion, expression all as good as possible, and with a natural, unaffected manner that is quite enchanting and yet not without dignity. She looks very young and the photographs do not at all do her justice. The Prince of Wales is in great admiration and is very proud of her and she, I hear from her ladies, is very much taken with him.
>
> I pray that this, certainly the most important day of his life, may prove to the young Prince the most auspicious also . . . Nothing can be more interesting than this young couple, who both seem as happy as possible, indeed their countenances are beaming, and quite delightful to see.

Even this happy event failed to change the Queen's prevailing mood, and her letters to Palmerston were still suffused with melancholy:

> REINHARDSBRUNN, SEPTEMBER 11: The Prince of Wales is engaged to Princess Alexandra of Denmark since Tuesday and the Queen hopes and trusts that this marriage, which was wished and indeed

almost settled by our most beloved Prince, may prove a blessing to the Prince of Wales and the country. The young Princess is indeed a lovely, sweet being whom it is impossible not to be pleased and struck with. To the poor Queen this event can no longer cause pleasure, for pleasure is for ever gone from her heart! But she is thankful for our son and our country to think there is a real prospect of happiness, that she can close her eyes—at no distant period, please God!—in peace and security. The Queen is to bring the young Princess back with her to England for a few weeks . . .

LAEKEN, OCTOBER 22: Lord Palmerston will know of the Queen's utter inability to get home from the dreadful weather which has prevailed since the very day we came here—and the amount of wind rendering it impossible for her to go—following the most perfectly beautiful weather, with only one bad day which we enjoyed for six weeks! The Queen is really so thankful for Lord Palmerston's having thought of proroguing Parliament to the beginning of November instead of the 24th October (tomorrow) and she thought quite far enough for else Parliament must have met, for return she could not. The gale has been terrific, and it blows again so much now that the Queen lives in real fear that we shall be still fixed here tomorrow. Fortunately there is nothing of such importance to make this delay of any consequence, but it is very inconvenient living on from morning to evening, for four days now, with almost all one's things gone on, and waiting to start; and though the Queen is most comfortable here and glad to be with her dear, kind, paternal, uncle, she is anxious, now that she has left dear Coburg,—her second home—to get back again to her own once so happy, now so desolate home, where she is surrounded by all belonging to her beloved husband and where all has remained as in those blessed days.

The Queen's nerves and strength and general health are just the same, and everything approaching to society or even having several of her own family together with her at her meals, is more than she can bear. But, trying and heartrending in many ways she found going to dear Coburg was, the many dear recollections of her beloved angel's childhood and youth (as well as of her dear mother), seeing the many scenes (so beautiful and peaceful in themselves), he so loved and the many kind old attached friends, high and low,—the hearing his native tongue—and the breathing of his native air—were soothing and sweet in their very sadness to her bruised spirit and her aching, bleeding heart!!—and she felt much leaving it . . .

On her return, Palmerston tried to console his sovereign:

> Viscount Palmerston presents his humble duty to your Majesty and in acknowledging the receipt of the letter of the 22nd inst. from Laeken with which your Majesty honoured him, begs to offer to your Majesty his sincere congratulations upon your Majesty's safe return; and he trusts that your Majesty may not have suffered materially from the very stormy passage which your Majesty must have had in crossing from the Scheldt . . .
>
> Your Majesty must have found your excursion to the Saxon Duchy interesting, and full of the most touching associations and recollections. Such occasions connected with the past, though in one sense painful, as bringing more strongly to the mind the consciousness of happiness gone by, are yet not unattended with something that soothes as well as afflicts, and the mental images of those who are gone are brought more vividly to the mind's eye, by the view of objects which memory associates with recollections of former happiness.

Sovereign and Prime Minister were by now engaged in an immense correspondence about the succession to the Greek throne. King Otho had finally been exiled to his native Bavaria and for months Europe was scoured for a suitable substitute. Nominally, Russia, France and Britain, as the three 'protecting powers', were under an obligation to exclude members of their own ruling families, but in the jockeying for influence, each was slow to acknowledge the fact. At one point the Greeks elected Prince Alfred, Queen Victoria's second son, almost unanimously to the throne. Some of Palmerston's comments to the Queen verged on the facetious:

> NOVEMBER 14, 1862: . . . The real truth as to the Greeks is that they are panting for increase of territory, although they acknowledge that the territory they have would bear three or four times its present population; and they own that their reason for thinking

of Prince Alfred was the hope that he would bring with him the
Ionian Islands . . .

DECEMBER 2: . . . Now as yet the Russian Government have
studiously evaded admitting that the Duke of Leuchtenberg is a
member of the Imperial family, and the only statement which
Prince Gortschakoff [the Russian Foreign Minister] has made on
the subject was that the question is a doubtful one and might be
argued in favour of the Duke. The accompanying letter from
Baron Brunnow would do credit to the General of the Jesuits, for
under pretence of giving a satisfactory explanation, it skilfully
evades the real question; is the Duke a member of the Imperial
family or is he not? When such pains are taken to shuffle out of a
plain answer to a simple question, which might be answered by a
simple affirmative or negative, it is impossible not to suspect bad
faith and unavowed views . . .

JANUARY 2, 1863: . . . The positive conditions which it would be
desirable to find to make an eligible candidate would be experience
in administration, and liberal constitutional principles, both of
which imply a certain maturity of age, not however beyond the
vigorous and active time of life. It is also desirable that the person
to be chosen should be connected with England, because the
Greeks seem to be so bent upon connecting themselves with your
Majesty's kingdom, that some among them have even conceived
the absurd idea of offering the crown to an English nobleman, if
it cannot be accepted by Prince Alfred.

Under these circumstances and taking into account all these
considerations, Viscount Palmerston would beg to submit that
Duke Ernest of Saxe-Coburg would be the best choice for England
and for Greece, and that it would be advisable to suggest him at
once to the Greeks if he should be willing to accept the offer . . .

The Duke succeeded in raising a whole host of difficulties,
demanding guarantees of his succession from the great powers,
both to the throne of Greece and in his own principality. Palmerston soon lost patience with him and wrote a small essay on his
attitude to the Queen:

. . . The Greeks want a permanent settlement, and a king who
would identify himself with Greece, and devote his mind and his

333

energies to the improvement, moral, material and political of Greece. But this desire would not be fulfilled by placing at the head of the nation a regent who was the ruler and sovereign of another and a faraway country; who looked upon himself only as a stop-gap, and whose future was in no degree identified with the future of the Greek nation. Known and announced as Regent for three or four years, the Duke would find impaired that legitimate influence which belongs to a sovereign in virtue of the permanence of his tenure; and he would find more and more every year that the ambitions and intrigues of men and of parties would be directed away from him and towards the designated successor.

But, moreover, it is not at all likely that the Greeks would give to their Regent King the power of appointing a successor. They would say that in a constitutional country such a right belongs to the parliament and not to the sovereign alone; and if they were asked to pass a law appointing as successor to the throne a young man of 18, they might not unreasonably say that they would rather make him their king at once, and appoint for him a Regency composed of Greek political men. The position of the Duke as King Regent would not be satisfactory to himself. If his thoughts and cares were during the three years of his Regency mainly directed to Coburg, as they probably would be, the duties of his Regency would be a burthen, and would not be heartily executed. If, on the contrary, he began to take a lively interest in Greece, which is not unlikely, he would feel much regret at having to retire to Coburg at the end of his three years.

For all these reasons it is submitted by Viscount Palmerston that yout Majesty could not well recommend to the Greeks to adopt the arrangement proposed by the Duke of Coburg and that the Duke should make up his mind either to accept the throne of Greece singly and permanently, if the Greeks should offer it to him on your Majesty's recommendation, or at once to say that he prefers to remain Duke of Coburg. Your Majesty would in the first case lose no time in recommending the Duke to the Greeks, and in the latter case your Majesty would at once proceed to endeavour to fix upon some other eligible candidate.

The Queen was equally out of sympathy with her relative and in the end the choice fell on the seventeen-year-old Prince William George of Denmark, brother to Princess Alexandra. He was to become as beset as his Bavarian predecessor, although he succeeded in maintaining his throne until his assassination in 1913.

The arrival of Princess Alexandra in England at the beginning of March 1863 produced in the Queen another spasm of sad recollection:

> . . . The Queen is indeed most deeply touched and gratified at the extraordinary exhibition of loyalty and affection exhibited on the occasion of the arrival of our future daughter, a tribute which she well knows, and wishes all should know, is owing to her great and good husband, who led the Queen in the right path and to whom she owes everything and the country owes everything! What joy, what pride would have filled her heart had he gone with his son this day and brought him and his lovely bride through the crowded streets to Windsor, and the Queen! Now he looks down, freed from the cares (which bow the Queen to the earth, unaided and unsupported and lonely and desolate in joy as in sorrow) on the result of this great game, life!
>
> The Queen wishes Lord Palmerston would take an opportunity of stating the Queen's feelings on this great demonstration, but also to say that those err who think that the wound can be healed by the marriage of our child!
>
> The sight of many happy young couples or of any happy couples is the one of all others which plunges daggers into the Queen's widowed heart for she is always alone and no one knows what a load of sorrow and of utter loneliness belongs to that saddest of names—a widow . . .

Plans were afoot to erect a public memorial to the Prince Consort. Palmerston's views on the form it should take were still influenced by his classical upbringing, in interesting contrast to the ornate edifice which in due course graced Kensington Gore:

> . . . Viscount Palmerston, when at Windsor, went to look at the drawings and plans for the proposed memorial and certainly cannot say that any of them appeared to him to be suitable.
>
> It seems to him that a memorial ought to be something simple and concentrated and that its leading character ought to bring forcibly to the mind of the beholder the memory and image of the person in whose honour it is erected. But all these plans fritter

335

away that leading idea by a multitude of complicated details; and the cost of executing such plans would be very great.

If Viscount Palmerston were to make any suggestion on the subject, he would say that what would appear to him to be most appropriate would be an open Grecian temple placed between Rotten Row and the carriage drive. The temple to consist of a cupola, supported by a circle of columns, with a statue of the Prince Consort of heroic size in the centre upon a suitable pedestal. The temple to be placed upon a raised platform with steps to ascend it and such accompanying and subordinate ornaments as might make a graduated transition from the temple to the surrounding open place, without detracting from the unity of the memorial, or drawing away attention from the principal figure and main object of the structure . . .

The amount to be voted by Parliament for the memorial was exciting a certain amount of controversy, but the Queen's opinions in the matter were peremptory:

The Queen is glad to hear that Lord Palmerston proposes to give notice on Monday for a vote in aid of the national memorial to the beloved Prince. But she trusts that he will not propose any sum so utterly unworthy of the House of Commons and the country as £30,000. Lord Derby, to whom the Queen will now write on the subject, himself mentioned £50,000 as a fitting sum for Parliament to vote—and every opinion which the Queen had heard on the subject points to that as the very lowest sum which it would become the House to appropriate to such an object. The saving is really a paltry one, and the Queen trusts that her ministers will not place themselves in the position of having possibly to resist an amendment having for its object to make the vote more worthy of the country.

The decision as to the nature of the design having been left to the Queen, it is as well not to bring up this question with the other more pressing one of the money to be voted . . .

After much lobbying and delay, the required sum was finally voted unanimously, and the Queen sent Palmerston a bound copy of her late husband's speeches in gratified acknowledgement. His reply was couched in the slightly fulsome terms he sometimes adopted on such occasions, but the Prime Minister was now in his eightieth year, and could afford to look back with a sentimental eye to the troubled decades of his service to the Queen:

> Viscount Palmerston presents his humble duty to your Majesty and begs to tender his grateful thanks for your Majesty's gracious letter and for the highly interesting volume which your Majesty has been pleased to send him. That volume he will always prize as a most valuable possession; doubly valuable, first on account of the record which it contains of the high and brilliant intellectual powers of a Prince for whom he felt an ever increasing admiration, and the most sincere and respectful attachment, and secondly on account of what is written in the title page by a sovereign towards whom he feels the truest devotion and for whose sorrow he feels a sympathy more deep than words could adequately express . . .

CHAPTER XII

'Pilgerstein is Gouty'

As THE YEAR 1863 DREW TO A CLOSE, THE QUEEN AND PALMERSTON became embroiled in the last great clash of his life. With the failing health of the King of Denmark, the whole question of Danish or German sovereignty over Schleswig-Holstein was re-opened. This led to the Prusso-Danish War and the defeat of Denmark.

The exchange of letters between the Queen, Lord Palmerston and Earl Russell on the subject would alone fill a substantial volume. It also forms that part of the Victoria/Palmerston correspondence which has been most fully published. Only so much will be repeated here as is necessary to convey the flavour of the altercation.

Both parties emerge from the episode with diminished credit. The Queen, for her part, adhered so blindly to her late husband's precepts concerning the desirability of a strong Germany, if necessary led by Prussia, and the need for Prussia and Britain to forge a firm friendship, that she cannot be acquitted of the charge of exceeding her constitutional prerogatives in opposing by every means British intervention on behalf of Denmark.

Palmerston had to endure a shattering blow to his position and prestige. Now nearly eighty, his intellectual powers were failing, although his physical buoyancy remained, to outward appearance, relatively unimpaired. His control of an otherwise unremarkable parliamentary session had been due more and more to the tolerance and affection of supporters and opponents alike. Thwarted by Queen and Cabinet in his desire for direct intervention, Palmerston became increasingly lost in the labyrinthine manœuvres and intrigues by which Prussia gained her ends—the reincorporation of Holstein and the German-speaking part of Schleswig into the German Confederation.

338

Threatening, trusting, disingenuous and baffled by turns, his only support came from Earl Russell, who finally proved his ineptitude as Foreign Minister. But if the two old men were hood-winked by the machiavellian Bismarck, it is only fair to say that the Queen misread the future Iron Chancellor's final intentions for Prussia even more calamitously. But then she lived another thirty-seven years to regret the impetus she had given to German nationalism, and Palmerston's days were now numbered.

The issue, stated briefly, was this: Schleswig and Holstein were still nominally independent duchies occupying the neck of the Danish peninsula. Schleswig had a predominantly Danish-speaking population, the Holsteiners spoke German. The two territories had long been linked by dynastic and administrative ties, although Holstein was nominally a member of the German Confederation and Schleswig was not. Schleswig acknowledged Danish suzerainty, into which Holstein was drawn—a position confirmed by the London Protocol of 1852 after the previous crisis in their affairs. In November 1863, King Frederick VII of Denmark died and his successor, Christian IX, the father of the Princess of Wales, immediately became involved in a dynastic and constitutional crisis, with Prussia pressing once again for the incorporation of the two duchies in the nascent German empire.

King Christian promulgated a new constitution for his realms which the German Federal Diet refused to recognise. Hanoverian and Saxon troops entered the two duchies to protect German rights and the Duke of Augustenburg revived the claims his father had renounced in 1852. Palmerston, who favoured the Danish cause as a means of preventing Germany from emerging as a strong North Sea and Baltic power, even went so far as to state at the end of the year that those who attacked the rights and independence of the Danes would find that it would not be Denmark alone with which they would have to contend.

The Queen was horrified by such language. The situation had become sufficiently critical by January 1, 1864, for her to write a formal letter to Earl Russell for the attention of the Cabinet:

The subject on which the Cabinet is to meet tomorrow is so

important, and the possible consequences of the course on which it may decide so serious, that the Queen, in her anxiety lest England should become involved in any war that may ensue between Germany and Denmark, must again write to Lord Russell, asking him to show her letter to the Cabinet.

The Queen regrets that the Governments of Austria and Prussia should have thought themselves justified by the conduct of Denmark, with respect to the Duchies of Holstein and Schleswig, in withholding their unconditional recognition of King Christian IX, according to the stipulations of the Treaty of London. And she regrets still more the extreme course pursued by the minor States of Germany, and more especially by those which had acceded to that Treaty.

But she thinks the following considerations should be borne in mind:

1. Denmark is admitted to have glaringly violated, as regards both Holstein and Schleswig, not only the specific engagements contracted by her with Austria and Prussia in 1852, but the promises and assurances repeatedly given by her to the German powers since 1848, that she would respect the ancient rights and privileges of those duchies.

2. The right of the German Confederation to interfere in Holstein—a Federal State—is not disputed; nor that just grounds exist for such interference.

3. Austria and Prussia have farther, by the admission of the English Government, an international right to demand the fulfilment of engagements internationally contracted with them by Denmark with regard to Schleswig; and if these engagements are not only not fulfilled, but directly violated, to consider such violation a direct and just cause of war.

4. The new order of succession cannot be said to have been legally established, either in Holstein or Schleswig. It was never submitted to the States of either of those duchies, nor accepted by the people.

If, therefore, the people of those duchies, taking advantage of the presence of the Federal Troops, shall declare in favour of the Prince of Augustenburg, much as the Queen may regret that the arrangements of 1852 (which, however, she and the beloved Prince Consort always deprecated as unjust) should not be carried into effect, she can never consent to become a party to a war undertaken for the purpose of imposing upon those people a sovereign whom they violate no engagement or allegiance in rejecting.

Nor, should war ensue between the German powers and Denmark, in consequence of the violation by the latter of her promises respecting Schleswig, could the Queen consider that any obligation rested upon England to come to the assistance of Denmark.

The Queen hopes her ministers will give these considerations their most serious attention; for she must repeat that she will not willingly give her consent to any course which may tend to involve England in war on this question.

The Queen trusts, however, that the Conference which has been proposed for the settlement of the question may be agreed to, and that it may succeed in effecting such a compromise as will be satisfactory on both sides; and in the meantime she hopes the Federal troops will not cross the Eider, and that thus hostilities may be avoided.

Palmerston thought Prussia demanding and wholly in the wrong and did not like the pro-German tone in the Queen's letter. In as bold a reproof as even he had ever administered, he countered her arguments in a memorandum of his own, adding:

Viscount Palmerston can quite understand your Majesty's reluctance to take any active part in measures in any conflict against Germany, but he is sure that your Majesty will never forget that you are sovereign of Great Britain . . .

The Queen retreated temporarily behind Sir Charles Phipps' pen:

The Queen, who is very tired this evening, has directed me to write to you in her name to say that her minute to the Cabinet was founded entirely upon her deep sense of her duties as the sovereign of this country, which prompts her to endeavour to save her people from being unnecessarily hurried into the horrors of war.

The ties of the Queen to Germany would naturally make her treat and speak of that nation, its rulers and its people kindly and without violence, but in every letter that she has written upon this subject she has looked to the welfare of her own subjects.

The Queen would be glad to hope that the question would be settled with justice to both parties to it and for this purpose is desirous of considering dispassionately and impartially the statement of wrongs and claims advanced by each.

However, when the Queen heard that Earl Russell had been telling Count Bernstorff, the Prussian Ambassador, that Britain would go to the aid of Denmark, she returned to the attack:

The Queen has read with the greatest alarm and astonishment the draft of a despatch to Sir A. Buchanan and Lord Bloomfield, in which Lord Russell informs them that he has stated in conversation to Count Bernstorff that, in the event of the occupation of Schleswig by Prussia to obtain a guarantee of the withdrawal of the proclamation of the joint constitution, Denmark would resist such an occupation and that Great Britain would aid her in that resistance. The Queen has never given her sanction to any such threat, nor does it appear to agree with the decision arrived at by the Cabinet upon this question.

The occupation of Schleswig by the Prussian troops may be commenced any day, and if resistance is to be made it must be immediate upon the invasion and take place upon the frontier.

England cannot be committed to assist Denmark in such a collision, which would be an entirely different contingency from that assumed in Lord Russell's draft (as arranged at the Cabinet), in which the German forces would place the Duchy of Schleswig in the possession of the Duke of Augustenburg. The occupation of Schleswig by the Federal troops, if it takes place, would be for the purpose of obtaining a guarantee for the withdrawal of an illegal incorporation of that duchy with Denmark, which Great Britain has throughout declared ought to be withdrawn, and it appears to the Queen that, of all pleas for plunging this country into war, this would therefore be the least defensible.

The point at issue has besides no reference to the provisions of the Treaty of 1852; but, on the contrary, the demand to King Christian, for the withdrawal of the proclamation of the joint constitution, could only be made upon the admission that he had succeeded to the Government of Schleswig.

The Queen has declared that she will not sanction the infliction upon her subjects of all the horrors of war for the purpose of becoming a partisan in a quarrel in which both parties are much in the wrong. She cannot allow a decision of such fearful importance to be thus incidentally arrived at, and she appeals to Lord Palmerston to prevent such rash declarations at the moment when her Government are proposing to the other signatories of the Treaty of 1852, equally concerned with herself in maintaining its stipulations, a deliberate and careful examination of the question in all its bearings, with a view to its peaceable solution.

Palmerston's answer took the form of a survey of the whole situation:

Viscount Palmerston presents his humble duty to your Majesty and has had the honour of receiving your Majesty's communication of this day upon the subject of Lord Russell's accompanying draft. Your Majesty will perceive that the passage in the second page, to which your Majesty objects, is not the report of a statement made by Lord Russell to Count Bernstorff at the interview to which the despatch relates, but purports to be a statement then made by Count Bernstorff of what he understood Lord Russell to have said upon some former occasion, with regard to which Count Bernstorff's memory might be right or wrong, and it is probable that Count Bernstorff may have understood as a positive declaration that which was only the indication of a possible one. Lord Russell is, of course, well aware than an actual decision on such a matter as that in question, does not rest with any single member of the Government, but with the Cabinet and with your Majesty . . .

As to the statement that Denmark would resist the invasion of Schleswig, that is merely the statement of what would certainly happen unless the invading force were so great as to be irresistible; but the Danes are a brave and noble race and would probably fight against any odds. Your Majesty deprecates the horrors of the war, but the Germans, at this moment, seem bent upon wantonly inflicting those horrors, whatever they may be, upon the un-offending and peaceful Danish population of the Duchy of Schleswig. The Germans are acting like a strong man who thinks he has got a weak man in a corner and that he can bully and beat him to his heart's content. But that is not the conduct of brave or generous minds, and it sometimes happens in real life, as it does in a romance, that the wicked giant finds that his intended victim meets with unlooked-for support. Lord Russell stated to Count

343

Bernstorff in the latter part of his conversation that 'in his own opinion England could not consistently with her honour allow Denmark to perish without aiding in her defence'. It seems to Viscount Palmerston that Lord Russell was perfectly justified in thus stating his own personal opinion. In that opinion Viscount Palmerston heartily concurs; and he is persuaded that it would be shared by every impartial and right-minded man in your Majesty's dominions.

Your Majesty seems to consider an invasion of Schleswig, part of the Danish dominions, for the ostensible purpose of taking a material guarantee for the revocation, as regards Schleswig, of the constitution of last November, as a natural and legitimate proceeding, but does not your Majesty remember that it was a similar proceeding by Russia, when she invaded the Danube Principalities, as a material guarantee, that roused the indignation of Europe, drew down the condemnation of Great Britain and led directly to the war against Russia? There cannot be a principle more dangerous to the maintenance of peace, or more fatal to the independence of the weaker powers, than that it should be lawful for a stronger power, whenever it has a demand upon a feebler neighbour, to seize hold of part of its territory by force of arms, instead of seeking redress in the usual way of negotiation; and the day might come when such a principle, established by Prussia, might be fatally retorted upon her by France, by the seizure of the Prussian Rhenish provinces.

Prussia might indeed say that she has made the demand and has not obtained redress, but the demand, made in December, that the constitution should be revoked by 1st January, when it was plain to the commonest understanding that what was asked was an absolute impossibility, was only setting up a mockery as an apology for an outrage. The Germans are already wrong-doers in Holstein, where they have no legal right to be. Execution in Holstein was decreed in order to obtain the revocation of the Patent of March 1863; that Patent was revoked before execution took place, and the revocation ought to have stopped execution. But violent ambition and reckless bad faith prevailed, and execution, though become utterly groundless and illegal, was made; and for what real motive? In order to hold Holstein till the Diet can determine who is the legitimate Duke of Holstein. But the Diet has no more right or competence to decide that question than to decide who shall

be Emperor of Austria, or who shall be sovereign of England.
There is nothing whatever in the Federal Act of 1815, or in the
final Act of 1820, which invests the Diet with the power which it
thus assumes. The treacherous manner in which that illegal occupation of Holstein, under the name of execution, has been made
use of, for the purpose of endeavouring to revolutionise the duchy,
has been so well stated in Lord Russell's despatch, that it is unnecessary to dwell upon it, but no one could wonder if, after such
an example of perfidy, the Danes should determine to make every
possible effort to prevent a similar course from being pursued in
Schleswig.

Your Majesty seems to suppose that the whole question as to
war or peace, as arising out of a German invasion of Schleswig,
would be settled on the frontier and that, if no resistance were
made, or if resistance were overcome, there would be no possibility of friendly assistance to the Danes. But Viscount Palmerston
would beg to submit that the course of things would be very
different. Assuming that the Prussians entered Schleswig and
obtained possession of it, as what is called a material guarantee for
the compliance of Denmark in a just demand for the revocation of
the Schleswig constitution, it is to be observed that such an invasion
would rouse the national pride of the Danes and would make it
more difficult for the Danish parliament, by whom alone the
revocation can be made, to yield to demands made at the point of
the bayonet, than to concede to the friendly advice of allied
powers.

It is possible that the Germans see this, and that it is with them a
motive for action, as they evidently seek not a settlement but a
quarrel. But Schleswig once occupied by German troops, new and
unjust demands would be made upon Denmark, with which Denmark could not be advised to comply and revolutionary movements would have been incited in Schleswig, as in Holstein, under
the shelter of the German troops.

The Germans, that is to say the Prussians, would then be summoned to go out of Schleswig, the constitution having been
legally and constitutionally repealed and the original pretence for
invasion having ceased—Prussia would refuse, as Russia refused
to go out of the Danube Principalities, and France, seeing the
advantage which such a state of things afforded her, would turn
against Prussia the example thus set by Prussia, and occupy as a

material guarantee the Prussian Rhenish provinces, following in all things the example set her by Germany and getting up in these provinces demonstrations in favour of union with France. England could not under such circumstances lend any assistance to Prussia and Prussia would pay a heavy penalty for her want of good faith. The whole French nation would be as clamorous for the Rhine as the Germans are for what they call Schleswig–Holstein and, disunited and unorganised as the German armies are, the frontier of the Rhine would be finally obtained by France.

Your Majesty says you are desirous of not inflicting on your Majesty's subjects the horrors of war; fortunately for the people of your Majesty's dominions, their insular position secures them from these horrors. But the course now pursued and further intended by Germany has a direct tendency to bring down these horrors upon the German nations and the policy recommended to your Majesty has a direct tendency to avert such calamitous result.

The Queen evaded the political issue while maintaining her personal attitude:

The Queen has received Lord Palmerston's letter of the 8th [January 1864]. He will agree with her that no good could result from her entering into a discussion with him as to the relative merits of the conduct of Germany or Denmark.

Lord Russell states in his despatch that he had wondered at the patience shown by Germany during eleven years of ill-usage of his German subjects by the late King; but this patience formed a striking contrast to the impatience shown during the short time in which the present King has been upon the throne.

That is a statement to which the Queen will make no objection, though there are many reasons for this conduct. But the Queen considered and considers it to be her duty to remonstrate against the declaration by Lord Russell to the Prussian Ambassador that Great Britain would assist Denmark in resistance to occupation of Schleswig by the Prussian troops. Such resistance, wherever it took place, would be war, and the assistance of England would involve her in that war.

His declaration of assistance was stated to have been made without the sanction of the Queen or the concurrence of the Cabinet, and she felt herself compelled to call Lord Palmerston's attention to it; but she certainly had neither the intention nor desire to enter into any controversy, always disagreeable to her, upon the general merits of the Dano-German question.

Lord Palmerston will not have failed to observe that the conversation, in which Count Bernstorff repeated what Lord Russell had said to him on a former occasion, is reported by Lord Russell to the Queen's Ambassadors at Vienna and Berlin as very interesting, but without any denial of its accuracy or retraction; and her representatives at those Courts might therefore undoubtedly have been led to believe that this was the decision at which the Queen and her Government had arrived.

The Queen thinks that this draft should be brought before the Cabinet for their consideration.

As events soon proved, the Queen's remonstrance had provided the turning point. The Cabinet, with Granville working busily on them on the sovereign's behalf—and using his position as Liberal leader in the House of Lords to keep the Queen apprised of their mood and deliberations—had no stomach for a war over Schleswig-Holstein. Parliament and country were probably with them in adopting a negative attitude. Once the decision not to intervene had been taken, Palmerston became powerless when Prussian and Austrian forces entered Schleswig on February 1.

The Queen was indefatigable. She summoned Lord Derby, the Opposition leader, impressed her views on him and extracted a promise that the Tories would not make Schleswig-Holstein a party matter. Thus armed, she directed a final warning to the Prime Minister before the debate in the House of Commons on the situation:

> The Queen approves the suppression of the paragraph she objected to. She is relieved at Lord Palmerston's not undertaking the journey here tomorrow, on the eve of the opening of Parliament, as she dreaded his catching cold, or bringing on a fresh attack of gout, when all his strength and vigour are required to meet the fatigues of the session.
>
> As the Queen will, however, not see Lord Palmerston, she wishes to tell him, in confidence, that when she saw Lord Derby the other day, she took an opportunity of telling him how important she thought it that this unlucky and difficult question of

Schleswig–Holstein should not be made a party one—in which he entirely agreed, and added he thought it absolutely necessary that all parties should be extremely cautious in their language in Parliament on the subject.

The Queen feels sure Lord Palmerston will fully concur in this and that she need not impress this further on himself and the other members of the Government.

The quarrel is now beyond our reach and we must wait to see the march of events. A time will very soon arrive when our advice, and possibly our mediation, will be asked; and if it is given with perfect impartiality, and a due regard to the interests of all parties, and the wishes and rights of the peoples concerned, [it] may conduce to the peace and permanent security of Europe. But till this time arrives, the Queen cannot but think that far the most dignified course for England will be to remain passive.

The Queen would wish Lord Palmerston to let Lord Russell see this letter.

The Queen's determined attitude still rankled with Palmerston, but she had turned the tide against him and he knew it. He tried one last blustering protest, although his bluff had been called:

Viscount Palmerston presents his humble duty to your Majesty and has communicated to Lord Russell your Majesty's letter. Lord Russell and Viscount Palmerston would abstain as much as possible tomorrow from any strong expression of the opinions they entertain; but if they should be attacked in debate they must defend themselves according to circumstances; and Viscount Palmerston cannot undertake to conceal the opinion, which he has this day expressed to Count Apponyi [the Austrian Ambassador] and to Count Bernstorff, that the invasion of Schleswig, after a promise made that the demands made by Austria and Prussia for the revocation of the constitution as it regards Schleswig should be accomplished as soon as constitutional forms will allow, is a most unjustifiable proceeding, and throws a heavy responsibility on the Austrian and Prussian Governments for the bloodshed, loss of life and destruction of property which this invasion will occasion. If the demands made had been refused, the two powers would have had a fair ground for war, but to make war to obtain the concession of demands, a compliance with which is solemnly promised, is an act of violence which cannot be justified . . .

348

The following day he was compelled to report:

> Viscount Palmerston presents his humble duty to your Majesty
> and begs to state that the debate in the House of Commons on the
> Address passed off without an amendment or any very serious
> attack on the Government, but with what may be called a talking
> which lasted till midnight . . .

Towards the end of February, when it appeared as if the Austrian
Government might send some part of its navy through the English Channel to support operations in Denmark, Palmerston
erupted again in a tremendous tirade to the Queen about the
iniquity of German intervention. His impotence only made him
the more angry:

> . . . It is quite intelligible and reasonable that the British Govern-
> ment should hesitate to send 20,000 British troops, and more
> could not be got together, to face the hundreds of thousands which
> Germany, if united, could oppose to us; and even with the co-
> operation of 30,000 Danes and 20,000 Swedes, our aggregate force
> would not numerically be a match for the enemy, though possibly,
> in a narrow country like Jutland and Schleswig, the advantage
> might be on our side. But that England, the first and greatest
> naval power, should allow an Austrian fleet to sail by our shores,
> and go and conquer and occupy the island capital of a friendly
> power, towards which we are bound by national interests and
> treaty engagements, would be a national disgrace to which
> Viscount Palmerston, at least, never would stoop to be a party. It
> makes one's blood boil even to think of it; and such an affront
> England, whether acting alone or with allies, ought never to
> permit . . .

This broadside was too much for the Queen, who replied through
Sir Charles Phipps:

> The Queen has been unwell all day to-day, suffering from a very
> bad headache, and has directed [me] to acknowledge for her the
> receipt of your letter of to-day—as she is quite unable to write
> herself.
> Her Majesty directs me only to add that her Majesty's sole wish
> and endeavour is to prevent, if possible, a general war—and to

349

obtain such a settlement of the differences between Germany and Denmark as may ensure the best probability of a secure and lasting peace.

But the Queen felt strong enough to write to the King of Belgium, saying:

> I am well nigh worn to nothing with vexation, distress and worry, and I have asked General Grey to tell you all about the conduct of those two dreadful old men . . .

With the calming of the parliamentary storm, the coming of spring and the *fait accompli* in Denmark, the correspondence between the Queen and Palmerston began to acquire a less exacerbated tone. In March, he was able to report:

> . . . It is rather indicative of the quiet state of domestic politics that the House of Commons should spend the whole evening in talking about a court martial, the result of which is generally approved and the verdict of which nobody says ought to be reversed . . .

By the middle of April, the Prussians and Austrians were in possession of the whole territory in dispute, and Russell and Palmerston had to content themselves with convening in London a conference of the great powers to settle peace terms. The exchanges between Prime Minister and sovereign provided evidence of their reconciliation:

> . . . The Queen proposes going on the 19th or 20th to Osborne till 9th May and then coming back here for a few days and going (should nothing very urgent or alarming prevent it) to Scotland on the 13th for a short while, inclusive of the Whitsuntide holidays— but being back here by 8th June. The Queen would not undertake this journey did she not feel that she must try and prevent a more rapid diminution of health and strength than has already taken place—by complete change of air. In Scotland, though the depression and desolation and sorrow are ever the same, she will be a great deal in the open air, and she feels it almost a duty to try and enable herself to go on for a short time longer (for she cannot think it will be long) with her arduous public duties. Of course if her absence at that time were to cause any difficulty or be detrimental to the interest of the country, she would not go to Scotland.

Her health and nerves have, however, suffered severely from the anxiety and hard work of this past winter and she feels very unwell, and more in want of change of air than ever. The Queen has no intentions of going abroad this autumn.

... Viscount Palmerston does not anticipate the occurrence of any state of things which could interfere with your Majesty's intended excursion to Scotland. The telegraph and railways have so shortened distances, and facilitated communications, that it is very unlikely that anything should happen while your Majesty will be in Scotland, the decision with regard to which could not wait, without any detriment to the public service, till your Majesty's pleasure could be taken, and any slight inconvenience, if any such should arise, would be as nothing when set in the balance against an arrangement which may reasonably be expected to contribute in any degree towards recruiting your Majesty's health. These unfortunate difficulties between Germany and Denmark must necessarily have added greatly to the ordinary anxieties belonging to your Majesty's position, and it may be hoped that the bracing air of the Highlands may prove beneficial to your Majesty's health, which cannot but have suffered from the mental strain which the events of the last few months must have produced.

Full harmony was not yet restored and they clashed again over a minor point. When Palmerston fulminated at length to the Queen about her objection to the appointment of one of his nominees to a vacant bishopric, she replied:

... It would be very disagreeable to her to answer that letter and to prolong a discussion which has taken a tone so different to that which Lord Palmerston is in the habit of addressing her ...

During the same period, Palmerston could not resist writing a distinctly double-edged letter to the Queen concerning public criticism of her pro-German attitude:

... Viscount Palmerston is always unwilling to touch upon subjects which may not be agreeable to your Majesty, but still he has duties to perform, which his devoted attachment to your Majesty and his deep sense of gratitude prevent him from shrinking from. The accompanying part of a recently set-up paper has been put into his hands. It contains much falsehood and misrepresentation and it is deserving to be put into the fire. But this paper, and others which have been mentioned to Viscount Palmerston, tend to show that an impression is beginning to be created that your Majesty has expressed personal opinions on the affairs of Denmark and Germany which have embarrassed the course of the Government. Nothing can be further from the truth, for in all that has been done, or abstained from being done, the views and policy of the Government have been suggested by their own sense of public duty and have met with the sanction and approval of your Majesty, in the most constitutional manner. But it would be a great evil if public opinion were to divest your Majesty of that proper and essential protection which the Constitution secures for the sovereign, by making the responsible ministers answerable for all that is done or not done; and if your Majesty's personal opinions and views were to become the objects of criticism or attack. Your Majesty has no doubt been duly careful as to the degree and manner in which your Majesty's opinions and views have been expressed, but it might be well that no indiscreet expressions from persons about your Majesty should give any countenance to such remarks as those in this newspaper.

The Queen countered sharply:

> ... As long as the Queen exercises her functions for the good of the country alone, and according to that Constitution which has through her reign been her sole guide, she must be content to see unjust remarks in obscure newspapers and must continue to disregard them. She quite agrees with Lord Palmerston that it ought to be put into the fire.

The next day, using the somewhat derogatory nickname by which Palmerston was known in her family—a literal German translation of his name—the Queen commented acidly in a letter to her uncle in Brussels: ' . . . Pilgerstein is gouty, and extremely impertinent in his communications of different kinds to me . . .'

In June the crisis flared up again, with the sudden rejection by M. Quaade, leader of the Danish representatives to the peace talks, of arbitration terms. Earl Russell again advocated British intervention in their favour, arousing the Queen to a further frenzy of protest, but this time she had the support of Palmerston, who was growing weary of the whole unprofitable *imbroglio*. The Queen was quite laudatory in her Journal entry:

> JUNE 21: Saw Lord Palmerston as soon as I arrived and found him very sensible, wonderfully clear-headed and fully alive to the extreme dangers of the situation. Showed him a telegram from Copenhagen, which made it clear that the Danes were not inclined, at any rate, to accept arbitration in its complete form, which of course would render it useless. He did not apprehend the great danger of the whole of Germany being united as one man against us, though he thought matters most serious. The greatest danger he saw from France joining us was dragging us into a war, in which she would claim the Rhine and possibly revolutionise the whole of Italy. He also entirely agreed with me that it was very doubtful whether we could do anything, for nothing but naval assistance could be given, and that only for three months. Would that not therefore be more humiliating for England than doing nothing at all? He felt this very strongly and said the Danes were the most obstinate people he knew; 'they are not an intelligent race and very *borné*.' He had told Quaade again and again that they were going to their own destruction, for no one would help them. The very outside of any assistance they could get from here would be by sea, and that was very doubtful. He still hoped that matters might be arranged peaceably, the difference being so very small, and no stone should be left unturned to effect this.

The Government managed to scrape together a majority in the House of Commons to support its passive attitude, an armistice was duly signed and the last great crisis in Palmerston's parliamentary life had been surmounted. Until his death the following year, few events of moment troubled the public scene and his correspondence with the Queen seldom transcended the exchange of essential business. They disagreed briefly over the appointment of a new Lord-Lieutenant of Ireland and the award of the Garter to the King of Denmark and the Grand-Duke of Hesse, but by January 1865, Palmerston was congratulating the Queen on the felicity of her reply to the Empress of France, declining a suggestion that she should contribute to a fund for re-building the Holy Sepulchre at Jerusalem:

... Viscount Palmerston, not knowing whether your Majesty has kept a copy or memorandum of what your Majesty proposes to write, returns the letter which he has received from your Majesty, but begs to have it again as a model of good feeling remarkably well expressed.

The old gentleman's once impeccable writing had now become spidery indeed, with the onset of his usual winter attack of gout. His reports on the desultory proceedings in Parliament now seldom exceeded a single sheet of paper, although he could still rouse himself to a sharp reminder, when he felt the Queen was exceeding her prerogatives, even in a minor matter:

> Viscount Palmerston presents his humble duty to your Majesty and begs to be allowed respectfully to submit for your Majesty's consideration, that the circular lately sent by Sir Charles Phipps by your Majesty's commands to the directors of railways, although its object was good and its recommendations unexceptionable, should, according to established rule, have been sent by the Board of Trade or by the Home Office. It is required by the principles and practice of the British Constitution that for every public act of the sovereign there should be some responsible official adviser, and there is an obvious advantage to the monarchical institution that some official person should always be interposed between the sovereign and the subject with regard to public acts of the sovereign, in order to secure the sovereign against personal criticisms or argumentative and controversial communications. The Board of Trade or the Home Office might equally have given it to be known that your Majesty was animated by a desire that your Majesty's subjects in general should have the benefit of those precautions which are taken by railway arrangements for the security of your Majesty's person.

> The Queen has received Lord Palmerston's letter of yesterday's date. She fully acknowledges the constitutional doctrines laid down by Lord Palmerston, they are well known to the Queen and have always been acted upon by her.
> But the letter written at her command by Sir C. Phipps was not, as Lord Palmerston supposes, a general circular to all railways, nor was it ever intended for publication. It was the expression of her

personal feeling upon a subject on which, for her family and servants of all kinds, she felt a peculiar interest, and was addressed to the directors of those railways by which the Queen and the members of the royal family usually travel. Such letters upon topics relating personally to the Queen she has upon several occasions caused to be written without their obtaining publicity. The directors of those railways understood its object and its nature, and it was not by any of the bodies to whom it was addressed that it was made public.

Palmerston's old sense of humour had not deserted him, as two extracts from his parliamentary reports for March showed:

> . . . It is remarkable that although Parliament has been sitting a month, and some questions of importance have been discussed, such as the state of Ireland and the malt duty, the Leader of Opposition has not yet opened his mouth, but the Government have no reason to complain of this . . .

> . . . The discussion showed how fond members of the House of Commons are of talking, and how little they are restrained from doing so by entire ignorance of the matters they wish to talk about. Nobody but Mr. Layard appeared to understand the functions of the Foreign Office, and nobody but Mr. Milner Gibson those of the Board of Trade . . .

Nor had his hearty cynicism diminished his chivalry towards political opponents:

> Viscount Palmerston presents his humble duty to your Majesty and begs to state that Mr. Romilly, Chairman of the Board for auditing the public accounts, having served many years and finding his health beginning to fail is desirous of retiring. Viscount Palmerston begs to submit for your Majesty's gracious approval that this office may be offered to Mr. Cobden. The duties are important and the salary has been £1,600 a year and might upon a new arrangement of the business be raised to £2,000. Mr. Cobden's circumstances are not good and he might be glad to accept such a retirement, especially as his health is not strong enough for constant parliamentary attendance. No injury to the public interest would arise from his ceasing to be a member of the

House of Commons. It may be doubtful, however, whether he would accept the offer, but the making it would be useful, and would be well taken by Mr. Cobden's friends, though not perhaps by Mr. Bright . . .

Sir Charles Phipps replied for the Queen:

The Queen has commanded me to answer your letter of yesterday's date for her, and to say that her Majesty thinks that no harm could result from offering to Mr. Cobden the Chairmanship of the Audit Office.

Mr. Cobden has always been employed by the Government and his removal from the House of Commons would not be any disadvantage . . .

The doughty old Free Trader did not live to enjoy his sinecure. Barely two months later Palmerston was reporting:

Viscount Palmerston presents his humble duty to your Majesty and begs to state that he was requested this morning to say something at the meeting of the House on the death of Mr. Cobden, and accordingly he did so on the motion for going into Committee of Supply. Mr. Disraeli did the same and Mr. Bright said a few words, evidently much affected by the loss of his friend . . .

Parliament was reaching the end of its term, but the prospect of new elections found no sign of flagging energy in the octogenarian Prime Minister. At the end of June he informed the Queen:

Viscount Palmerston presents his humble duty to your Majesty and begs to state that the progress made in the public business before the two Houses of Parliament is such that the prorogation and dissolution may probably take place on Thursday of next week. Lord Redesdale wishes the session to be prolonged for some days beyond that time, in order that some contested railways Bills now before the House of Lords may be disposed of, but it does not seem to Viscount Palmerston to be right that the whole of the United Kingdom should be exposed to the trouble and expense attendant on a delay of the dissolution, merely for the convenience or advantage of some squabbling railways companies; and it is probable that, with the fine weather now prevailing, the harvest will begin earlier than usual, and it is desirable that the elections should not be delayed so as to clash with the operations of the harvest.

It is therefore the intention of Viscount Palmerston, in answer to a question that is to be put to him this evening, to say that in all probability the prorogation and dissolution will be Thursday of next week.

In July the Government was returned with a handsome majority, and the old man appeared to attack his administrative duties with undiminished vigour. The Queen sent him a kind note from Osborne in August, before leaving for a visit to Coburg:

> ... The Queen starts in an hour with fair weather. She hopes to hear of Lord Palmerston's continued good health, and that he will take great care of himself.

> Viscount Palmerston presents his humble duty to your Majesty and begs to be allowed to return his thanks for your Majesty's gracious mention of his health. He deems it a duty which he owes to your Majesty to do his best to maintain that health which is essential for the performance of the duties of the post which your Majesty has been graciously pleased to confer upon him ...

The last letter of consequence that Palmerston wrote to his sovereign showed that his bluff prejudices had barely altered in the course of sixty years in public life:

> ... The meetings of the French and English squadrons at Cherbourg, Brest and Portsmouth have gone off with success even beyond expectation, and the Duke of Somerset says that the French were surprised at the real cordiality of their reception. The political advantage of these meetings will be felt on both sides of the Atlantic. On this side of that ocean the good feeling manifested in both countries, both by the naval service and by the civil population, will serve to promote essentially the security for peace, and it will dispel in France the mistaken belief that the English nation entertain a settled hatred of France and Frenchmen. It is worth remark that the French navy have always been better disposed towards England than the French army, and this is not unnatural. The French army feel that the British army has stripped from the French brow laurels gathered in every field of European

357

warfare and that, having beaten in every battle those French troops who had beaten everybody else, the English army ended by defeating the Emperor Napoleon himself, and sending him prisoner to St. Helena. In this case the pain of defeat was aggravated by the mortification of losing a pre-eminence acquired by a long series of victories and conquests. But France never pretended to be a predominant naval power, and she looked upon her naval reverses as events happening in the natural order of things, and there was no feeling of wounded pride or mortified vanity to sharpen the pain of national disaster. Added to which, it may be said that there is less of vanity and more of simplicity of character belonging to the naval than to the military profession.

On the other side of the Atlantic the effect of these meetings cannot fail to be wholesome. There is nothing which the North Americans dislike more, as an obstacle to their schemes, than a cordial union between England and France; and as the tendency of the human mind is always to exaggerate the bearing and importance of events not clearly understood, the Americans will look upon these meetings as a sort of preliminary defensive alliance between the two countries, and they will accordingly be less likely to wish to pick a quarrel with either.

He was spending the parliamentary recess at Brocket, once the seat of his long dead friend and colleague, Lord Melbourne, and now in the possession of Lady Palmerston. His health was beginning to fail, but in the last letter in his own hand to the Queen, written on October 4, his handwriting was once more firm and clear:

> Viscount Palmerston presents his humble duty to your Majesty and begs to submit for your Majesty's gracious approval that Lord Camden may be appointed your Majesty's Lieutenant for Brecknockshire in the room of Colonel Watkins deceased.

On the same date, the Queen was writing from Balmoral on the perennial subject of her children's matrimonial and financial affairs. Her third daughter had now become engaged:

> The Queen, knowing the interest Lord Palmerston takes in everything that concerns the welfare and happiness of her family,

wishes now to mention a subject on which for many reasons she has hitherto said nothing.

Lord Palmerston is aware of the desire of the Queen, a desire occasioned by the absolute necessity of the case, to find such a marriage for Princess Helena as would enable her to reside for the most part, if not entirely, in England, and thus to continue to be the Queen's comfort, which is indispensable to her, of her society and assistance. Lord Palmerston also knows that the Queen has never allowed political considerations to interfere in arranging marriages for her daughters, with what she and the beloved Prince believed to be for their happiness.

And it is under the conviction that the step she has now taken will be both for her own comfort, and the happiness of our daughter, and would have been entirely approved by the Prince, that she has given her consent to the marriage of Princess Helena with Prince Christian of Holstein Augustenburg, younger brother of the present Duke.

The character of the Prince stands very high. In spite of the personal considerations that might make such an alliance to be unwelcome to the Prince and Princess of Wales, they have received the communication of what is intended most kindly. The Prince willingly accepts all the Queen's conditions as to residence in England, and the Queen looks forward most hopefully to the happiest results from the proposed marriage.

Prince Christian will come over after Christmas, before which time no formal declaration can be made, and the Queen must ask Lord Palmerston still to consider this communication as confidential. The marriage itself cannot take place before the summer.

For the first time in 28 years, Palmerston failed to give the Queen's business his immediate attention. His seemingly inexhaustible vitality was suddenly fading fast, and on October 18 the masterful old man, lucid and uncomplaining to the end, quietly died. It was Princess Helena—'Lenchen'—who brought the news to her mother.—The Queen had been sending anxious enquiries by telegraph from Balmoral, but when she came to make her terse diary note of the event, the prejudices formed through two decades of recurring strife with the strongest political figure of the mid-nineteenth century still coloured her last comment:

Lenchen met me on the top of the stairs, when I came in, with the news of poor Lord Palmerston's death, which had taken place this morning at a quarter to 11. Strange, and solemn to think of that strong, determined man, with so much worldly ambition,—gone! He had often worried and distressed us, though as Prime Minister he had behaved *very well*. To think that he is removed from this world, and *I* alone, without dearest Albert to talk to or consult with!

Appendix of Sources

R.A. X 61 = Royal Archives and reference number.
R.A. QJ = Royal Archives, Queen Victoria's Private Journal.
B.P. = Broadlands Papers.
J.M. = 'The Letters of Queen Victoria' (John Murray, London, 1907 and 1926).

PAGE	CHAPTER I	PAGE	
7	R.A. A 8/9 23.vi.1837	19	R.A. A 9 9.v.1839
8	B.P. 24.vi.1837	20	B.P. 7.x.1839
8	R.A. A 8/9 2.vii.1837	20	R.A. A 10 15.xii.1839
8	R.A. A 8/9 3.vii.1837	20	B.P. 21.i.1840
9	R.A. A 8/9 18.vii.1837	20	B.P. 28.i.1840
9	B.P. 22.vii.1837	21	B.P. 30.i.1840
9	R.A. A 8/9 22.vii.1837	21	B.P. 3.vi.1840
9	B.P. 6.viii.1837	21	B.P. 10.vi.1840
9	R.A. A 8/9 6.viii.1837	21	B.P. 12.vi.1840
9	B.P. 12.viii.1837	23–4	B.P. 26.ix.1840
9–10	R.A. A 8/9 18.viii.1837	24	R.A. G I 11.x.1840
10–13	B.P. 6.vii.1837	24–5	B.P. 12.x.1840
13	B.P. undated	25	R.A. G I 8.xi.1840
13	B.P. 7.x.1837	25	B.P. 9.xi.1840
13–15	R.A. A 8/9 8.x.1837	25–7	R.A. G I 11.xi.1840
15	R.A. A 8/9 28.i.1838	27–9	B.P. 11.xi.1840
15	R.A. QJ 24/5. ii.1838	29	R.A. G I 1.ii.1841
16	R.A. QJ 6.v.1838	29	B.P. 2.ii.1841
16–17	B.P. 11.vii.1838	29–30	R.A. A 10 4.ii.1841
17	B.P. 13.vii.1838	30	B.P. 30.v.1841
17	R.A. A 9 13.vii.1838	30–1	R.A. A 10 30.v.1841
17	R.A. A 9 17.vii.1838	31	B.P. 30.viii.1841
17	B.P. 16.i.1839	31	R.A. A 10 31.viii.1841
17	R.A. A 9 16.i.1839		
18	R.A. A 9 27.i.1839		
18	R.A. A 9 19.iv.1839		CHAPTER II
18	R.A. A 9 5.iii.1839	34	R.A. C 25 16.vii.1846
19	B.P. 9.v.1839	35	B.P. 30.vii.1846

APPENDIX OF SOURCES

APPENDIX OF SOURCES

APPENDIX OF SOURCES

APPENDIX OF SOURCES

APPENDIX OF SOURCES

APPENDIX OF SOURCES

APPENDIX OF SOURCES

Index

INDEX

Balmoral Castle, 94, 125, 127, 205, 267, 294, 327, 329–30, 358–9
Baring, Sir Francis, 158, 177
Barrot, Odillon, 26, 28
Bavaria, 64, 89, 332
Beatrice, H.R.H. Princess, 215
Beaumont, M. de, French Republican Ambassador in London, 93, 94, 95, 102
Bedford, Duke of, 97, 122
Belgium; becomes an independent kingdom under King Leopold (1830), 7, 16, 18, 22, 23, 91, 101, 140, 287
Bentinck, Mr., 289
Berkeley, Admiral, 195
Bernstorff, Count, Prussian Ambassador, 342, 343, 344, 347, 348
Bessarabia, 188, 189, 192
Bethell, Sir R., 259
Bismarck, Prince, 339
Bloomfield, Lord, 287, 289, 342
Bouverie, Mr., President of Board of Health, 184
Bowyer, Sir George, 293, 294
Brand, Mrs., later Lady Dacre, 121
Bresson, Comte de, French Ambassador in Madrid, 40, 43
Bright, John, 214, 215, 299, 300, 356
Bruce, Lady Augusta, Lady-in-Waiting to Queen Victoria, 324
Brunnow, Baron, Russian Ambassador, 142, 333
Buchanan, Sir Andrew, 342
Buchanan, Mr. James, American Envoy in London, 193, 194
Buckingham Palace, 5, 182
Builders' strike, 265–6
Bulwer, Sir Henry Lytton, British Minister in Madrid, 24, 37, 39, 42, 43, 44, 62, 76, 77, 78, 88
Buren, Mr. van, 17

Cabrals, Portuguese, 46, 53, 54, 58, 59, 60, 61
Cambridge, H.R.H. George, Duke of, 3, 179; appointed Army Commander-in-Chief, 205, 208, 217, 225, 244, 246
Camden, Lord, 358
Campbell, Sir Colin, 217, 218
Canada, 18, 33, 226, 308
Canning, George, 6, 7, 139
Canning, Lord, 162, 163; appointed Governor-General of India, 177, 304
Canning, Sir Stratford, British Envoy at Constantinople, 110, 111, 116
Cape of Good Hope, 201
Cardwell, Mr., 162, 258, 260
Carnarvon, Lord, 165
Catholic Emancipation, 6
Cavour, Count, 254
Cecille, Admiral, French Ambassador in London, 106
Charles Albert, King of Sardinia, 73, 75, 76, 82, 83; defeated by Radetzky at Custozza, 90; concludes armistice with R., 92; is again defeated by R. and abdicates, 105–6, 260
Charlotte, H.R.H. Princess, daughter of William IV, 3
China, 30, 212, 213, 218, 220, 296, 297
Christian de Holstein Glucksburg, Prince, 9, 71
Christian IX, King of Denmark, 339, 340, 342
Christina, Queen Mother of Spain, 38, 39, 62, 90
Cinque Ports, 207, 302, 307
Civil War, American, 307–11, 321–2, 323, 325, 328, 329
Clarence, H.R.H. Duke of, 3
Clarendon, Lord; as Lord Lieutenant of Ireland, 97, 114, 123, 144; as Foreign Secretary (1853–8), 148, 150, 159, 160, 161, 162, 163, 189, 190, 191, 192, 204, 205, 231; out of office, 256, 257, 258, 259, 260 292
Clark, Sir James, 312, 313, 314, 316, 317
Cobden, Richard, 182, 212, 214, 215, 258, 259, 260, 298, 300, 355, 356

INDEX

INDEX

Pedro V, heir to the Portuguese throne, 51, 312

Peel, Frederick, 165, 171, 215, 216

Peel, Sir Robert, 1, 19, 31, 32, 33, 34, 119, 165, 198, 237, 290

Peel, Sir Robert, son of Sir Robert, 171

Persigny, Count, French Ambassador, 261, 263, 264, 267, 271, 272, 274, 275, 276, 299, 300

Phillimore, Dr., 177, 309

Phipps, Colonel Sir Charles, 132, 133, 312–21, 325, 326, 327, 330, 341, 349, 354, 356

Piedmont, 73, 82, 87, 95, 261, 264, 267, 269, 272, 275, 276, 277

Ponsonby, Viscount, Ambassador in Vienna, 74, 101

Portugal; revolt against Queen Maria, (1846), 45–58. Also: 7, 22, 23, 35, 64, 78, 79, 83, 88, 129

Prince Consort Bill (see Chapter VIII)

Progresista Party, Spain, 89

Prussia; sponsored the Duke of Augustenburg as successor to the Danish throne, 70–1; defends Holstein against Danish attack, 108–9; Prusso-Danish war (1863–4), 338–350; peace conference convened, 350; armistice signed, 353. Also: 22, 23, 67, 72, 83, 89, 129, 130, 131, 287, 288

Quaade, M., 352, 353

Quadruple Alliance (1834), 54

Radetzky, Marshal, 73, 74, 82, 90, 92, 106

Raglan, Lord, 163, 167

Ratazzi, Signor, 323

Redesdale, Lord, 356

Reform, Parliamentary, 1, 148–52, 228–9, 257, 285, 286, 289, 290, 299

Resolute, Arctic Discovery Ship, 206–7

Revue Retrospective, 88

Ricasoli, Baron, Italian Prime Minister, 323

Roebuck, Mr. 156, 166, 168, 169

Roman Catholic Charities Bill, 293–4

Romilly, Mr., 355

Russell, Lord John (later Earl Russell), Home Secretary (1837), 1, 2; attempts to form a government (1845), 34; Prime Minister, 54; is asked to stop ministerial intrigue in Portugal, 78–80; receives complaints from the Queen and Prince Albert about Palmerston, 90, 92, 96–7, 104–5, 114–17, 118–19, 120–121, 122, 123, 131; defends Palmerston, 104, 120, 122; requests that M. Kossuth shall not be received by Palmerston, 132; agrees on the dismissal of Palmerston, 133–7; his government defeated, 138; joins Lord Aberdeen's government (1853), 144; Leader of the House of Commons, 148, 149, 150, 152, 153; government defeated (1855), 157; asked to form a government but fails, 158–161; out of office, 162; appointed Colonial Secretary under Palmerston, 170; represents Britain at Crimea peace talks in Vienna, 175; faces censure on return and resigns, 182–4; refuses to take office under Lord Granville, 257; Foreign Secretary under Palmerston (1859), 258; supports the further liberation of Italy, 279; withdraws his Reform Bill, 290; accepts a peerage, 304. Also: 99, 100, 106, 107, 127, 129, 212, 232, 238, 249, 254, 255, 256, 259, 260, 261, 262, 264, 265, 271, 274, 276, 277, 280, 281, 282, 297, 299, 300, 305, 306, 310, 321, 327, 338, 339, 340, 342, 343, 344, 345, 348, 350, 352

Russia; renewed hostilities against Turkey, 148–9; the Crimean War (1854), 153; death of Czar Nicholas, 172; fall of Sebastopol, 185; peace negotiations, 188–9;

377

INDEX

Russia—*continued*
Treaty of Paris signed (1856), 192.
Also: 14, 15, 23, 67, 72, 89, 110,
111, 112, 125, 173, 190, 191, 206,
227, 287, 288, 332, 333

SARDINIA, 63, 73, 75, 86, 254, 260, 262,
278. See also under Charles
Albert and Victor Emmanuel,
Kings of Sardinia
Sarim Effendi, Turkish Ambassador, 15
Saxe-Coburg, Duke Ernest of, 333,
334
Schleswig-Holstein; the Danish suc-
cession question, 70–1, 108–110;
invasion of Schleswig by Den-
mark, 108–10, 125–6; loss of inde-
pendence after the Prusso-Danish
war, 338 et seq.
Scott, General Winfield, 311
Scully, Vincent, 265
Sebastopol, 173, 177, 183, 185, 187
Selwyn, Mr., 293
Seville, Enrique Duke of, 36, 37, 38, 40
Seward, William Henry, 311, 321–2
Seymour, Sir George, 207
Seymour, Sir Hamilton, British Envoy
to Portugal, 50, 54, 55, 56, 57, 58,
59, 61, 78, 79, 80
Shelburne, Lord, 204
Shrewsbury, Lord, 84
Sicily, 85, 99, 104, 129
Sinope, 149, 152
Smith, Vernon, President of the Board
of Control, East India Company,
171, 177, 217, 228, 231
Solferino, battle of, 260
Solyman Pasha, 25
Somerset, Duke of, 300, 301, 311, 357
Soult, Marshal, 26, 28
Southern, Mr., Legation Secretary,
Portugal, 47, 48, 49, 51, 53, 57
Spain; government overthrown, 33,
the Spanish marriages, 36–43, 88,
97; requires withdrawal of Sir
Henry Lytton Bulwer, 76–7. Also:
7, 16, 23, 35, 44, 55, 58, 62, 64, 80,
83, 88, 91, 129, 287

Spooner, Mr., 293
Stanley, Lord, 136
Stewart, Professor Dugald, Edinburgh
University, 5
Stockmar, Baron, 4, 10, 12, 22, 32, 46,
114, 123, 237
Stowell, Lord, 308
Sussex, Duke of, 1, 3
Sutherland, Duchess of, 12
Switzerland, 63, 116, 281
Syria, 24, 25, 28, 33

TAHITI, seizure by the French, 33,
88
Tallenay, M. de, 72, 73, 80, 81
Taylor, Mr., 329
Taylor, Sir Herbert, 11
Temple, the Hon. Sir William, 205–6
The Times, 43, 44, 104, 186, 187, 203,
290
Thiers, M., French Prime Minister, 23,
24, 26, 27
Treaty
—of London (1852), 71, 339, 340, 342,
343
—of Paris (1856), 192
—of Utrecht (1713), 36
—of Vienna, 64, 94, 100
—of Zurich, 272, 274, 275
Trent affair, 308–11, 312, 321–2
Turgot, M., French Foreign Minister,
132, 133
Turin, 85, 86, 87, 141
Turkey; defeat of Mehemet Ali at Acre,
23–4; 26, 27, 29, 34, 110, 111;
Russian hostility and destruction
of Turkish fleet at Sinope, 148–9;
outbreak of Crimean War (1854),
153, 189
Tuscany, 263, 265, 266

VANE, Lord Adolphus, 329
Venice, 73, 74, 75, 82, 83, 89
Victor Emmanuel, King of Sardinia,
254, 264
Victoria, Duke of, Regent of Spain, 88
Victoria, H.R.H. Princess Royal, 234–
237, 243, 252

378